NICE JEWISH GIRLS

NICE JEWISH GIRLS

A LESBIAN ANTHOLOGY

Edited by

EVELYN TORTON BECK

Revised and Updated Edition

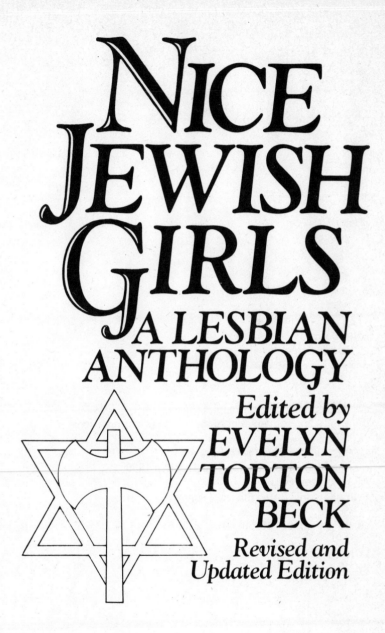

Beacon Press   Boston

Beacon Press
25 Beacon Street
Boston, Massachusetts 02108-2800

Beacon Press books
are published under the auspices of
the Unitarian Universalist Association of Congregations.

96 95 94 93 92 91 90 89   8 7 6 5 4 3 2 1

LCN: 89-42596
ISBN: 0-8070-7905-7

This book is dedicated
to the memories of

BLANCHE GOLDBERG

10 June 1945–15 July 1981

Founding member,
Jewish Lesbians of Madison, Wisconsin,

who said, when hearing of her illness,
"I still have work to do on this planet."

and

RUTH BLEIER

17 November 1923–8 January 1988

Founding member,
Lysistrata, a Feminist Restaurant,
and author of *Science and Gender*,

who might well have said with Emma Goldman,
"If I can't dance, it's not my revolution."

With this book we are continuing their work.

aleyhen hashalom

עליהן השלום

Contents

Jewish Identity: A Coat of Many Colors

If I Am Only for Myself, What Am I?

That's Funny, You Don't Look Like a Jewish Lesbian

Family Secrets

If I Forget Thee O Jerusalem

Appendix: Cast a Critical Eye

Acknowledgments

To the First Edition:

There are things one reaches for, and then occasionally there are things that come when one is ready for them. The idea for this anthology came to me, not in a dream, but at a workshop on Jewish women's studies at the 1979 conference of the National Women's Studies Association. It took the form of a brief but exceptionally clear message from Gloria Z. Greenfield, publisher of Persephone Press, printed neatly on a scrap of paper: "Would you be interested in developing a Jewish lesbian anthology?" I was at once thrilled and terrified. Though it did not take me long to say yes, it took several years for this work to be completed.

An anthology is, by definition, a collaborative effort; this one even more so. I want first to thank Gloria Z. Greenfield, my senior editor at Persephone Press, for having the vision to conceive this book, for believing in it, and sticking with it even when the going got rough. Her help in the editorial process was substantial and invaluable. Moreover, without her energy and enthusiasm, the book would still be in-process instead of in-print. Next, I want to thank Pat McGloin, co-publisher of Persephone Press, who was responsible for layout and text design, and who assisted in all aspects of the preparation of the volume. I want to thank both Pat and Gloria for opening their home to me in the zero hours of manuscript preparation and for taking such good care of me.

I want to thank Persephone's indefatigable and unfailingly good-humored staff: Alexandra Chasin for assisting in the general editing; Camille LeFevre and Mary Wright for copy-editing; Eileen Brady for typesetting; Anne Kornblatt for helping prepare the glossary.

At moments, this anthology threatened to engulf my life and the lives of those around me. Most especially, I want to thank Sue Lanser who more than anyone lived with the *tsores* and *naches* of this book, and who never failed to offer me emotional and moral support, and words of wisdom when I needed them. I am also grateful for her expert help in proof-reading the manuscript.

I would like to acknowledge the help of Irena Klepfisz whose work I had long admired. Through the anthology I came to know her as a friend and to count upon her sound advice and warm support (ministered miraculously over the long-distance telephone). I thank Judy Waterman for suggesting a reorganization for my introductory essay. I thank Joan E. Biren for feedback and support. I thank Lynn Gorchov and Laurie Baron for helpful references.

I want to give special thanks to the Madison Jewish Lesbian Group for providing years of a loving environment which allowed me to explore and affirm my Jewish lesbian identity.

I thank all the contributors for their cooperation and courage.

I thank our parents and grandparents and all those Jews who came before. Few of us have any sense of family history that extends further back than two generations. This book acknowledges our historical unrootedness as it helps to root us now, as Jews and as lesbians.

I thank our ancestors for their determination to survive.

February 1982

To the Second Edition:

I want to thank Nancy K. Bereano, editor of the Crossing Press Feminist Series, for seeing this book back into print with skill and enthusiasm. I want to acknowledge the wisdom and support of *Di Vilde Chayes,** who pushed the boundaries of my thinking and helped me remember the connections between different struggles without ever losing sight of the specificity or justice of our own. I also feel supported by the dozens of Jewish lesbian groups which have been forming across the country.

World events have dramatically changed the context in which this book exists. The Israeli invasion of Lebanon, the horrors of Sabra and Shatilla and all that followed in their wake occurred *after Nice Jewish Girls* was published. For obvious reasons then, the book does not make any reference to these events. Because bringing the individual essays up to date was not a realistic choice, I want to acknowledge the possibility that some contributors would have formulated some things differently if they were writing today. While I myself am even more critical of Israel's current internal and foreign policies than I was two years ago, I nonetheless reaffirm my belief in Israel's right to continue to exist, even if that country has proven to be no better than other nation-states. I claim solidarity with those progressive groups within Israel (particularly the peace movement and lesbian/feminist currents) which are committed to working toward a just and peaceful solution in the Middle East—a solution that would assure the survival of Palestinian Arabs as well as Jews.

The response to *Nice Jewish Girls* has been overwhelmingly positive. The book has generated lively discussion and controversy, which I consider to be healthy. That Judaism is changing heartens me. The *Jerusalem Post* (November 20-26, 1983, p. 19) carried a review of *Nice Jewish Girls;* in lesbian/feminist circles, non-Jewish women are beginning to form groups dealing with their anti-Semitism; and in the Fall of 1983, the faculty of the Jewish Theological Seminary (Conservative branch of Judaism) voted to ordain women. My optimism in these troubled times can perhaps best be explained in Jewish terms. Hope is the Jew in me who affirms belief in Jewish survival against the odds. It is this spirit that informs the second edition of *Nice Jewish Girls* as it goes to press in 1984/5744.

January 1984

* *Di Vilde Chayes* (Yiddish), literally, "the wild beasts." It is the name by which our Yiddish-speaking mothers tried to control our behavior and make us into the "nice Jewish girls" we were supposed to become — as in, "Go comb your hair. You look like a *vilde chaye!*" It is the name we gave to the support/study group to which I belong. The other members are Nancy K. Bereano, Melanie Kaye/Kantrowitz, Irena Klepfisz, Bernice Mennis, and Adrienne Rich.

Acknowledgments to the Third (expanded) Edition

The major acknowledgment for the 1989 edition is the recognition that, in spite of setbacks, our work truly matters and that there *has* been movement. The "L" word has become increasingly speakable within many Jewish communities, and the "J" word is being talked about in more complex ways among feminist activists and theorists.

In the seven years that mark the time span from the 1982 edition, I have been sustained by a wide network that is at once personal, political, and professional. Warm and expert help in preparing this edition has come from Deborah Chasman and Thomas Fischer, editors at Beacon Press. Loving support has come from my friends and colleagues in the Women's Studies Program at the University of Maryland–College Park, and from close personal friends and family members across the country—in Washington, D.C.; Brooklyn, New York; Madison, Wisconsin; Oakland, California; and Ithaca, New York. I want to name Rona Eisner here, because my work with her has given me greater strength, courage, wisdom, and a greatly expanded capacity to trust. And I want especially to celebrate my mother, Irma Torton, whose support of my work as a Jewish lesbian seems to increase as she and I grow older.

Finally, I want to acknowledge the loving friendship, wisdom, and expert editorial advice of L. Lee Knefelkamp, known in this volume by her chosen Jewish name of Chaya Shoshana. I give thanks to each and every one of these people individually and collectively. Without your support I could not continue to do this work.

E.T.B.
May 1989

Why Is This Book Different from All Other Books?

Evelyn Torton Beck

Why? I'll tell you why. According to Jewish Law, this book is written by people who do not exist. I assure you, it's all very logical: we're not proscribed because we don't exist. If we existed, believe me, they'd be against us.

Wait a minute. Who are *they* and who are *we*? And what does Jewish Law have to do with it?

They, in this case, are the *rabbonim*,* the interpreters of Jewish Law.

We, us, are the Jewish lesbians.

The Law is the Law. It doesn't mention us.

Actually, it is not only the *rabbonim* who have been unable to imagine us. Let me tell you a story. Very often this year, when people asked me what I was working on, and I answered, "A book about Jewish lesbians," my answer was met with startled laughter and unmasked surprise bordering on disbelief, "Are there *many*?"—as if the juxtaposition Jewish/lesbian were just too much. To me, these responses had the force of warnings.

I got the message. Or rather, it got to me. While I fought against silencing myself completely, I did begin to hesitate before answering, to assess the safety of the terrain. I began to understand the limits that the dominant culture places on "otherness." You could be a Jew and people would recognize that as a religious or ethnic affiliation *or* you could be a lesbian and some people would recognize that as an "alternative lifestyle" or "sexual preference," but if you tried to claim both identities—publicly and politically—you were exceeding the limits of what was permitted to the marginal. You were in danger of being perceived as ridiculous—and threatening.

*All Yiddish and Hebrew expressions are translated in the glossary.

Jewish Invisibility

In order to feel fully safe I need to feel known. How so? Is
visibility safety? Complex questions. Uncomfortable, uneasy answers, stirring up old hurts, old angers, old fears.

In Vienna in 1938, when I was five years old and Hitler came
to power, visibility was not safe. Schools were closed to me, as
were parks, stores, restaurants. Once I was sent to buy butter
because I was blonde and did not look Jewish. Men came and
took my father away. I am told that while the men waited for
my father to get his coat, I walked right up to one of them, put
my foot next to his, and said, "See, we have the same shoes, only yours are much bigger."

I did not know why or where my father was being taken, nor
how long he would be gone. Later I was told: to the camps—to
Dachau, to Buchenwald. My mother took me with her to the
Gestapo when she tried to get him released. After a year she
succeeded; I don't know how or why. My family history is a
series of gaps, leaving questions to mark the spaces: What happened to my father while he was gone? Who took us in after the
Nazis evicted us from our apartment? How did we get by after
they confiscated the small business my father had painstakingly
built up over the years? How did my father get out of the
camps? My parents talked about those years, selectively. And
not often.

But I remember one story well: when my father was still in
the camps, my mother had arranged to have me, the elder child,
sent to England where British citizens were taking in "endan-
gered" European children. According to my mother, it had been
easy to place me because I was so pretty (did not *look Jewish*,
did she mean?). But I never went; she needed my father's permission—which he refused to send. Though he did not know
if he would ever see any of us again, my father refused to split
the family, even to save me. As it turns out, the one who didn't
get saved was my grandmother. When the exit visas arrived, there
were only four—two for the parents, two for the children. If I
had been sent to England, the fourth visa could have been used
to save my grandmother. But who could have known that there
would be such choices? My mother, an only child very attached
to her mother who lived with us, later rationalized that painful
decision: "It's just as well poppa didn't let you go to London. . . .
You were such a nervous child, you would never have survived

the Blitz." Always when I heard that story I felt that I had been saved at someone else's expense: survivor's guilt is a high price for a child to pay.

I do not remember an entire year, my sixth, in Italy. I barely remember the long ocean voyage to New York on the last boat allowed out of Italy. I remember only sea-sickness and June 10, 1940, the date of our arrival; I remember measles on shipboard and how they had to mask my face with powder or we would all be sent back. *Having to hide: a sure sign of danger.*

Jewish invisibility is a symptom of anti-Semitism as surely as lesbian invisibility is a symptom of homophobia.

Combatting invisibility. At first it seemed an easy task. I would talk to Jewish groups about homophobia. I would talk to lesbian groups about anti-Semitism. I would talk to both groups about the need to affirm and accept difference. I would remind each group that invisibility has a trivializing, disempowering and ultimately debilitating effect on its members. And both groups would remember and understand.

But it hasn't been that simple, for each group has absorbed some of the myths and distortions about the other without any apparent consciousness of irony. How is it possible to move from this bind? To make ourselves heard and known? *If I say that Judaism is more than a religion, as lesbianism is more than a sexual preference, I begin to tap the complexity.* Being Jewish informs a woman's consciousness from the time she is young until she grows old, no matter how far from religion her family may be. Add to this the consciousness of a lesbian identity, and you create yet different patterns of seeing and experiencing the world. For Sephardic Jews and Jewish lesbians of color, the angles of vision become more multiple and more complex.

For many of us, unexpectedly, the experience of coming out as lesbians was a crucial step toward our coming out as Jews. The experience of being outside the bounds of society as a lesbian makes a woman more willing to acknowledge other ways in which she stands outside. It becomes increasingly harder to ignore the signals of outsiderhood. And soon one doesn't want to.

While most of us have some idea of what is meant by "coming out as a lesbian," the process of "coming out as a Jew," especially for a lesbian-feminist, is less easily defined and even less easily put into practice. I believe that all of the contributors to this anthology reject the patriarchal aspects of Judaism—yet it is not always easy to separate the elements in what is an old, multi-layered, complex, and sometimes contradictory culture.

To be born a Jew is to be born into a group with its own religious practices and beliefs, as well as a particular value system and code of ethics. Few represented here are seriously interested in transforming the religion, yet most of us respond with deep emotion to the holidays that punctuate the Jewish calendar and create the framework for traditional Jewish life. Some of us have created our own woman-identified Jewish rituals. Some are avowed atheists. Yet all of us are Jews. Some are struggling with denials and erasures, forced assimilations, silences and shame. Others take pride and pleasure and great joy from our Jewish identities. For some, this identity lies in the link with radical political traditions: Jewish activism in the Bund,* the American labor union movement, the civil rights movement, the anti-war movement, the feminist movement, the struggle for gay and lesbian rights. For yet others it is the Jewish love of and respect for learning; the pull of Jewish music—the insistent rhythms and the sweetly sad melodies; the special foods we eat. Some of us value most our Jewish gestures and intonations; our intensity and passion; our blending of the comic with the tragic; our ability to laugh at ourselves; our ability to survive. Our shared wisdom, shared fears and hopes, shared sense of history, shared languages and literature; our oral story-telling tradition.

To be born a Jew is to be part of a unified culture that is also extremely diverse. Jews are of all races and have settled on all continents, in all economic classes and on all points of the political spectrum (though traditionally Jews have participated in radical and liberal politics in numbers much larger than their proportion in the population—a fact that has been used against us by political conservatives[1]). Historically, Jews have been proud of our non-homogeneous thinking and our skills in seeing complexity. "Three Jews, four opinions," is a maxim quoted with pride.

What kinds of knowing do we share? Most Jews, I would venture to say, have some sense of the Jewish tradition of prayer and study; many feel behind them the weight of the Bible; the Law (oral and written); Talmudic disputation (*pilpul*)—affectionately referred to as hair-splitting; Jewish mysticism; the ancient prayers and songs which many of us were taught as children

---

*Yiddish abbreviation for "General Jewish Workers' Union in Lithuania, Poland and Russia," a Jewish socialist party founded in Russia in 1897.

that float in our heads—we sing their melodies, even if we no longer understand or accept their meanings.

Jews have been connected to a variety of languages wherever they have lived: ancient Hebrew, the language reserved for prayer and study; Yiddish or Ladino* (the vernacular for Ashkenazi and Sephardic Jews, respectively); as well as the languages of the host countries in which Jews have found themselves. Some of us learned modern Hebrew, the language of the State of Israel, a language that was developed as a defiant gesture of Jewish liberation from victimhood in Eastern Europe, where Jewish existence was precarious and pogroms an accepted fact of life. Though Yiddish was denigrated in Israel because of its association with life in the *shtetl*, it is the language of some of our parents and many of our grandparents. Those of us who grew up hearing Yiddish or Ladino in the home have a very emotional response to it and know at least a few words of those languages.**

An important part of what we know together is the history of Jewish survival and thus the history of anti-Semitism, which over the centuries has taken on various and often contradictory forms that have affected women as well as men, sometimes differently. These categories are not neatly separable, and frequently they overlap:

religious: Jews are despised and abused as heretics, infidels, and Christ-killers, and are accused of murdering Christian babies for ritual purposes.

social: Jews are treated like pariahs, undesirables; they must abide by laws restricting where they may live and

---

*See glossary for further details.

**Yiddish was the connecting link for Ashkenazi Jews from around the year 1000. World War II completed the destruction of the culture that gave rise to Yiddish (an erosion that had been begun by pogroms and assimilation). For Ashkenazi women, Yiddish is of particular significance because its name is *mame loshn,* the "mother tongue" or the "mother's tongue." It belonged to the women; its literature was developed (by men) so that women, who were not trained in Hebrew, would be able to read. It is associated with warmth, emotion, home, nurturing, and rootedness—even in exile. Like women, Yiddish was elevated (often sentimentalized, especially after World War II), but also denigrated. It was seen as impure (a dialect of German, rather than a language of its own), unacademic, and overly emotional.

Ladino (also known as Judeo-Spanish, Judezmo or Spaniolish) is the name of the Hispanic language spoken and written by Jews who were expelled from Spain in 1492, and is used as the vernacular for Jews in North Africa, the Balkan states, Turkey, the Middle East, the United States, and Latin America.

how they may earn their living; trade guilds and social groups are closed to them because of their undesirable characteristics. They are made to wear special hats or badges to set them apart.

political: Jews are scapegoats, held responsible for all the contradictory evils in the world; Jews are "Communists," Jews are "Capitalists."

economic: Jews are Shylocks, "operators" who succeed by devious means; Jews are untrustworthy, unreliable, materialistic, penny-pinching swindlers.

psychological: Jews become the repository of the fears and fantasies of the majority; the dominant culture's desire to assimilate the Jew is projected onto the Jew as "the Jewish plot to take over"; the Jew is said to be loud, pushy, aggressive, devious; against such a giant, force becomes necessary and justifiable.

sexual: Jews are the incarnation of sexuality; the Jewish woman is seen as the temptress, associated with exotic sexual practices; the Jewish male is the defiler of Christian women. The Jewish male is impotent; the Jewish woman is sexually withholding.

racial: Jewish blood is unclean, impure; Jews are undesirable, degenerate, dirty, smelly, suspect, peculiar, etc.

Even if we don't know all the details of this history, we know this story; it is imprinted on our psyches at an early age. How different this list reads if I cast it into the "we" voice: "We are despised and abused. . . we are pariahs. . . we are undesirables . . . we are the incarnation of sexuality. . . we are unclean. . . *we, we, we. . . .*"

Responses to Anti-Semitism

It is not the belonging to many groups that is the cause of the difficulty, but an *uncertainty* of belongingness.[2]
K. Lewin, *Resolving Social Conflict* (1948)

I was pained but not surprised to feel invisible as a lesbian among Jews. I was terribly disappointed and confused to feel invisible as a Jew among lesbians.

While lesbian-feminists have increasingly begun to acknowledge diversity, anti-Semitism is still not taken seriously in the lesbian-feminist movement. Anti-Semitism has not been included *by name* in the important litany of "isms" against which the movement has pledged itself to struggle: sexism, heterosexism, racism, classism, ageism, able-bodyism.

Some lesbian-feminist theorists claim that anti-racist work subsumes the fight against anti-Semitism, but I have not found that to be true in practice. For example, in an otherwise excellent workshop on "Racism and Lesbianism" held at the 1981 National Women's Studies Association (NWSA) Conference, in a discussion of the Ku Klux Klan, the Klan's anti-Semitism was not even mentioned until I brought it up. When I did, it was acknowledged (the speakers clearly knew a great deal about this aspect of Klan activity), but once the question was answered, the subject was rapidly dismissed. Was the question inappropriate to the session? Isn't it vital for us to make connections between oppressions? To see in what ways anti-Semitism, racism, and other forms of oppression are different and alike?

Actually, my experience in this session was rather positive. More often, the attempt to include anti-Semitism in discussions of racism is rejected and sometimes met with a sense of outrage that Jews are trying to take over *again*. There was, in fact, some initial resistance to having a forum on anti-Semitism at the 1981 NWSA Conference where the overall theme was "Women Against Racism." And I have been distressed to find that many gentile lesbian-feminists with otherwise highly sensitive political awareness, are reluctant to give attention to anti-Semitism, to understand how it operates, and to consider seriously their participation in it. For it seems unlikely that any individual can altogether avoid internalizing the prejudices of the dominant culture.

An instructive though particularly painful example of how anti-Semitism has been supported by the lesbian-feminist movement (even if out of ignorance and insensitivity) is provided by the controversy surrounding the charges that Z. Budapest's *The Holy Book of Women's Mysteries, Part II* is anti-Semitic.[3] Among other instances cited is the following offensive passage:

> The Jews carried a deep burden of guilt about what they had done to Lilith, the Great Goddess, and to cherubs in general. Lilith cursed them as a result, and in effect told

them that nothing would go right for Jews again until her worship had been reinstated. Could this be the final solution to the Middle East crisis?[4]

This passage, which is blatantly anti-Semitic, not only blames the Jewish people for bringing Jew-hating upon themselves, but also suggests that they deserve it. Even worse, Budapest seems to support Hitler's "final solution" to the Jewish question—the annihilation of all Jews. The fact that several of Budapest's coven sisters and supporters are themselves Jewish in no way mitigates the anti-Semitism of this passage; in fact, it serves to highlight the ways in which some Jewish women have internalized anti-Semitism.

In response to a letter from Naomi Dykestein protesting the anti-Semitism in Budapest's book, Z. Budapest was at first extremely defensive and even insulting, using the explicitly anti-Semitic epithet "little dyke princess" to discredit her critic, and insisted that the charges of anti-Semitism were simply an excuse for "trashing." In response to continued public pressure from Jewish women (whom she referred to as the "Jewish Mafia") and concerned others, Budapest eventually inserted an author's note that reads in part: "I regret that passages in my book have been understood as anti-Semitic. This was not, and is not, my intention. The use of 'final solution' (on p.197) was an anti-Semitic act and most regrettable." Several follow-up letters to feminist newspapers express dismay and dissatisfaction with Budapest's retraction. Budapest neither analyzes her own words, nor explores the feelings behind them. Instead, she shifts the responsibility for her own anti-Semitism. In another letter published in the feminist press, Budapest claims that her initial defensiveness stemmed from issues of "personality" and the "unpleasant circumstances surrounding the charges." It is important to understand that this feeble explanation, which entirely obscures and evades the issue of anti-Semitism, is typical of the way anti-Semitism operates to discredit the victim. Such patterns of reversal should not be legitimated, since they serve to silence those who would speak out.

Unfortunately, this is not the only recent instance of anti-Semitism in the feminist movement. The November 1981 issue of *Feminist Bookstores' Newsletter* carried the following "joke" in its media hotline: "Then it was off to the WOMEN IN PRINT CONFERENCE where I learned that feminist publishing is controlled by JEWISH-WORKING-CLASS-LESBIANS and the

4-H." (This conference was held in 4-H headquarters in Washington, D.C.) That same issue also carried a complaint about ". . . coming home to criticism that we were uncaring of women and were anti-Semitic for not having books on the shelf that are o.s.i.* at the publishers. This is a true story." In the first instance, the "humor" plays on the myth that the New York publishing industry is run by Jews; the Jewish reference in the second accuses Jewish women of being insensitive, unreasonable, and overly demanding. Is the Jewish reference in any way essential, or is it simply an easy way to discredit the complaining women?

While we can take some comfort from the fact that one of the authors of these thoughtless remarks was responsive to criticism and has since published letters of protest in the February issue of the Newsletter, such painful incidents will in the future be avoided only if gentile women are willing to examine their conscious and unconscious anti-Semitism in the same way that white women (including Jewish women) must examine their racism.

In response to an upsetting confrontation between Jewish women and women of color in a New England regional Women's Studies Conference,** Cherríe Moraga (*et al.*) wrote in *Gay Community News*, "We don't have to be the same to have a movement, but we *do* have to be accountable for our ignorance. In the end, finally, we must refuse to give up on each other."[5]

The risks for both Jews and gentiles of entering into a dialogue were painfully demonstrated at an all-day workshop on "Jewish Lesbians and Anti-Semitism" held in Madison, Wisconsin in May 1979. At one point in the day, the Jewish lesbians asked that the group be divided, because the gentile lesbians' stories about their anti-Semitic backgrounds were creating great anxiety and pain for the Jewish women. While everyone understood the need to separate at that time, the non-Jewish lesbians were loathe to discuss their anti-Semitism with each other and found it difficult to do so; some expressed jealousy of the developing close ties they sensed among the Jewish lesbians who were, for the first time, coming together around their common heritage, as lesbians *and* as Jews. Yet we have come to understand that white women must work on their racism with each other, that such education is not the burden of women of color.

*Out-of-stock indefinitely.

**For details see Gloria Z. Greenfield's essay "Shedding" in this volume.

And the feeling of exclusion, though understandable, does not differ in kind from some heterosexual women's responses to lesbian bonding.

Why is it often difficult to see parallels? Do we resist seeing them? Need one oppression cancel out another? Would the recognition that it is not *either/or* but *both/and* be too overwhelming? What would happen if we admitted that oppressed groups can themselves be oppressive? In the face of this complexity, a few facts remain clear: oppression is never less oppressive simply because it takes a different form. Success has never protected Jews from anti-Semitism. Even those Jews who considered themselves more German than Jewish were annihilated by the Nazis. Ironically, when Jews have succeeded in integrating into a society, it has been used against them: suddenly every Jew becomes "the rich Jew," the penny-pinching, exploiting miser. The great American dream, "from rags to riches," is simply not acceptable for Jews, whose success is somehow always tainted. Moreover, if at certain moments in history some Jews have entered into the mainstream, it is only because some powerful groups have "allowed" it; often this is done with the purpose of using Jews as a buffer and/or as an easy scapegoat when one is needed. It is an age-old pattern for Jews—*today*, allowed in, perhaps even encouraged; *tomorrow*, ignominiously thrown out.[6] Many people fail to understand the implications of this recurrent fact of Jewish history, and even some Jews fall for the mirage, taking the surface for the whole, refusing to acknowledge the precariousness of Jewish existence. Is that why, even now, I feel I have to justify my concern? *To prove that any form of anti-Semitism is always a real danger?*

Everywhere the overriding message seems to be: Forget about anti-Semitism. Or if you do see it, ignore it. This attitude prevails even in some parts of the Jewish community, particularly among those Jews who are the most politically conservative and feel they have the most to lose. "The American Jewish Committee said today it would be a 'mistake' to interpret recent trouble as signalling a 'new and dangerous wave of anti-Semitism in the United States. . . . On balance. . . the Jewish position in the U.S. remains secure despite 377 anti-Semitic incidents reported in 1980.' "[7] By the end of 1981 that number had more than *tripled*. How many incidents went unreported? The Human Relations Commission of Maryland's traditionally liberal Montgomery County (which saw a particularly large rise in racist and anti-Semitic incidents) estimates that only one out of ten persons reports harassment to the police. Understandably, anti-Semitism is very frightening, especially to those Jews who, despite an exterior pose of calm, believe it is always there, lurking just beneath the surface. (Jewish folk-"wisdom" warns: "Scratch a *goy* and find an anti-Semite.") Still, many Jews who are willing to recognize the existence of anti-Semitism seem to feel that the best survival tactic is to remain silent; possibly then things won't get much worse.

Such debate over strategy is not new. It shook and almost split the Jewish community of Milwaukee, Wisconsin, when in the 1970s the Nazi party was particularly active in that city.* It is in this light that we must understand the furor over the recent publication of Jacobo Timerman's book, *Prisoner Without A Name, Cell Without A Number*,[8] in which the Jewish Argentinian publisher and editor not only exposes the tortures to which he was subjected in an Argentinian jail for two and a half years, but also accuses the leaders of the Argentinian Jewish community of passively accepting the widespread anti-Semitism which is condoned by their government. As a *Jewish* liberal, Timerman was singled out by his jailers and became the butt of specifically anti-Semitic abuse, both physical and verbal. While his speaking out has been criticized and his character discredited by some Jews in the United States, Israel, and Argentina, no one denies the accuracy of his report concerning his treatment in jail.[9] Perhaps those Jews who are most angry at Timerman for speaking out do not want to put their own worst fears to the test: that even if Jews speak out, no one will listen or care; that even if anti-Semitism is acknowledged, it will be dismissed as less important than other oppressions. Less important *to whom?*

The discounting of anti-Semitism is itself anti-Semitic. Through such denial the victim is made to doubt the evidence of her experience (that's how women have been driven crazy by men); and to feel shame: shame for being a victim; shame for complaining when there are "larger" issues at stake; shame for speaking out; shame for keeping silent.

What's left, it is said, is social anti-Semitism, which isn't as serious as political anti-Semitism.[10] We are told that white-

---

*When the Nazi Party distributed anti-Semitic literature in front of Jewish-owned stores, the Jewish community could not agree on strategy: some Jews felt it best not to call attention to the incident, to ignore the leafleters in the hopes that they would go away. Others wanted to protest. Those who were against the protest feared that protesting might incite others to greater anti-Semitic acts.

skinned Jews can always pass. Why is the possibility of "passing" so insistently viewed as a great privilege open to Jews, and not understood as a terrible degradation and denial?[11] The prevailing mood, even in the lesbian-feminist movement, urges us to ignore the vulnerability we feel and the invisibility we experience *as Jews.*

The Jewish Image in Lesbian-Feminist and Feminist Literature

To a great extent the energy for this book came from my desire to break the silence and the cycle of confusion: to refuse any longer to feel like a victim, to raise the issue. I had to find out whether the lesbian-feminist movement would accept me *as a Jew.* Whether it would join me in my fight. Whether *my* fight was also *our* fight. During the last seven years I had given a great deal of energy to the lesbian-feminist movement and had come to feel more at home among lesbian-feminists than I had ever felt anywhere before—until I realized that my Jewish identity was relatively invisible unless I made a point of mentioning it.

I had managed to rationalize my shock and dismay when I found the narrator of *Rubyfruit Jungle* describing the fat Jewish girl Barbara Spangenthau as someone who "always had her hand in her pants playing with herself, and worse, she stank. Until I was fifteen I thought that being Jewish meant you walked around with your hand in your pants."[12] In 1974, as an emerging lesbian, I didn't want to admit that the movement's leading fiction writer was basing her humor on age-old anti-Semitic stereotypes. I simply couldn't afford to take it in. So I kept silent. In those early years of struggle it seemed unworthy to make a fuss. And worse—it seemed divisive. I could not yet claim my anger. I wanted too much to belong.

Bertha Harris' novel *lover* shocked me by its reliance on Jewish stereotypes, associating Jews with violence, sex and money. Jewish physical characteristics are consistently seen as exotic and dangerous:

> Her face was both aristocratic and Jewish. Had there ever been a Romanov Jew? Frequently her face blazed with teeth and light. "She has what they call Russian hair," Rose-lima said. Her hair was pale, and lethal, like an electric chair.[13]

Flynn, one of the major characters, is fascinated by the story of a Puerto Rican man who, ". . . likes to fuck young Jewish girls up the ass."

He commits sodomy on young Jewish girls, so that they may repent of the sins of their slumlord daddies. Their fathers, he tells them, owned the rat-filled tenements of his youth. Parting their buttocks, the young girls remind themselves that this is going to hurt him more than it hurts them. It is only to revenge himself.[14]

The justification of sado-masochism in this passage is not only anti-Semitic and racist, but also utterly anti-feminist in its conception. Moreover, in Harris' novel, Jewish history is degraded:

When they feel like it. . . the twins. . . roll in the mud; they drink a bottle of beer; they enact. . . an elaborate game in which only they are the survivors of the holocaust and must perform heroically at sex so that the race may be renewed.[15]

Furthermore, Gertrude Stein, who denied her Jewish identity, is discredited as "Miss Moneybags."[16]

Even in 1981 while I was preparing this anthology, I hesitated to protest publicly the anti-Semitic and racist stereotypes in Noretta Koertge's *Who Was That Masked Woman?*, a novel that not surprisingly was hailed by Bertha Harris as "the legitimate heiress to the throne of *Rubyfruit Jungle*."[17] This is a book in which most of the Jewish characters are ostentatiously rich, superficial, and sexually promiscuous. It is also a book that contains the following observation made by the narrator:

Take the Jews—they aren't very well liked but they do okay—get into *Who's Who* and all that stuff while the Poles stay down in Cicero and work in the steel mills—and the blacks—they're even worse off. What makes the difference? Is it a case of native intelligence or cultural heritage or what?[18]

The responses to the one review (Amy Hoffman's in *Gay Community News*, December 26, 1981) that criticized the book for its anti-Semitism and racism only served to confirm my doubts about speaking out. The following letter contains essentially all the excuses made for the book in what is probably their most offensive articulation:

You'll have to excuse me. I am not physically challenged. Neither am I a woman of color. . . .   *Who Was That Masked*

Woman? spoke very directly to my experience. Why can't you East Coast theorists [*code for Jewish?*] leave us Midwestern ex-WASPs alone? We're gay too, you know. We can't help it if we aren't multiply oppressed. Amy Hoffman owes Noretta Koertge an apology.[19]

Only recently has there been any public support for Hoffman's criticism. It took the form of a particularly thoughtful, well-documented letter from the lesbian publisher Pat McGloin, who concludes, "Any writer who calls herself a lesbian-feminist must be accountable to the images she perpetuates in her writing. Readers, writers, publishers, bookstores and reviewers have the responsibility to demand accurate portrayals of all of our lives."[20]

Anti-Semitism may also thoughtlessly be perpetuated even when Jews are more fully integrated into the body of a literary text and not simply objectified as peripheral "others." This occurs whenever portrayals of Jews, though plentiful, are limited to negative characteristics. For example, while there are quite a number of Jewish characters in Jan Clausen's short story collection *Mother, Sister, Daughter, Lover*, not one of them has any positive attributes. The story "Daddy" provides a good illustration. The father and his fiancée—we are pointedly told—"are all Jewish" and are stereotypically rich and crude: they have money, a house with two bathrooms, vacations in Florida, a color TV, and they perpetuate sexist roles. What are we to conclude from the fact that Daddy's lesbian ex-wife, who is portrayed as poor and "politically correct" in her values, is only "part Jewish"?[21]

Another subtle, and therefore more insidious form of anti-Semitism occurs when Jewish experience is trivialized, appropriated, or falsified. Clausen's story "The Warsaw Ghetto" provides an example of such trivialization. In this story, the Warsaw Ghetto Uprising is referred to only in an annoyed comment concerning the behavior of a gentile child: "What would we have done with you in the Warsaw Ghetto?" "What's a Warsaw Ghetto?" the child responds.[22] The Jewish narrator doesn't explain that in this armed Jewish uprising in 1943, every Jew in the Ghetto (over 56,000) was either killed outright by the Nazis or deported to extermination camps.[23]

Looking at Koertge's *Who Was That Masked Woman?* from this perspective, we see that she not only appropriates and trivializes, but also falsifies the atrocities committed by the Nazis against Jews. Having broken her leg, the main character Tretona contemplates the wonders of the Kutschner rod technique being used to heal her—a technique she claims Nazi scientists had developed on American GIs: "She tried to figure out if it wasn't good after all that the Nazis had done the experiments."[24] This seemingly harmless question entirely obscures the fact that it was overwhelmingly *Jews* who were used for grotesque medical experiments by Nazi doctors. While the author makes these remarks in the voice of her character, she cannot slough off the responsibility for perpetuating a false, "cleaned up" picture of history. Such insensitivity is dangerous, especially since the narrator in no way discredits or questions the character's integrity in thinking that it might have been "good after all that the Nazis had done the experiments."

That virtually no reviews of these highly-praised and widely-read authors mention anti-Semitism is a symptom of how little consciousness there is of this issue. Fortunately, excellent guidelines that would help raise consciousness are available. Paul E. Grosser and Edwin G. Halperin in *Anti-Semitism: The Causes and Effects of a Prejudice*, include an extended discussion of how to analyze anti-Semitism in works of literature while keeping in mind the integrity and responsibility of the artist. Their guidelines read in part:

> Unflattering descriptions of Jews and Jewish life in literature or other artistic creations, although not the work of anti-Semites and possibly accurate concerning the authors' experiences, might reflect an acceptance of anti-Semitic stereotypes and thinking common to the day, and in any case, serve to reinforce them. . . .
>
> Art does not exist in a vacuum. . . . The inclusion of Jewish villains, stereotyped Jews, or unflattering portraits of Jewish life in novels or works of art can be justified because they can and do exist or are the artists' vision of truth. But from a moral perspective—given the background of anti-Semitism and its consequent latent potential and accepting the premise that the inclusion of such portraits will, however indirectly, add to that potential—justification should rest on a broader base.
>
> This argument admittedly demands much of the artist. It necessarily limits the range of creative definition. It does, however, also expand the role of the creative person. It challenges the writer to consider the impact of the written word. In short it demands the artist to be a whole person with social as well as artistic integrity.[25]

The feminist press has also been surprisingly silent (though there has been much talk in private) about the anti-Jewish feeling expressed in the following lines in Judy Simmons' poem "Minority" which appeared in *Conditions: Five, The Black Women's Issue.*

Mine is not a People of the Book/taxed
but acknowledged; their distinction is
not yet a dignity; their Holocaust is lower case.[26]

The public silence may be due to the discomfort these lines have caused, because they threaten the possibility of coalition between Black and Jewish women. The editors of *Conditions:Five* do, however, seem to be aware of the problem with Simmons' trivializing perspective on Jewish oppression and they have appended a note to that effect. However, a note by itself does little to combat the real difficulty in this poem or in this attitude. What is needed is an on-going dialogue between Jewish women and women of color, a dialogue which has just barely begun.[27]

Better communication might perhaps have kept sociologist Iva E. Carruthers from using a classically anti-Semitic stereotype in order to make a point about the women's movement in her essay in the anthology *Sturdy Black Bridges*. Carruthers' essay attacks the white feminist movement for "assaults to African familyhood; the theory for which is emerging from a predominantly Jewish elite group."[28] Moreover, one hopes it is only ignorance and not malice that made Carruthers use the term "Aryan" to include both Jews and Asians. It is particularly painful and offensive for Jews to be included in the Aryan race, since six million Jews were killed under Hitler (and hundreds of thousands more tortured) solely because they were *not* Aryans. Familiarity with the facts of even only comparatively recent history and a degree of compassion would help eliminate this kind of anti-Semitism.

It seems incredibly ironic that the strong presence of Jewish lesbians (many with radical activist backgrounds) in the lesbian-feminist movement goes essentially unrecorded and unnoticed in any positive way by Jews and gentiles alike. Few lesbians have recorded the Jewish lesbian presence to any extent, and they are all Jewish writers: Nancy Toder, Elana Dykewomon (Nachman), Melanie Kaye, Irena Klepfisz, Alice Bloch, Ruth Geller, Harriet Malinowitz, Martha Shelley. The near invisibility of Jewish energy in the lesbian-feminist movement may itself be a result of anti-Semitism, real or feared: a response to the fear that if Jews were more visible *as Jews*, they would be accused of controlling the movement. Because Jews are present, yet invisible, it has been difficult to feel comfortable about claiming Jewish lesbian identity, especially when, year after year, many of our feminist businesses urge us to buy our Christmas presents early. *Us? Our?* Again the nagging question. Should I make a fuss? It seems so unnecessarily touchy. After all, Jews are only a small minority. Then I remember. Whenever I "made a fuss" (i.e., raised the issue of lesbian invisibility) at a feminist session where the speakers failed to include lesbians in their presentations, I had the support of the lesbian community. It was understood that the discomfort was to be *theirs*, not ours. Speaking out now, as a Jew, would there be the same lesbian support? And when I finally did mention, in words carefully chosen not to offend, that I was... having difficulty... with the... implicit assumption... that we all... celebrated Christmas... with the erasure... of my Jewish culture and heritage... was it my own discomfort I was experiencing because I was publicly identifying myself as a Jew, or was I responding to others' discomfort with my Jewishness?

Nice Jewish Girls

> All the forces of civilization had worked against this, still it happened.
>
> Elana Nachman, *Riverfinger Women*[29]

I started this project in a spirit of optimism, rooted in my pleasure (and relief) at finally having found a sense of congruence for the pieces of my life. I have since become increasingly sobered by the ramifications of what it can mean to want to say: I am a Jewish lesbian. The truth is that it is extremely difficult to identify oneself as a Jew outside the long shadow of anti-Semitism. It is like trying to imagine what it would feel like to be a lesbian in a non-homophobic world. So this book has become the exploration of complexities, as well as a celebration of our survival.

The anthology is a mosaic of our lives—past and present. Many of us describe and analyze what it was like to grow up Jewish (and lesbian) in different parts of the United States, South America, Europe and Asia. Not all of us were born in this country. All but two of us now live in the United States.

Some of us experienced World War II directly, but all of us were touched by the Holocaust; there is hardly a Jew who did not lose some relatives under Hitler. The oldest of us is close to sixty-five, the youngest in her twenties.

We came out as lesbians at different stages of our lives. Not surprisingly in a culture that is obsessed with survival, a number of us have been married. At least five of us are mothers; one of us has a Jewish lesbian daughter,[30] another a Jewish lesbian aunt.[31] Others among us are thinking about bearing children and wondering what it would be like to bring them up as the Jewish children of Jewish lesbians.

Probably the single most insistent theme in this book, repeated with variation and from many different angles and perspectives, directed at both non-Jewish lesbians and non-lesbian Jews, is the desire of the contributors to be "all of who we are." In proper Jewish tradition, we ask many questions. It is our way of coming to know. So we ask, collectively, in different voices, genres, and styles: What does it mean for us to identify as Jewish lesbians? In what ways have we internalized our Jewishness? How are we, as Jews, different from each other (by place of birth, life history, relationship to tradition, race, class, age), and in what ways are we the same? What sparks of recognition fly between us when we meet as Jewish lesbians? What values and cultural habits do we share? What kinds of pride do we take in being Jewish? What fears do we share? What shame? How have we internalized myths and stereotypes, particularly about Jewish women? What similarities do we share with lesbians from other ethnic groups?[32] How are we different? How have Jewish survival skills helped us learn to survive as lesbians? What are the peculiarly Jewish roots of our radicalism? Though the women included here actually represent a spectrum of political beliefs, I suggest that it is a radical act to be willing to identify publicly as a Jew and a lesbian.

We also explore our relationships and attitudes toward family, community, children, traditions, separatism, gay synagogues, Israel, Jewish men, gentile lesbians (white and of color, as friends and lovers), "passing" (nose jobs, name changes, and the like), spirituality, the history of our people. Initially I had envisioned essays on Jewish lesbians under Hitler (on which there is silence, even in books that deal with Hitler's treatment of homosexuals); on lesbians in the Kibbutz movement (on that issue too there is absolute silence); and on participation of Jewish lesbians in the American labor movement, alluded to only in passing in *The*

Jewish Woman in America: "There is evidence that a small number of Jewish women in the labor movement became involved in same sex relationships, some of which lasted a lifetime. One of these couples even adopted a child."[33] It is my hope that some historian will follow this lead and find out the details of these Jewish lesbian lives. Yet, for how many other lesbian Jews was the evidence destroyed? I have observed an incremental invisibility at work: Jewish history, itself not written into the mainstream, is compensatory history, written mostly by Jewish men, who also leave out Jewish women. The new field of women's history has ignored Jewish and lesbian experiences; lesbian history has not focused on Jews, and Jewish women's history has avoided the lesbian dimension.

With this anthology we have made a start. We have recorded Jewish lesbian lives in pictures, poems, fiction and essays. We have made theories about our lives. We recognize that although in the past we have often experienced a double or triple vulnerability and a sense of isolation—as the only lesbian among Jews, the only Jew among lesbians, the only Jewish lesbian of color among white Jewish lesbians, the only Sephardic Jew among Ashkenazi—we now know that we are not alone. We exist as part of a rapidly growing grassroots movement of Jewish lesbian-feminists, creating an informal network of local consciousness-raising, support, and study groups. We have even produced two issues of a Jewish lesbian newsletter *Shehechiyatnu,* the editorship of which is intended to rotate from city to city.[34]

The work has already had an impact on the lesbian-feminist community. More people acknowledge the need to deal with anti-Semitism as a separate issue. Fewer people are ready to say that anti-Semitism is dead. A greater sense of Jewish pride is emerging. Jewish lesbians have become more thoughtful about themselves *as Jews* and more aware of the absence or presence of other Jews. A dialogue has begun.

What I hope is that this book will also open a dialogue with the *rabbonim.* Well, maybe not the *rabbonim,* but with members of the Jewish community-at-large. I'd like them to *shep naches* from our contributions to Jewish life. I'd like to hear them say *"mazel tov"* instead of *"oy gevald"* when they see we've made a book of our own. Actually, we are just like them, only different. Robin Tyler describes her Jewish connection:

> I was always very Jewish—all my relatives are very Jewish and I was raised Jewish. I'll never forget the time when

somebody said, "you shouldn't wear that suit, you're too butch and that gives a bad impression." I said, "Margie Adam wears a suit," and they said, "that's different." I said, "you mean I'm too Jewish." All of a sudden, because I talk with my hands and I talk loudly, it's called butch. In my family it was called—you know—my Aunt Betty.[35]

I want Robin's Aunt Betty and my mother to be proud of us, to recognize us as their offspring.

l also want the radicalism of the very outrageous, very outspoken, very political lesbian-feminists, Maxine Feldman, Robin Tyler,[36] Alix Dobkin, and Linda Shear to be recognized as part of the Jewish radical-activist tradition in Eastern Europe. As comics, Feldman and Tyler follow the tradition of Jewish storytellers and wedding jesters (who warned the brides against marriage), whose job it was to keep the community laughing and crying, revealing it to itself:

> Jewish women within the movement have often been the ones to change their names. . . . My last name is obviously very Jewish. Someone once asked me why I hadn't changed my name. I said to them, "I think you better check your anti-Semitism. Why haven't you asked Meg Christian?"[37]
>
> —Maxine Feldman

Yes, tradition. It's probably not what our foremothers had in mind, but then, did *they* ask their parent's permission to leave the old country? And where would they be if they had? Jewish humor runs very deep in Jewish culture. It is widely believed that for oppressed groups humor is a weapon, a way of getting back. But who are you getting back at when the joke is on you? No, humor is a mask. You laugh so nobody will see you cry. Yet Jewish laughter in the midst of pain is also healing and empowering. We have also learned to laugh at ourselves. It has become a tradition.

Tradition. The Jewish lesbian community in Madison, Wisconsin recently had a painful opportunity to merge Jewish tradition with lesbian-feminist beliefs. It was at the memorial service for Blanche Goldberg, one of the founding members of the Madison Jewish-lesbian group. Her funeral was as lesbian as it was Jewish. About one hundred and fifty women (and a few men) attended the service. Blanche had wanted to die at home and the lesbian community (with the help of Madison Hospice

Care) had helped her to do that. After experiencing the painful months of her slow dying, the community wanted to both mourn her death and celebrate her life. Rabbi Alan Lettofsky, who had supported a dialogue about Jewish gays and lesbians at the University of Wisconsin Hillel (and had thus won our confidence), agreed to lead services. He was, at all times, sensitive to our needs and wishes. He knew who we were and who Blanche was. He had visited Blanche's home and had talked with her lover. In his eulogy, he acknowledged the loving care the lesbian community had given to Blanche. He also said it was more than any single family would be able to provide.

In the chapel, a large Jewish star replaced the cross. Tapes of women's music played in the background while the mourners gathered. Purple ribbons decorated the pulpit. The prayers were only as long as necessary, and Alan had feminized the Hebrew so it was clear that a *woman* had died. Blanche was an orphan, but her lover's mother and brother had come, had *wanted* to be there. Just before the service began, while a small circle of intimate friends—her immediate family—went through the traditional ceremony of cutting the black ribbon pinned to our clothes (the symbolic act of rending the clothes, the Jewish sign of mourning), the tape played Holly Near singing, "There is something about the women." After the blessings, we stood up and spoke about Blanche's life, of what she had done and what she still would have wanted to do. We said the word *lesbian*. We said the word *cancer*. We said the *Kaddish*. Blanche had died young, but we didn't only cry at her funeral. We also laughed, out of our pain, but also out of our Jewishness.

Unexpectedly, the bringing together of our lesbian and Jewish identities at this ceremony of mourning was healing and strengthening. Here, there was no "uncertainty of belongingness," here all was trust. If only it were possible to keep that trust alive and bring it into the dailiness of our lives. If this anthology were to make that just a little more possible, then I would sing, as Jews do at the Passover Seder, *dayenu*, "it is enough."

Endnotes

[1]Jews have been singled out as especially likely to be traitors to their country. For example, see the Dreyfus trial in France where Dreyfus was framed on charges of espionage in 1894, pardoned in 1898 and finally cleared in 1906. See also the trial of Ethel and Julius Rosenberg in the United States who were executed on charges of treason in 1953, and Adrienne Rich's poem "For Ethel Rosenberg" in *A Wild Patience Has Taken Me This Far* (New York, 1981), pp. 26-30.

[2]Quoted by Judith Weinstein Klein in *Jewish Identity and Self-Esteem: Healing Wounds Through Ethnotherapy* (1980), p. 16. Available from the American Jewish Committee ($2.75).

[3]My summary is based on the exchange of letters in the following feminist and lesbian-feminist publications: *off our backs* XI:6 (June 1981), 28-29; XI:8 (August/September 1981), 30-31; XI:10 (November 1981), 30; and *The Lesbian Insider/Insighter/Inciter*, No. 4 (July 1981), p. 10.

[4]Z. Budapest, *The Holy Book of Women's Mysteries, Part II* (Los Angeles, 1980), p. 197. Changes scheduled for next edition.

[5]Letter to the editor, *Gay Community News* VIII:32 (March 7, 1981), p. 4.

[6]In the Middle Ages Jews were encouraged to become money lenders—an occupation forbidden to Christians by the Church. "In Central Europe during and after the Renaissance, Jews commonly served princes and governments as financiers or financial advisers. Many of these 'court Jews' fell from favor to disgrace, exile, or the executioner's axe when the king or princeling needed a scapegoat to appease popular resentment against his misrule—or wanted a quick and sure way to cancel his debts." *The Many Faces of Anti-Semitism*, published and distributed by the American Jewish Committee, Institute of Human Relations, revised edition 1978, p. 18.

[7]*The Washington Post* (April 27, 1981).

[8](New York, 1981), translated from the Spanish by Toby Talbot.

[9]This controversy was widely publicized in all the major American newspapers. See, for example, "Timerman's Charges Anger Jews in Argentina, U.S." *The Washington Post* (June 22, 1981), A:1, 5-7.

[10]I believe it is shame and self-hatred that motivated the letter from Sandy Katz, Shelley Kushner and Louise Brotsky, who make offensive statements about Judaism and Zionism, and object to the fact that the November 1981 issue of *Big Mama Rag* had given equal weight to racism and anti-Semitism. They believed this to be wrong because "it focuses so much energy and attention on fighting anti-Semitism, confusing it with the fight against racism and white supremacy in the United States." *Big Mama Rag* (December 1981), p. 3. One wonders how anyone can wholeheartedly fight the oppression of another group when, in order to do so, she finds it necessary to denigrate and deny her own oppression.

[11]See Michelle Cliff, *Claiming an Identity They Taught Me to Despise* (Watertown, Mass.: Persephone Press, 1980), an exploration of her experience as a light-skinned Jamaican woman. See also Cherríe Moraga (*et al.*) in *This Bridge Called My Back*, ed. Cherríe Moraga and Gloria Anzaldúa (Persephone Press, 1981).

[12]Rita Mae Brown, *Rubyfruit Jungle* (Plainfield, VT: Daughters, 1973), p. 12.

[13]Bertha Harris, *lover* (Plainfield, VT: Daughters, 1976), p. 96.

[14]Harris, p. 23.

[15]Harris, p. 84.

[16]Harris, p. 118.

[17]Bertha Harris, quoted on the back cover of the paperback edition of *Who Was That Masked Woman?* (New York: St. Martin's, 1981).

[18]Noretta Koertge, *Who Was That Masked Woman?* (New York: St. Martin's, 1981), p. 178.

[19]*Gay Community News* XI:25 (January 16, 1982), p. 4. This letter is signed by Joni Peters, Zanesville, Ohio.

[20]*Gay Community News* XI:26 (January 30, 1982), p. 4.

[21]Jan Clausen, *Mother, Sister, Daughter, Lover* (Trumansburg, NY: The Crossing Press, 1980), p. 18.

[22]Clausen, p. 12.

[23]Of the 500,000 Jews confined in the Warsaw Ghetto between 1941 and 1943, 490,000 Jews were either murdered or incarcerated in extermination camps. When Warsaw was liberated in 1945, only two hundred Jews remained. For more detailed information, see Helen Fein's *Accounting for Genocide* (New York: The Free Press, 1979).

[24]Koertge, p. 65.

[25]Paul E. Grosser and Edwin G. Halperin, *Anti-Semitism: The Causes and Effects of a Prejudice* (Secaucus, NJ: Citadel Press, 1979), pp. 302-303.

[26]*Conditions: Five, The Black Women's Issue* (1979), p. 93.

[27]See transcribed tapes by Beverly Smith with Judith Stein and Priscilla Golding, " 'The Possibility of Life Between Us': A Dialogue Between Black and Jewish Women," *Conditions: Seven* (Spring 1981), pp. 25-46.

[28]"War on African Familyhood," by Iva E. Carruthers in *Sturdy Black Bridges* (Garden City, NY: Doubleday, 1979), edited by Roseann P. Bell, Bettye J. Parker, and Beverly Guy Sheftall, p. 9.

[29](Plainfield, VT; Daughters, 1974), p. 9. Elana Nachman has since changed her name to Elana Dykewomon.

[30]See my essay, "Daughters and Mothers: Three Generations," in this volume.

[31]See "The Letters from My Aunt," by Maida Tilchen with Helen D. Weinstock in this volume.

[32]See note 27. See also "Face-to-Face, Day-to-Day—Racism CR," Tia Cross, Freada Klein, Barbara Smith and Beverly Smith in *Top Ranking: A Collection of Articles on Racism and Classism in the Lesbian Community*. Compiled by Joan Gibbs and Sara Bennett (February Third Press, 1980), pp. 65-69.

[33]*The Jewish Woman in America*, by Charlotte Baum, Paula Hyman and Sonya Michel (New York: New American Library, 1975), p. 161.
Although the authors minimize the lesbian experience by suggesting that the women turned to each other because of their common devotion to the labor union and because of the dearth of men, this book nonetheless provides very valuable information about the Jewish woman in Europe and the United States. It also offers an excellent analysis of the negative stereotypes and suggests probable causes for their development.

[34]"*Shehechiyatnu* is a feminized version of the Hebrew from a prayer of joy and thanksgiving which is traditionally recited at times of celebration. . . . It means '*who has brought us life*,' " from the first issue (4 Heshvan, 5740; October 25, 1979, Boston). The second issue was published in Madison, Wisconsin on March 24, 1981. The editors write, "In addition to money, we need a group of Jewish dykes in another city to volunteer to edit and distribute the next issue. If no group volunteers, *Shehechiyatnu* will die young." As of February 1982, no new group has volunteered.

[35]From an unpublished interview with Robin Tyler by Evelyn Torton Beck, Washington, D.C., September 19, 1980.

[36]Robin Tyler was born Arlene Chernick but changed her name so her family would not discover she was performing on the Jewish Sabbath.

[37]"Give Me That Ol' Lesbianism!" Interview with Maxine Feldman by Cindy Rizzo, *Gay Community News* X:4 (April 19, 1980), pp. 8-9.

Still Different (1989)
Evelyn Torton Beck

To link the editions of *Nice Jewish Girls* with another death is not what I had envisioned. But in January of 1988 Ruth Bleier, an important member of the Madison Jewish lesbian community, died.

Ruth was the first lesbian mother I had ever known, the first Jewish lesbian I ever met, the first feminist activist I knew at the university. But because in 1970 I had not yet developed lesbian ways of seeing, I (mis)interpreted her living with another woman and both their children as nothing more than an "arrangement of convenience."[1] Ruth was a very private person who did not make public declarations about her multiple identities even while fund-raising for her most ambitious project, the building of Lysistrata, A Feminist Restaurant, which would also serve as a communal meeting and safe dancing space for women. But if you got to know her, you knew she was proud to be a woman, a scientist, a doctor, a mother, a grandmother, a lover of women, an activist, and a Jew. By her passion for justice and her commitment to women and other oppressed groups, she claimed her Eastern European heritage of radical Jewish politics.

In January 1988, in the Great Hall of the University of Wisconsin, where Ruth Bleier had taken great pleasure in listening to Adrienne Rich read her poem "Sources" only five years earlier, several of Ruth's communities gathered to mourn and honor her. I inscribe her name in this book so she will not be lost to Jewish history.

How Is This Year Different from All Other Years?

How else to measure the distance between 1982 and 1989? All weekend, in preparation for writing this introduction to the new edition, I have been going through my very disorderly files, nonetheless finding a folder containing all forty-four reviews of

Nice Jewish Girls, which included nine from the Jewish press.
All positive. Many more than we ever thought we would get.
Good: we spoke and were heard. But among my papers I also
found the programs we distributed at the many Jewish-lesbian
cultural events that were organized to celebrate the publication
of the anthology, to which hundreds of people came, mostly—but
not all—lesbians."[2] Then I came upon the "writs of excommunication" that were distributed outside our Boston reading by a
self-styled "Supreme Rabbinic Court of America" in Silver
Spring, Maryland, and an unsigned single-spaced tract from New
York City, crammed with dire scriptural warnings and headed,
"How do you plead, guilty or innocent?" A question.

In 1982 it was a question many *rabbonim* still felt they had
the right to ask. And in a way they were not entirely mistaken,
for in 1982 we were more tentative about our rights as Jews. In
the seven intervening years we have learned to demand to be
heard, seen, respected, included—yes, celebrated—by our people.
We know we offer something different: other voices, other ways
of seeing and understanding the world that expand possibilities
for the Jewish people, ways that will help, not hinder, our collective survival as Jews. By our activism as "out" lesbians and "out"
Jews, by serving as leaders of feminist movement in many arenas,
we represent the legacy of the "prophetic minority" among our
radical foremothers and fathers.[3] In the chapter on contemporary
lesbian activism in *Another Mother Tongue,* poet/theorist and historian of gay culture Judy Grahn writes of Jewish lesbians in
ways that support this assertion.

> As I think about my experience of the Lesbian/feminist
> movement from 1969 until the present, 1983, the
> number of Jewish Lesbians I can think of who have
> been catalysts, organizers, founders of institutions,
> writers, poets, artists, analysts, and general thinkers
> is virtually legion . . . they joined every movement for
> social justice in America . . . in many cases they led
> these movements, helped connect them to each other.
> . . . They came out in droves . . . often founding some
> particular aspect of [the movement] as a new entity.[4]

But in 1989 I cannot write about us as a "we" with such equanim-
ity; I cannot speak in the name of all "Jewish lesbians" or all
"Jewish lesbian-feminists." Like the Jewish people, Jewish lesbian-feminists are both one and many. In the years between these

two editions the differences among us have become more apparent. And if these differences have not irrevocably divided us, they have made us understand that Jewish lesbian community—if we are to have it—must be built around more than the fact of our being Jewish and lesbian.

This realization was a deep disappointment to some Jewish lesbians, who had hoped or believed that simply bringing these identities together would resolve most general life problems and all Jewish ones. When it did not: when even Jewish lovers did not mean trouble-free relationships, when the needs for *feminist* rituals could not be met even in gay/lesbian synagogues, when some Jewish lesbians "came out" as s/m lesbians, when some Jewish lesbians began having babies (by insemination or adoption),[5] when some continued to identify as separatists,[6] when our opinions on Israel did not mesh, when Jewish lesbian "converts" to Judaism began to name themselves in the litany of Jewish difference,[7] when Jewish Lesbian Daughters of Holocaust Survivors created a separate network,[8] it became clear that even as lesbian feminists, we were many different kinds of Jews.

In this we are very like other Jews— only a quasi-comforting thought. How could we have thought that by our difference as lesbians we could resolve the differences that have historically divided Jews, that we could answer *the* question that has been challenging (plaguing) Jews for centuries? Especially when adding "lesbian" (or "lesbian-feminist") only complicates the question. It has been easier to know what we are fighting against than to agree about what we are trying to build. *Nice Jewish Girls* was a powerful catalyst for the search, but it provided no answers to that haunting question.

What Does It Mean to Be a Jew?

In this process of looking back it occurred to me to reread my notes for what was one of the first public presentations I ever gave in an *all*-lesbian environment following the publication of *Nice Jewish Girls*. From a lesbian perspective, the setting could not have been more benign—the Women's Coffeehouse in Minneapolis, run by a politically aware group of lesbians who offered a substance-free environment. Yet, as my notes tell me, and as I so clearly remember because the memory is etched into my mind by the knots that were in my stomach, I was terrified to speak to what I knew would be a mostly non-Jewish audience.

Of What Was I Afraid?

In those years, we had not yet built any bridges of safety between ourselves and non-Jews in the lesbian community. *Nice Jewish Girls* was the first plank, but we did not yet know if the scaffolding would hold. I had been scheduled to read poetry by Jewish lesbians and to speak about the process of editing the book and the responses to it. While I had no objective reason to be more afraid of speaking as a Jew to a "mixed" group of lesbians than I was of speaking as a lesbian to a "mixed" group of Jews (which I had done the previous evening), I discovered that I felt far more vulnerable as a Jew than I did as a lesbian. I said, "Speaking out as a Jew in a lesbian space feels like the riskiest act of my life, because my survival as a lesbian, my ability to continue to speak out as a *lesbian* Jew, depends on the continuing support of the lesbian community." And I was not at all sure I had it—as an "out" Jew. Today I feel more clarity about what I can realistically expect from any community: some support from some people some of the time. No one community is truly "home," but Jewish lesbian space still feels the closest to it, most of the time.

Although we have catalyzed major changes in perception, to some degree in both Jewish and lesbian communities we are still the "other" whose presence has to be remembered by acts of will. But for the most part our existence is known, spoken, often taken into account. Women's concerts are no longer scheduled for Jewish holidays. Women think to ask for the dates. *Nice Jewish Girls* sits on the shelves of many Hillels and some Jewish Community Center libraries. The major difference between those who see us and those who do not is their degree of *feminist* consciousness, not whether they are Jewish or lesbian.

Yet such optimism tells only half the story. Jewish presence continues to be omitted from what seem to be strongly feminist and lesbian-feminist publications. Even in the few months since I completed my overview, "The Politics of Jewish Invisibility."[9] new examples have come to my attention. For example, it is still a shock (and a deep disappointment) to find no mention of Judaism in the 1988–89 "Feminism and Religion" issue of *Connections: an International Women's Quarterly,* which excused itself in the fine print on the grounds of "a lack of provocative material and a shortage of Hebrew translators."[10] Equally maddening is the omission of Jewish/Gentile relationships in a recent self-help book for lesbian couples, especially since cultural and religious differences become especially potent during the annual Christmas siege. It is hard not to get angry or to believe that the omissions are deliberate, for the process is slow and terribly uneven. It requires a balancing act to take in the gains without losing sight of the continuing omissions.

Now that the general silence has been broken it is sometimes hard to recall how it once engulfed us and how loud our voices sounded. But in 1982 we could not be sure of how we would be received or heard, even in lesbian-feminist space. This was not sheer paranoia. Historically, it has not been safe to be a Jew. And some of what I was afraid of in "coming out" as a Jew in the lesbian community did happen, not in Minneapolis but in other lesbian spaces.

Like the time in East Lansing, Michigan, when a woman interrupted a workshop I had been asked to lead on "building community across cultural differences" to tell me that much as she "liked and respected" me, I was making her "ill, *physically ill*," because I was "*taking control* of the workshop." I was stunned and a little confused, because I had been especially invited to be a leader; it never occurred to me at the time that she found me offensive as a leader simply *because I was a Jew*. It took a woman of color to suggest that possibility. When the assault occurs before understanding sets in, its effects take a long time to heal.

An incident in upstate New York also took me entirely by surprise and felt like an ambush or a set-up. I was dining in a restaurant with two lesbians from the area (who were not Jewish but were intrigued by *NJG*); I was about to write a check for my portion of the bill when one of them suggested that if I paid for all three of us by check, they could reimburse me in cash, and I could write the whole meal off on my income tax. When I said I thought this was a very clever idea, the one who had suggested the plan remarked proudly, "*And I'm not even Jewish!*" I was so stunned I could not speak. When hours later I confronted her (very gingerly) with my pain, she defended herself by saying she has a Jewish friend who always makes such jokes. We did not see each other again.

One of my greatest disappointments came from one of my lesbian students who knew my work and had often heard me speak on Jewish themes. In late December I ran into her, and after an intense conversation (raised Catholic, she had discovered that one of her grandparents was Jewish) she wished me "Merry Christmas." Though I was disappointed in her lack of sensitivity, I nonetheless smiled and said my usual, "Thanks, I don't celebrate Christmas, but I'll try to have a happy holiday." My response led to a very lengthy discussion, which I thought brought some deeper understanding. But as she bid good-bye for what would be the rest of the academic year, she said, smiling, "Happy Easter." I believe I called her back to say I was not smiling. Because we live life "in the small," such incidents gather weight cumulatively.

One of the results of editing *Nice Jewish Girls* has been my realization that most non-Jews know virtually nothing about Jewish history, culture, or religion. Such ignorance leads to the fear of mis-speaking, while fear of mis-speaking keeps people from asking questions or learning. The non-Jewish students in my lesbian culture classes (where I began to teach *NJG*) were the first to tell me how confused and mystified they were, how difficult they found it to grasp that one could be a cultural Jew without being a practicing, religious one; how strange it was to them that "Jewish atheist" was a meaningful construct.

Still, they told me stories. Because many of them had never known a Jew in their small rural communities, they had grown up with the idea that they knew nothing of anti-Semitism. Yet one student could tell me that when she went off to college, her brother warned her to be careful, because with a family name like Buchholz, she might be taken for a Jew. Like the anti-Semitism that recently was imported into Japan (where there are virtually no Jews), or its reemergence in a virtually Jew-free Poland, it turns out that anti-Semitism is quite portable and can easily exist independent of Jewish presence.

In that coffeehouse in Minneapolis I was not afraid of deliberate or malicious anti-Semitism. But when you are presenting yourself as a Jew in a mostly non-Jewish environment, you never know how it will break out.

How to Measure the Distance?

I like to think that if either anti-Semitism or homphobia broke out today I would respond with less temerity and greater authority. Our collective voices have created an environment in which I feel more entitled to speak. The *Tikkun* conference that took place in New York City in December 1988 is a good case in point. It was a conference intended to bring progressive Jews together, yet no special sessions on gay and lesbian Jews had been planned (though some people from the gay/lesbian community had been invited to speak as individuals on other panels). Pressure from lesbians and gay men resulted in a last-minute panel that brought together four speakers and more than one hundred people. The sense that we had a right to be visible both to ourselves and to the rest of the community was palpable and effective.

Seven years after the initial appearance of *Nice Jewish Girls* our sense of entitlement in Jewish progressive space is strong. This has been fostered, among other efforts, by the New Jewish Agenda feminist task force that produced a pamphlet discussing homophobia in the Jewish community,[11] and other coalitions that Jewish lesbian and gay communities have successfully forged with synagogues. The New York chapter of the National Council of Jewish Women supports a Jewish lesbian affinity group. The Jewish Caucus fulfills that role in the National Women's Studies Association, which is so influential for feminist thinking. *Nice Jewish Girls* has created a space for Jews in the lesbian/gay community.

In response to a call I made at the *Tikkun* workshop for stories of Jewish lesbian lives, I got a letter from a New York City painter and art teacher, Bea Kreloff, who is a political activist, a lover, a grandmother, and the mother of a gay son. Her words provide a good example of how collectively we have ourselves prepared the ground on which we now stand. At age 64, she writes, "I'm living exactly as I wish with the raised consciousness of feminism, over the socialist, Marxist, political conscience I grew up with, enlarged by gay liberation, empowered by my lesbianism, all of it coated with the best of the Jewish ethics and culture of my Jewish tradition. It's all come together now."

But there are still Jews for whom it doesn't come together so easily. I hear of and meet Jewish lesbians in Austria, Holland, Germany, Australia, the United States, whose Jewishness was hidden from them, or who had been taught to hide it from others. Some had been baptised by their parents to protect them; others had felt a special kind of vulnerability without knowing why. But baptism doesn't protect you from loving women or from feeling like a Jew once your roots are uncovered. For many of these women, *Nice Jewish Girls* provided an opening, a way back, a beginning. For me, the book has been an anchor whose very physical presence is a comfort. It is unthinkable that it would ever go out of print, and I am pleased that Beacon has placed it in its Jewish feminist series, next to *The Tribe of Dina* and a new anthology of writings by lesbian and gay Jews.[12]

Endnotes

[1]Some details of this tragicomic misunderstanding are detailed in my essay "Daughters and Mothers, Three Generations" in this volume.

[2]In Boston, in New York City, in Los Angeles, in San Francisco, in Chicago, in Madison, Wisconsin, in Washington, D.C., and elsewhere.

[3]For a discussion of this legacy, see Gerald Sorin, *The Prophetic Minority: American Jewish Immigrant Radicals, 1880-1920* (Bloomington: Indiana University Press, 1985).

[4]Judy Grahn, *Another Mother Tongue: Gay Words, Gay Worlds* (Boston: Beacon Press, 1984), pp. 186-191.

[5]A recent *New York Times* article discusses the lesbian "baby boom." Because of the greater pressure on Jewish women to produce children, it may well be that Jewish lesbians are choosing to have or adopt children in greater proportion to their numbers in the population. Two new anthologies include essays and poetry by Jewish lesbians. See *Politics of the Heart: A Lesbian Parenting Anthology*, ed. Sandra Pollack and Jeanne Vaughn (Firebrand Press, 1987) and *We Are Everywhere: Writings by and About Lesbian Parents*, ed. Harriet Alpert (The Crossing Press, 1988).

[6]See "Lesbian Separatist Statement from the Closing Session of the Jewish Feminist Conference, held in San Francisco, May 1982"; "Owning Jewish Separatism and Lesbian Separatism," Billie Luisi Potts, 1982; "One More Contradiction," Naomi Dykestein, 1983; "Journal Entry," Elana Dykewomon; and entries by Alix Dobkin and Liza Cowan in *For Lesbians Only: A Separatist Anthology*, ed. Sarah Lucia Hoagland and Julia Penelope (Onlywomyn Press, 1988).

[7]For a fuller discussion by a Jewish convert see "Living in the In-Between," by Chaya Shoshana (L. Lee Knefelkamp) in this volume. I recognize that some converts prefer the term "Jews-by-choice," but I concur with Lee, who argues that all Jews choose daily whether or not to live or identify Jewishly.

[8]This group organizes two retreats annually. One of their members is currently soliciting material for an anthology of writings and photos by JLDHS, partners, and interested others, tentatively entitled *The Hour of the Rooster, the Hour of the Owl.* For further information, contact Catherine O. Lohr, P.O. Box 6194, Boston, MA 02114.

[9]See *NWSA Journal* Vol. I, No. 1 (1988), pp. 93-102.

[10]No. 28 (1988-89). This excuse is flimsy, untrue, totally unsatisfactory and simply points up the board's ignorance.

[11]*Coming Out, Coming Home.* $.50 a copy, $35 for 100. Can be ordered from New Jewish Agenda, 64 Fulton St., #1100, New York, NY 10038.

[12]*Twice Blessed*, ed. Christie Balka and Andy Rose (Beacon Press, 1989). For further thoughts on Jewish lesbian feminist community see my essay "Naming Is Not a Simple Act: Jewish Lesbian Feminist Community in the 1980s" to appear in that anthology (Fall 1989).

from **Bashert***

Irena Klepfisz

These words are dedicated to those who died

These words are dedicated to those who died
because they had no love and felt alone in the world
because they were afraid to be alone and tried to stick it out
because they could not ask
because they were shunned
because they were sick and their bodies could not resist the
    disease
because they played it safe
because they had no connections
because they had no faith
because they felt they did not belong and wanted to die

These words are dedicated to those who died
because they were loners and liked it
because they acquired friends and drew others to them
because they took risks
because they were stubborn and refused to give up
because they asked for too much

These words are dedicated to those who died
because a card was lost and a number was skipped
because a bed was denied
because a place was filled and no other place was left

These words are dedicated to those who died
because someone did not follow through
because someone was overworked and forgot
because someone left everything to God

**ba shert'*: inevitable, (pre)destined.

because someone was late
because someone did not arrive at all
because someone told them to wait and they just couldn't
    any longer

These words are dedicated to those who died
because death is a punishment
because death is a reward
because death is the final rest
because death is eternal rage

These words are dedicated to those who died

Bashert

These words are dedicated to those who survived

These words are dedicated to those who survived
because their second grade teacher gave them books
because they did not draw attention to themselves and got lost
    in the shuffle
because they knew someone who knew someone else who could
    help them and bumped into them on a corner on a Thursday
    afternoon
because they played it safe
because they were lucky

These words are dedicated to those who survived
because they knew how to cut corners
because they drew attention to themselves and always got picked
because they took risks
because they had no principles and were hard

These words are dedicated to those who survived
because they refused to give up and defied statistics
because they had faith and trusted in God
because they expected the worst and were always prepared
because they were angry
because they could ask
because they mooched off others and saved their strength

because they endured humiliation
because they turned the other cheek
because they looked the other way

These words are dedicated to those who survived
because life is a wilderness and they were savage
because life is an awakening and they were alert
because life is a flowering and they blossomed
because life is a struggle and they struggled
because life is a gift and they were free to accept it

These words are dedicated to those who survived

Bashert

From One Generation to Another

Daughters and Mothers: Three Generations

Evelyn Torton Beck

An Autobiographical Sketch (1980)

I have a piece of lesbian history I haven't quite known what to do with.

Sometimes you know something is important and ought to be shared, and yet the uncertainty of where you might find the right place to publish it and the fear that it might not be accepted anywhere keeps you from putting it down on paper. This has been true for me and the story I've been carrying around in my head for a long time now.

The story is the story of my life. My life and my daughter's. I am EviB—the lesbian name my lover gave to me. It is a name I especially like, with its warm and playful evocation of Gertrude Stein and Alice B. Toklas. In the name I am both Gertrude and Alice. I am a community woman and a university professor. I am Jewish and a mother. I am a Jewish lesbian who is the mother of a Jewish lesbian. And if the world were a different place, and my mother not so hooked into the patriarchy, I'd be the daughter of a lesbian, too.

It was my mother who taught me to love women. Not by loving me or by encouraging me to love women, but by her own unwitting example—the intense, life-long ties she shared with her women friends. I saw the closeness and the caring, even as she faithfully spouted what she believed to be her truths: Love men, they are our only salvation. Fear men, they are the dangerous enemy. She dreamed of male heroes, yet lived in a safe world of women. In real life, my father provided protection and sustenance. My memory is that other men were there only as essential backdrop and for occasional flirtation.

My daughter was an active lesbian in her teens. I envy her the freedom she took—I did not give it to her. If I had not been so fearful; if I had lived in other times; if my own mother had not been so watchful or so judgmental, especially when I was in my early teens, I'd have been freer to be the lesbian I was. I would not have had to spend long hours in the library agonizing, proving that I wasn't what I feared I was, knew I was, and talked myself out of being—loving women intensely, passionately, often obsessively, yet denying what this meant.

The best friend of my childhood years turned out to be a lesbian. I didn't know it in the years we shared a great passion for our seventh-grade English teacher; saving our money to buy her a costly gold bracelet, planning and writing about it all summer long, she at camp and I at home. (My friend spent twenty years in therapy, she later told me.) When she came out at age fourteen, it was a neighborhood scandal, talked about at length and in detail, at least in my home, primarily by my mother, who seemed to know everything about it. I can no longer clearly differentiate what I knew for myself from what my mother told me, how much my mother really knew from what she made up or guessed. I do remember some fragments.

My friend was involved with an older woman who lived on the next block with another woman. (How old was older? Twenty-five? Thirty-five?) Did my mother really suggest they seduced her? Probably. Were they really gym teachers, or am I making that up? My friend, herself, told me the police frequently bothered them when they were together in the car. Sometimes they were able to use someone's apartment. Did I know what they did? Did I guess or imagine? I distinctly remember one detail. She told me they always need a lot of tissues. I didn't *exactly* know what for, but I've never forgotten that detail either. I must have known something. Sometime later my friend told me her friend had deflowered her and she had bled. I sensed she was proud of this detail, but I'm not sure I believed she was telling me the truth. Did I think she invented these details just for my sake? How much did I really grasp? I myself was still totally sexually inactive at the time (except for masturbation, which I had learned young and liked a great deal and was terribly ashamed of). I disliked intensely what seemed to be the necessary making out at parties and always tried to get out of participating. Usually, I succeeded. At home, over and over again, my mother repeated that my friend was disgusting. What she did was disgusting. When I was disobedient, it was my friend's fault. She was a bad influence. Her mother was a communist, a divorcee who worked outside the home, what else could you expect?

In spite of my mother, we remained friends. A few years later she told me the details of her love affairs with women at college. How her lovers would touch her in the dark in bed, how they would touch her in bed but refuse to kiss her. How they would, in the daylight, withhold their love and pretend they didn't know her. These stories have stayed with me (till now I had no idea how indelibly) for nearly thirty years. I found it hard to understand why these lovers acted so strangely. If either of us had any inkling, we did not say. I doubt that the word *lesbian* ever crossed our lips, even while she was telling me these stories. I only remember clearly that she was badly hurt and terribly confused. We had no analysis, no names, no vocabulary (not in the early fifties on the streets of Brooklyn) with which to talk about women's love for women. The best I could offer her (and this I did willingly, eagerly) was to listen. In thinking myself back to those years, it dawns upon me that her stories with their muted eroticism must have aroused me then, mildly, as they do now in the retelling. And I feel ashamed at feeling pleasure from what caused her pain. And at my own cowardice.

We've more or less lost touch now, but she was resigned and a little bitter when I last saw her, a few years ago, after a lapse of fifteen years. The long therapy had not erased the hurt. "I am neither," she said, when I asked her if she was still involved with women. "I cannot dissociate women from how bad and crazy I felt all those years." I remembered then how desperately she had tried to make life with a man work for her. More than once she had seriously contemplated marriage, but it never happened. I knew it was all wrong, but never once in the many years we exchanged letters did I dare express my doubt, did I dare say what I knew in my guts to be true: "Why are you trying to be what you are not?" No, I remained silent, foolishly polite, frequently encouraged her in her pursuit of marriage, and was disappointed with her every disappointment. Now she claims to have found peace in withdrawing from sexual intimacy altogether, and I feel angry for her, for myself, for all of us. Of course she is still a lesbian. Has never been anything else. It doesn't seem fair for her to have to believe she is "neither."

In a way, I was luckier. I masked myself in ways that protected. I think if I had come out then, as my friend did, in the late forties, I would be worse than "neither." I feel sure I would have cracked. My mother would have seen to that. She was so relentless, and I so tied to her approval. I fully believed she would lock me up or throw me out (the latter now doesn't seem very likely—she was too fiercely possessive to let me go). Being poor and new immigrants, we did not believe in or have access to psychiatrists. Instead, thinking to save me, she would not have hesitated to destroy me herself. My need for protection was very real, and for a time my mask worked. True, I continued to fall in love with women all my life (I never did outgrow that passion), but I was able to marry a man. And live with him for twenty years. And bear two children, one of whom is now a lesbian and has been since she was thirteen.

It feels hard to have to say I didn't help her become one. No, if truth be told, I'd have stopped her at the time if I could have. I did try. And so did her father. This is the hardest thing to admit, to set down on paper: I tried to keep her from becoming a dyke. I thought it would ruin her life. I really did. We threatened to call the police if she continued to see her lover. (I had no idea then of the power of the law or the enormity of our threats.) I didn't even really believe that they were lovers—my thirteen-year-old child and the twenty-one-year-old woman who was her mentor. I only knew that they loved each other and had made plans to sleep together. We kept them apart (or thought we did).

We joke about it now, she and I. Her friends all told her I must be a closet case to know so much and care so passionately. They were right, of course, but I was exceptionally obtuse. It took me years to really take in the fact that my daughter made love with another woman (not merely love, *sex*), even after she and her second lover had been living together for two years. And sleeping in one bed. And appearing with a group of Jewish lesbians in a protest at Hillel. I was utterly naive and heavily defended. Ridiculously, after I came out, I kept it from my daughter for a whole year (or thought I did). In fact, she knew and the whole community knew. (Was I ashamed to admit how very wrong I had been when she was thirteen?) One of the mothers I had run to in a panic about my daughter was herself the lesbian mother of a lesbian, only I didn't know it at the time, in spite of the fact that she was sharing her life with a woman. I can hardly bring myself to imagine how she experienced our assault; she met it with silence. We wanted her to *do* something, anything, to warn the other parents, to stop the affair. We did manage to call the youth-group parents together; I don't remember how they calmed us down. From the relatively safe distance of a decade, I can almost see the humor of the situation. That the lesbian mother (who is now also a colleague) speaks to me at all often amazes me. We almost never mention those times. I think they embarrass us both.

Today my daughter is twenty-three. That she is a lesbian comforts me. Whatever her struggles, I don't worry she will give her power away to the patriarchy. I trust and respect her and her lover and the many women who are her friends; I count myself among them. We share much these days. I also know that her example paved the way for me. In trying to understand her, I found myself facing myself and my marriage. I clearly remember the day when our family shrink (a patriarchal but sensible man who knew she was a lesbian) said of my young teen-age daughter, with particular emphasis on the first and last words, "*She's* O.K., but what about the two of *you*?" That day marked the beginning of my liberation and my slow return to the lesbian self I had abandoned years ago.

Of course it didn't happen all at once. The process was slow, sometimes painful, and helped enormously, crucially, by my growing economic independence. First, I had to free myself from the mask of heterosexuality I had so earnestly assumed. Only then could I begin to explore my love for women. But I was not going to burn all my bridges at once. Comical as it now seems, I prepared the way by systematically announcing my intentions to my heterosexual friends. It worked. Making love with a woman felt like the most natural thing I had ever done. (That still makes me angry, since all my life I had been led to believe the very opposite.)

In one sense, the transition was easy; my emotional life had never ceased to be with women. That fact had caused me some discomfort while I was married, since it did not fit my picture of marriage. (Now and then my husband complained about it, but I didn't admit it to him. It must have made him feel just slightly crazy.) On the whole, it was a problem I could dismiss with relative ease. Some kindly, well-meaning shrink had once told me, in the early years of my marriage, that if I was successful in having orgasms with men, I could not possibly be a lesbian. I'm not so sure how deeply I believed him. It continued to seem strange to me that I always wanted to express my feelings for women by touching them, but I dutifully held back. (I don't think I ever mentioned these details to my shrink, which may have helped him in his diagnosis.) It also seemed odd to me that the only words that seemed accurately to describe certain of my feelings for women were the "inappropriate" words, "I am in love with. . . ." Instinctively, I knew better than to mention these feelings to anyone but my oldest, dearest, most trustworthy, unquestionably heterosexual friend. I don't think she really knew what to make of my confession either, but I know it helped me enormously that she listened and did not say it was a terrible thing. (Very like the role I played in listening to my childhood lesbian friend.) The word *lesbian*, of course, was never mentioned.

Fortunately, I had never fallen in love with my confidante, though I loved her deeply (and still do). No doubt that saved our friendship. I remember how relieved I was (even at age eighteen when we first met) that I did not have "those" feelings for her. I so much wanted to be her friend, and knew from experience how burdensome those feelings could be and how peculiarly they sometimes made me behave. (My passions for women always felt like some dread disease I had contracted and could neither control nor get rid of.) I was terribly ashamed of these feelings and at the same time treasured them as my most valued possession, my secret source of joy, comfort, and nourishment, right through the years of my marriage.

As I read and reread these pages, I realize how long and cumbersome the process of coming-to-myself has been. I am now forty-six. I came out five years ago. It frightens me to think that without the lesbian/feminist movement, without the example of my own daughter (and other brave women I admire and respect), I might still be in the closet *to myself*, might still believe in the absolute normality of heterosexuality, despite the strong evidence of my own feelings. I ask myself as I read this: Is it possible that without the support of a movement I might never have come out? Merely continued to inexplicably and inappropriately fall in love with women? A part of me believes this could have happened, unless I had ever fallen in love with a woman who knew herself to be a lesbian (and knew me for one too). Or would I have run away from even such an opportunity?

Recently, one of the women I was in love with years ago told me I had once asked her to go to bed when I was still married, and she had refused. I have absolutely no recollection of such a conversation, but the longing and the desire were certainly there, perhaps for us both; I suspect more was communicated between us than either of us ever acknowledged in words. But as I said before, even as an adult, I was exceedingly naive. She was a painter. I modeled for her, both in the nude and while nursing my son. Over the years she produced hundreds of portraits and sketches of me. In oils, in pencil, in pastel. For hours each day, for days on end, I sat while she painted and we talked. I understood well what this time meant to me; I never thought to ask what it meant to her. (Perhaps we made love after all, without touching.)

I have no way of knowing what shape my life might have taken without the influence and support of a lesbian/feminist movement. I only know with certainty that the last five years of my life have been for me the most fully lived. The years of greatest growth and deepest opening, of real congruence with myself. And for this richness, this happiness (unexpected, but actively sought for), I am grateful.

I came out to my mother about three years ago. She knew before I told her. (Her antennae are ever up.) In fact, I did not tell her. She asked. The very first thing she wanted to know was which of us was the man, I or my lover? When I told her we were not at all into roles, she was incredulous, particularly about sex. How was it possible, she wanted to know. "Who decides what to do?" She constantly brings up the subject of homosexuality (sometimes playfully) and as constantly puts it down. Just the same, letting her know was the most freeing thing I have ever done for myself. I no longer wait for her approval. She accepts me, as best she can, with some severe reservations—what she refers to as the "big big BUT." Her sense of humor saves her for me. I have come to understand that she is not simply judging me, that she is also jealous—of the obvious closeness with my lover, of the nurturing we give each other. In her ironic vision, she faults our love as a "mutual admiration society." She is slightly peeved. If we can be so gentle and loving to each other, why can't everyone else (in the heterosexual world she knows) be equally so? She says this in tones that could be called accusing. It was not the model for her marriage nor one she ever envisioned. We do not talk well. She has not learned to love me, nor has she ever loved herself. About these things, I am sad.

As for me, in coming out I finally gave birth to the woman I had been carrying for decades. She has learned to love herself as she has allowed herself to love and be loved by another woman. I am glad to share her life. I like her and am glad she finally told her story. My story.

Further Thoughts (1987)

I feel very protective of this essay. It is more private than anything else I have ever published, and exposing it to public view in an anthology likely to have a wide audience makes me feel particularly vulnerable. When it first appeared in 1980, I had not yet fully taken in the fact that if you write something down and send it out for publication, it will, if published, very likely be read. Such "innocence" makes it considerably easier to write of delicate matters in your own voice.

It should not then be surprising that this essay means more to me than any other writing I have produced. Together with the introductory essay to this volume, it is implanted in my mind as the very core of my autobiography. In rereading my own words today, I am struck by how deeply I knew and trusted that I could not speak as a mother without speaking almost at the same time, in counterpoint, as a daughter. I still appreciate the way I wove together themes I have since pursued independently in greater depth, but I am amazed at what I did not highlight at all. The fact that I am a Jew is clearly present but not foregrounded; I did not pursue what it meant to be a Jewish daughter and Holocaust survivor, a Jewish lesbian mother of a Jewish lesbian daughter, themes that still wait to be further developed. Nonetheless, it is impossible for me to rewrite this essay today without violating the truths of my life as I understood them at the time. What this essay suggests, but does not analyze, needs to be explored independently. For example, I have only recently begun to deal with the fact that when speaking in a public, nonlesbian forum, I feel a distinct discomfort at revealing that I have a lesbian daughter. This, in spite of the strong comfort this fact gives me in private and in safe (i.e., nonhomophobic) environments. What to do with the filter that makes me see myself as peculiar in the eyes of others? Why should I, for even one minute, have to worry that my family has "gone too far" by containing a lesbian daughter *and* mother? To what extent is this particular fear connected to my own history as a survivor? Who determines the limits of the acceptable? How to combat this defensiveness in myself? How to speak of my lesbian daughter naturally, with ease and pride, the way I now speak easily as a lesbian and a Jew?

My son and his wife recently provided a hopeful counterpoint to this sense of dis-ease. At their wedding this summer, they invited me and my partner, my daughter and her partner, to sit up front with the wedding party, together with the other close relatives. The fact that two of the couples were of the same sex was unmarked in any way, and I felt a good deal of pride that their love for us made it possible for them to refuse to see through any filter but their own.

To return to the past. Some facts in the essay as I wrote it then have changed and can easily be brought up-to-date.

Eight years have gone by. My daughter is now thirty-one, and I have just turned fifty-four. We still have only gingerly discussed the difficult years of her coming out. We are friends, but respectful of the distance we need in order to remain close. I had hoped that the occasion of the republication of this essay might provide an opportunity for us to talk about the past in greater depth, but we seem not to be ready for such intimacy. [*Editor's note:* See "Mother and Daughter, Jewish and Lesbian: A Conversation (1989)," p. 16.] Yet my daughter appears to take pride in my writing and has willingly given her permission for the inclusion of this essay, which is, after all, as much about her as it is about me. I have never shown it to my mother who, in the intervening years, has learned to love me better, and has allowed her "big big BUT" to undergo some considerable shrinkage. She seems to have made peace with my life in spite of her own determination to resist what could be construed as absolute affirmation. She sees that I am genuinely happy and is happy for me; is finally even proud of my accomplishments.

The friend who claimed that she was "neither" heterosexual nor lesbian has since accepted her lesbian self in more positive ways, though she still lives a heavily closeted life in relative isolation.

My first lesbian lover who named me EviB is now a deep and abiding friend. I have found a life-partner, whose love and trust are the foundation for my life, my loving, and my work in the world.

On Passing: From One Generation to Another

Nina Rachel

I find myself   always between the rock and some
                        kind of hard place.
When   white is rock   and the hard places are
                        brown and beige and black.
I fall in   between.
Caught by neither   and seeing no place   of my own.

Out   on the streets of Vienna, 1938
5 years old
Sent to buy butter   blond curls hiding the yellow
                        star worn over her heart
Hiding the fear   of what if you're caught
                        out there   looking like one of
                                            them.

It didn't stop them from arresting the father, from
    killing the grandmother outright.
They didn't pass   she died.

Growing up in fear   I learned anger
Knowing even before knowing   that I was not
                        supposed to be
Should be dead
Should be grateful.

Living in anger   I would never try to pass,
                    never learn all the ways of
                                white.

And if they called out
     "kike" or "big-nosed hairy-legs Jew"
         I would not run   also
         did not fight
But died a thousand tiny deaths in places still
    frozen inside.

Anger hides despair.

Passing   is pain and fear.
Curled up completely still
Hands and feet and head tucked inside
Hoping your outside looks a lot like
    rock
        wondering when you'll be found out
        and knowing that you don't belong.

Choosing life   I walk upright   and hope my brown curls
                do not hide the Mogen David
                around my neck.

Mother and Daughter, Jewish and Lesbian: A Conversation (1989)

Evelyn Torton Beck and Nina Rachel

For several years we had been talking about "doing something together" because we thought that our experiences and inter-actions as a mother and daughter who were both Jewish and lesbian would be of interest to others. The new edition of *Nice Jewish Girls* seemed to provide an ideal opportunity.

But it wasn't easy to get started; we live on opposite coasts, and neither of us was willing to begin this conversation on the telephone. Even though we were both quite nervous about stir-ring up the past, we decided to spend a few days together, leaving ourselves the option of "not writing anything if it doesn't work out." Once we were in the same space, we did begin to talk, and by mutual agreement Evi took notes (unobtrusively). We did this for several hours at a time, letting the conversation take us where it would, not forcing ourselves to "stick to the topic."

After a day or so, Evi put our conversation into the computer and began transcribing and editing the material. This method worked well for Evi's words, but Nina's did not sound like her; so Nina took the outline and rewrote it in her own language, reorganizing and clarifying where necessary and—amazingly—learning to use the computer in the process. Then we read our writing out loud and made more changes together.

This process was surprisingly smooth and without tension, though we were both exhausted by the work and the feelings it had evoked. What began as a somewhat stiff interaction evolved into a warm and relaxed conversation.

Although we had no set agenda, our conversation as Jewish

lesbians reflects one of the major struggles in Jewish life today: what does it mean to call oneself a Jew, particularly a secular Jew?

* * *

Evi: What does it mean to you to be a Jewish lesbian?

Nina: In thinking about my Jewish lesbian identity, I have to say that the part about how to be *Jewish* has been and continues to be more of a struggle for me than how to be lesbian. Whatever part Jewish culture plays in my life, it is clear that my participation is and can only be as a lesbian.

The development of a strong lesbian identity was certainly not easy in the face of real parental horror at my coming out. In fact, both of you made it as difficult as you could for me to even see my friends; with words and actions you told me just how horrible a lesbian choice would be. For a couple of years I tried to go out with boys, tried to convince myself that my love for Cathy was a fluke—that I could be equally interested in men as in womyn. It didn't work.

By the time I was sixteen, it was clear that my life would be with womyn. I also got a much longed-for work permit, a job and out of your house. When I started college the following fall, my life was already centered in the gay world: in the streets, in the classroom, and, of course, in the bars.

E: So how do you feel about being Jewish?

N: How to be Jewish has been a more puzzling problem. I feel like I take a soap-box stand on being Jewish and how important it is to me. Although I can be really vocal and quite adamant in my opinions, I often feel that I don't have enough concrete knowledge of Jewish culture to back up my beliefs.

E: But you learned Hebrew when we lived in Israel for a year.

N: That's true, but if I were to trace a language that connected me to my culture, it would be Yiddish. The culture that I came from was *yiddishkayt*, not Hebrew or Israel. Secular *yiddishkayt* barely exists today, and the Yiddish language is dying out because parents are not teaching it to their children. This really upsets me. I feel like the path back to my culture is falling away.

E: Do you really think you would have wanted to learn it when you were little? That you would not have resented our trying to teach it to you?

N: I don't know. My fantasy would be to have learned it as I learned English, as a native tongue. You know, I have a lot of anger at Jews who assimilate and are not interested in Jewish culture. I was taught by you that Jews who assimilate have sold their souls and that that is one of the most horrible things one could do. But you didn't teach me what it means *not* to assimilate. You didn't teach me what it means to *be* a Jew. What the substance of that is.

E: But that is exactly what I feel! I am so public a Jew and don't know nearly enough. And though my father sent me to a religious Hebrew school (which I hated) and then to a secular Yiddish school (which made more sense to me), today I am still struggling to make *being* Jewish meaningful. But I am really shocked and surprised that you feel that way too.

N: Well I do. I feel a strong spiritual connection to a heritage I do not honestly know very much about. At Jewish gatherings and events, I often pretend to know what's going on. I've learned to listen carefully and to learn as much as possible without actually asking questions and admitting to what I don't know. Most people think that I know far more about Jewish tradition than I really do. It's the picture I've worked hard to present. There are times when I am inspired to go out and learn more. At our gay/lesbian synagogue in San Francisco there is a womyn's Torah study group and a Havurah. There are also Yiddish classes at Hillel in Berkeley. But I feel overwhelmed, as if I could never learn all this in a lifetime.

E: But I feel that way too. I also have to look up the details of Jewish history or the holidays. It is my experience that almost every Jewish lesbian feels she doesn't know enough. I wonder if that comes from a model deep in traditional Jewish culture that says Jewish authenticity means total immersion. In Jewish study there is no such thing as "knowing enough." But I'll bet you don't know as little as you think you do.

N: But what I want to know is why wasn't I taught more of what you knew?

E: I think I was rebelling against what I had been forced to learn, and at the time it didn't seem very meaningful. And how much did I really know? Whatever they "taught" me, I actually "learned" very little. I have been teaching myself ever since. It has become my life's work. I've always hesitated to ask you—but do you think your study of aikido is a displacement of your interest in Jewish culture, and search for a community?

N: That is entirely possible. It has certainly seemed easier to commit myself to daily study of aikido (which I do) than to any consistent study of Jewish tradition. But I do see a connection between the two studies. I find that the practice of aikido resembles Torah study. In both practices humility is what is needed in the face of something much greater than oneself. The aikido master, like the Talmudic scholar, after 35 years of study says, "I think I am beginning to understand . . ." the interpretation of a phrase, a movement, or the connection of a word to the whole, of a single motion to the complete form. And the world aikido community is much like the world Jewish community, in that wherever you go, you can find a place where you will be welcomed.

E: When did your Jewish identity become so important to you?

N: As far back as I can remember, it's always been strong. When I was a young kid, I was always very conscious of our Jewishness, but especially after we came back from Israel. I wanted to be a part of a community.

E: Oh, so when you said you wanted to go to Hebrew school, maybe you really meant it.

N: (with ironic laughter) Yeah!

E: And we didn't let you go. Dad was from a strongly atheist background and was very much against it. We would have had to join a Temple, which also cost a lot of money. And I had heard it wasn't a very good school.

N: Well I really wanted to belong to something Jewish. Remember when we lived in England for a year, I told everybody at school I was Orthodox. I always wore a Jewish star and a *chai* and refused to go to school assemblies and say Christian prayers.

E: I guess I thought that you had gotten a sense of what it meant to be Jewish because we talked about it at home all the time.

N: That's true. But talking about it was no substitute for actual experience.

E: That's painful to hear.

N: But I did associate Jewish culture with the progressive socialist politics that you and Dad shared.

E: You are right. We did bring you up with a sense of being different; that was one thing your dad and I had in common, a sense of being outsiders. We didn't either of us conform and didn't encourage you to.

N: Well it certainly wasn't easy for us, but life got really tough in 1966, as I was entering the sixth grade, when you bought a house in an upper-middle-class, repressively white, racist, anti-Semitic neighborhood. Thankfully, we never wanted to join the country club because I'm sure the membership there did not include Jews, socialists, or antiwar/civil-rights activists. All of which we were.

E: I didn't think of it that way. I had no sense that the neighbors might be upset with us!

N: It's not a clear memory, but I think we were also harassed because before we even moved in, we rented the house out for the summer to a visiting family who happened to be black. Then *we* moved in and we didn't look like anything they had ever seen before either. It felt to me as though we looked as different from the neighbors as humanly possible. Remember how Micah wore his hair in a pony tail and the kids put a pink ribbon on his desk? Did you know that he got beat up almost every day on his way home from school and I defended him? It was very hard.

E: Do you think it would have been different in another neighborhood?

N: Maybe a little. But it was hard growing up Jewish and different in Madison, Wisconsin. There were very few Jews—in junior high school I was one of only two Jews in my class, and the other girl was trying as hard as she could to be invisible. She taunted and teased me right along with the other kids. I was living in a community where being Jewish was not popular, to say the least. And I knew that the worst thing in the world was to be a Jew and deny it. This was a serious dilemma. When the protests in school and the antiwar activity started, I also began my first love affair, and I acted on what I was taught. In our house, being different was OK, even desirable, so I didn't see that anything I was doing was any different from what I had been taught. Why would there be anything wrong with acting on your beliefs even if they were different from what everyone else was doing?

E: And we supported your rebellion, up to a point. But then it went further than we were comfortable with. Especially when you were coming out as a lesbian and we freaked out. In all this, did you feel good about being Jewish? I think we gave you some sense of pride.

N: Oh yes, I was certainly proud of it.

E: And we always celebrated Chanukah; we lit candles every night and gave you little presents.

N: But we stopped after a while. I always thought you did it mainly because that's what one should do when one had children, so the children should have a celebration instead of Christmas.

E: Well that was true. And Dad used to call it "Chanuka-instead." It really is a minor holiday.

N: I know. I always tell people that. When they wish me Merry Christmas and I say I don't celebrate Christmas so then they wish me Happy Chanukah, I always say "Don't make a big thing of it, it's really only a minor holiday. It's not a Jewish Christmas."

E: What about Seders?

N: I always liked the Seders at Ima's and Poppa's. There was a nice warm feeling about them. I liked being in New York.

E: Did you understand what they meant?

N: Not really, but I liked them.

E: They always made me very tense; I was afraid there would be fights.

N: Well I do remember Uncle Eddie trying to kill Ima a few times.

E: (uncomfortable laughter) Do you remember the big Seder in Israel at the home of Rahel and Yehuda Lapidot? You were vegetarian then and broke your diet because of the huge amount of meat on the table.

N: (laughter) Yes. I remember that well. I liked that a lot. The Seder has become one of the most meaningful rituals of my life.

E: What about Rosh Hashanah and Yom Kippur? I don't think we made a big fuss about that then.

N: I don't remember observing the Holy Days until the ninth grade, when I insisted on going to services. I remember that I knew it was within my rights to take off from school and so I did. I went to services at Hillel with one of my friends for an hour or two, but mostly this was just a legal way to skip school.

E: We did go to Hillel for some other holidays.

N: We used to go at Purim I remember. I always liked that. Dad spoke at the *latke-humantasch* debate every year.

E: And when Grandma Minnie was alive she always made latkes. Do you remember that?

N: Yes. I liked to go to her house too.

E: So being lesbian and being Jewish were never really separate for you? And coming out as you did in the late 60s, did you not have to work through homophobia?

N: Of course I did. You always have to work that through. And you never ever get rid of it entirely, even today. But being Jewish was always a fact of my life. I never questioned *whether* I was Jewish, just *how* to be Jewish.

E: Me too. Maybe I was always struggling with what that fact meant. But it seems to me that it became much more urgent, once I became public as a lesbian and grasped how that put me at risk. Becoming visible as a lesbian made me less safe in the world but more secure in myself, so maybe I could face the un-safety of being Jewish. I had struggled so hard for so many years to be heterosexual. You didn't have to struggle with that.

N: I did. I tried to be heterosexual for at least two years when I was 15 and 16. I tried to be in love with this one [male] or that one. I always blamed it on the very clear message I got from you and Dad that what I was doing was all wrong and horrible. But I don't know if I would have had that struggle anyway.

E: Well, we certainly didn't make it any easier for you.

N: But not feeling safe as a Jew *ever*, seemed more obvious to me because anti-Semitism got me much sooner than homophobia. I think there was anti-Jewish feeling even in my grade school, which was more ethnically mixed than the schools I later attended. I remember I came home from kindergarten and complained that they were making us say the Lord's Prayer before juice and cookies, and you went to school and protested. I am not sure how they treated me after that. And do you remember I had these two friends Tina and Maria, and when I realized they were German I ran home screaming that their father was a Nazi!

E: You must have imbibed a lot more at home than I realized. I only remember that faintly. How did I respond?

N: You tried to explain that not all Germans were Nazis. But I was terrified.

E: You ended up in some way replicating my life!

N: (wry smile) I think that would be a safe statement.

E: What do you think that is, a repetition compulsion?

N: I'd much rather believe in something like agreements I made with you before I was born.

E: I believe that's possible. Part of my freak-out at becoming a mother, and especially birthing a girl child, had to do with my history with anti-Semitism and the sense of being unwanted and slated for murder. If I had no right to live, how could I have the right to reproduce another like me? That must have been a terrifying idea. And you know, I gave birth to a Jewish girl child in a virulently racist and anti-Semitic place where I felt I had no right to be.

N: And anti-Semitism was more openly acceptable at that time.

E: Yes, your birth was in non-safety.

N: And the experience of that anti-Semitism was intensified by your childhood memories of it.

E: I hadn't thought about it that way, but I think you are right. And I transmitted all that to you. Did I talk about my experiences a lot? About my past?

N: I don't remember. I feel like I always knew some things but don't remember being told directly. I remember watching concentration-camp footage on TV with Ima the summer before we went to Israel. She told me to leave the room but I wanted to stay.

E: I never knew she watched them. We were not even allowed to talk about the camps. She always made us feel she could not take it. Because she had left her mother behind. What stories do you remember?

N: I don't even know if these are true, but I remember hearing that you got the measles on the boat and had to wear pancake makeup or they would send you all back. You had the responsibility for whether the family would be saved. I don't remember hearing much about Ima's mother who was killed or my aunts and uncles, but I always believed I was named for Tante Anna. Nina is really the name Anna.

E: Those stories are true. And maybe subliminally you were named for her. She survived the Holocaust but was dying of cancer just when you were born.

N: I always believed she was the one we left behind. I didn't know much about Rachel, the other great aunt I was named for.

E: Rachel was your dad's mother's beloved sister who died before you were born. Do you think Dad's experiences had any effect on you?

N: Yes. His father died when he was 11 years old, leaving him to parent his three-year-old brother; this greatly affected his life and ours. From him I learned "don't trust anybody but yourself." He grew up in poverty and his parents were communists. I was proud of that. From both of you I learned that I was capable of doing anything that I set out to do. Both your experiences of striving for what you believed in were powerful examples for me.

E: Were you aware of the different kinds of Jews that your two sets of grandparents were? That caused a lot of tension. I was brought up more traditionally; Dad was brought up as an atheist with strong Jewish progressive *yiddishist* left politics.

N: I wasn't aware of the rift between my grandparents, but I was always proud of Dad and the political work he was doing.

E: I think that kind of work has a particularly Jewish cast to it. I think Jewish lesbian-feminists are also carrying on that tradition. What did you think of Jewish-lesbian organizing in the 1970s when we lived in Madison?

N: I had a bad attitude towards it.

E: Because I was in it?

N: I am not sure. Probably. Before you were out as lesbian I think I was more involved. Then for many years I was more heavily into the bar scene than the political scene.

E: I was very surprised when I later found out that you had kept your interest in things Jewish. And very pleased. In a way I hoped you had figured out some answers.

N: I kept it from you for a long time.

E: I kept my interest in Jewish things from my father, because he had pressured me when I was young. After my father died, when I finally told my mother I was working as a Jew and a lesbian in Jewish communities, she said to me, "Don't think you are doing Jews a favor." Individuation is complicated.

N: Yes, I have a hard time telling my story without first telling yours and Dad's stories.

E: As I recall, our house was very liberal. I think we believed in gay rights and believed people should be who they are—as long as it wasn't my children. (laughter) It is still very hard for me to separate out all the turbulence of the '60s, the rebellion against parental authority, the dope I discovered you were taking, the youth group leaders I trusted, and then your falling in love with one of the leaders who was a lesbian. So I freaked out, but I can't swear that I wouldn't have freaked out anyway.

N: You have to look at all those things in their context for what they were. You thought the youth group was responsible, but everybody was doing drugs. And I had this idea when I was about 10 or 11 that I was never going to get married or have kids, and I knew I didn't like kissing the boys.

E: Did you think of yourself as a lesbian?

N: Somewhere around the sixth grade I began to wonder, does this mean I am a lesbian? So obviously, I had heard the word.

E: Were you scared?

N: A little, not terribly. You know, when we lived in England and I went to that all-girl's school, the girls all held hands and kissed one another. I remember thinking that this was great.

E: When I finally came out as a lesbian myself, how did you feel about it?

N: My first thought was, "Can you do it somewhere else please?" I was angry and thought you had a lot of nerve. When I came out as a lesbian it was a terrible thing, but when you came out in a big political way, it was supposed to be great! You came bursting onto the scene. "Here I am superdyke, well-known, visible," in what I had grown to call my community.

E: Because of my position as a professor and activist?

N: Yes, and because you were oblivious to the fact that I had been politically and socially active in the gay community for years. I remember once seeing you at a rally and you were happy to see me there. What you said was, "It's really nice to see you getting

more involved in politics"—as though I hadn't been. My truth
was that I'd been out there for years. You were really the new-
comer.

E: I guess I wasn't very sensitive. Did I give you the feeling that
the way I was doing it was the only way to do it? But wasn't there
a part of you that was pleased? When I talk to younger lesbians,
they are always very excited at the idea of a lesbian mother.
Lesbian mothers also seem to be pleased if their daughters are
lesbians. I feel like that. I worry about you less.

N: There's a part of me that is pleased now but was not at the
time. As lesbians we have always lived in very different worlds.
How we live on a daily basis is very different. Our ideas of what
we should do as lesbians are very different and have always been,
in terms of lifestyle and political choices.

E: Being lesbians makes for some common bond, but you think
the differences in lifestyle are more powerful?

N: Here is a good example of what I mean. We are both interested
in womyn's music. You took an academic approach, studying and
teaching about the music; let's face it, you live in academia. My
approach was to work on the festival in Michigan for 10 years,
to work as distributor of womyn's music and to bring these
womyn into my life as friends. We take entirely different ap-
proaches to the same issue. I sometimes thought you were studying the things I was living.

E: That is a powerful statement. I hadn't perceived as much difference, but I see what you mean. But I do call myself an activist.

N: I don't mean to imply that you are not. I don't mean to say
that what you are doing is not useful or worthwhile. It's just
different. In the last few years I have grown to appreciate your
contributions to the lesbian community. Now I am very proud of
your work. I think I started feeling proud when I helped proof
the first edition of *Nice Jewish Girls*. But you have some funny
ideas. I used to get annoyed when you said, "A lesbian wouldn't
do *that*," whatever was not in your experience. I see lesbians as
being a more diverse group. What they share is a primary relationship with womyn, but in all other things there is great
variety.

E: You mean my knowledge and experience of lesbianism is entirely within the context of the lesbian-feminist movement? I

don't know or even appreciate lesbian culture outside the realm of feminism?

N: Exactly, and that's part of why I maintained a certain distance from you over the years. Recently you have been more willing to look beyond your own world and I have been more willing to risk sharing with you. I probably feel most connected to you when I read your work or listen to you lecture. You often can clarify the very things I am trying to talk about and work with in my life.

E: Well you know you were a role model to me when I was coming out. Once I got to know you better and came to believe in your strength and courage, that gave me the strength to become the lesbian I always was. (long pause) I feel really good that we were able to have this conversation now. Who would have thought it possible?

If I Am Not for Myself, Who Will Be?

from **Perspectives on the Second World War**

Irena Klepfisz

listening to conversations   over brandy
i am always amazed at their certainty
about the past   how it could have been
different   could have been   turned around
with what ease   they transport themselves
to another time/place   taking the comfort
confidence of an after dinner drink

          it would be too impolite
of me to say   my mother hid with me
for two years among ignorant peasants   who
would have turned us in   almost at once   had
they known who we were   who would have watched
with glee while we were carted off   even though
grandad had bounced me on his knees and fed me
from his own spoon   and my mother is a frightened
woman

          it would be too impolite
to say   you do not know yourselves   you do not know
others

fifteen minutes from the Kar Kare Klinic*

Elana Dykewomon

JEWS should not live where I live
on the coast of oregon   we should move somewhere
when i was a kid
they said l.a. was safe, but it isn't anymore
not safe for kids windows to sport menorahs
in new york where my grandmother
was an old jewish womon
a gang of white girls pushed her
into the gutter, broke her hips

they paint it on the sides of buildings
all over the states
all over the world
it keeps on reappearing
doesn't go away
every other day i clip it out of the newspapers
once we were in the flamingo cafe in new orleans
a group of highly painted secretaries were talking
—mama knows all about the jews   she dated one—

it's
easy to make this list
places where jews should not in live:
in germany   in egypt   in portland
in yreka   in utah   in paris
in ghettos

---

*Between 1979 and 1983, my partner Dolphin and I were the only Jewish lesbians on the southern Oregon coast for hundreds of miles. The Kar Kare Klinic was owned by the organization its initials indicate. Shortly after this poem was written, the lone Jewish tailor in the town (fifteen minutes in the other direction) had his shop burned down. In 1983 we moved to Oakland.

outside of big cities   like skokie
in cuba   in the south
even miami isn't so great
in oakland they bait jews at their workplaces
& i dont expect it's easier in uganda
new zealand any
catholic protestant muslim or hindu nation
in the soviet union
in spain algeria chile bolivia buenos aires
el salvador nicaragua cape verde
south africa   canada poland
a jew should not live alone
a jew should not live with other jews
it provokes attention
a jew should not live in the native lands of others
a jew should not live in israel
jews are not israelis, they're just immigrants
they should have stayed out
should have stayed out of boston
out of singapore and canton
they should get out of california

we should leave southern oregon

Some Notes on Jewish Lesbian Identity*

Melanie Kaye/Kantrowitz

That I am lesbian is my usual awareness. My close people are almost all lesbians, mostly not Jewish. I live in Santa Fe, among gentiles; and though I am lonely for Jews, I don't go to *shul*, and never did; and don't pray, or even know the prayers. I think Israel a boiling contradiction; and besides, they don't give queers citizenship.**

But the rise of Klan activity, Reagan and his white-on-white cabinet, synagogues bombed in France, have me in a sweat. Dreams of the camps. I need to know the network I may be forced to count on. I want to know the tradition, what binds us besides danger.

Jewish Tradition

This year I made a menorah from a stick of wood, hammered in nine nails, eight and one for the special candle (angry I'd forgotten its name). Lighting the candles each night, I remember Chanukah with my parents and sister, the presents (a little one each night, and a big one on the last night). We never said prayers, though my father, raised orthodox, must have known them. I remember their menorah, a music box in its base played the *Hatikvah*. I thought all menorahs played the *Hatikvah*; and this Chanukah, each night as I light the candles I hum, can't

*I would like to thank Michaele Uccella for her grueling editing and intellectual, political and emotional inspiration and sustenance (not to mention physical assistance in meeting publication deadline).

**Israel is hardly unique in its discrimination against gays, though predictably more than a fair share of criticism is directed against Israeli policy. As a Jewish lesbian, I find homophobia in Israel[1] especially heartbreaking when I consider that the Nazis would have killed me for being gay as well as Jewish (estimates on how many homosexuals were imprisoned in the Nazi death centers range from the conservative figure of 220,000 to 900,000).

keep from humming the *Hatikvah*. My body feels warm: for thousands of years people have lit candles to celebrate freedom, millions of Jews are doing it right now.

On the seventh night I rushed out early and forgot to light the candles; later discovered it was the eighth and last night, and I'd missed it. I had started Chanukah a day late. I felt ridiculous; and deprived. So friday at sundown I lit a candle for the sabbath and stood in front of it, wanting to do something special—but what? wondering, what is it we do, we Jews on friday night when we light candles—what is precious in this, is it just centuries and endurance? All I could imagine doing was crossing myself, which made me very nervous, evoking my imprinting; to do anything christian is to sin, not against god but against jewishness; to betray my people.

Liberals and pacifists often challenge the notion of "one's own people." Liberals "don't like labels"; pacifists say, "face your enemy with love."[2] Both say, "people are people." I think Jews are haunted—intelligently so—by spectres of cattle cars packed to the top with our people. Some of who I am roots in the knowledge, as early as I can remember: there are people who did not want us to exist—millions of them. For these people, there is no love. It's easy for me to think in terms of "my people" and "our enemies."[3]

I learned this way of thinking from my parents; both are antireligious, fierce in their hatred of everything German, suspicious of the gentiles (though they are polite and try not to say goyim), and passionate in their communication of certain truths: never cross a picket line; all men are brothers (*sic*); nothing is more important than school (corollary: the best job you can get is teaching; security, and the same hours as your children).[4]

Of course, there would be children. I think I am a disgrace to my family, as a lesbian, as a childless woman. Also, I am to them a nice girl: though instead of providing for my parents, I occasionally need to borrow from them, at least I have an education and write books. The content of these books is not so important to them; one uncle bought two copies of my poetry book, which celebrates women who kill abusive men.

My family are good people: they would take care of me, any of them; they welcome my (gentile) lover as if she were a husband (to her discomfort!); they do not disown—family is family. I sometimes feel ready to dissolve in a great wash of tears because I have no child to contribute to this brave pool of survivors. As if I owe these parents aunts uncles cousins a birth—for those who died?

The grandparents are all dead now, and none of us born in this country knew their families, only great-uncle Abram who barely spoke english—all the rest died in the camps, except one cousin was saved and shipped off to Israel (Palestine, then), the only survivor from the old world (and I know he would take care of me too).

Maybe because I can't imagine very far back, having no language to remember with, no name for my grandmother's *shtetl*, or even for her mother or father, no photographs, maybe for these reasons those of my family who still live loom for me with such solidity. A child would bind me to them, would give both me and the child this solidity: there would always be thanksgiving and people to have birthdays with, celebratory and irritable, people who overeat and go on diets, who play mah jongg and poker, or who avoid these things, but all of us would *know* these things. I feel a visceral tug of family, especially at a distance. I choose to live far from them, among lesbians, women who are all somewhat outside the cultures which raised us. Jewishness is a leitmotif in and out of my brain; not the main theme.

But sometimes—a tv program called "Kitty: Return to Auschwitz"; the sound of a yiddish melody I don't know by name but have heard in the air, in my sleep, my whole life; a crossword puzzle, twenty-four down, "German Chancellor," the answer is "Hitler"—something forces my awareness not that I am Jewish—I am always Jewish—but that others are not.

for example, excerpts from journal, May 1980

> *writing—i stop to pee—in the bathroom through the door i can hear m's radio, news, jewish school in hebron attacked, five dead, how many wounded? in 1929 the jews fled hebron, escaping an arab massacre. now the israelis settle there. i am crying, in part because the non-jewish world—the goyim—will explain and justify the killings with and through hatred of jews, will not care much because it's only jews. on the left, pro-arabs; on the right, nazis. i feel alone.*[5]

or, a month later:

> *i meet r., a dyke visiting from arkansas—i hadn't thought to ask myself, is she jewish? but her car*

*sports a huge star in the rear window. i ask if she's
not afraid to be so identifiable, especially in the south.
she says, "i decided it was time to come out." the
thought scares me. invisibility is sometimes a comfort. at the same time i see how the star made our
conversation possible—that we welcomed each other
as jews because i knew she was jewish and would
welcome me.*

I begin to identify myself as Jewish, often—not in visual ways
but with words; I discover Jewish women everywhere—yes, like
coming out.

Jewish Identity

Historically, Jewish people have vacillated between forced
identification and forced assimilation. A brief chronology:

1215	The church's Fourth Lateran Council decrees that Jews must wear distinctive dress (a large hat, a yellow or crimson circle over the heart to mark them as targets).
1290	Jews expelled from England.
1306	Jews expelled from France.
14th-15th c.	Jews expelled from German countries.
1492	Jews expelled from Spain.
1800s	In France, under the revolutionary government, and in Germany: passports and identification cards marked to identify the Jews.
1804	Jewish Statute passed in Russia, obliging the Jews to—among other things—take last names (patronyms), against their own custom and in keeping with the gentile way.[6]
1850	Russian Jews ordered to stop wearing their traditional dress: men had to cut their *peyes* (long sideburns); women to stop shaving their heads on the eve of marriage.[7]
1938	Jews in Germany who had changed their names (before 1933) were forcibly re-

stored to their "original" names; all
Jews had to take the middle name Sarah
(for females) or Israel (for males); new
babies had to be named from a government list.[8]

Jews in Germany had to get their passports
stamped with a big red J.

1940   Jews in Germany had to get their ration
cards stamped with a big red J.

1940s   Jews in Germany and throughout Reich-
occupied territories had to wear a Jewish
star as mandatory public identification.

1940s   Jews deported to the camps.
(and earlier)

Exposed or isolated, deprived of our culture or locked into it,
our powerlessness to define ourselves culminates in the camps:
take Primo Levi, a chemist, deported from Italy to Auschwitz in
1943, one of millions: "Levi's number—174517—was tattooed
on his left arm in a swift and slightly painful operation. . . . Only by showing the number could 174517 get bread and soup."[9]
Levi speaks:

Nothing belongs to us anymore; they have taken
away our clothes, our shoes, even our hair; if we
speak, they will not listen to us, and if they listen,
they will not understand. They will even take away
our name: and if we want to keep it, we will have to
find in ourselves the strength to do so, to manage
somehow so that behind the name something of us,
of us as we were, still remains.[10]

Jewish Names

Jews have always had to exist "behind the name." In the new
world too, many of us, like other immigrants, lost our names or
heard them mutilated, out of gentile ignorance, laziness, or
hostility. Some of us shed our names like a ragged coat.

My father's name is Kantrowitz, my mother's Wolfgang
(I slip over the ordinary erasure of female to male name).
He changed his name to Kaye just before the first child—my sis-
ter—was born in 1942. My mother tells how she threatened to

name the baby Forsythia if he didn't change it, Forsythia Kantrowitz. I have heard her tell this story a dozen times at least; always there is an assumed comicality about the name. My father says everyone called him Mr. K. anyway, at the vacuum cleaner store where he did sales and repair. for business. because Kantrowitz was too long, too hard to say.

(think about Gloucester; McLoughlin)

(think about 174517)

At the dyke bar in Portland I tell Amy Kesselman my best Jewish friend that I'm thinking about taking back my mother's maiden name—as far back as I can go through the women—or my father's name—or both. "Kaye is a made-up name," I say, "It has no history." Amy, historian, tells me, "Just because a history isn't pretty doesn't mean it isn't history."

Kaye is both history and closet. history of a kind of closet. Kaye is Kantrowitz Kaminsky Keminetsky Kowalsky Klutz Korelowich Ka. . . .

(think about asking every Jew you know: what *was* your name?)

I recently met a woman who knew me through my written work. "Oh," she said, "I expected you to be tall and blond." I joked "I must be doing something wrong"—but it made me feel funny.

Also recently, a woman asks my name and I find myself about to say, Melanie Kantrowitz, just to hear it, to test her face. If I called myself Melanie Kantrowitz, no one would ever expect me to be tall and blond.

I grew up laughing at names that were typically ours—not Deborah or Naomi, bible names, but old-fashioned names like Yentl, Sadie, Rivka. My whole generation of girl children born Jewish mid-forties NY city was named Susan Ellen Judy and sometimes Jane. Any given school class would have its Ellen C., Ellen R., Susan A., Susan L., Susan W., Jane S., Jane L. . . .

But whatever the name, if you looked like a Jew, you couldn't hide.

Looking Like a Jew

In the Jewish resistance, women did much of the courier, weapon-gathering, smuggling, communication, and guide work—in part because they could pass more surely than the men, who might be asked at any moment to drop their pants. The many Jews—women and men—who did pass testify to how many Jews look "Aryan."

Yet at least one woman resistance fighter was stopped leaving the Warsaw Ghetto because she had a Jewish nose.

This historical flash may put into perspective the painful, expensive operation which men (often Jewish ones) make jokes about—the nose job. In the heyday of Barbra Streisand, it's hard to remember that every Jewish teenage girl of my generation whose nose "looked Jewish" longed for another chance. Parents who could pay, paid. When my cousin Susan turned fifteen, she got a nose job. When I saw her a week later, she still looked like someone had beat the shit out of her—her face bruised, puffy—and a swollen nose which, a few months later, "reverted." More money, more nose-breaking, more pain. Again, it reverted. She had her nose re-done three times. I can't remember what it looks like now, whether or not the nose job was "successful."

> We all knew Jewish noses were ugly. Never asking, "*why* ugly?" or answering, "because Jewish."[11]

When I was a tiny girl, my aunt Edna said of me, "look at that, a nose like a *shiksa*." I snuck into the bathroom to stare in the mirror, sobbing, "I don't look like a *shiksa*, I don't"— this, before I knew what a *shiksa* was. But later I took a strange sickish pleasure in "my nose" and would tell people what my aunt had said, partly to make them notice my nose.

Through my teens and halfway through my twenties I was setting and sometimes bleaching, sometimes straightening my hair. What I did to my eyebrows will be understood only by those women who also have black bushy eyebrows. I was not trying to look like a *shiksa*—I was trying to look pretty.

> (why ugly? because Jewish.)

I was also trying to sound pretty (cultured).

Sounding Like a (Low Class) Jew

Sometime around ninth grade, words like *yenta shmate bubbe* began to embarrass me. I—as I thought of it then—aimed higher. What I meant by this was vague but included museums, foreign films, and an escape from Brooklyn—dates, engagement parties, weddings at temples with booze and cocktail franks and long-line bras and girdles and dyed-to-match shoes and a band playing Anniversary Waltz while uncles made cracks about wedding nights. It also meant escape from a six-days-plus-two-nights-work-week selling longline bras and girdles in "the store"—my father's and his sister's business, where all of us worked, full, part-time, summers, christmas, at various times in our lives.

And words like *shmate* trapped me—no matter who said them—marked, stripped and revealed me. I came from people who talked *like that*. I came from them and would be stuck with their lives. In case I needed proof of the connection between their lives and that accent, I had only to attend C.C.N.Y. and discover that in order to graduate, I had to learn NOT to talk *like that*.[12]

But last night I sang yiddish songs with a dozen Jewish women. L., a woman in her twenties was teaching us the words, I was moved by her pleasure in the words, the sound and lilt—pretty. She seemed like a daughter I might raise, braver and less scarred—the sounds she speaks, her inflections are the very sounds I grew up trying not to make: *zuntig, bulbes*

muntig, bulbes

dinstik un mitvokh, bulbes [13]

In these songs the ways words sound good is to sound *like that*, not "uneducated english," but yiddish, a language.

I borrow from L. a book, *Der Yidisher Lerer* (*The Yiddish Teacher*). My eyes have always wobbled at the sight of hebrew or arabic letters, but the first word in this book is *bubbe*; the second is *mame*. These words leap from my blood, my mouth knows how to say them. At two letters a day I'll have the alphabet in a couple of weeks. *shvester. zogt. vaser. vos vill di bubbe? di bubbe est a zeml.* my tongue.

In the Jewish Women's Group I have felt ashamed of my ignorance—of hebrew, of religion. I've muffled words to songs rather than ask anyone to slow down. Passover with these women, each of us reads something from the service, adding something of her own. I talked about my grandmother Helen Wolfgang who had just died that week—how she had left Poland as a teenager and was rebellious against religion because Jewish orthodoxy had been stifling to her freedom—how we always had a seder at her house, but with bread on the table as well as matzah. One woman—bless her—said, let's drink to her—what was her name? But from many others there, I felt disapproval so clear it was visceral. I thought, many of these women were raised by professional parents, sent to hebrew school, taught cultural pride. A poor Jew trying to climb out of her class learns to associate her lowerclassness with her jewishness (also her femaleness).

I notice in the group that P. who knows hebrew commands much respect. She's been researching Jewish ceremony, looking to recreate a matriarchal religion, and she performs an evening prayer for us, closing the shabbes, something to do with the new moon. All the while she holds and rocks and tips the glass of wine (which is really grape juice, none of these women drink) she has poured very full; and L. whose house it is and whose rug it is not keeps bending over P. to steady the glass, her face showing anxiety about the juice and the rug but P. will not sip off the top, she keeps waving her arms and the juice slops dangerously to the edge and some drops spill on the blanket, yes, on the rug, but there's no stopping P. as she performs the ritual—

(and I think, this is why I don't like religion, she is wonderful in the rabbi role, absorbed and holy, but *she* won't have to clean up the spilled juice)

I also notice that P., in her knowledge of hebrew and religion, those arenas of Jewish male activity, is more heeded than L. who is younger, softer, and knows yiddish and hundreds of songs, and worries about her friend's rug. The hierarchy of hebrew over yiddish, male over female, rich over poor replicates here.[14] If you're going to be Jewish, at least be refined; not female, especially not Jewish female.

Acting Like a Jewish Woman

As Jewish women, we are often blamed for our strength. When I became a lesbian and no longer had to care what men, Jewish or otherwise, thought of me, I came into my power. As a lesbian, I learned fast and ecstatically that women liked me to be strong. I began to enjoy, build, and relax into my full self.

On the other hand, a few months ago, I was applying for jobs and was interviewed by an all-women's collective for one job, and by english department faculty (women and men) for another. I found myself comfortable with the "english" people—the school was a city college, and most of them were either Jewish or very accustomed to women "like me." With the women's collective members—several of whom were lesbians— I had an eerie sense of unbalance. None of them were Jewish; I was a surprise to them.

This unbalance can explode into bitter repercussions. In one group, several of the women were having a hard time with "my style." It had never occurred to me to count noses. but I counted noses. They didn't look Jewish. Most of the women troubled by me had been sent to expensive colleges by their fathers; they spoke with well-modulated voices, and they quaked when I raised mine. They didn't understand that to me anger is common, expressible, and not murderous. They found me "loud" (of course) and "emotional." Interestingly, I got along fine with all the women of color in the group, one therapy buff, and one middle class wasp woman who was also a dyke and a radical and my best friend at the time—and who hipped me to the covert anti-semitism (she explained since *she'd* been afraid of me, she could recognize it in others).

But I'm talking not just about differences and fear of difference. I'm talking also about power to suppress difference. Why ugly?

So when women say things like
she has a "difficult" style
as well as
aren't all Jews rich? (or, the more sophisticated version, aren't all Jews middle class?)
or, there are *so* many Jewish teachers writers filmmakers Jewish women in the women's movement[15]

or, when they don't say these things but assume them, we are not being paranoid if we hear familiar themes: pushy, loud, moneygrubbing, exploitative, and—especially—there we are taking over again, in the schools, the art world, even the movement.[16]

Nor are we being paranoid if we point to anti-semitism, in the United States, or in the women's movement; and they say it isn't really. Or, as happened last year in San Francisco, tell Jewish women wanting to meet as Jews, that this is divisive, that Jews are "really" white; or "really" European.[17] Or, if they hint that "all that" is over now, why are we making a fuss.

Or, if their ignorance compels us to explain that gentiles persecuted the Jews for thousands of years before the Nazis got efficient at it;[18] and that a year after the Nazi defeat, in Kielce, Poland, a mob stormed a Jewish community center and killed, out of the tiny number of surviving Polish Jews who remained in Poland, forty-one Jews. And that pogroms then erupted all

over Poland. That even now, with a Jewish population of five to
eight thousand (from 3.5 million pre-Hitler), anti-semitism rises
again, accelerates, in Poland.[19]

I am pulled back to the theme of danger as the shared Jewish
identity. As Jewish women, we need also to define ourselves by
ourselves, on our own terms.

Jewish Women

As women and as lesbians we have learned to reclaim names
like
dyke
bitch
manhater
golddigger
shrew
harpy
whore
cunt
amazon
(even) lesbian
even *woman* had first to be reclaimed from a place of
squeamishness.[20]
As Jewish women and Jewish lesbians, we need to reclaim
words like
pushy
loud
politico
power trippy
cheap
dominating
garish
sexy
emotional
always screaming
bossy
scary temper
difficult style
(and, of course) Jewish mother
(and) Jewish princess

Take Jewish mother. Who accuses her of the heinous crime—of
let's face it—pushiness? Often, Jewish men; especially those who
have climbed out of her class because of her help. Ironic, too,

that success often comes to Jewish boys through an education which teaches them to be ashamed of their jewishness, and of their mothers. Perhaps the familiar put-downs of Jewish women by Jewish men stem from male resentment of the strong mother; indignity that a successful Jewish man, unlike his idealized wasp counterpart, has to contend with uppity women.[21]

As Jewish women, we need to look at our people with our own eyes. To see Judith, who saved the Jewish people; she flirted with the attacking general, drank him under the table; then she and her maid (whose name is not in the story) whacked off his head, stuck it in a picnic basket and escaped back to the Jewish camp. They staked his head high over the gate, so that when his soldiers charged the camp, they were met by their general's bloody head, looming; and ran away as fast as their goyishe little feet could run. Then Judith set her maid free, and all the women danced in her honor.[22]

That's a Jewish princess.

Or Anzia Yezierska, who told, in yiddish-like english, stories of Jewish immigrants, especially women's struggles for love, freedom, and education. Of her work, she wrote: "It's not me—it's their cries—my own people—crying in me! Hannah Breineh, Shmendrek, they will not be stilled in me, till all America stops to listen."[23]

That's a nice Jewish girl.

Or Violette Kaye, who recently when I asked, ashamed, to borrow money for an airline ticket back east, and she said, of course; and then told me they're retiring, and I said, this isn't a good time for any of us, and she said, listen, if I have it, and I do, it's yours.

That's a Jewish mother. (mine.)

Jewish Foremothers

I began with the holocaust. I want to know how it happened—not how the Jews let it happen (the question sprouts so easily on gentile tongues) but *how* did it happen? I come from people who were killed like that, for that. An odd identity, but a compelling one.

Especially I need the stories of resistance laced through the horror, as an amulet, inspiration, and warning. To know that our efforts at resistance came too late, too frail for six million. To swear "never again" uncertain of what this oath might entail; but in some corner of my brain on guard.

Most stories of the holocaust, like most other stories, have been told by and about men. I don't reject them for this, they are Jewish and mine. But as a woman, I need to know about the women, and that many Jews fought back, as they could, Jewish women among them.

To fortify myself, I collect names and as much information as I can find. About women who fought inside the camps. Say their names.

> Rosa Robota; Esther, Ella, and Regina, all hanged for crucial parts in the Auschwitz resistance.

or, Sala Lerner who fought at Sachsenhausen.

or, Mala Zimetbaum, the "Runner," who had worked in the Belgian underground, was caught and sent to Auschwitz, and escaped, and inspired the women to wait, to survive, to believe that liberation would come; though she was caught again and killed.

or, Olga Benario and Charlotte Eisenbletter, who gathered the women's resistance at Ravensbrück.

—that there was a *Woman's Resistance* at Ravensbrück—

or, Fania Fenelon, a member of the Auschwitz women's orchestra, privileged to survive—and anyone who survived the camps was privileged (and lucky); she played Beethoven's Fifth at Birkenau, for the prisoners to delight in the signature tune of the Free French Broadcasts; and arranged a Jewish (therefore, forbidden) song as a march, so the prisoners marched to a Jewish song, while the SS tapped their feet, ignorant.

or, Kitty's mother, who survived as a hospital worker at Auschwitz, and hid her sick daughter under a mattress with a dead body on it; who hissed at her, *run, run,* because those who could run, when the commandant said *run,* survived.

and Kitty herself, who worked the gas chambers, and doesn't lie about it; who stole from the dead (only from the dead) and hoarded the gold to buy explosives to blow up the Auschwitz ovens. They blew up one of the Auschwitz ovens.

and the hundreds—thousands?—of women who fought in the Warsaw Ghetto Uprising—like Niuta Teitelboim, known in the resistance as Wanda "of the braids," who organized a women's detachment, guided Jews out and smuggled weapons into the ghetto, often posed as a whore or shy girlfriend to gain access to Nazi officials and kill them;

blew up Nazi trains and clubs, robbed a bank; was tortured and killed by Nazis, but not before she smuggled
out a note, assuring her comrades that she wouldn't betray them.

or Mira Fuchrer, a factory woman's daughter, polished speaker,
practiced in surviving where she wasn't meant to. Her
comrades describe her as a sprite, everywhere at once.
She said, we'll stay alive only by resisting every rule we
possibly can.

or Dvorah Baron, a rich man's daughter, blond, with a nose like
a *shiksa*—an expert messenger because she could pass;
emerged first from a bunker on the fourteenth day of the
uprising, using her looks to shock the Germans into paus-
ing while she threw a grenade in their faces.

or Regina Fudin, the champion guide of the Warsaw sewers.

or Zivia Lubetkin, a commander of the ZOB; when she escaped
from the ghetto, she almost killed a fellow commander because his orders left behind some of her people.

or Pola Elster, captured fighting in the Brushmaker's District of
the Ghetto; crammed into a cattle car with hundreds of
people, for days, mothers with thirsty babies two three
four days in the car giving the babies piss to drink, the only fluid, and watching the babies die in convulsions; Pola
Elster suggested they file down the window bars and try
to escape. The others were afraid it would make things
worse—but how, she wondered, could they get worse?[24]

In the book where I learn about the Warsaw Ghetto Resistance,
there are pictures of these women. I read their stories; study
their faces, turn to the introduction to see who was actually interviewed, who survived. Almost forty years later I feel pain at
each discovered death. I stare especially at the picture of Pola
Elster. Her hair is short, slicked back, she's wearing a tie. She
looks like a dyke. I ponder the contradiction that some of my
Jewish people will think I'm being insulting and disrespectful
to suggest this.

I read about Krysia Frimer, whose brother was a resistance
fighter but he forbade her to join because it was too dangerous—
yet she was killed first. I mourn all the women deprived of the
right to fight back, who were not thereby saved; and all the
women whose names have not survived, who took messages
food weapons in and out of the ghetto, who whored to the
soldiers leaders cops for somebody's life freedom food information, who kept themselves and their children alive.

Those were Jewish women. I come from women who fought
like that.

I want a button that says *Pushy Jew. Loud Pushy Jew. Loud
Pushy Jew Dyke.*

Santa Fe, New Mexico
Summer 1980 - Winter 1981

Endnotes

[1]"Jews who are homosexual are not allowed to obtain Israeli citizenship under the Israeli law of return. . . ." (Miriam Socoloff, Leo Schlosberg,
and Jeffry [Shaye] Mallow, "Why We Write About Gay Liberation," in
Chutzpah: A Jewish Liberation Anthology [San Francisco: New Glide
Publications, 1977], p. 28).

[2]See Barbara Deming, *Prison Notes* (Boston: Beacon Press, 1966), for
a sensible and moving account of non-violent struggle in the South. But
the perspective is that of a white, who can choose to enter the struggle.

[3]See Andrea Dworkin's useful concept of "primary emergency" in
Woman Hating (New York: E.P. Dutton, 1974), p. 23; also my column in
Sinister Wisdom 8 ("Scrambled Eggs: Politics as an Act of Love").

[4]In fact, I am a teacher (though I teach mostly college-level, above my
parents' aspirations; and though being a public lesbian creates a considerable fly in the ointment of security).

[5]It's odd, considering how active Jews have been on the left, that positions and attitudes taken by radicals toward the Jews have rarely reflected
Jewish interest. We find among radicals all the anti-semitism prevalent in
other quarters; for example, in late nineteenth century Russia, some radicals "adopted the tactic of fusing class with national antagonism": one
"revolutionary" group issued a leaflet praising pogroms and urging the
"honest Ukrainian people" to rise up against "the kikes." See Milton
Meltzer, *World of Our Fathers* (New York: Dell, 1974), pp. 206 ff. See
also Susan Schechter, "To My Real and Imagined Enemies, and Why I
Sometimes Can't Tell You Apart," and Steven Lubet and Jeffry Mallow,
"That's Funny, You Don't Look Anti-Semitic: Perspective on the American Left," both in *Chutzpah.*

[6]Meltzer, *World of Our Fathers*, pp. 38 ff., notes that until this point,
the Jews of Eastern Europe had used hebrew names; and that distinctions
between two Jews of the same given name were made through common
sense—nicknames, street where you lived, your wife's or husband's name—
not through patronyms. Russian Jews got to choose their surnames. In
Austria, Jews had to select from a list which included some deliberately
offensive names.

[7]This kind of regulation, where women are forbidden a practice of
"their" culture which is oppressive to them, evokes ambivalent feelings.
The issue, as usual, is choice.

[8]The list of acceptable names specifically excluded hebrew names (e.g., Esther, Ruth, Adam, Daniel); and included names like Scharne, Scheindel, Schneine, Schewa (for girls); and Faleg, Feibisch, Feisel, Feitel (for boys). See Raul Hilberg's flawed but infinitely useful *The Destruction of the European Jews* (New York: Harper & Row, 1979; c. 1961), pp. 119-120. All information in this brief chronology not otherwise cited is from Hilberg. Hilberg's "flaw" is rigid adherence to his thesis of Jewish passivity, in the face of clear evidence of courageous and sometimes effective Jewish resistance. See Milton Meltzer, *Never to Forget* (New York: Dell, 1976), pp. 135-189; and Yuri Suhl's inspiring collection, *They Fought Back: The Story of Jewish Resistance in Nazi Europe* (New York: Schocken Books, 1975; c. 1967).

[9]Meltzer, *Never to Forget*, p. 121.

[10]Quoted, *Ibid*.

[11]"What's a weed? A weed is a plant you don't want." Michaele Uccella, conversation, Summer 1979.

[12]When I went to City College of New York (the sixties) students—who were mostly working and lower-middle class immigrant once-removed children—were required to pass four units (two to four classes) of speech, where the emphasis was on learning not to dentalize (sound consonants harshly, against your teeth); dentalization is characteristic of yiddish, italian, polish, russian, etc.

[13]"sunday, potatoes/monday, potatoes/tuesday and wednesday, potatoes," yiddish folk song.

[14]Hebrew, the language in which educated male Jews spoke to god; yiddish, the tongue to which (Ashkenazi) women and poor men are restricted. So yiddish was the people's tongue; also, to some Jews, a brand of exile. The split among activist Jews tended to occur along political lines: Bundists (intent on building worker consciousness) opted for yiddish; Zionists chose hebrew. Survivors of the Warsaw Ghetto Uprising report that in the hidden bunker at Mila 18 on the nineteenth day of battle, an argument broke out about the merits of yiddish vs. hebrew! In Dan Kurzman, *The Bravest Battle: The 28 Days of the Warsaw Ghetto Uprising* (New York: Pinnacle Books, 1980). The book is irritatingly slick but invaluable for details of conversations, events, photographs of resistance fighters.

[15]Some women who teach women's studies report being questioned about why there are "so many lesbians on the reading list," when, in fact, there may be three or four articles out of twenty-five or so. Sometimes "so many" equals "too many" equals "any." On the other hand, the Jews' honorable commitment to intellectual and, especially, political work is either idealized (*all* Jews do these things) and/or considered a sign of our tendency to take over. "It was never dealt with in a way that might have helped us to understand it or that might have helped us to feel good," Ruth Balser, "Liberation of a Jewish Radical," in *Chutzpah*.

[16]Evidence indicates that quotas often and still function to exclude Jews. See Alfred Kazin's remark that Lionel Trilling was hired as THE Jew at Columbia University, in *New York Jew* (New York: Alfred Knopf, 1978). In my own time, Columbia one year abandoned quotas for stu-

dents, with the result that they were flooded by New York Jews (all males, of course).

[17]It's depressing that these women, many of whom had burned out trying to explain to male lefties their need to meet as *women*, couldn't generalize.

[18]See Hilberg, *The Destruction of the European Jews*, pp. 1-30.

[19]See, for example, an article in a recent *New York Times*, "Anti-Semitism Without Jews? A Polish Riddle," by John Darnton, March 15, 1981, IV: 4.

[20]*Mother* (Jewish or not) is still unclaimed, charged with negativity, though on its way to more positive ground; it shows up as a positive word/ concept more in our art than in our conversations.

In a class I taught jointly with Paula King, we had the group list every bad word we could think of about women; the assignment was then to pick one and reclaim it ("Women As Creative Artists," Portland State University, Oregon, Women's Studies, Fall 1978). It would be interesting to do this with Jewish women.

[21]That women lose personal power in heterosexual relationships as their men gain class power in the society seems obvious. Upwardly mobile in earning power and/or self-image, men want their due. See discussion in *The Jewish Woman in America* by Charlotte Baum, Paula Hyman, and Sonya Michel (New York: Plume Books, 1976), pp. 235-261, an excellent source.

[22]I am indebted to J.J. Wilson for this story, from her presentation on women artists (published as *Women Artists*, co-authored with Karen Petersen [New York: Harper & Row, 1976]).

[23]Quoted in the introduction to *The Open Cage: An Anzia Yezierska Collection* edited by Alice K. Harris (New York: Persea Books, 1979), p. vi.

[24]These women's stories are available in Suhl and in Kurzman; in Fania Fenelon's *Playing For Time* (written with Marcelle Routier, translated by Judith Landry [New York: Berkley Books, 1979]); Kitty's story is from a recent PBS television broadcast of the film Kitty made of her return to Auschwitz, to teach one of her sons about Auschwitz. Zivia Lubetkin survived and went to Israel after the war and, with others, founded *Kibbutz Lochamai Hagetaot* (Ghetto Fighters' Kibbutz) in Western Galilee.

Anti-Semitism in the Lesbian/Feminist Movement

Irena Klepfisz

In the summer of 1981, I wrote to Womanews, *a New York City-based paper, about its silence and apparent indifference to the growing anti-Semitism in this country, a silence and indifference which I consider anti-Semitic itself. Though my letter was sparked by specific articles in one of its issues, it could in fact have been addressed to almost any of the major feminist or lesbian/feminist papers, most of which have been equally silent on this topic.*

In response to my letter, Womanews *focused its December 1981 issue on Jewish women and anti-Semitism. The article that follows (minus specific criticisms of* Womanews' *response to my letter) appeared originally in that issue together with other pieces by Jewish women.*

In *Prisoner Without A Name, Cell Without A Number,* the Argentinian Jew Jacobo Timerman answers the question "whether a Holocaust is conceivable" in his country, in this way:

> Well, that depends on what is meant by Holocaust, though no one would have been able to answer such a question affirmatively in 1937 in Germany. What you can say is that recent events in Argentina have demonstrated that if an anti-Semitic scenario unfolds, the discussion on what constitutes anti-Semitism and persecution and what does not will occupy more time than the battle itself against anti-Semitism.

Timerman's statement can easily be applied to the situation here in the United States where, I believe, an "anti-Semitic scenario" is on the verge of developing. And like so many other issues of the "mainstream," this one is being mirrored in the les-

51

bian/feminist movement. Repeatedly, I find that I am preoccupied not with countering anti-Semitism, but with trying to prove that anti-Semitism exists, that it is serious, and that, as lesbian/feminists, we should be paying attention to it both inside and outside of the movement.

My experience with this is much like shadowboxing, for the anti-Semitism with which I am immediately concerned, and which I find most threatening, does not take the form of the overt, undeniably inexcusable painted swastika on a Jewish gravestone or on a synagogue wall. Instead, it is elusive and difficult to pinpoint, for it is the anti-Semitism either of omission or one which trivializes the Jewish experience and Jewish oppression.

Even when confronted with these attitudes, the lesbian/feminist response is most likely to be an evasion, a refusal to acknowledge their implications. This was the case when I wrote to *Womanews* over its repeated silence on anti-Semitism. Though conceding previous omissions the collective typically resisted a deeper analysis: "Your anger is understandable, but the tone of your letter is puzzling. *An oversight, considerable as it is, is not necessarily a sign of insensitivity much less intentional silence*" (italics mine). In a movement that has focused on the meanings of oversights, silences, and absences and that has rigorously examined how they are functions of oppression *no matter what the intent*, this type of defense and excuse is very difficult for me to absorb, much less accept.

I am aware that there are many Jewish women actively participating in the lesbian/feminist movement and that makes the situation even more painful and dangerous. For it is clear that what I am confronting here is not just anti-Semitism of non-Jews, but of Jews as well.

I recently heard a Jewish woman complain about what she perceived to be a lack of pride among Jewish lesbian/feminists. Though in agreement with her observation, I felt angry with her complaint. For what philosophy, emerging out of this movement, I asked, has encouraged the development and sustaining of such pride? What strategies evolved against the growing oppression in this country have included the strategy for countering anti-Semitism, a strategy that would enable Jewish women to feel some self worth? What theory of oppression, formulated by either Jews or non-Jews, has incorporated an analysis of the history of anti-Semitism outside of the movement and within it, a theory that would reflect a caring for the fate of Jews? And how often have Jewish lesbian/feminists heard anyone declare: "I am committed to this struggle not only because I am a lesbian, but also because I am a Jew"?

The truth is that the issue of anti-Semitism has been ignored, has been treated as either non-existent or unimportant. And, therefore, I am not surprised that pride is low among Jewish lesbian/feminists. For that kind of evasion, that kind of stubborn refusal to focus can only breed low self-esteem, can only increase defensiveness about drawing attention to oneself, can only encourage apologies for distracting others from "more important" issues, can only instill gnawing doubt about whether anti-Semitism exists at all.

Yet clearly the opportunities to connect anti-Semitism with other oppressions have been with us for as long as we have been concerned with the rise of fascist activity in this country. On each occasion in which outrage has been expressed over the ideologies and goals of the Ku Klux Klan, of the American Nazi Party, of the accelerating Christian movement—on each of these occasions there was an opportunity to bring up the issue of anti-Semitism, for each of these has been and continues to be unequivocally anti-Semitic. Yet such interconnections have not been made. And Jewish women have not been insisting that they be made.

There have been a few who have sensed that something is wrong about this, but even they have been hesitant to bring it up, as if by doing so they would be just causing trouble. How is such hesitancy possible among women who have passionately devoted themselves to fighting *every* form of oppression? How can anyone, given our goals and ideals, even doubt the correctness of challenging anti-Semitism?

I believe that Jewish lesbian/feminists have internalized much of the subtle anti-Semitism of this society. They have been told that Jews are too pushy, too aggressive; and so they have been silent about their Jewishness, have not protested against what threatens them. They have been told that they control everything; and so when they are in the spotlight, they have been afraid to draw attention to their Jewishness. For these women, the number of Jews active in the movement is not a source of pride, but rather a source of embarrassment, something to be played down, something to be minimized.

For these women, it is enough that their names are Jewish. Their Jewishness never extends any further. Their theories and viewpoints are never informed by Jewish traditions and culture, or by Jewish political history and analysis, or even by Jewish oppression. In short, there is nothing about them that is visibly Jewish except their names—and that is simply a form of identification, of labelling. No, Jewish women have not been visible in this movement as Jews. They have been good, very good. They have not drawn attention to themselves. And I, a lesbian/feminist proud of her Jewishness, am as sick of it, as I am sick about it.

I think it is time that Jewish and non-Jewish women focused on this issue and got it into perspective. I think it is time for all of us in this movement, Jews and non-Jews alike, to examine our silence on this subject, to examine its source. And Jews especially need to consider their feelings about their Jewishness, for any self-consciousness, any desire to draw attention *away* from one's Jewishness is an internalization of anti-Semitism. And if we want others to deal with this issue, then we ourselves must start to develop a sense of pride and a sense that our survival *as Jews* is important.

If someone were to ask me did I think a Jewish Holocaust was possible in this country, I would answer immediately: "Of course." Has not America had other Holocausts? Has not America proven what it is capable of? Has not America exterminated others, those it deemed undesirable or those in its way? Are there not Holocausts going on right now in this country? Why should I believe it will forever remain benevolent towards the non-Christian who is the source of all its troubles, the thief of all its wealth, the commie betrayer of its secrets, the hidden juggler of its power, the killer of its god? Why should I believe that given the right circumstances America will prove kind to the Jew? That given enough power to the fascists, the Jew will remain untouched?

There are many, and Jews are among them, who do not accept my view. But I am firm in my belief. Not out of panic. Not out of paranoia. I believe it because of what I know of American history and of what I know of Jewish history in Christian cultures.

I am a lesbian/feminist threatened in this country. I am also a European-born Jew, born during the Second World War, a survivor of the Jewish Holocaust. That historical event, so publicized and commercialized in the mass media, so depleted of meaning, has been a source of infinite lessons to me, lessons which I value.

Fact: It took *four* years before the Jews of the Warsaw Ghetto could learn to trust each other and overcome their hostilities toward their divergent political philosophies; it took *four* years before they could pool their energies and resist the Nazis in what has become known as the Warsaw Ghetto Uprising. And before that, while the Zionists would not speak to the Socialists, and while the Socialists would not speak to the Communists, the Nazis were creating more and more efficient death camps and more and more Jews were being exterminated.

Fact: When the Jews finally staged the uprising in April, 1943, the Polish underground refused them almost every form of assistance. Even though they were facing the same enemy, even though their country was occupied, the Poles could not overcome their anti-Semitism and join the Jews in the struggle for the freedom of both groups, and instead chose to stage a *separate* Polish uprising more than a year later.

These two facts concerning this event in Jewish history are permanently etched on my consciousness. (1) The oppressed group divided against itself, incapacitated, paralyzed, unable to pull together while the enemy grows stronger and more efficient. (2) Two oppressed groups facing a common enemy unable to overcome ancient hatreds, struggling separately.

And I think about these two facts whenever I hear about a completely Jewish demonstration against the American Nazi Party in the midwest and then hear about a completely Black demonstration against the same American Nazi Party, this time on the east coast.

And I think about these two facts also in terms of this movement, the lesbian/feminist movement, consisting of diverse groups with diverse needs and diverse experiences of oppression.

I want the issue of anti-Semitism to be incorporated into our overall struggle because there are lesbian/feminists among us who are threatened in this country not only as lesbians, but also as Jews. If that incorporation simply takes the form of adding us on to the already existing list of problems, then it will be merely tokenism and lip service. But if it includes self-examination, analysis of the Jew in America, and dialogues between Jews and non-Jews, then I think this movement will have made a real attempt to deal with the issue.

The following are some questions that I think both Jewish and non-Jewish women might consider asking in trying to identify in themselves sources of shame, conflict, doubt, and anti-Semitism. They should keep in mind that the questions are designed to reveal the degree to which they have internalized the anti-Semitism around them. I hope that by examining their own anti-Semitism, Jewish women will conclude that anti-Semitism, *like any other ideology of oppression*, must *never* be tolerated, must *never* be hushed up, must *never* be ignored, and that, instead, it must *always* be exposed and resisted.

1) Do I have to check with other Jewish women in order to verify whether something is anti-Semitic? Do I distrust my own judgment on this issue?

2) When I am certain, am I afraid to speak out?

3) Am I afraid that by focusing on anti-Semitism I am being divisive?

4) Do I feel that by asking other women to deal with anti-Semitism I am draining the movement of precious energy that would be better used elsewhere?

5) Do I feel that anti-Semitism has been discussed too much already and feel embarrassed to bring it up?

6) Do I feel that the commercial presses and the media are covering the issue of anti-Semitism adequately and that it is unnecessary to bring it up also in the movement? Am I embarrassed by the way anti-Semitism/the Holocaust is presented in the media? Why?

7) Do I have strong disagreements with and/or am ashamed of Israeli policies and, as a result, don't feel that I can defend Jews whole-heartedly against anti-Semitism? Is it possible for me to disagree with Israeli policy and still oppose anti-Semitism?

8) Do I feel guilty and/or ashamed of Jewish racism in this country and, as a result, feel I can't defend Jews whole-heartedly against anti-Semitism? Is is possible for me to acknowledge Jewish racism, struggle against it, and still feel Jewish pride? And still oppose anti-Semitism?

9) Do I feel that Jews have done well in this country and, therefore, should not complain?

10) Do I feel that historically, sociologically and/or psychologically, anti-Semitism is "justified" or "understandable," and that I am, therefore, willing to tolerate it?

11) Do I feel that anti-Semitism exists but it is "not so bad" or "not so important"? Why?

12) Do I believe that by focusing on the problem of anti-Semitism I will make it worse? Why?
13) Do I feel that Jews draw too much attention to themselves? How?
14) Do I associate the struggle against anti-Semitism with conservativism? Why?
15) What Jewish stereotypes am I afraid of being identified with? What do I repress in myself in order to prevent such identification?

Jewish Identity:
A Coat of Many Colors

Interracial Plus

Josylyn C. Segal

I am the daughter of an American Negro/Native-American mother (an accomplished dancer) and a Russian/Roumanian Jewish father (a jazz drummer). My parents' marriage did not last long; they separated after their characters became incompatible (contrary to the often expressed assumption that they separated because of "racial problems"). After living with my mother during my first eight years, I chose to live with my father.

Having the surname "Segal" and living with my father gave me the impression that I was automatically Jewish. Although my father was not a practicing Jew, I knew he believed in one G-d. Throughout my childhood I heard Yiddish conversation and melodies and watched my father turn his nose at the thought of drinking milk with a hamburger. When I was twelve I joined B'nai B'rith Youth.

Three weeks after I became a member, the community rabbi telephoned my father and informed him that since my mother was not Jewish, I was not Jewish, and consequently could not belong to B'nai B'rith Youth. It is difficult to describe the depth of my emotional trauma when I was told that I was not Jewish. I had always believed, indeed taken for granted that I was Jewish.

Being ejected from the youth group, and learning later that other members lobbied the national headquarters in my favor, evolved into a dramatic ordeal. Given the option, I decided to convert to Judaism in order to be accepted as a "real," full-fledged Jew according to Jewish Law. The conversion, in Orthodox tradition, involved studying Jewish Law, history, observance and lifestyles, as well as anti-Semitism. My conversion acted as a catalyst for an even deeper sense of my Jewish heritage and identification.

Being a part of everything that I am—an interracial Jewish lesbian—makes me a target for a wide range of bigoted attitudes.

My choice to relate with whomever I choose—and not exclusively align myself with Blacks because of my skin color or with Jews because of my religion—disturbs most Americans. I can relate with Blacks and I can relate with Jews. My vantage point affords me a unique and invaluable perspective on Jewish racism and Black anti-Semitism.

When I enter both traditional and gay American synagogues and participate in religious services, I often receive stares of "What is *she* doing here?" Then, after the congregation witnesses my fluency with the Hebrew prayers, I am accosted with "What *are* you?" or "Where did *you* learn to daven so well?" And, of course, the "more aware" light-skinned Americans have trouble accepting Jews who do not fit into the stereotyped Ashkenazi image.

Nobody assumes that I am Jewish; I do not "look" Jewish. This makes me privy to quite a range of freely spoken anti-Jewish attitudes. Black Americans, as part of the gentile majority, tend to share universal misconceptions about Jews.

In my experience, the oppressive stereotypes associated with Jewish Americans outnumber those associated with Black Americans. That is *not* to say that Jewish oppression is more severe than Black oppression; rather, the history of Jewish oppression is far older than the history of Black oppression. The longer a people have been oppressed, the longer the list of oppressive stereotypes associated with them.

Yet, if I suggested to most Black Americans that Jews are an oppressed people, I would receive looks of agitated disbelief; most Black Americans perceive Jews as exploitative and wealthy whites. At one time I believed that if the history of Jewish oppression were made available to Black Americans, their hostility towards Jews would decrease. After being labeled "A Black That Acts Jewish" and "A Jew That Looks Black," I believe that, paradoxically, Black anti-Semitism is more prevalent among the younger, educated, less religious.

I have met many angry Black Americans who have discovered the Palestinian Liberation Organization (PLO) as an ideal vehicle for projecting their anti-Semitism. Even though the PLO is remote and abstract to most Black Americans, I have been accosted countless times by Black Muslim men (who have conveniently chosen their version of Islam) telling me that as a Black woman, I should support the PLO. When I respond—all in one breath—that I believe that the Arab refugees need a home, that I am Jewish, and that I support the State of Israel, I am informed that I should not support Israel because if and when the Arab countries impose another oil embargo, my Black brothers and sisters will suffer more than my Jewish brothers and sisters.

The State of Israel evokes a myriad of emotions for me. I see a small country besieged by the entire world, with a scattered and oppressed people—connected by persecution and the Torah— fighting to justify her right to exist. My love for Israel runs deep and strong. Yet, I am angered by Israel's blatant racist patterns and practices.

During my first visit to Israel, I recognized the extent to which white racism has penetrated the Jewish community. I found that Jews of Europe, North America, South Africa and Australia are often quite overt with their bigotries toward darker Jews (Arab, Sephardic, Oriental and Ethiopian). I was appalled when I first witnessed an American Jewish tourist comment on the common sight of Arab Jews begging in Jerusalem's Jewish Quarter, *"They're* Jewish? They can't be *Jewish. . .* they're so *dirty!"*

I have since become aware of the class differences between light-skinned and dark-skinned Jews. The Jews that I saw working in sanitation were consistently Arab. They receive a lower wage than the average European Jew.

The European Jews who were instrumental in the founding of Israel were responsible for imposing European-Jewish values on Arab-Jewish culture. One of my former professors at Brandeis University, Dr. Paul Flor, theorized that the European Jews were thus reacting to the anti-Semitic stereotype of Jews as "dirty, dark and smelly." He contended that the Arab-Jewish cultures reminded European Jews of an image portrayed and exploited during the Holocaust.

European Jews supervising immigration into developing towns and communities did not prohibit Arab Jews from entrance. However, Arab-Jewish cultures were expected to assimilate. For example, the supervisors designated that many French, Hungarian, Syrian, and Moroccan Jews would live in a community designed by European city planners. The simple fact of variance in family-size between Arab and European cultures was ignored. As a result, contemporary Israeli society is abundant with communities that are quite impoverished. The European family with two children in a two-bedroom apartment has been able to leave the community and ensure their children's education. In contrast, the Syrian family in an identical two-bedroom apartment with thirteen children remains in the town; their children attend schools that promote European values. The children become alienated and truancy increases. With scant education, upward financial mobility becomes impossible.

This scenario is somewhat parallel to the United States. How can Israel make such blunders, paralleling the "American Way"? In response to my question, I am often told, "When there is a question of war, we are all Jews, and we all fight together," or "Give Israel time... it is a new country." These responses are unacceptable.

Still, my *Jewishness* has never been questioned by Israeli Jews. Their society has a pervasive understanding that Jews come from everywhere, in all shapes, classes and colors. This gives me, as an interracial Jewish lesbian, a special comfort when I question the whereabouts of my homeland. My American Sephardic Jewish friends share a similar comfort in experiencing Israel as homeland.

With roots in two oppressed and misunderstood cultures, I have a unique perspective on the Black-Jewish conflict. Black Americans do not have the "white-skin" privilege afforded to most American Jews. The Black American's transformation of frustrations and grievances into anti-Jewish aggression may suggest an envy of seeing another minority "get over."

In order for there to be any bonding, Black and Jewish Americans need to confront and demythicize their stereotypes of each other, acknowledge different needs and conflicting interests. Without compromise, negotiations and coalition action, both groups will continue to distrust each other and never realize that they share the same oppressor.

My strength is my interraciality; it permits me to comfortably (though not necessarily successfully) challenge, confront, and educate the ignorant about the "other," and to dispute misconceptions about what I am *supposed* to be (i.e. either I should know how to dance and play sports, or I should have a stash of money). I can talk food. Ask me about hominy grits, knaidlach, hamhocks, greens, kreplach, latkes, ribs, sweet bread, tzimmes, matzo brei, and chitterling. And I'll tell you that I am both hungry and vegetarian.

How a Nice Jewish Girl Like Me Could

Pauline Bart

Growing up Jewish in New York during the rise of fascism and the Holocaust meant growing up with a political consciousness. The radio was always turned to news programs, since news could mean life or death. I knew all about Franco and the Spanish Civil War, and I thought that the world was made up of Irish Catholics and Jews since all my teachers were Irish Catholic.

When I first arrived in kindergarten I asked my teacher, Miss McEvoy, if she were Irish or Jewish. She was on the wrong side, so it did not surprise me when she spoke of the infant Jesus at Christmas. My parents, however, were surprised and complained.

I went to school B.E.—before ecumenicism. Pluralism had not yet been invented and we were still considered a melting pot rather than a salad bowl. So my ninety-eight percent Jewish school had to sing Christmas carols. I led strikes in my row against singing the words I decided were too religious. No Jesus, Mary or Holy Virgin. Developing a political consciousness was rewarded in my family.

East Flatbush, Brooklyn, 1936. In honor of Armistice Day, I had to bring a present to school for a hospitalized World War I veteran. In response to the present my mother selected, I said "When my children ask me for presents to give to the soldiers who were hurt fighting Hitler and Mussolini I will give them something nicer." This prescient observation was immediately sent to the Yiddish *Daily Forward*. Pauline Bart, girl *chochem*, was first published in the first grade.

Before Pearl Harbor, a teacher proudly declared that she had attended an America First (isolationist) rally. I told my parents. They called the principal. He called me in. The teacher got in trouble. I later got in trouble.

It was St. Patrick's Day in Winthrop Junior High School. The United States had already formally entered the War. I had heard on the radio that Nazi spies were using Ireland as a base. I knew it was bad for the Jews. The teacher asked if anyone was not wearing green. She then embarked on a project of greening the class. I refused to be greened. It became a school scandal. One Jewish teacher supported me, noting that we did not wear blue and white on Jewish holidays.

I was never silent. Not then, not during the fifties, not now.

It is Erev Yom Kippur 1972. My lover, who has just returned from spending Rosh Hashanah with her family, and whom I have missed desperately (I got a kitten but it didn't work), tells me that she cannot sleep in the same bed with me. I promise that I won't "do anything" but she says that it doesn't matter. It is The Law. Since she has a degree in Talmud my case is hopeless. The next day she goes to the traditional, rather than the alternative services at a college campus and waits for the tenth man to arrive before they start. I tell her that she must confront the Jewish religious establishment and use her talmudic training to make Jewish feminism possible. She refuses. Confronting the Jewish establishment on religious issues is bad for the Jews. Later she temporarily refuses to join Jewish Women for Affirmative Action because that too was bad for the Jews. I tell her that she won't be able to go to Israel because I will denounce her to the Embassy as a Lesbian and the Law of the Return does not apply to homosexuals. She cries. I am stunned because she never cries. I later write that she keeps her life in separate kitchen cabinets. In fact she is now a closet kosher since she can pass—indeed have high status—by being a vegetarian.

It is my sabbatical and I am in Paris, invited by a French sociologist to meet with French feminists. I put on my non-designer jeans and orange "A woman without a man is like a fish without a bicycle" T-shirt, and arrive at the prestigious address. The table is set for high tea and the women are all wearing knit dresses, nylons and heels (this was before the "dress-for-success" epidemic hit). Some of the women teach at the Sorbonne; some have been active in International Women's Year, which I learned from *off our backs* was a fraud. I feel superior to them, for they are bourgeois feminists.

I see an interesting painting on the wall and ask about it. The hostess informs me that she had it painted with symbolic representations of parts of her life. She tells me what the various objects signify. When she gets to the lower left-hand corner, she says, "The barbed wire represents Auschwitz and that is my concentration camp number." I no longer feel superior.

My next stop is Amsterdam and I am speaking at the Women's Center about women and health issues, noting the dangers of the Pill. After the talk a woman concludes that the only logical solution is to become a lesbian. An obvious dyke, wearing a large Jewish star, remarks that this kind of reasoning worries her. We talk and she takes me to the club where gay men and lesbians meet. She tells me that the lesbians are about to separate, which makes her sad, because she believes in pushing the boundaries back, not closing them. We arrange to meet the next day; she will take me to the museum and show me why Rembrandt was a greater artist than his contemporaries.

After the museum I assume the role of Pauline Bart, girl sociologist and intrepid interviewer. I ask her how she survived the war; she tells me that she was sent from Christian family to Christian family. I mention that she does not look Jewish. She says, "Of course not. If I looked Jewish I'd be dead." She gets a terrible headache and I feel guilty and stupid.

We return to her apartment where I learn of her role in the founding of Israel's gay liberation movement. She left after finding it impossible to live openly as a lesbian. In Israel she was in *galut* because she was a lesbian and in Amsterdam she is in *galut* because she is a Jew.

She tells me that on the Amsterdam tram people make nasty remarks when they pass the prosperous Jewish section which is prosperous only because the Jews received reparations for their losses during the Holocaust. She tells people, "You know how they got that money. Would you like to have gotten it that way?" She is clearly a woman who would have led strikes in junior high school. I have missed the last tram. We spend the night together. I feel as if I have come full circle.

It is Erev Rosh Hashanah 1979 and I am driving home feeling somewhat disconnected. I have never felt any need to do anything special for the High Holy Days, taking pride in only celebrating the festivals of freedom, Hanukkah and Pesach. I am listening to Chicago's educational radio station when they announce a special holiday service written by a distinguished Jewish academic. I know that distinguished academic. I also know his daughter. She stayed in a brutal marriage rather than avow her lesbianism because of "what it would do to her father." I turn the radio off. There is no way that program could have any positive meaning for me.

Just as I was taught always to ask, "Is it good for the Jews?" I now ask, "Is it good for women?" I do not understand the

women who write about battered husbands and are then surprised that their data is used against battered women; who write
about connections between rape and the menstrual cycle and
are surprised when that too is used against women. I am never
surprised. They are always looking for Christian babies' blood
in the matzah. They will always use anything they can against us.

Nor do I understand women who are surprised when supposed "pro-feminist" men act sexist. My mother said, "Scratch
a goy and you find an anti-Semite." I say, "Scratch a man and
you find a sexist." Sometimes I refer to men as the goyim.

I count woman winners
Like my mother counted Jewish names.
Rhodes Scholars, Nobel laureates, White House "fellows."
So they're not all my sisters—
They're my ethnic group.

Some of Us Are Arabic
Rachel Wahba

Throughout my childhood, my father joked about our being "Wandering Jews." It was his way of lightening our burden with what I believe was a combination of historical pride and a search for connectedness with the Jewish People in the face of identity-lessness as stateless "gaigin."*

I am a Sephardic/Arabic Jewish immigrant of Egyptian and Iraqi parents. Born in Bombay, India, I grew up Stateless** in the Japanese cosmopolitan city of Kobe.

Living in a city with an international population representing many walks of life was an incredibly enriching experience, and it was difficult living as a brown-skinned Eastern Jew. At a very young age, I learned—from the racist international schools I attended, the color-coded Arabic world of my parents, and Japanese society—that it would have been much easier as a light-skinned Ashkenazi.

In my youth, I spent a great deal of energy learning how to pass as a New York Ashkenazi Jew. I have always felt affinity with New York Jews, and two of my closest childhood friends were from Brooklyn and the Bronx. When I first arrived in the United States, I was thrilled when people mistook me for American-Ashkenazi and asked me where I got my "tan." I can pass for Ashkenazi not only because of my familiarity with the dominant (Western) culture, but also because of the Ashkenazi Assumption.

Although Arabic and North African Jews comprise approximately sixty-seven percent of Israel's population, we are a minority within a minority. Jewish history, culture, food—

---

*Japanese pejorative for "foreigners."

**No citizenship or passport. By 1957, all Egyptian Jews residing outside of Egypt lost their citizenship, including the four thousand who were expelled in 1956.

"Jewish" anything—has been defined by Western/Ashkenazi Jews. It is not surprising, then, that even after I tell people I am an Arabic Jew, many continue to assume that I come from a Yiddish background. Arabic was spoken in my home, and I never tasted a bagel with cream cheese and lox until I came to the United States. Our customs, food, language and music are Middle-Eastern and Judeo-Arabic. On special occasions we drink Turkish coffee after dinner out of tiny espresso cups, and we don't know from Yiddish and gefilte fish!

Both my parents left their respective homelands with the knowledge that they would never return. Since the inception of Islam, life for the Arabic Jew has been an insecure existence marked by daily humiliation—periodically culminating in anti-Jewish riots, massacres, rape, torture, plunder and expulsion. On the street, a Jew could be hit on the head by any Moslem passing by. This ritual, called *chtaka* (accompanied by a special sacramental phrase[1]), is one example of the prevailing attitude towards Jews living in Arab lands.

My father left Egypt when the conditions for Egyptian Jews began to deteriorate visibly. In 1938, serious anti-Jewish riots took place in towns with Jewish populations, particularly Alexandria, Cairo and Mansoura. The situation continued to worsen during the next decade with arrests, torture and massacre of Egypt's Jews. In 1956, four thousand Jews were expelled and their property and possessions were confiscated. The once flourishing Jewish communities were extinguished as Egypt's Jewish population diminished from 75,000 (1948) to 350 (1974).[2]

I was raised with my mother's vivid memories of hiding in neighbors' homes, running from one rooftop to another as she fled from Baghdad's anti-Jewish mobs,* and going to bed with her shoes on for weeks afterward. My family also worried constantly about our uprooted Egyptian relatives living in poverty in Israel, and the safety of our other relatives trying to leave Iraq, my mother's country of origin. There, where Jewish communities existed since Biblical times, the Jewish population was being dramatically diminished from 135,000 (1948) to 2,500 (1971) to 400 (1974).[3] The Jewish communities in other Middle-Eastern and North African countries met with similar fates. Those of Tunisia, Yemen, Aden, Algeria and Libya are now almost extinct, and the few thousand remaining Jews in Syria are

---

*Known as the "Rashid Ali Riots" of June 1941. 175 Jews were estimated as murdered, 1,000 wounded, and it is unknown how many were raped and tortured. Jewish homes and businesses were destroyed and looted.

not permitted to emigrate. Morocco has the largest remaining Jewish population in the Arab world today.[4] My mother could not return to the Middle East to live in a country surrounded by hostile Arab states, so we could not consider the logical solution to our statelessness: *aliyah* to Israel. And so we waited, for twenty years, for immigration to the United States since the U. S. quota for Egyptian nationals was very low.

As an Arabic Jew and stateless immigrant, my perspective on being Jewish differs from most American Jews'. As second and third generation, they are distanced from the pogroms and *shtetls* of Europe, the anti-Jewish mobs and the "Jewish Quarters"[5] of the Middle East and North Africa. Feeling isolated, I have to explain myself more often than I care to; occasionally, I lapse into an old childhood fantasy of being Susan Goldberg, my best friend from the Bronx. Then I would not have to feel so "different," like a minority of one!

And yet I am not alone. I straddle two support systems: the lesbian community and my family of origin—my extended family. My family is very close and important to me. From them I receive validation as an Arabic Jew and the connection to my background that I cannot find in the lesbian community. Although my parents do not fully understand my lesbianism, they accept it. I am not torn by choosing between them and my lifestyle.

My Jewish identity has always been solid. Coming from a background of anti-Semitic missionary schools with crucifixes hanging in every room and living in a country where assimilation was not an option, I could not forget or ignore who and what I was. Unlike my "American" Jewish daughter, my being a "Stateless" Jew gave me no country to claim. I could not belong to a country *and* be "Jew-ish"; I *was* a "Jew." In the fifth grade, I wanted to crawl under my desk to hide when my class read aloud the poem "Man Without A Country." My mother purposely emphasized a strong Jewish identity in my brother and myself partially to alleviate the sense of disenfranchisement and non-belonging in a world where everyone was supposed to have a country.

As a Jew, I identify with all Jews as a People. We not only share similar cultural values, but also a common history of oppression—whether Eastern or Western, Sephardic or Ashkenazi. And we share a common destiny. Yet, I am often asked, "What do you mean you are an 'Arabic Jew'? Isn't that a contradiction?" The contradiction is in the question, especially when it

comes from another Jew. It is particularly invalidating when it
is asked at a Jewish lesbian-feminist gathering. Although I am
there to connect and identify with other Jewish lesbians, it is
enormously difficult to feel connected while feeling invisible! I
feel safer with people who care to know more about Arabic
Jews. Too often we Sephardim are used opportunistically as a
weapon with which to attack Israel. (Nearly every time I mention Israel, someone will too quickly label Israel "racist" for its
shabby treatment of its Sephardim. Otherwise, I hear very little
acknowledgement from anyone regarding the Sephardim. Israel's treatment of the Sephardim is inexcusable and definitely
racist, but to use the Sephardim to make Israel a villain feels
opportunistic to me.)

There is no contradiction in being an Arabic Jew. There are
no divided loyalties, no country to pledge allegiance to. For
centuries Arabic Jews have been a disenfranchised minority,
"foreigners" carrying identity cards or badges in their native
lands. Always second-class citizens and vulnerable to the whims
of oppressive regimes, Jews have been a People without a country. Historically, the Jews of North Africa and Arab states have
had only their Judaism to fully identify with. The Magen David
has been our symbol, and Israel our historic homeland. Judaism
has been our culture, history, religion, spirituality, and nationality.

Endnotes

1Albert Memmi, *Jews and Arabs* (Chicago: O'Hara, Inc., 1975), p. 21.

2Martin Gilbert, *The Jews of Arab Lands: Their History in Maps*
(Board of Deputies of British Jews, 1976), map 9.

3*Ibid.* map 5.

4*Ibid.* maps 6, 7, 8, 10, 11, 12. Jewish populations diminished in Morocco
from 285,000 (1948) to 20,000 (1974); in Tunisia from 110,000 (1948)
to 2,000 (1974); in Yemen from 55,000 (1948) to 500 (1974); in Aden
from 8,000 (1948) to nil (1974); in Libya from 38,000 (1948) to 20
(1974); in Algeria from 140,000 (1948) to 500 (1974); and in Syria
from 29,770 (1943) to 18,000 (1946) to 4,000 (1974).

5Jewish ghettos in the Middle East/North Africa.

Split at the Root
Adrienne Rich

For about fifteen minutes I have been sitting chin in hand in front of the typewriter, staring out at the snow. Trying to be honest with myself, trying to figure out why writing this seems to me so dangerous an act, filled with fear and shame, and why it seems so necessary. It comes to me that in order to write this I have to be willing to do two things: I have to claim my father, for I have my Jewishness from him and not from my gentile mother; and I have to break his silence, his taboos; in order to claim him I have in a sense to expose him.

And there is of course the third thing: I have to face the sources and the flickering presence of my own ambivalence as a Jew; the daily, mundane anti-Semitisms of my entire life.

These are stories I have never tried to tell before. Why now? Why, I asked myself sometime last year, does this question of Jewish identity float so impalpably, so ungraspably, around me, a cloud I can't quite see the outlines of, which feels to me without definition?

And yet I've been on the track of this longer than I think.

In a long poem written in 1960, when I was thirty-one years old, I described myself as "Split at the root, neither Gentile nor Jew, Yankee nor Rebel."* I was still trying to have it both ways: to be neither/nor, trying to live (with my Jewish husband and three children more Jewish in ancestry than I) in the predominantly gentile Yankee academic world of Cambridge, Massachusetts.

But this begins, for me, in Baltimore, where I was born in a hospital in the Black ghetto, whose lobby contained an immense, white marble statue of Christ.

---

*"Readings of History" in Adrienne Rich, *Snapshots of a Daughter-in-Law*. W.W. Norton, New York, 1967, pp. 36-40.

My father was then a young teacher and researcher in the department of pathology at the Johns Hopkins Medical School, one of the very few Jews to attend or teach at that institution. He was from Birmingham, Alabama; his father, Samuel, was an immigrant from Austria-Hungary and his mother, Hattie Rice, a Sephardic Jew from Vicksburg, Mississippi. My grandfather had had a shoe store in Birmingham, which did well enough to allow him to retire comfortably, and to leave my grandmother, on his death, a small income. The only souvenirs of my grandfather, Samuel Rich, were his ivory flute, which lay on our living-room mantel and was not to be played with; his thin gold pocket-watch, which my father wore; and his Hebrew prayerbook, which I discovered among my father's books in the course of reading my way through his library. In this prayerbook there was a newspaper clipping about my grandparents' wedding, which took place in a synagogue.

My father, Arnold, was sent in adolescence to a military school in the Tennessee mountains, a place for training white Southern Christian gentlemen. I suspect that there were few if any other Jewish boys at Colonel Bingham's. Or at "Mr. Jefferson's university," in Charlottesville, where he studied as an undergraduate. With whatever conscious forethought, Samuel and Hattie sent their son into the dominant Southern WASP culture, to become an "exception," to enter the professional class. Never, in describing these experiences, did he ever speak of having suffered—from loneliness, cultural alienation, or outsiderhood. I never heard him use the word, "anti-Semitism."

It was only in college, when I read a poem by Karl Shapiro beginning: "To hate the Negro and avoid the Jew/is the curriculum" that it flashed on me that there was an untold side to my father's story of his student years. He looked recognizably Jewish, was short and slender in build with dark wiry hair and deepset eyes, high forehead and curved nose.

My mother is a gentile. In Jewish law I cannot count myself a Jew. If it is true that "We think back through our mothers if we are women" (Virginia Woolf)—and I myself have affirmed this—then even according to lesbian theory, I cannot (or need not?) count myself a Jew.

The white Southern Protestant woman, the gentile, has always been there for me to peel back into. That's a whole piece of history in itself, for my gentile grandmother and my mother were also frustrated artists and intellectuals, a lost writer and a lost composer between them. Readers and annotators of books, note-takers, my mother a good pianist still, in her eighties. But there was also the obsession with ancestry, with "background," the Southern talk of family, not as people you would necessarily know and depend on, but as heritage, the guarantee of "good breeding." There was the inveterate romantic heterosexual fantasy, the mother telling the daughter how to attract men (my mother often used the word "fascinate"); the assumption that relations between the sexes could only be romantic, that it was in the woman's interest to cultivate "mystery," conceal her actual feelings. Survival tactics, of a kind, I think today, knowing what I know about the white woman's sexual role in the Southern racist scenario. Heterosexuality as protection, but also drawing white women deeper into collusion with white men.

It would be easy to push away and deny the gentile in me: that white Southern woman, that social Christian. At different times in my life, I suppose, I have wanted to push away one or the other burden of inheritance, to say merely, *I am a woman; I am a lesbian.* If I call myself a Jewish lesbian do I thereby try to shed some of my Southern gentile guilt, my white woman's culpability? If I call myself only through my mother, is it because I pass more easily through a world where being a lesbian often seems like outsiderhood enough?

According to Nazi logic, my two Jewish grandparents would have made me a *Mischling, first-degree*: non-exempt from the Final Solution.

The social world in which I grew up was Christian virtually without needing to say so; Christian imagery, music, language, symbols, assumptions everywhere. It was also a genteel, white middle-class world in which "common" was a term of deep opprobrium. "Common" white people might speak of "niggers"; *we* were taught never to use that word; *we* said "Negroes" (even as we accepted segregation, the eating taboo, the assumption that Black people were simply of a separate species). Our language was more polite, distinguishing us from the "rednecks," or the lynch mob mentality. So charged with negative meaning was even the word "Negro" that as children we were taught never to use it in front of Black people. We were taught that any mention of skin color in the presence of colored people was treacherous forbidden ground. In a parallel way, the word "Jew" was not used by polite gentiles. I sometimes heard my best friend's father, a Presbyterian minister, allude to "the Hebrew

people," or "people of the Jewish faith." The world of acceptable folk was white, gentile (christian, really) and had "ideals"
(which colored people, white "common" people, were not supposed to have). "Ideals" and "manners" included not hurting
someone's feelings by calling her or him a Negro or a Jew—naming the hated identity. This is the mental framework of the
1930's and 1940's in which I was raised.

(Writing this I feel, dimly, like the betrayer: of my father,
who did not speak the word; of my mother, who must have
trained me in the messages; of my caste and class; of my white-
ness itself.)

Two memories: I am in a play-reading at school, of *The
Merchant of Venice*. Whatever Jewish law says, I am quite sure
I was *seen* as Jewish (with a reassuringly gentile mother) in that
double-vision that bigotry allows. I am the only Jewish girl in
the class and I am playing Portia. As always, I read my part
aloud for my father the night before, and he tells me to convey,
with my voice, more scorn and contempt with the word "Jew":
"Therefore, Jew. . . ." I have to say the word out, and say it
loudly. I was encouraged to pretend to be a non-Jewish child
acting a non-Jewish character who has to speak the word "Jew"
emphatically. Such a child would not have had trouble with the
part. But *I* must have had trouble with the part, if only because
the word itself was really taboo. I can see that there was a kind
of terrible, bitter bravado about my father's way of handling
this. And who would not dissociate from Shylock in order to
identify with Portia? As a Jewish child who was also a female I
loved Portia—and, like every other Shakespearean heroine, she
proved a treacherous role model.

A year or so later I am in another play, *The School for
Scandal*, in which a notorious spendthrift is described as having "many excellent friends. . . . among the Jews." In neither
case was anything explained, either to me or to the class at
large about this scorn for Jews and the disgust surrounding Jews
and money. Money, when Jews wanted it, had it, or lent it to
others, seemed to take on a peculiar nastiness, and Jews and
money had some peculiar and unspeakable relation.

At this same school—in which we had christian hymns and
prayers, and read aloud through the Bible morning after morning—I gained the impression that Jews were in the Bible and
mentioned in English literature, had been persecuted centuries
ago by the wicked Inquisition, but that they seemed not to
exist in everyday life. These were the 1940's and we were told

a great deal about the Battle of Britain, the noble French Resistance fighters, the brave, starving Dutch—but I did not learn of the resistance of the Warsaw Ghetto until I left home.

I was sent to the Episcopal church, baptized and confirmed, and attended it for about five years, though without belief. That religion seemed to have little to do with belief or commitment; it was liturgy that mattered, not moral passion. Neither of my parents ever entered that church, and my father would not enter *any* church for any reason—wedding or funeral. Nor did I enter a synagogue until I left Baltimore. When I came home from church, for a while, my father insisted on reading aloud to me from Thomas Paine's *The Age of Reason*—a diatribe against institutional religion. Thus, he explained, I would have a balanced view of these things, a choice. He—they—did not give me the choice to be a Jew. My mother explained to me when I was filling out forms for college that if any question was asked about "religion" I should put down "Episcopalian" rather than "none"—to seem to have no religion was, she implied, dangerous.

But it was white social christianity, rather than any particular christian sect, that the world was founded on. The very word "christian" was used as a synonym for virtuous, just, peace-loving, generous, etc. etc.* The norm was christian: "religion: none" was indeed not acceptable. Anti-Semitism was so intrinsic as not to have a name. I don't recall exactly being taught that the Jews killed Jesus; "Christ-killer" seems too strong a term for the bland Episcopal vocabulary; but certainly we got the impression that the Jews had been caught out in a terrible mistake, failing to recognize the true Messiah, and were thereby less advanced in moral and spiritual sensibility. The Jews had actually allowed *moneylenders in the Temple* (again, the unexplained obsession with Jews and money). They were of the past, archaic, primitive as older (and darker) cultures are supposed to be primitive: Christianity was lightness, fairness, peace on earth, and combined the feminine appeal of "the meek shall inherit the earth" with the masculine stride of "Onward, Christian Soldiers."

Sometime in 1946, while still in high school, I read in the newspaper that a theatre in Baltimore was showing films of the Allied liberation of the Nazi concentration camps. Alone, I

---

*In a similar way the phrase "that's white of you" implied that you were behaving with the superior decency and morality expected of white, but not of Black people.

went downtown after school one afternoon and watched the
stark, blurry but unmistakable newsreels. When I try to go
back and touch the pulse of that girl of sixteen, growing up in
many ways so precocious and so ignorant, I am overwhelmed by
a memory of despair, a sense of inevitability, more enveloping
than any I had ever known. Anne Frank's diary and many other
personal narratives of the Holocaust were still unknown or un-
written. But it came to me that every one of those piles of
corpses, mountains of shoes and clothing, had contained, simply,
individuals, who had believed, as I now believed of myself, that
they were meant to live out a life of some kind of meaning, that
the world possessed some kind of sense and order; yet *this* had
happened to them. And I, who believed my life was intended to
be so interesting and meaningful, was connected to those dead
by something—not just mortality but a taboo name, a hated
identity. Or was I—did I really have to be? Writing this now, I
feel belated rage, that I was so impoverished by the family and
social worlds I lived in, that I had to try to figure out by myself
what this did indeed mean for me. That I had never been taught
about resistance, only about passing. That I had no language for
anti-Semitism itself.

When I went home and told my parents where I had been,
they were not pleased. I felt accused of being morbidly curious,
not healthy, sniffing around death for the thrill of it. And since,
at sixteen, I was often not sure of the sources of my feelings or
of my motives for doing what I did, I probably accused myself
as well. One thing was clear: there was nobody in my world
with whom I could discuss those films. Probably at the same
time I was reading accounts of the camps in magazines and
newspapers; what I remember was the films, and having questions that I could not even phrase: such as, are those men and
women "them" or "us"?

To be able to ask even the child's astonished question *Why
do they hate us so?* means knowing how to say "we." The guilt
of not knowing, the guilt of perhaps having betrayed my parents, or even those victims, those survivors, through mere curi-
osity—these also froze in me for years the impulse to find out
more about the Holocaust.

1947: I left Baltimore to go to college in Cambridge, Massachusetts, left (I thought) the backward, enervating South for
the intellectual, vital North. New England also had for me some
vibration of higher moral rectitude, of moral passion even, with

its seventeenth-century Puritan inner scrutiny, its Abolitionist righteousness, Colonel Shaw and his Black Civil War regiment depicted in granite on Boston Common, its nineteenth century literary "flowering." At the same time, I found myself, at Radcliffe, among Jewish women. I used to sit for hours over coffee with what I thought of as the "real" Jewish students, who told me about middle-class Jewish culture in America. I described my background—for the first time to strangers—and they took me on, some with amusement at my illiteracy, some arguing that I could never marry into a strict Jewish family, some convinced I didn't "look Jewish," others that I did. I learned the names of holidays and foods, which surnames are Jewish and which are "changed names"; about girls who had had their noses "fixed," their hair straightened. For these young Jewish women, students in the late 1940's, it was acceptable, perhaps even necessary, to strive to look as gentile as possible, but they stuck proudly to being Jewish; expected to marry a Jew, have children, keep the holidays, carry on the culture.

I felt I was testing a forbidden current, that there was danger in these revelations. I bought a reproduction of a Chagall portrait of a rabbi in striped prayer-shawl and hung it on the wall of my room. I was admittedly young and trying to educate myself, but I was also doing something that *is* dangerous: I was flirting with identity.

One day that year I was in a small shop where I had bought a dress with a too-long skirt. The shop employed a seamstress who did alterations, and she came in to pin up the skirt on me. I am sure that she was a recent immigrant, a survivor. I remember a short, dark woman wearing heavy glasses, with an accent so foreign I could not understand her words. Something about her presence was very powerful and disturbing to me. After marking and pinning up the skirt she sat back on her knees, looked up at me, and asked in a hurried whisper: "You Jewish?" Eighteen years of training in assimilation sprang into the reflex by which I shook my head, rejecting her, and muttered, "No."

What was I actually saying "no" to? She was poor, older, struggling with a foreign tongue, anxious; she had escaped the death that had been intended for her, but I had no imagination of her possible courage and foresight, her resistance; I did not see in her a heroine who had perhaps saved many lives including her own. I saw the frightened immigrant, the seamstress hemming the skirts of college girls, the wandering Jew. But I was an

American college girl, having her skirt hemmed. And I was frightened myself, I think, because she had recognized me ("It takes one to know one," my friend Edie at Radcliffe had said) even if I refused to recognize myself or her; even if her recognition was sharpened by loneliness, or the need to feel safe with me.

But why should she have felt safe with me? I myself was living in a false sense of safety.

There are betrayals in my life that I have known at the very moment were betrayals: this was one of them. There are other betrayals committed so repeatedly, so mundanely, that they leave no memory trace behind: only a growing residue of misery, of dull, accreted self-hatred. Often these take the form not of words but of silence. Silence before the joke at which everyone is laughing: the anti-woman joke, the racist joke, the anti-Semitic joke. Silence and then amnesia. Blocking it out when the oppressor's language starts coming from the lips of one we admire, whose courage and eloquence have touched us: *She didn't really mean that: he didn't really say that.* But the accretions build up out of sight, like scale inside a kettle.

1948: I come home from my freshman year at college flaming with new insights, new information. I am the daughter who has gone out into the world, to the pinnacle of intellectual prestige, Harvard, fulfilling my father's hopes for me, but also exposed to dangerous influences. I have already been reproved for attending a rally for Henry Wallace and the Progressive Party. I challenge my father: "Why haven't you told me that I am Jewish? Why do you never talk about being a Jew?" He answers measuredly, "You know that I have never denied that I am a Jew. But it's not important to me. I am a scientist, a Deist. I have no use for organized religion. I choose to live in a world of many kinds of people. There are Jews I admire and others whom I despise. I am a person, not simply a Jew." The words are as I remember them, not perhaps exactly as spoken. But that was the message. And it contained enough truth—as all denial drugs itself on partial truth—so that it remained for the time being unanswerable, even though it left me high and dry, split at the root, gasping for clarity, for air.

At that time Arnold Rich was living in suspension, waiting to be appointed to the professorship of pathology at Johns Hopkins. The appointment was delayed for years, no Jew ever having held a professorial chair in that medical school. And he wanted it badly. It must have been a very bitter time for him, since he had believed so greatly in the redeeming power of excellence, of being the most brilliant, inspired man for the job. With enough excellence, you could presumably make it stop mattering that you were Jewish; you could become the *only* Jew in the gentile world, a Jew so "civilized," so far from "common," so attractively combining Southern gentility with European cultural values that no one would ever confuse you with the raw, "pushy" Jews of New York, the "loud, hysterical" refugees from Eastern Europe, the "overdressed" Jews of the urban South.

We—my sister, mother and I—were constantly urged to speak quietly in public, to dress without ostentation, to repress all vividness or spontaneity, to assimilate with a world which might see us as too flamboyant. I suppose that my mother, pure gentile though she was, could be seen as acting "common" or "Jewish" if she laughed too loudly or spoke aggressively. My father's mother, who lived with us half the year, was a model of circumspect behavior, dressed in dark blue or lavender, retiring in company, ladylike to an extreme, wearing no jewelry except a good gold chain, a narrow brooch, a string of pearls. A few times, within the family, I saw her anger flare, felt the passion she was repressing. But when Arnold took us out to a restaurant, or on a trip, the Rich women were always tuned down to some WASP level my father believed, surely, would protect us all—maybe also make us unrecognizable to the "real Jews" who wanted to seize us, drag us back to the *shtetl*, the ghetto, in its many manifestations.

For, yes: that *was* a message—that some Jews would be after you, once they "knew," to rejoin them, to re-enter a world that was messy, noisy, unpredictable, maybe poor—"even though," as my mother once wrote me, criticizing my largely Jewish choice of friends in college: "some of them will be the most brilliant, fascinating people you'll ever meet." I wonder if that isn't one message of assimilation—of America—that the unlucky or the unachieving want to pull you backward, that to identify with them is to court downward mobility, lose the precious chance of passing, of token existence. There was always, within this sense of Jewish identity, a strong class discrimination. Jews might be "fascinating" as individuals but came with huge unruly families who "poured chicken soup over everyone's head" (in the phrase of a white Southern male poet). Anti-Semitism could thus be justified by the bad behavior of certain Jews; and if you did not effectively deny family and community, there would always be a cousin claiming kinship with you, who was the "wrong kind" of Jew.

I have always believed his attitude toward other Jews depended on who they were. . . . *It was my impression that Jews of this background looked down on Eastern European Jews, including Polish Jews and Russian Jews, who generally were not as well educated.* This from a letter written to me recently by a gentile who had worked in my father's department, whom I had asked about anti-Semitism there and in particular regarding my father. This informant also wrote me that it was hard to perceive anti-Semitism in Baltimore because the racism made so much more intense an impression: *I would almost have to think that blacks went to a different heaven than the whites, because the bodies were kept in a separate morgue, and some white persons did not even want blood transfusions from black donors.* My father's mind was racist and misogynist, yet as a medical student he noted in his journal that Southern male chivalry stopped at the point of any white man in a streetcar giving his seat to an old, weary, Black woman standing in the aisle. Was this a Jewish insight—an outsider's insight, even though the outsider was striving to be on the inside?

Because what isn't named is often more permeating than what is, I believe that my father's Jewishness profoundly shaped my own identity, and our family existence. They were shaped both by external anti-Semitism and my father's self-hatred, and by his Jewish pride. What Arnold did, I think, was call his Jewish pride something else: achievement, aspiration, genius, idealism. Whatever was unacceptable got left back under the rubric of Jewishness, or the "wrong kind" of Jews: uneducated, aggressive, loud. The message I got was that we were really superior: nobody else's father had collected so many books, had travelled so far, knew so many languages. Baltimore was a musical city, but for the most part, in the families of my school friends, culture was for women. My father was an amateur musician, read poetry, adored encyclopaedic knowledge. He prowled and pounced over my school papers, insisting I use "grown-up" sources; he criticized my poems for faulty technique and gave me books on rhyme and metre and form. His investment in my intellect and talent was egotistical, tyrannical, opinionated and terribly wearing. He taught me nevertheless to believe in hard work, to mistrust easy inspiration, to write and rewrite; to feel that I *was* a person of the book, even though a woman; to take ideas seriously. He made me feel, at a very young age, the power of language, and that I could share in it.

The Riches were proud, but we also had to be very careful. Our behavior had to be more impeccable than other people's. Strangers were not to be trusted, nor even friends; family issues must never go beyond the family; the world was full of potential slanderers, betrayers, *people who could not understand.* Even within the family, I realize that I never in my whole life knew what he was really feeling. Yet he spoke—monologued—with driving intensity. You could grow up in such a house mesmerized by the local electricity, the crucial meanings assumed by the merest things. This used to seem to me a sign that we were all living on some high emotional plane. It was a difficult force-field for a favored daughter to disengage from.

Easy to call that intensity Jewish; and I have no doubt that passion is one of the qualities required for survival over generations of persecution. But what happens when passion is rent from its original base, when the white gentile world is softly saying: "Be more like us and you can be almost one of us"? What happens when survival seems to mean closing off one emotional artery after another? His forebears in Europe had been forbidden to travel, or expelled from one country after another, had special taxes levied on them if they left the city walls, had been forced to wear special clothes and badges, restricted to the poorest neighborhoods. He had wanted to be a "free spirit," to travel widely, among "all kinds of people." Yet in his prime of life he lived in an increasingly withdrawn world, in his house up on a hill in a neighborhood where Jews were not supposed to be able to buy property, depending almost exclusively on interactions with his wife and daughters to provide emotional connectedness. In his home, he created a private defense system so elaborate that even as he was dying my mother felt unable to talk freely with his colleagues, or others who might have helped her.

I imagine that the loneliness of the "only," the token, often doesn't feel like loneliness but like a kind of dead echo chamber. Certain things that ought to, don't resonate. Somewhere Beverly Smith writes of women of color "inspiring the behavior" in each other. When there's nobody to "inspire the behavior," act out of the culture, there is an atrophy, a dwindling, which is partly invisible.

I was married in 1953, in the Hillel House at Harvard, under a portrait of Albert Einstein. My parents refused to come. I was marrying a Jew, of the "wrong kind" from an Orthodox Eastern European background. Brooklyn-born, he had gone to Harvard, changed his name, was both indissolubly connected to his childhood world, and terribly ambivalent about it. My father saw this marriage as my having fallen prey to the Jewish family, Eastern European division.

Like many women I knew in the fifties, living under a then-unquestioned heterosexual imperative, I married in part because I knew no better way to disconnect from my first family. I married a "real Jew" who was himself almost equally divided between a troubled yet ingrained Jewish identity, and the pull toward Yankee approval, assimilation. But at least he was not adrift as a single token in a gentile world. We lived in a world where there was much intermarriage, where a certain "Jewish flavor" was accepted within the dominant gentile culture. People talked glibly of "Jewish self-hatred" but anti-Semitism was rarely identified. It was as if you could have it both ways, identity and assimilation, without having to think about it very much.

I was moved and gratefully amazed by the affection and kindliness my husband's parents showed me, the half-*shiksa*. I longed to embrace that family, that new and mysterious Jewish world. It was never a question of conversion—my husband had long since ceased being observant—but of a burning desire to do well, please these new parents, heal the split-consciousness in which I had been raised, and, of course, to belong. In the big sunny apartment on Eastern Parkway, the table would be spread on Saturday afternoons with a white or embroidered cloth and plates of coffee-cake, sponge-cake, *mohn*-cake, cookies, for a family gathering where everyone ate and drank—coffee, milk, cake—and later the talk eddied among the women still around the table or in the kitchen, while the men ended up in the living-room watching the ball-game. I had never known this kind of family, in which mock insults were cheerfully exchanged, secrets whispered in corners among two or three, children and grandchildren boasted about, and the new daughter-in-law openly inspected. I was profoundly attracted by all this, including the punctilious observance of *kashruth*, the symbolism lurking behind daily kitchen tasks. I saw it all as quintessentially and authentically Jewish, and thus I objectified both the people and the culture. My unexamined anti-Semitism allowed me to do this. But also, I had not yet recognized that as a woman I stood in a particular and equally unexamined relationship to the Jewish family and to Jewish culture.

There were several years during which I did not see, and barely communicated with my parents. At the same time, my father's personality haunted my life. Such had been the force of his will in our household that for a long time I felt I would have to pay in some terrible way for having disobeyed him. When finally we were reconciled, and my husband and I and our children began to have some minimal formal contact with my parents, the obsessional power of Arnold's voice or handwriting had given way to a dull sense of useless anger and pain. I wanted him to cherish and approve of me not as he had when I was a child, but as the woman I was, who had her own mind and had made her own choices. This, I finally realized, was not to be; Arnold demanded absolute loyalty, absolute submission to his will. In my separation from him, in my realization at what a price that once-intoxicating approval had been bought, I was learning in concrete ways a great deal about patriarchy, in particular how the "special" woman, the favored daughter, is controlled and rewarded.

Arnold Rich died in 1968 after a long deteriorating illness; his mind had gone and he had been losing his sight for years. It was a year of intensifying political awareness for me, the Martin Luther King and Robert Kennedy assassinations, the Columbia University strike. But it was not that these events and the meetings and demonstrations that surrounded them, pre-empted the time of mourning for my father; I had been mourning a long time for an early, primary and intense relationship, by no means always benign, but in which I had been ceaselessly made to feel that what I did with my life, the choices I made, the attitudes I held, were of the utmost consequence.

Sometimes in my thirties, on visits to Brooklyn, I sat on Eastern Parkway, a baby-stroller at my feet: one of many rows of young Jewish women on benches with children in that neighborhood. I used to see the Lubavitcher Hassidim—then beginning to move into the Crown Heights neighborhood—walking out on shabbas, the women in their *sheitels* a little behind the men. My father-in-law pointed them out as rather exotic—too old-country, perhaps, too unassimilated even for his devout sense of Jewish identity. It took many years for me to understand—partly because I understood so little about class in America—how in my own family, and in the very different family of my in-laws, there were degrees and hierarchies of assimilation which looked askance upon each other—and also geographic lines of difference, as between Southern Jews and New York Jews, whose manners and customs varied along class as well as regional lines.

I had three sons before I was thirty, and during those years I often felt that to be a Jewish woman, a Jewish mother, was to be perceived in the Jewish family as an entirely physical being, a producer and nourisher of children. The experience of motherhood was eventually to radicalize me; but before that I was encountering the institution of motherhood most directly in a Jewish cultural version; and I felt rebellious, moody, defensive, unable to sort out what was Jewish from what was simply motherhood, or female destiny. (I lived in Cambridge, not Brooklyn, but there, too, restless, educated women sat on benches with baby-strollers, half-stunned, not by Jewish cultural expectations, but by the American cultural expectations of the 1950's.)

My children were taken irregularly to Seders, to Bar Mitzvahs, and to special services in their grandfather's temple. Their father lit Hanukkah candles while I stood by, having relearned each year the English meaning of the Hebrew blessing. We all celebrated a secular, liberal Christmas. I read aloud from books about Esther and the Maccabees and Moses, and also from books about Norse goblins and Chinese grandmothers and Celtic dragon-slayers. Their father told stories of his boyhood in Brooklyn, his grandmother in the Bronx who had to be visited on the subway every week, of misdeeds in Hebrew school, of being a bright Jewish kid at Boys' High. In the permissive liberalism of academic Cambridge, you could raise your children to be vaguely or distinctly Jewish as you would, but Christian myth and calendar organized the year. My sons grew up knowing far more about the existence and concrete meaning of Jewish culture than I had. But I don't recall sitting down with them and telling them that millions of people like themselves, many of them children, had been rounded up and murdered in Europe in their parents' lifetime. Nor was I able to tell them that they came in part out of the rich, thousand-year-old, Ashkenazic culture of Eastern Europe, which the Holocaust destroyed; or that they came from a people whose secular tradition had included a hatred of oppression and a willingness to fight for justice—an anti-racist, a socialist and even sometimes a feminist vision. I could not tell them these things because they were still too blurred in outline in my own mind.

The emergence of the Civil Rights movement in the sixties I remember as lifting me out of a sense of personal frustration and hopelessness. Reading James Baldwin's early essays, in the fifties, had stirred me with a sense that apparently "given" situations like racism could be analyzed and described and that this could lead to action, to change. Racism had been so utter and implicit a fact of my childhood and adolescence, had felt so central among the silences, negations, cruelties, fears, superstitions of my early life, that somewhere among my feelings must have been the hope that if Black people could become free, of the immense political and social burdens they were forced to bear, I too could become free, of all the ghosts and shadows of my childhood, named and unnamed. When "the Movement" began it felt extremely personal to me. And it was often Jews who spoke up for the justice of the cause, Jewish civil rights lawyers who were travelling South; it was two young Jews who were found murdered with a young Black man in Mississippi. Schwerner, Goodman, Chaney.

Moving to New York in the mid-sixties meant almost immediately being plunged into the debate over community control of public schools, in which Black and Jewish teachers and parents were often on opposite sides of extremely militant barricades. It was easy as a white liberal to deplore and condemn the racism of middle-class Jewish parents or angry Jewish schoolteachers, many of them older women; to displace our own racism onto them; or to feel it as too painful to think about. The struggle for Black civil rights had such clarity about it for me: I knew that segregation was wrong, that unequal opportunity was wrong, I knew that segregation in particular was more than a set of social and legal rules, it meant that even "decent" white people lived in a network of lies and arrogance and moral collusion. In the world of Jewish assimilationist and liberal politics which I knew best, however, things were far less clear to me, and anti-Semitism went almost unmentioned. It was even possible to view anti-Semitism as a reactionary agenda, a concern of *Commentary* magazine or, later, the Jewish Defense League. Most of the political work I was doing in the late 1960's was on racial issues, in particular as a teacher in the City University

during the struggle for Open Admissions. The white colleagues
I thought of as allies were, I think, mostly Jewish. Yet it was
easy to see other New York Jews, who had climbed out of poverty and exploitation through the public school system and the
free city colleges, as now trying to block Black and Puerto Rican students trying to do likewise. I didn't understand then that
I was living between two strains of Jewish social identity: the
Jew as radical visionary and activist who understands oppression
first-hand; and the Jew as part of America's devouring plan in
which the persecuted, called to assimilation, learn that the price
is to engage in persecution.

And indeed, there *was* intense racism among Jews as well as
white gentiles in the City University, part of the bitter history
of Jews and Blacks which James Baldwin had described much
earlier, in his 1948 essay on "The Harlem Ghetto"*; part of the
divide-and-conquer script still being rehearsed by those of us
who have the least to gain from it.

By the time I left my marriage, after seventeen years and
three children, I had become identified with the women's liberation movement. It was an astonishing time to be a woman of
my age. In the 1950's, seeking a way to grasp the pain I seemed
to be feeling most of the time, to set it in some larger context,
I had read all kinds of things, but it was James Baldwin and
Simone de Beauvoir who had described the world—though differently—in terms that made the most sense to me. By the end
of the sixties there were two political movements, one already
meeting severe repression, one just emerging—which addressed
those descriptions of the world.

And there was, of course, a third movement, or a movement-
within-a-movement—the early lesbian manifestos, the new visibility and activism of lesbians everywhere. I had known very
early on that the women's movement was not going to be a
simple walk across an open field; that it would pull on every
fibre of my existence; that it would mean going back and
searching the shadows of my consciousness. Reading *The Second Sex* in 1950's isolation as an academic housewife had felt
less dangerous than reading "The Myth of Vaginal Orgasm" or
"Woman-Identified Woman" in a world where I was in constant
debate and discussion with women over every aspect of our lives
that we could as yet name. De Beauvoir had placed "The Les-

Notes of A Native Son, Beacon Press, 1955.

bian" on the margins, and there was little in her book to suggest the power of woman-bonding. But the passion of debating ideas with women was an erotic passion for me, and the risking of self with women that was necessary in order to win some truth out of the lies of the past was also erotic. The suppressed lesbian I had been carrying in me since adolescence began to stretch her limbs and her first full-fledged act was to fall in love with a Jewish woman.

Some time during the early months of that relationship, I dreamed that I was arguing feminist politics with my lover. *Of course*, I said to her in this dream, *if you're going to bring up the Holocaust against me, there's nothing I can do.* If, as I believe, I was both myself and her in this dream, it spoke of the split in my consciousness. I had been, more or less, a Jewish heterosexual woman; but what did it mean to be a Jewish lesbian? What did it mean to feel myself, as I did, both anti-Semite and Jew? And, as a feminist, how was I charting for myself the oppressions within oppression?

The earliest feminist papers on Jewish identity that I read were critiques of the patriarchal and misogynist elements in Judaism, or of the caricaturing of Jewish women in literature by Jewish men. I remember hearing Judith Plaskow give a paper called "Can a Woman Be a Jew?" (her conclusion was, "yes, but. . . ."). I was soon after in correspondence with a former student who had emigrated to Israel, was a passionate feminist, and wrote me at length of the legal and social constraints on women there, the stirrings of contemporary Israeli feminism, and the contradictions she felt in her daily life. With the new politics, activism, literature of a tumultuous feminist movement around me, a movement which claimed universality though it had not yet acknowledged its own racial, class and ethnic perspectives, or its fears of the differences among women—I pushed aside for one last time thinking further about myself as a Jewish woman. I saw Judaism, simply, as yet another strand of patriarchy; if asked to choose I might have said (as my father had said in other language): *I am a woman, not a Jew.* (But, I always added mentally, if Jews had to wear yellow stars again, I too would wear one. As if I would have the choice to wear it or not.)

Sometimes I feel I have seen too long from too many disconnected angles: white, Jewish, anti-Semite, racist, anti-racist, once-married, lesbian, middle-class, feminist, exmatriate Southerner, *split at the root*: that I will never bring them whole. I would have liked, in this essay, to bring together the meanings of anti-Semitism and racism as I have experienced them and as I believe they intersect in the world beyond my life. But I'm not able to do this yet. I feel the tension as I think, make notes: *if you really look at the one reality, the other will waver and disperse.* Trying in one week to read Angela Davis and Lucy Dawidowicz;* trying to hold throughout a feminist, a lesbian, perspective—what does this mean? Nothing has trained me for this. And sometimes I feel inadequate to make any statement as a Jew; I feel the history of denial within me like an injury, a scar—for assimilation has affected *my* perceptions, those early lapses in meaning, those blanks, are with me still. My ignorance can be dangerous to me, and to others.

Yet we can't wait for the undamaged to make our connections for us; we can't wait to speak until we are wholly clear and righteous. There is no purity, and, in our lifetimes, no end to this process.

This essay, then, has no conclusions: it is another beginning, for me. Not just a way of saying, in 1982 Right-wing America, *I too will wear the yellow star.* It's a moving into accountability, enlarging the range of accountability. I know that in the rest of my life, the next half-century or so, every aspect of my identity will have to be engaged. The middle-class white girl taught to trade obedience for privilege. The Jewish lesbian raised to be a heterosexual gentile. The woman who first heard oppression named and analyzed in the Black civil rights struggle. The woman with three sons, the feminist who hates male violence. The woman limping with a cane, the woman who has stopped bleeding, are also accountable. The poet who knows that beautiful language can lie, that the oppressor's language sometimes sounds beautiful. The woman trying, as part of her resistance, to clean up her act.

My gratitude to Michelle Cliff, whose work forced me to examine my own "passing"; to Elly Bulkin and Gloria Z. Greenfield, for the Jewish women's workshop at Storrs, Connecticut, June 1981; to Evi Beck, Maureen Brady, Michelle Cliff, Gloria Z. Greenfield, Irena Klepfisz, Judith McDaniel, for criticism of the first draft; and to Elana Dykewomon and Melanie Kaye, for their words.

*Angela Y. Davis, *Women, Race and Class*, Random House, 1981; Lucy S. Dawidowicz, *The War Against the Jews 1933-1945* (1975), Bantam Books, 1979.

Living in the In-Between
Chaya Shoshana
(L. Lee Knefelkamp)

My name is Chaya Shoshana. I am a different kind of Jew. I am a convert, and I have learned that my very existence often makes people uncomfortable—Jews and Gentiles alike. Conversion was at once the most deeply personal and the most public and communal commitment that I ever made. I am grateful for this chance to write about my experience, but I do so with the dis-ease that personal revelation usually evokes.

I have always experienced myself as one who lives in the in-between. In my own profession I live between theory and practice: between the ideal of a community of scholars and the pragmatic reality of daily university life, between the hope for the future and the work of the present. I spend a great portion of my life on airplanes, flying between speaking engagements that matter to me—and now, flying between my two homes, my work and my love. Yet this existence has always felt familiar to me.

The daughter of parents touched by war, I spent my childhood moving from place to place, learning to live in the in-between that three fathers and sixteen different schools imposed on a young life. It wasn't until I went to college that I ever lived in one place for four consecutive years.

My life was enriched by the experience. Living in urban and rural communities, southern and northern, eastern and north-western, in this country and abroad, I learned to both respect and ignore ordinary boundaries. And I learned that for all that I was a part *of* in this world, I was also apart *from* a good share of it most of the time. I never felt home . . . or at home. In fact I have felt truly at home only in the past four years, when I have been able to integrate myself as a lesbian and a Jew with the tangible reality that I am loved well by my partner and love her well in return.

91

I believe I began my journey to Judaism when I was 10 and living in Japan. My family's Japanese home on the mountain overlooking Kamakura was surrounded by gardens and fish ponds. I was always slipping outside the garden gate and exploring the mountain paths that beckoned to me. One day I came upon a small Shinto temple and graveyard. While resting on the temple steps I looked up and saw a wide stream of light coming down from the heavens and through the trees into the graveyard. Every 10-year-old who has ever gone to Christian Sunday school will tell you THAT light signifies that God is present. My family had embraced many Christian denominations, but most recently I had been assured that there was only one true religion (Missouri Synod Lutheran) . . . and THE light was shining on the catechism book to prove it. As I saw it then, I had two choices: either God was everywhere and there was no single true religion, or the LIGHT didn't signify God's presence after all. I chose the light. Life was never to be the same. In essence it became a true spiritual journey, one that led me to Judaism and to become a Jew.

While in college I began studying at a nearby synagogue and continued my studies in the Peace Corps and graduate school. I had married in the Peace Corps, and my husband and I encouraged each other's separate religious identities. We didn't really talk much about our differences, but we lived with them in a kind of silent peace. After I began my university teaching career I decided it was time to join the Jewish community. I went to my Hillel Rabbi, told him of my background and my intent to convert, and asked to study with him. He turned me away. I told him that I knew he had to turn me away three times but that I would keep coming back—so couldn't we just save time and get started? We began what was to become a great friendship, going for long walks, studying texts, discussing insoluble problems, working on High Holy Day services. Many of our conversations centered around the reasons that would draw someone into Judaism, that drew me into Judaism. He listened, questioned, understood that while I was not born a Jew, my Judaism *was* an integration of my life experiences and the result of how I had come to make meaning in the world.

As a developmental psychologist, I see life as a series of phases; each new phase contains all that has gone before and the kernels of what will come after. I see my whole life as leading to conversion and see conversion as one of the most significant transformational events of adulthood. It has influenced everything that has come after.

Some of the most important time of my nomadic youth was spent on a farm in the rural Midwest. I was transformed by the experience. I loved the land, the changing of seasons—especially the hard work of planting, tending, and waiting to see if there would be a harvest. I loved taking care of the hundreds of animals. And I loved living with the awesome realities of nature—a nature of terror and destruction, a nature that gave the words "nutrient" and "nurturance" profound meaning. The rural experience ties you to the land and the landscape. You learn to read the skies and the clouds, the color of the earth when it's tilled, the size of the crops in the field, the condition of the animals under your care. Your life is merged with the seasons; your rhythm is tied to the rhythm of the agricultural year. Each season has a different focus and literally forces self-reflection and contemplation. To this day I live my life around the seasons of the year, a way of being that ties my present life as a Jew to the meaningful events of my past.

Judaism is an early pagan religion bound to the rural experience and to the seasons of the agricultural year. We often forget that, living as we do in the diaspora with a centuries-old history of being forbidden to till the land. The urban/suburban American Jew is largely ignorant of the Jewish presence in American rural history and often has genuine difficulty understanding the agricultural imagery and meaning of Jewish writings about the holy days. One of the ironies of being the particular convert I am is that what would seem to set me apart from the modern Jewish experience—my ties to rural America—is what helped draw me to it and makes me feel a part of that experience. Apart from, a part of: living in the in-between.

Change has been the constant of my life. When one grows up as I did, experiencing many types of environments, many cultures, and many changes in family structure and members, the need for community is immense. I was drawn to the reality of a communal identity that would travel *with* me, a community that existed both as an identifiable entity in the world and as something contained *within* me. I was drawn to be a part of the delicate relationship between the larger community and the self, and the knowledge that one truly could not exist without the other. We gather together on holy days not just for ourselves as individuals, but because the community could not exist without us. Each person is responsible for the active affirmation and continuation of the community regardless of the particulars of location or culture. And each person is bound by the admonition to live according to the Jewish communal ethic of activism in the world. We know, in whatever personal way, what it means to be strangers in a strange land, and we are bound by the knowledge of our own human experience to act to protect the stranger, to protect the "other" in our midst. We must repair the world—physically, interpersonally, intellectually, spiritually, ethically. And each of us must select an appropriate way to do this work. I found that vision of the activist community made up of activist individuals to be both powerful and compelling. I also resonated to Jewish theology, but I do not find it comfortable to discuss my spirituality or my spiritual odyssey in public.

As a Jew I became whole: tied to the seasons, a necessary member of the community, and bound by an ethic of activism. As whole as I am, I am helped to be whole by remembering that I am a different kind of Jew. I lived a childhood and adolescence influenced by non-Jewish culture and experience, unmarked by threats of anti-Semitism. I am fortunate to be able to trace my family history over many generations, and I have grown up knowing five generations of family members. I would never deny that history, that living part of who I am.

After a year of walking and discussing such issues with my Hillel Rabbi, I was ready to take the formal step of conversion. By this time I had been living Jewishly for over a decade and was deeply involved in Hillel work as well as in other forms of Jewish activism. Conversion was still an enormous step. How could I really join the Jewish community? Would I be welcome? How would my family react to this formal declaration of identity? My colleagues? My friends? The Jewish community?

Conversion is not a solitary act. No one can join a community that does not wish her to join. No community can annex an individual against her will. The very act of conversion signifies the mutual recognition of individual and community that they are bound together, a part of one another. The act of conversion signifies that the "other" is now part of the "we." All elements of the conversion ceremony emphasize the communal nature of this extraordinary rite of passage. I was examined by a Bet Din, a court of three Rabbis (in my case a Conservative, a Reform, and a Reconstructionist) who engaged me in a long and wide-ranging discussion of my Judaism. I then immersed myself in the Mikva, prayers were recited, and I emerged a Jew. In the naming ceremony I took the name Chaya Shoshana, daughter of Sarah, Rachael, Leah, and Ruth. I became a member of the "Holy Community," Kehillah Kedoshah. I thought my journey had ended, that I was home. I was wrong. I am a different kind of Jew.

Different. How? Not because my relatives sing Christmas carols—many other Jews grew up singing Christmas carols. Not because my warm memories of Shabbos candles, eating, and receiving the blessings given to children are not memories of my own childhood home—many other Jews found warmth and comfort in that scene in *someone else's* house, just as I did. Not because I grew up ignorant of the laws and customs and unique experiences of my people—many other Jews grew up without that sustaining and identity-forming knowledge. Not because I came to claim Judaism and my identity as a Jew in adulthood—many other Jews share in that profound, frightening, fulfilling experience.

Different. How? Because I am not a born Jew endowed with the birthright of authenticity. Different because others ask me to explain or justify my Judaism and my presence in the community, whereas born Jews carry with them the assumption of authenticity. (One of the most common statements I hear when longtime Jewish friends or colleagues learn of my conversion is, "I thought you were a *real* Jew.") Different because my very presence, very existence as a Jew serves as a catalyst for questions: Who is a Jew? What is a Jew? I am a living projective technique. My presence often causes discomfort and raises issues of trust and safety. My presence as a member of the community causes the members to stretch the limits and the definitions and the assumptions of Jewishness.

Although I must tell you: I believe now that we are ALL "different" kinds of Jews. One of my closest and dearest friends did not find out she was Jewish until well into her adulthood. Her parents had escaped the Nazis, established themselves in the United States, and did not inform their three daughters until one memorable New Year's Eve at a family gathering. She and her sisters have children of their own who know that they are Jewish but grapple with what that really means in the context of their lives. Just as their mother and I do. We spend hours sitting on each other's couches talking, questioning, confronting our sense of the meaning of Judaism and being Jewish in our lives. I am more knowledgeable about things Jewish. She is a born Jew who knows very little of Judaism. I embrace many religious, home-based rituals of Jewish life. She, too, has built a home of ritual, deeply based in familial relationships but centered more in the cycles of the secular and Christian calendars. We are two women

who came to be Jews in adulthood. One discovered her Jewish
identity abruptly. One came to her Jewish identity through years
of searching, study, and commitment. I claim my Jewishness and
make it a part of everything I do. She never denies her Jewishness, but does not make it central to her life. Each of us has
helped the other understand the meaning of being Jewish. Each
of us has helped the other struggle with questions of identity in
her own life . . . questions that include sexuality, career changes,
professional directions, the meaning of committed relationships,
the continuity of family, and the role our friendship plays.

If the fundamentalists have their way, my friend would be
eligible for Israeli citizenship under the Law of Return and I
would not. The recent Orthodox demand that the Law of Return
be amended to *exclude* all non-Orthodox converts raises fundamental questions of authenticity. All born Jews can return regardless of religious tradition. Only converts are required to meet
an additional test of Orthodoxy. This demand on the part of the
Orthodox is, I believe, a fundamental challenge to the legitimacy
of pluralistic traditions within Judaism and a fundamental challenge to the communal nature of conversion itself. The fate of the
"other" convert within the Jewish community is a bellweather
for the fate of any "other" within the community. The recent
debate about the Law of Return has been searingly painful, but
it has brought to voice attitudes about conversion that too often
have existed in silence.

Indeed, I still feel a kind of quiet terror when I tell people
that I am a convert to Judaism. In groups of Jews my statement
is often met with an embarrassed silence, a quick change of subject, and a complete erasure of the reality of my voice. In groups
of non-Jews the initial silence is quickly followed by the demand
to know why someone would do such a thing. Both Jews and
non-Jews commonly pose questions of a negative nature: Why
would someone take on a minority identity? What would possess
(note the wording) someone to deny their real identity and become something else? What could possibly be so compelling as to
warrant such a step? And both groups tend to assume that one
would convert only because of a relationship; rarely do they consider that one would convert as an individual on one's own, that
there would be in Judaism something so positive and passionately compelling as to draw people to it as a commitment, a way
of life, a way of being in the world. My experience as a convert
is an exact parallel to my experience as a lesbian in the world.
"Coming out" as a convert involves choices, dangers, and rewards

parallel to those of coming out as a lesbian. I believe that negative reactions or embarrassed silence on the part of Jews with respect to conversion is a manifestation of fear of the "other" and some degree of internalized anti-Semitism—just as I believe that negative reactions and embarrassed silence on the part of heterosexuals is a manifestation of fear of the "other" and some degree of homophobia. And I am convinced that negative reactions of non-Jews to Jewish conversion is a manifestation of anti-Semitism. Judaism is not seen as attractive and compelling any more than lesbianism is seen as attractive and compelling.

The Jew who has converted risks loss of family at worst, and a period of estrangement and misunderstanding at best. Family members often see the conversion as a denial of family values, upbringing, and way of life. Holidays become problematic. Relationships take on more complexity. The need for truth-telling and communication becomes compelling, while wariness and mistrust increase due to the loss of old assumptions. The Jew who has converted is seen as a different and somehow alien person in the body of the old and familiar child, sibling, loved one. It is not uncommon for parents to deny the reality of the conversion or to suffer feelings of guilt and blame for not having succeeded in the proper socialization of their child. (This is especially true if the individual has converted on her own and not in the context of a relationship.) My own parents were deeply troubled by my conversion, believing that I had lost my soul and that I had denied my own life and upbringing. My sister displayed a supportive reaction (and a calming effect on my parents) because she had always found me to be highly individualistic. My favorite aunt and her daughter, my favorite cousin, were deeply supportive, asking sensitive and empathic questions, seeking to understand and to celebrate something that obviously meant so much to me. My parents would not tell anyone else in the family, nor would they tell any of their friends. It was to be kept secret at all costs.

Most Jewish readers of this book will not have had to come out as Jews to their parents and family. Many of them will, however, have faced the issue of coming out as lesbians, and I believe they'll recognize both the fears and the reaction patterns that I have described. My family responded to my lesbianism much as they did to my Judaism. Coming out as a lesbian so many years after becoming a Jew added a further layer of "otherness" to our efforts to love and understand one another. They had more fears for me as a lesbian in the world than as a Jew in the world, but the issue of being different, being "other," being a strange person in a familiar body carried through both sets of reactions.

Painful as those experiences were, they were anticipated. Anticipation brings with it a sense of protective preparation. What I was not prepared for was the difficulty I faced as a convert in Jewish lesbian circles and the difficulty I faced as a lesbian in Jewish circles. Once again I confronted the reality of living in the in-between—of being a person who never totally fit into any group. Here the source of pain was that the very experience of being an "other" did not seem to enable individuals to be empathic about another "other" identity. Coming out as a Jew or as a lesbian carried a sense of threat and fear of being misunderstood or dismissed regardless of the fact that I would be coming out to a group of individuals who had lived and shared experiences of being "other" themselves. This was a profound realization.

The reality of my own experience led me to redouble my efforts to become an effective educator around issues of individual differences and diversity. It is my life's work. I have a will to be whole, to be the integrated sum of my individual parts, to use my insights as a wandering outsider to forge a sense of self-worth and affirmation from the *inside* of myself. I have a will to enable the different parts of myself to confront one another. Because it is impossible to reconcile all the conflicts, I seek not to resolve them but to maintain a constant, intense internal dialogue. I choose Judaism and I will be a Jewish, feminist, lesbian Jew within my Jewish community and in the world. We will confront one another in a lifelong creative tension that has the possibility of profoundly transforming the life of the community as well as my own life. I choose to be a Jew who converted and to continue to make that choice an affirmation of myself and my community. I choose to be a Jew every day. So does every other Jew I know. We are all Jews by choice. We are all strengthened by the daily making of that choice. I am stronger, more whole, more constantly joyful, surer of my work in the world because of that choice.

This essay would not be complete without a few words about the most important experience of my life—the ongoing, life-affirming dialogue that I have with my partner. Partners in life and encouragers of each other's life work, we are different kinds of Jews. We once did a presentation called "Dialogue of Difference" in which we outlined our differences in background and experience. She is a Holocaust survivor, a woman of Vienna who has literally wandered the world, forged a truth-telling identity, and come to be in partnership with a Midwestern American Jewish convert. The miles of distance between us are significant—we have talked long and late into countless evenings about our similarities and our differences. We have struggled to make it safe for her to trust me and for me to trust her. She no longer makes or condones disparaging remarks about "goyim," knowing that I was a "goy" and members of my family are "goyim." I no longer react to cultural differences with automatic fear and resistance. We confront class differences, culture differences, and religious differences—as Rich would say—all the time expanding the possibilities of truth between us, the possibilities of life and love between us. Because of who *we* are together and the strength and joy that *we* make possible, we each can claim our own past and see it as a living part of ourselves. No convert can exist denying her past. If one's past is erased, one is dead to oneself . . . and therefore to others. We greet each day knowing we are different kinds of Jews and that part of our work in the world is to make that reality a safe reality . . . in our home and in the world.

I live a joyful life. My family now affirms my Judaism and my life with my partner. I can experience Vienna and Brooklyn. She can spend Thanksgiving on a Midwestern farm, ride horses, and load bales of hay. We have traveled the miles of distance between us and now live together in the in-between. All things are truly possible.

A Coat of Many Colors
Savina Teubal

On both my mother's and father's sides my heritage is Syrian. However, my mother was born and raised in Manchester, England, while my father came from Aleppo, Syria.

A daughter of the upper-middle class, my mother took to Victorianism like a duck to water. Her peers were Middle Eastern Jews, mostly Syrian, who had acquired the elitist touch of the British. She was born the year Victoria died, when the Empire was at its zenith, imposing the queen's mores on the rest of humanity.

My father, then an uneducated and impoverished young man, was propelled with his brothers to the shores of Argentina in search of fortune. In the course of his quest, my father spent twenty years in Manchester where he met and married my mother.

During the same twenty years my brothers and I were born, but shortly afterward we were all transferred to Argentina, where my mother instituted a crash course in British culture for the entire family. The veneer acquired by my father's family can be credited to the forbearance of my formidable mother, who lived like a queen, whose elegance and poise were legendary, and whose influence greatly embellished and dignified the financial stature achieved by my father.

Beneath the glitter of the elite, we lived a life of recently settled Arab nomads. In Argentina, we rode in Cadillacs instead of on camels and lived in large houses instead of tents. The religious climate in our household was strict, almost fanatic, except that we prayed to HaShem instead of Allah. Our guests were served the traditional sweetened Turkish coffee and sat for hours, the men in one room talking business and the women in another exchanging sociabilities. Except during special high-ranking functions the guests who frequented our home were

Syrians from Aleppo, direct or via Manchester, Milan, Paris or Rome.

We children were discouraged from making friends at school, and strongly encouraged to find friends within the tribal unit. As I grew up I realized that I was to choose a husband from within the boundaries of our subculture, that is Argentina's Arab-Jewish community from Aleppo. It would have been acceptable for me to marry an Egyptian or a Baghdadian, but never an Ashkenazi! It goes without saying that the thought of marrying a Christian was preposterous. Marriage as my lot in life was never questioned by my parents. Higher education was unthinkable.

My education was nonetheless fascinating. I attended a traditional British girls' school which had excellent tuition in literature, the arts and sports. Afternoons were devoted to Spanish school. My extracurricular activities were Hebrew, music and dance. On Saturdays we ate lunch to the strains of Verdi, Puccini, Bizet, et al., a tradition of my mother's. Saturday afternoons, on the other hand, were spent listening to my father's Arabic records, which for many years were incomprehensible to me. Music subsequently became the most meaningful bridge with which to integrate my varied background. Today I am equally moved by Arabic love songs, Italian opera, European symphony or Israeli or Argentine folk music. I can express myself adequately in most European languages and Hebrew, but not in Arabic.

Arabic was spoken at home by most of the visiting Syrians and by my parents when they did not want the children or servants to understand the conversation. When my father was angry at us he shouted in Arabic, so I did learn some curse words. I also learned how to ask for money and express endearments. Speaking Arabic in public was generally considered common and vulgar by the British elite in our community, particularly my mother's family. My mother was the eldest of eight siblings and the only one who affirmed her Arabic heritage. Her family, especially the younger ones, generally felt uncomfortable with their Jewish identity.

At a certain point in my life I realized that I too had to accept or reject my Arabic-Jewish identity. The Jewish part was not so difficult. Both my mother and father identified very strongly with Jewish traditions, and so did the rest of our community. My mother's family, on the other hand, had little respect for my father's insistence on Arab subculture and Jewish ritual. Though they ate at his table, they sneered and made fun of him and his family behind his back. In their attempt at Westernization, they felt obliged to suppress and attack their own Arab core.

Since my education was British I identified with my mother's British family, and to some extent I also looked down on my father. To regard my father as inferior was tempting, since he treated me as an Arab sheikh would treat his daughter: strictly and uncompromisingly, as an object to be sold in the marriage market. My British education and daily contact with the sophisticated South American urban life forced me to rebel against my father's bedouin-like restrictions, which were as foreign to me as the Arabian Nights.

It took a great deal of introspection before I accepted my British education with its Latin American overtones while rejecting the snobbism and the critical elitist attitude of the Victorians. I incorporated the Arab heritage with its strong tribal ties, basic emotional warmth, rich poetic culture and philosophical relation to nature.

As a lesbian, I have only recently begun to shed some light on the value of my Jewish heritage. The most important aspect of my Jewish upbringing was the communality; the Jewish ritual was a true gathering together, a communal sharing, a time to give as well as take. Everyone was included, old and young, men and women, married and unmarried. Each participant had a very important role to play.

Belonging is a form of identification. One may identify as a lesbian, but lesbianism has little reclaimed history and no traditions. There are no celebrations to mark the stages in the life of a lesbian, her initiation or her union with another, no coming-of-age rituals, weddings, or lesbian gatherings at the birth of a child. Even at her death, a lesbian's life-long commitment to another woman may be contested or made invisible by omission.

Many years ago I ended a relationship with a lover and felt alone. It was Pesach, and I travelled six thousand miles to spend this holy day of liberation with my mother. I felt an overwhelming need for the familiar—to recognize and be recognized. I wanted to hear the age-old Sephardic chants at Seder, with tonalities and pronunciation I could relate to. I yearned for the Syrian food, stuffed onions or vine-leaves; *haroset* made with dates, not apples. I could not have filled that void in the same way with my lesbian friends. Of course, had it not been Pesach, I would not have thought of going to my mother's. Judaism is an important link to my past—not a religious link, but an emotional and cultural one.

Integration is a state of mind. While watching the late Egyptian President Anwar Sadat and the Israeli Prime Minister Menachem Begin warmly making peaceful overtures in the Knesset, tears welled in my eyes; this event had touched the very depth of my soul. My struggle for integration was symbolically enacted in the arena of Middle Eastern politics. Within my being, the circle of integration had been completed and was being sanctified from without.

If I Am Only for Myself,
What Am I?

Kaddish

Melanie Kaye/Kantrowitz

and when I told the woman—a survivor, a fighter in the Warsaw
Ghetto Uprising—about the Holocaust conference in Maine, and
how many of the people there had known *nothing*, she said, *They
still know nothing.*

> *Yisgadal v'yiskadash sh'me rabbo,
> b'olmo deevro chiruseh v'yamlick
> malchuseh*

if I said kaddish for each one

if I were to mourn properly
I would not be done

If I were to mourn
each artist seamstress *schnorrer* midwife baker
each fiddler talker tailor shopkeeper
each *yente*   each Communist   each Zionist
each doctor pedlar beggar Bundist rabbi
each prostitute   each file clerk   each lesbian
each fighter   the old woman in the photograph from
Hungary   holding the hand of the child whose
socks droop   each Jew

> *b'chayechon uvyo-mechon, uv'chayey
> d'chol beys yisroel*

I would not be done   yet
it was more than death   was more   the people's
heart   a language I have
to study   to practice speaking with
old people   songs   to collect   transcribing
from records or from the few

who know   a culture   which might have died
in this country   which eats culture   a death
we call normal   a culture   *astonishing*
in its variety   a taste   a smell   a twist of song
that was   *Vilna*
              Odessa
              Cracow
              Covner-Gberna
              Warsaw
these were once Jewish sounds

*

baagolo uvizman koreev, v'imru omen

Tuesday my father died   Wednesday
the rabbi   who never met my father   met with us
my mother   my father's sisters   the daughters
5 minutes before the funeral was to begin
to prepare the eulogy   He asked
if my father had belonged to any organizations   if
people from   his place of business had come
and he said   since there were no sons
he   would say kaddish   for my father

and I did not tell the rabbi   my father was broken
before he died   I did not describe his twisted body   asbestos
in his lungs   I did not explain   my father worked
6 days plus 2 nights a week   paid
for my eyeglasses   cavities   penicillin shots
I did not say   he joined no temple
I did not say he loved the sound of Yiddish but
would not speak it
I did not mention he beat us   the children
but not his wife   I did not reveal his high point in life
a trip   with his buddies   to the Chicago World's Fair
in a '32 Ford   I did not say he changed his name   he was
Kantrowitz   he became Kaye   I did not say he built
a business   retail   and taught me
never cross a picket line

Y'he sh'meh rabbo m'vorach l'olam
ulolmey olmayo

I did not tell the rabbi   my father listened carefully
to all things Jewish

nor did I tell him
save your prayers

I said, *I will speak at this funeral*
and I did   to mourn him properly

*

*v'yespo-ar v'yisromam v'yisnaseh
v'yishador v'yishal-lol*

he taught me all men are equal before I knew
to suspect the words   before I learned
to fight with him to say   *people   all
people   daddy   and please   don't say
girl*

sh'med d'kud-sho b'reech-hu

About Hitler   I always knew
Chanukah   we lit candles   said
no prayers   but got presents   red sweaters   ball bearings   sang
no songs   but *Hatikvah*   played on the menorah like
it was   our song   I knew I belonged to Jews
I knew   I was part of Israel

*l'elo min kol birchoso v'shiroso
tushb'choso v'nechemoso daamiron*

and so I do
and so I am

and so   when I heard about children   women
families shot   stabbed at the table in   Shatilla
Sabra   I couldn't breathe
and I was   almost   too afraid   to mourn

let me be plain
Jews sent up flares
for christians   to kill by

let me absorb
yes   they are men   soldiers   also, my people   my father loved
all things Jewish   and should I disown?
I   who will be blamed   with the others   again

let me mourn   if anything
is holy   flesh
so readily torn   from the skeleton

let me rock   my body   like a scared child—
of what skin   what tongue   which people?
whose child is this?
the answer says if the child shall
live   die   suffer   kill

let me be strong as history
let me join those   who refuse
let there be time
let it be possible

> *b'olmo v'imru omen. Y'he sh'lomo rabbo
> min sh'mayo*

let no faction keep me
from those who suffer

let no faction keep me from those who needed a home
and found one

let no faction keep me from those
who need a home now

                              *

> *y'chayim olenu v'al kol yisroel.
> v'imru omen.*

and in Rome   where Jesus the dead Jew is raised
against us
as in Kansas   or California

a synagogue   blown up for being   a Jew place
a baby   blown up for being   a Jew baby
in *shul*   for the high holy days

> *Oseh sholom bimromo, hu'ya aseh*

if there's a Jew alive   if a sin is always Jewish sin   this baby
paid   again   nothing is expiated   there is
blood in the camps   the bulldozers come to push
bodies   into hiding   this is what men do
Gemayel is received at the UN   with applause
this is the Jewish problem

my father loved all things Jewish

a culture   *astonishing in its variety*   was

if I were to mourn properly
I would not be done

> *sholom olenu v'al kol isroel. v'imru
> omen.*

1983

kaddish, Jewish prayer for the dead, language: Aramaic.
schnorrer, a moocher
yente, a gossip, someone who has to put her two cents in all the time
Bundist, member of the Jewish socialist organization
Hatikvah, lit., "hope": the Israeli national anthem
Gemayel, President of Lebanon, head of the Christian Phalange Party

Note: All poems have sources, but with some, these sources are so
immediate that it seems only right to name them. *Kaddish* came to me
first through the work of the Argentinian Jew Mauricio Lansky, an
artist whose series of prints depicts simply and with extraordinary
beauty face after face; each print has a number like a concentration
camp tattoo. Also crucial was Irena Klepfisz's long prose poem *Bashert*
(published in *SW 21* and in her book *Keeper of Accounts*). Jacobo Tim-
merman's *The Longest War: Israel In Lebanon* taught me to be more
afraid of silence than of how speech will be used against Jews. The
many-faceted Israeli peace movement gives me necessary inspiration
and courage.

Resisting and
Surviving America*

Irena Klepfisz

As a child, my first conscious feeling about being Jewish was that it was dangerous, something to be hidden. For years I agonized over my visibility as a Jew, over the fact that I lived in a Jewish neighborhood, that my name was on lists of Jewish organizations and schools, that at a moment's notice I could be found, identified, rounded up. My sole comfort during that time was that I did not "look" Jewish—something which I clung to as my only means of escape.

My sense of danger was rooted in a total physical and emotional knowledge of the war. Yet this knowledge was acquired only after I came to America in 1949 at the age of eight. It was in New York—at the annual memorials for the uprising of the Warsaw Ghetto, during conversations among my mother's friends, in the books I was encouraged to read—that I absorbed the full horror and insanity of the camps and ghettos, absorbed them in such a way that they became first-hand knowledge. I reacted and lived as if I had been an adult in 1945, instead of a four-year-old child. It was especially in these early years in America—when the pain of survivors around me was unguarded and raw—that I learned in minute detail the ingenuity and capriciousness of the torturer, the powerlessness of the victim's reason and logic, and the necessity of a rigid life/death morality. As a child, I was old with terror and the brutality, the haphazardness of survival.

Ironically, those who taught me "not to forget" also provided me with a way of coping. And as melodramatic as it may seem, it was through literature. My first felt response to literature was in my Workmen's Circle Yiddish *Shule* No. 3 in the Bronx. There I absorbed an endless variety of Yiddish poems and songs.

*The first section of this paper was originally written in 1979 as a statement for the *Anthology of Contemporary American Jewish Poets* (unpublished).

I found that they touched me in a way that neither "The Ancient Mariner" nor "Evangeline" (which I was reading then in public school) ever touched me. Predominantly the poetry of labor, of poverty and ordinary struggle, their open rhymes and bare meters transformed what was painful into something not only bearable, but beautiful.

> I have a little boy
> A child so rare and fine
> That when my eyes behold him,
> I think the world is mine.
>
> But seldom, oh so seldom,
> I see him when he's at play;
> I see him only fast asleep
> When I return from a hard, hard day.*

As I grew older, I learned the full breadth of Yiddish literature; but this early introduction with its inherent political vision became as powerful an influence in my life as did the war.

Of course neither influence was always reflected in the American Jewish life around me. I was repeatedly dumbfounded by other children who insisted on calling themselves Jewish, but who did not know Yiddish, were not avowed atheists and socialists and who knew nothing of the war or of the Jewish Labor Bund. I tended to be quite cynical about them and dismissed them as fakes.

Things merge in strange ways and I do not want to falsify by making unnatural distinctions. Experience has obviously taught me that Jews are not the only ones in danger and that what is "undesirable" in me is not limited to my Jewishness. As an adult I have nurtured what I consider to be a mature, healthy paranoia, one which I cling to as an important means of survival. As a writer I still cherish poetry that tells a story, especially the dramatic monologue. I still value most a poetry that deals with people, especially those alienated and out of the mainstream—the overworked and dreamless, Third World, women, gay—a subdued, earnest poetry that expresses their feelings, their struggles, the conditions of their lives.

---

*From Morris Rosenfeld's "My Little Boy"; translation mine.

February 1981

Dear Evelyn:

You've asked me to add something to the statement I wrote for the *Anthology of Contemporary American Jewish Poets*. To add something about being a lesbian, a Jewish lesbian.

As usual with this kind of thing, I feel I can't simply add a statement, that I have to start over again, to start from the very beginning. And as usual, my feelings are not exactly the same as when I first wrote over a year ago.

It is not that I have re-evaluated or have changed my ideas, only that at different moments I focus on different aspects of some of these issues. My feelings about being a Jew, especially being an American Jew, and more recently about being an American Jewish lesbian, are not all completely clear or logical to me. They seem for the most part to be tangled and inter-locked and I guess I will present them that way—not to do so would seem to me to falsify. I am sure certain statements will seem contradictory. Perhaps to some even offensive. But I will try to be honest here, as honest as I can allow myself to be.

One of the things most evident to me about my feelings is that I have rarely expressed them. It is not that I have disguised them, but merely that I have for the most part remained quiet about them. There are many reasons for this. For one, I have sensed that people are simply fed up with what Jews feel. Sensing this, I have not been eager to make myself vulnerable. I have also been silent because, unlike what maybe some people would assume, I feel critical of certain segments of the Jewish popula-tion and how they function in America. I do not often express these criticisms because of the persistent and more recently flourishing climate of anti-Semitism in America. Since I have not seen any strong concern over this anti-Semitism (except per-haps from the most conservative elements in the Jewish com-munity, those often labelled extremists and hysterics), I have been afraid to express my own misgivings lest they be inter-preted as anti-Semitic. To criticize in an atmosphere of dislike or even indifference is to play into anti-Semitic strategies. I refuse to do that.

One reason I am willing now to write about the mixture of feelings that I have is that I trust you and trust the anthology. It feels safe to say many of the things I want to say.

Let me begin with the silence that stems from my sense that people are tired of hearing about what Jews feel. This silence hides my extreme pain, frustration and rage with non-Jews and

Jews alike. The source of people's impatience, I believe, is the Holocaust. I find it almost impossible to write that word, because here—in America—the word has lost almost all meaning. And the fault lies with both non-Jews and Jews. It lies with the "American way of life," with the process of Americanization, with American big business, with commercialism, with posing, with artificial feelings.

I am convinced that the reason that people are turned off of the Holocaust—I can barely believe that I just now wrote *"turned off of the Holocaust"*—and yet that seems the most appropriate language to describe the phenomenon since the Holocaust has been like a fad, a rock group losing its original sound, a fashionable form of dress that outlives its popularity—I am, I repeat, convinced that people are turned off of the Holocaust, because it has been commercialized, metaphored out of reality, glamorized, been severed from the historical fact.

Yet despite this "turn off," I find—and am repeatedly stunned by it—that people (again non-Jews are guilty of this repeatedly) insist on dredging it up. Writers, for example, who have no feelings or connection to the war, insist on it as literary metaphor, as an epigraph, as some kind of necessary addition. A casual allusion to Auschwitz. An oblique reference to the Warsaw Ghetto. Somehow this "sprinkling" of Jewish experiences is thought to reflect sensitivity, a largeness of heart. And of course it does not. It is simply the literary Holocaust, the Holocaust of words that have nothing to do with fact. It is nothing more than pose. I must say that my teeth grind whenever I see these gratuitous gestures—usually devoid of any Jewish context, devoid of any sense of the Jewish experience or history.

I am also furious with the Holocaust of American Big Business. The Holocaust of glamour. Of movie stars. TV stations. Of sloppy books that sell millions of copies and make reputations and millions and millions of dollars. This Holocaust is awarded Emmys, Oscars, Tonys, Best-Jewish-Book-of-the-Year awards. This phenomenon of co-opting is, of course, not atypical. It is very, very American. It is the process of mainstreaming whatever seems real and genuine, whatever seems threatening. It is a process of dilution, of wringing any reality or feeling out of true suffering or need or ideal. It is cheapness, vulgarity. And repeatedly it rouses my rage and disgust.

Am I making any sense? It is hard to write this. But I've been thinking a lot about it lately, about the corruption here in America, how everything becomes big business, how everything

becomes diseased. Everything. Manufacturers roll up their
sleeves and we're inundated with buttons, slogans, black arm
bands, yellow ribbons, six candles.

Both Jews and non-Jews have depleted the meaning of the
word Holocaust in this way. But Jews, by themselves, have also
had their own special role. Their own Holocaust has been preserved as the Holocaust of spectacle, show biz, of song and
false ritual. Of services at Temple Emanuel on Fifth Avenue
among silk scarves and fur coats. Of condolence telegrams
from candidates on the campaign trail. Of Presidential declarations. Of operatic arias. It is the Holocaust of finally organizing,
of having meetings and dues and committees. Of gaining status
and respectability through incorporation and tax-exemption.

I am sick of all of it. Sick and angry because I know it has
absolutely nothing to do with what my family and I experienced during the war; it has nothing to do with what millions
of Jews experienced during the war.

And so I rage internally when I hear or sense that people are
tired of or fed up with the Holocaust.

And worse. I feel robbed, robbed of a true sense of loss, a
true sense of mourning, a true sense of suffering and surviving.
I am not sure I can explain this properly. But this hype of the
media, of publishing houses, etc. has robbed me of the possibility of really mourning the losses of my life, of even defining
them or articulating them properly. How can I say to people
that for the survivors with whom I grew up the Holocaust never
ended? That all my life I will feel the loss of never having
known my father, never even having a photograph of him after
the age of seventeen. That all my life I will feel the loss of aunts
and cousins and grandparents I never knew. That my mother
still stacks shelves and shelves of food—*just in case*. That twenty
years after the war, when some plaster fell down from the living
room ceiling, she froze with fear because she thought we were
being bombed. That when a friend's child died—the mother, incredulous at this unexpected death, said to me: "Irena, I thought
I had already paid for all my children's sins. I paid for them during the war. I told God. This, what I went through, is for my
children's sins." That another friend committed suicide just
when it seemed she had settled into her American life. That
even I, just recently, after surgery, expressed my sense of viola-
tion through dreams about the war.

None of this has anything to do with the Holocaust that people are "turned off" of. It is ordinary, undramatic and ever pres-

sent. The Holocaust was not an event that ended in 1945. At least not for the survivors. Not for me. It continued on and on because my mother and I were alone. Because my father's family no longer existed and I was its sole survivor. It continued on in the struggle of extreme poverty that we experienced in the early years in this country. It continued on and on, coloring every thought I had, every decision I made. It continued on in the Bronx, on ordinary streets, at the kitchen table. It continued on invisible.

So you can understand that when I see that experience exploited, co-opted, when I sense people are fed up, how I want to rage at everyone: "You're fucking around with my pain, with my real pain, my real life. Forget the metaphor. Think about reality."

The real mourning, the real sense of loss has hardly ever been evoked or expressed, at least not recently. And as I said—Jews have participated in this falsification. I am not an expert on what happens to immigrant groups in America, but I have often felt that one way of assimilating, of entering the American mainstream, is to learn to package, to adopt big business techniques, to market. It is, of course, also the way to lose your spiritual identity. It's obvious how this has happened to labor and various minority struggles in this country. And it's happened to Jews as well. And I am pained by it, frustrated by it. It is such a horrendous mistake. But Jews have done it. Have pushed into the mainstream and thought themselves safe, deluded themselves—for no matter what, they are not part of the mainstream, no matter the money or the position. When it comes to the bottom line, the Moral Majority is Christian. So is the Ku Klux Klan. So is the Nazi Party. And I am completely stymied that large segments of the Jewish population have not absorbed these simple basic facts.

I am also angry that Jews have somehow, during this process, gotten stuck—I'm not sure if that's the right word, but I don't know how else to express it. They have been unable to absorb the experience of the Holocaust, have not learned how to transcend the catastrophe. They've mistakenly thought that to transcend means to forget the past, that to think about the present is to abandon the past. That too is a painful mistake, a grave mistake for Jews in America, because it's kept many of them from universalizing their experience, from joining with others who have experienced oppression—not perhaps an exact duplication of Jewish oppression, but nevertheless oppression.

Jews have made the mistake of thinking that we all must experience exactly the same thing; in doing so, they've severed themselves from many other people's suffering. And so I become angry because of course I want Jews to "know better"—feel they should "know better"—and am repeatedly disappointed when the evidence shows they are just like most people—they don't learn from experience or from history.

This is perhaps the most painful aspect for me of being Jewish, for I identify strongly as a Jew, am proud to be a Jew. And yet I sometimes feel so torn—so torn from the Jewish community, from the Jews I grew up with, who nurtured me, helped me. And yet I don't understand what America has done to them and how it has seduced them. The conservatism is there and really hard to accept. But it is there, definitely there with the mainstreaming.

So when you ask me to say something about being a Jewish lesbian, what can I say? You know of course that there are no Jewish lesbians because to begin with Jews are not supposed to be sexual. Especially Jewish women. So what the Jewish lesbian encounters are the typical conservative stances. Closed doors. Silence. Disgust. For this reason I have not publicized my lesbianism in Jewish circles. That is probably wrong. Probably homophobic. I have thought it pointless, self-defeating in certain instances. Often I have not said anything out of simple fear. I didn't want to experience the closed door, the disgust. At the same time I've been perfectly aware that you can't write and publish and keep these things a secret, especially if some people are already in on the secret. And so the secret spreads. Irena Klepfisz. Oh yes, she wrote those poems about the Holocaust. But you know she wrote those other poems too. Well, we can always pretend we didn't read them. No need to mention them. Let's just talk about those poems about the Holocaust. Powerful stuff. But did you continue reading past the first section? Did you read those other poems too?

At that moment I am an outsider, a lesbian, a *shiksa*. The Jewish community is not my community.

But as a Jew—as a Jew in a Christian, anti-Semitic society—the Jewish community is, and will always remain, my community.

Enemy and ally.

This is the confusion. Being Jewish. Being a lesbian. Being an American. It all converges. It is hard to separate out. It is like feelings about one's parents. Love and embarrassment. The painful realization that they are not perfect.

As I perceive the danger from the Right increasing, my identification grows even stronger. I want to buy a Jewish star to
wear around my neck. I can hear my mother's wry comment:
"What? Have you become a pagan?" Not unexpected from a
Jewish-socialist position. But it is true; for the first time in my
life, I want to wear a Jewish star. The time seems right for it.

But if the time is right for it, it is not only because reactionary elements in this country have made it so. There is a danger,
I believe, from the Left as well, and this includes the Jewish
Left—especially those in the Jewish Left who are embarrassed
about being Jewish. Who will only say that Jews are guilty of
this or that. Who never express any pride or love or affection or
attachment to their Jewishness. Who only declare their Jewishness after making an anti-Semitic statement, as if ending such a
statement with "Well, I'm Jewish" makes it all right, acceptable.
That too enrages me and frightens me. Those of the Left, Jew
and non-Jew alike, seem to believe what the Right has always
maintained—that Jews run the world and are, therefore, most
responsible for its ills. The casualness, the indifference with
which the Left accepts this anti-Semitic stance enrages me. It is
usually subtle, often taking the form of anti-Semitism by *omission.* Its form is to show or speak about Jews *only* as oppressors,
never as anything else. That is anti-Semitic. And I think it's
prevalent and it scares me, the repeated fault-finding in an
atmosphere of indifference.

I cannot end without affirming as strongly as I can my deep
feelings of identification and pride in being a Jew. It was Jews
that first instilled in me the meaning of what oppression and its
consequences are. It was Jews who first taught me about social-
ism, classism, racism, and about what in the fifties was called
"injustice." It is from Jews that I adopted ideals that I still
hold and principles that I still believe are true and must be
fought for and put into practice. It was from Jews that I learned
about the necessity for resistance. It was from Jews that I also
learned that literature was not simply fancy words or clever
metaphor, but instead it was deeply, intimately connected to
life, to a life that I was a part of. It is really almost impossible
to compress this inheritance into a single paragraph. But I know
its depth and vitality, and I know that I have absorbed it thoroughly into my consciousness.

I know also that often some Jews have not lived up to what
they themselves have expressed and taught others. I do not like
that and will not apologize for it. And I generally argue and
fight with them whenever I am with them and find they are

lacking. But I will not deny them. I am clearly their product, the product of a Jewish upbringing, of Jewish teaching, of the Jewish experience both here in America and Europe. That is not schmaltz, or nostalgia, or sentimentality. It is simply acknowledging and crediting Jews with what I consider to be my best self.

I said from the start it was not going to be very logical. Strong identification. Pride. Disappointment. And fear—fear of what is happening to the Jewish community from within, as well as what is happening to it from without. And these feelings are always with me. I write as much out of a Jewish consciousness as I do out of a lesbian/feminist consciousness. They are both always there, no matter what the topic I might be working on. They are embedded in my writing, totally embedded and enmeshed to the point that they are not necessarily distinguishable as discrete elements. They merge and blend and blur—for in many ways they are the same. My poem "Death Camp." My poem "From the Monkey House and Other Cages." Alienated. Threatened. Un-American. Individual. Defiant. To me they are ever present.

Afterthoughts: 1988

Since the publication of Nice Jewish Girls: A Lesbian Anthology *in 1982, there has been greater contact between Jewish lesbians and gays and the mainstream Jewish community. Things are better, much improved but not nearly what we'd like them to be. There are still many obstacles that impede satisfying relations between Jewish gays and heterosexuals. I discussed two of these in a speech I delivered in Chicago in November 1988 entitled "Jewish Lesbians, the Jewish Community, Jewish Survival." The occasion was a symposium, "Jewish Feminism—A Call to the Future," sponsored by the American Jewish Congress and Spertus College of Judaica.*

I know that Jews have special concerns that color their attitudes toward gays and lesbians, and I would like to address two of these. The first is the issue of demographics. There is great concern that intermarriage, the loosening of community ties, and weakening of Jewish identity are decimating the Jewish population. The Holocaust or *der khurbn* ravaged us; our children and the future generation are a major preoccupation. Certainly those of us who are children of *di lebn geblibene*, survivors, who have lived among survivors understand *di benkshaft*, the longing, yearning for continuity that was and remains the fabric of *undzere elterns khaloymes*, our parents' dreams. *Ikh bin di eyntsike lebn-geblibene fun der tates mishpokhe.* I am the only survivor of my father's family. I know the keen sense of loss behind *di khaloymes*, those dreams: the desire to pass on the names of dead relatives, the desire to regenerate the family.

I also know that the entire burden of fulfilling *di khaloymes* has fallen on *di yidishe froyen*, Jewish women, and has put great pressure on Jewish women to bear children. And though I understand the feelings and concerns that lie behind that pressure, I feel it is imperative for us to resist this special form of sexism, which reduces a Jewish woman's value simply to a biological function. We have to resist the view that the most significant contribution a Jewish woman can make to *undzer folk*, our people, is to give birth to a Jewish child.

This is an important issue and one that can serve as common ground for Jewish lesbians and their heterosexual Jewish sisters. Jewish lesbians are often confronted with the argument that they do not care about Jewish survival because we do not want to bear children, an argument that of course ignores the fact that many lesbians *do* have children. But aside from that, it is outrageous to suggest that those of us who have chosen to be childless are indifferent to Jewish survival. In fact we have a critical function to play in maintaining the survival of our community in every sphere of Jewish life, and bearing children is not always the best contribution we can make. I know of many women who possess hardly any Jewish identity, are entirely ignorant of Jewish history, religion, culture—they could have a dozen children but these children would be raised in a void.

Clearly the act of bearing a child is not a guarantee of Jewish survival, for *der khurbn*, the Holocaust, not only ravaged us physically through the murder of 6 million, it ravaged *undzer kultur, undzer gayst*, our culture and spirit. If Jewish identity is weakening in the United States, one cause is the destruction of Eastern European culture, a culture on which American Jews were extremely dependent, to which they turned for nourishment and strength. The result is that assimilation, alienation, and a thin fading Jewish identity have become our greatest enemies. Yet Jewish women and lesbians have a great deal to offer to counter these by the art they produce, by the institutions they establish and nurture (secular and observant, cultural and religious), by their acute political sense. I am thinking of my own commitment to Yiddish and to building a strong Jewish identity. I am thinking of my close friend and collaborator, the lesbian/feminist Melanie Kaye/Kantrowitz, who lives and teaches in a graduate program in Vermont and with whom I worked for four years on *The Tribe of Dina: A Jewish Women's Anthology* so that *all* Jewish women could discern their role in Jewish life and culture. Throughout the year Melanie gives workshops in the women's community on Jewish identity and relentlessly challenges anti-Semitism whenever and wherever she sees it. I am thinking of my friend, another lesbian, Evelyn Torton Beck, a mother of two, a teacher, scholar, and chair of Women's Studies at the University of Maryland in College Park. It was Evi who identified the influence of Yiddish theater on Kafka's writing and who brought to the surface Bashevis Singer's misogyny. I am thinking of my friend and lesbian Clare Kinberg, recently settled in Oregon, who works tirelessly to further peace between Israelis and Palestinians. I am thinking of my friend and lesbian Bernice Mennis, who lives in upstate New York and teaches non-Jewish students at the local community college about Jewish immigrant life through the stories of Anzia Yezierska. I am thinking of my friend and lesbian Marianna Kaufman, a librarian in Atlanta, Georgia, who always makes sure that her library is up to date in its Judaica section. I am thinking of my friend and lesbian Sharon Kleinbaum, who lived in Amherst, Massachusetts, and for a number of years served as the assistant director of the National Yiddish Book Center, which is helping to keep Yiddish and Yiddish culture alive. Sharon is now completing her rabbinical studies in Israel. I am thinking of Rabbi Linda Holtzman, a lesbian who teaches in Philadelphia and prepares men and women for their roles as teachers and rabbis. I am thinking of Elana Dykewomon, who with other Jewish lesbians founded a writer's group in Oakland that is trying to create a new American Jewish literature, one that acknowledges lesbian presence in the Jewish community. I am thinking of the Jewish lesbians in Northampton, Massachusetts, who with their Jewish heterosexual sisters are translating the biographies of Yiddish women writers so that they will finally become known to the American Jewish community and take their rightful place in Yiddish literature and history. I am thinking of the Jewish lesbians in Boston who are editing an anthology of their experiences as daughters of Holocaust survivors; they are determined the past will not be forgotten and are working toward a future that will help Jews heal. And I am also thinking of all the other Jewish lesbians who are afraid of being identified, but who work in mainstream Jewish organizations like the American Jewish Congress, the American Jewish Committee, Hadassah, the National Council of Jewish Women, the Workmen's Circle, YIVO Institute for Jewish Research—lesbians who live in fear of the community, but who nevertheless serve it through endless council and committee work in these organizations as well as in neighborhood synagogues and community centers.

What the Jewish community needs is more women, more lesbians like these, for it is they and their work that will help us be a prouder, stronger community, one able to resist the pull of the homogenizing Christian mainstream. It is lesbians like the ones I've just named who are actively helping guarantee Jewish survival, just as much as the Jewish women who bear Jewish children—perhaps even more.

I would like to raise one more issue that often emerges in a discussion of lesbians and gay men in relationship to the Jewish community. Frequently I have heard that Jews need to be careful whom they form alliances with, that they need to keep a low profile and, because of the unpopularity of gays, they need to avoid being associated with such a group. Again I understand the fear behind the argument. I too worry about Jewish visibility, especially when that visibility is associated with unpopular causes. I think any people that has been traumatized as we have been by the Holocaust or has experienced genocide naturally feels cautious and tentative in taking public stands. And yet we need to resist these fears and always strive toward the moral good, toward justice. In a way we have no choice. We are, after all, a small minority in this country, and we cannot struggle successfully if we struggle alone. This is the hard political reality. We need to be able to form alliances and to do that we must understand not only our own needs, but also the needs of others.

When gays are threatened, the Jewish community ought to be ready to defend them, for surely a threat to gays will ultimately extend to other minorities. At all times, including times of crisis, the Jewish community ought to be able to say: "Gays are our children, our parents, our friends and neighbors. We love them. They are our own." When the Jewish community can say that, when its leaders begin to speak out against homophobia, against sexism, against prejudice, it will become a true ally. The Jewish community will not only be protecting gays—it will be enriching itself by guaranteeing that the lesbians and gays in its own midst are able to participate fully in Jewish life.

Notes of an Immigrant Daughter: Atlanta

Melanie Kaye/Kantrowitz

you dream
of what it looked like
before the europeans came, before
they brought the africans, chained—
when native peoples rode hunted grew corn
& sang all over the many-nation's face:
cheyenne sioux cherokee pontiac comanche
winnebago passamaquoddy navajo mohican
apache kiowa hopi chickasaw

too many to name

1. a movie, BIRTH OF A NATION, called
"a classic." black women
have rolling eyewhites;* white women
are blond and rapeable
by black men. the ku klux klan
is the hero

when they show this movie in greensboro, north carolina
people—black & white—gather
to protest; five are shot dead
by local nazis
& the hero klan

the one time i was in atlanta
some rich white women told us, don't
go downtown at night
so we go downtown—
it's alive with black people, women, men
out on the streets after the movies or concert—
something to fear?

* The grotesque look of Black people in this racist film is explained by the fact
that they are really whites in blackface. Only in crowd scenes do a very few actual
Blacks appear. Michelle Cliff's suspicions led me to this information.

down here, death's face is white.
the one time i camped in alabama, i kept
thinking we're northerners
dykes & commies—
you catholic, me a jew

if we had no dog
if we had no gun
how could we sleep

klansmen on trial right now in greensboro
claiming self-defense

2. in france they're bombing synagogues
this country concerned as usual when
jews get killed says
nothing

and the summer we lived in maine
on the bedroom door someone had painted
in blood, swastikas—
we painted over their sick
breath—still
the house stunk

                    i can't go back
                    where i came from was
                    burned off the map

                    i'm a jew
                    anywhere is someone else's land

3. i dream: i'm climbing a ladder behind a young woman, blond,
dressed punk style; stitched on the leg of her jeans, in green &
pink letters, the words: *how will you die, who will you kill*

in the morning i read the news—in atlanta
black children
are being killed

a daycare center blows up

children go out to play or to the store &
disappear: fifteen missing or found
strangled, shot, or drowned or
dead—cause undetermined

                    for months they say these deaths
                    are not related

4. all over the nation is someone else's land
for example, the whole state of maine might have been
passamaquoddy nation, had the treaty
saved by a woman in a shoebox been honored
as written; had the people risked
everything   on the young ones' faith

they won millions of acres anyhow
and dollars, and the children
can all go to college
but first they learn their language
and their people's ways

5. a mother's voice booming across the TV miles
how many children going to lose their
lives mr mayor before you
do something

            the papers say the mothers just
            don't take care

mother of a murdered child, keening, they
didn't tell us about the danger, if
i'd known, i'd never have
let him out, my
baby be alive

            some people charge the mothers
            have done the killing

mother of children not yet dead shouts mr
mayor   we don't want to see you on TV
we don't want to see you next week
we want to see you
now about our
children

mother of a murdered child &
three still living, camille bell
says—if they were white children. . .

but, interrupts the white reporter, the
mayor the chief of police are
black (he means, aren't you
satisfied)

camille bell looks past him
says, these children were black
& poor

while newspapers i clip & save in a shoebox say
the klan practices guerrilla warfare
outside of atlanta
as outside nashville
as outside houston & dallas
as outside buffalo & kingston
as outside portland oregon
as outside youngstown ohio
the klan gathers

*how will we die
who will we kill*

klansmen on trial in greensboro
verdict: not guilty

if they were white children

if the mayor were on welfare
if the governor got pregnant
if the president had suckled babies instead of
sucking off the trilateral commission would
death's face be leering
all over the world

as in atlanta
where mothers
as always
teach children how to survive—
don't get in anyone's car   children   is that
correct— and to sing
with the preacher   in church
jesus loves the little children
all god's children in the world
red & yellow black & white
they are precious—

and in the sight of their mothers
they are precious—

mr mayor
mr president
mr chairman of the board

one of the klansmen acquitted in greensboro
has already been shot at

in atlanta
16 17 18 19 20 21 23 25 28 children
are dead or missing

and we want to see you
now
about our children

April 1981

6. don't   say it's
over   they
caught the killer
one black man

the white south stands on corners
with bibles
shaking hands

why whistle dixie
unless you like the tune

why call a restaurant "plantation house" unless
you mourn the demise

why move the people from their land
unless you want it

at a house named for plantations
i cannot eat

nor can i go back
my people were burned off the map

the flames still crackle
on crosses
in buffalo
portland
atlanta

all over the nation
our children are watching
to see
who we become

December 1981

Repeating History
Bernice Mennis

My Jewishness feels like a tangled web—almost too tangled and vulnerable to unravel. But there are a few strands that can be looked at, some words, stories, remembrances that can give a vague outline to an even vaguer picture of growing up in America as a Jew.

My parents repeated certain "lessons" so often that they almost became "truths." One lesson was that whenever there was *any* trouble, Jews should watch out. Growing up in the early 1900s in a small village outside of Kiev, my father, his family and the Jews in the village learned that unrest, poverty, natural or unnatural catastrophes, hard times, revolution, bad weather—anything could and did bring pogroms and attacks on Jews. Chaos, confusion, movement, change in the outside world created fear in my father's *shtetl*. It was this fear that impelled my father to leave Russia at the age of thirteen and, after a three-year wait in Roumania, to come to New York City.

Another "lesson" was that a Jew will always be seen as a Jew, no matter how assimilated s/he thinks s/he is. The German Jews—snobby, aristocratic, intellectual, "superior" to the East European Jews—identified as Germans, not Jews. They felt secure in their assimilation into German society, until the Nazis made them wear yellow stars, rounded them up, sent them to extermination camps, killed them. What happened to them was a lesson to all Jews: first, even the most assimilated (those most socially and financially secure) are still seen only as Jews; second, Jews are always vulnerable and at any point can be betrayed, scapegoated, and killed; therefore, a Jew must learn to recognize who is Jewish and who is not, to trust only Jews, to be wary of all non-Jews.

It was because of these "lessons" that the first, and sometimes only, question my father would ask about someone was: "Is s/he Jewish?" And although my response was and still is:

"What difference does it make?" I know that I myself am acutely conscious of who is Jewish and who is not when I walk into a room. My parents' "lessons" connected this information with survival, with the distinction between friends and enemies. I absorbed the importance of that information.

Watching television, my father would point out to me the Jewish comedians, the Jewish musicians, the occasional Jewish athlete. There was a feeling of pride when a Jew was publicly "good," but tremendous shame and guilt when a Jew was "bad." The feeling of collective responsibility and guilt was incredible. When Jack Ruby, a Jew, shot Oswald, my father panicked, fearing that it would set off reprisals against all Jews.

My "good" guys and "bad" guys are very different from my father's, but my almost instinctive reactions to them are the same. When I read about "good" Jews fighting for radical, humanitarian causes, I feel proud. But when I read about a corrupt Jewish landlord or businessman, or about an Israeli action of which I disapprove, I feel guilt, shame, responsibility. And fear—fear that all Jews, including me, will be blamed, punished. Each time there is some terrible crime committed, I fear that a Jew will be named the culprit.

Because my parents felt a collective guilt and fear, they tried hard to assimilate, tried hard not to stand out. While my sister and I were growing up, they pressured us to be more "American," to avoid being political, to go to college (but not graduate school), to marry and have children, to be like the typical American girl/woman. Although they learned the lessons of the German Jews, strongly identified as Jews and associated exclusively with Jews, although my father's accent and my relatives' ways distinguished them as "greenhorns" and non-Americans, my parents still wanted very much to vanish into the mainstream.

As a result, their pride in their Jewish identity was always undercut by the heavy sense of shame and self-hate that our country transmits to all immigrants, to all non-Western European, non-white peoples. For example, my father loved telling stories of life in the Russian *shtetl*, while my mother, born into a family that had just emigrated from Russia, also delighted in telling stories of her parents' settlement as the first Jews in Quincy, Massachusetts. Yet, whenever I would ask about the "Bintel Brief"—letters to *The Jewish Forward*—or life on the Lower East Side, my father would begin talking disparagingly of the ignorance of "greenhorns." Instead of feeling proud that he had worked two jobs, brought his entire family here from Russia, and supported our family on the income from a small tomato and banana stand at which he worked six days a week, twelve hours a day—my father felt ashamed of his accent, his misspellings, his work, his "greenhorn" ways. It is not surprising that this shame, this strong sense of inferiority and self-denigration was passed on to his children.

And I, "Americanized" like my parents, learned to be ashamed of them and of myself, of our looks, loud talk, ways of eating, ways of bargaining. I remember especially disliking my mother's "masculine" dominance over my father's "effeminate" weakness, her crazy focus on food and home, and her control over her children. She seemed to me the stereotypical Jewish mother of *Portnoy's Complaint*.

It was only much later that I realized how my acceptance of that picture of her was a real betrayal, fed by society's misogyny, its blame/hatred of all women/wives/mothers, and how it was specifically anti-Semitic. *The Jewish Woman in America*[1] shed some light. I was struck by the strength of Eastern European Jewish women; I thought about how hard it must have been for them to fit into the socialized role of the submissive, dominated American woman/wife/mother. In the village in Eastern Europe, it was common for the men to spend their days in prayer and study. Frequently, it was the women who dealt with matters of the world, bargained in the marketplace, struggled with the material realities of survival. A pot that could feed a family was a Jewish woman's triumph. To feed and to nourish, to give, to provide—these were acts of love and strength.

But what was valued in Europe was seen in America as masculine, loud, vulgar, pushy. The strength of these Eastern European Jewish women became something shameful, something to be held in check. When economic conditions allowed, the Jewish woman, like her American model, was told that her proper place was in the home. She was told that her strength and energy were to be directed, not to the larger outside world, but to children and housekeeping. Constrained and with no real outlet, forced into such narrow channels, that Jewish energy sometimes took bizarre forms. Realizing this now, I recognize my former betrayal of my mother as the classic pattern of blaming the victim, accepting the value judgments of the "oppressor."

After reading *The Jewish Woman in America*, I formulated a rather factless "theory" that a great number of lesbians sprang from the wombs of Eastern European Jewish women. Clearly those strong women—ashamed of their strength, critical of their daughters, socialized to want the acceptable American way for themselves and their children—had nevertheless managed to convey another message: "Be strong! Be independent! Be in the world! Don't be a *shmate* for any man!" This message was delivered neither openly nor clearly; rather it was intertwined with many other conflicting messages. Still, many of us managed to hear it and recognize our mothers' deeper and truer voices.

My fanciful theory was not, however, the only connection between my two strong identities—my Jewishness and my lesbianism.

At a Lesbian Survival Conference at Brooklyn Women's Center, I co-facilitated a workshop on "Lesbian-Straight Friendships" with a woman who then identified herself as straight. After the discussion she told me how shocked she was to realize why she had not come out as a lesbian—she did not want to be in another ghetto. When the lesbians in the group talked of common humor, dress, language, and the distrust of the "other," she recalled her pain growing up in a poor Jewish ghetto on Manhattan's Lower East Side. She did not want to be in another ghetto.

While the ghetto isolates, it also provides a home and family. I recall my parents claiming that if one spoke Yiddish, s/he could travel anywhere and find friends who would provide shelter. Despite vast national/cultural differences, the fact of Jewishness would create a bond.

As a lesbian, too, one could travel anywhere and find family. One could spot another, pick up on a conversation, visit a women's bookstore or coffee house or bar, call a switchboard, or refer to *Gaia's Guide*. And despite vast differences, the fact of lesbianism would often bring an immediate sharing, communication, understanding. Being an outsider enabled one to be inside.

When I left New York City for rural upstate New York, I expected isolation as a lesbian. Through various channels, I gradually met other lesbians. The circle widened into a group of forty lesbians called Adirondykes. My current community is not as large as the one I left in New York City, but it is a community that accepts, supports, nourishes. Despite our many differences, the fact of lesbianism creates a strong bond.

However, as a Jewish lesbian I still feel isolated. In New York City, many of my friends were daughters of Jewish immigrants.

The idiosyncracies of our families, our relationship to food, the way we shouted or debated, our hand gestures and body mannerisms, our humor—all felt like home. I miss that language, that shared knowledge which needs no explanation.

The assumption in most of the United States is that everyone is both Christian and heterosexual. When people make anti-Semitic comments, they include me in their assumed commonality of judgment. In response, I feel the need to "come out" as a Jew rather than pass, thus losing their acceptance of me as an insider, setting myself apart as the "other" with its objectification and judgment.

Today I put two letters in my mailbox—one to my Zionist Blue Cross/Blue Shield Medical Plan and one to the Gay Lobby. Each made me hesitate, for each exposes me to the mailman who reads the envelopes of all incoming and outgoing mail. I feared his judgment and gossip. I was clearly not a Christian wife/mother, but a Jewish lesbian—something sinful in this region of the Moral Majority.

The vehemence with which lesbians are hated, and which I have experienced, still surprises me. As a Jew, I have never felt that kind of hatred directly. But reading any history of extermination camps, of expulsion/massacre/torture in Spain, England, North Africa, Russia, Poland, and Argentina evokes similar shock and surprise. Why does our Jewishness seem so intolerable? I know that at certain historical moments, when conditions worsen with unemployment, poverty, fear and frustration, people need someone or something to blame. Individual prejudices become transformed into societal and historical "solutions." Those in power validate certain channels for hatred; it is their safety mechanism, diverting frustration and rage away from political action and revolution. Historically, the designated channels have been homophobia, anti-Semitism, racism, and sexism. In different countries and at different times, the targets shift, but there remains a universality to these hatreds. In my father's words: "At any point, for any reason, we can be attacked."

Because the attacks seem so illogical and irrational, we can become haunted by the question: How could so many people, acting so strongly, be wrong? As victims, we often internalize hateful judgments: as homosexuals, we are "perverse" and "disgusting"; as Jews, we are "pushy" and "materialistic." However, the internalization is often more subtle. In order to avoid attacks we become our own police, out of fear as well as self-hate,

willing to judge and restrict those of us who are "bad": the obvious Jews (Hassidim), the obvious lesbians (butches and
femmes).

I remember attending a Lesbian and Gay Pride march in
Boston, where Maxine Feldman—wearing a very fine three-piece
suit—and Clover (a gay man)—wearing assorted dresses and fancy attire—emceed the rally. They were both wonderful in their
humor, warmth, political awareness. And I remember feeling
very conscious that just a few years earlier I would have been
ashamed to have them publicly represent me to the straight
world. As I betrayed my mother by accepting "their" judgment
of her, in an earlier phase of my lesbianism I betrayed my lesbian
friends who refused to ask for approval. In both situations I
was experiencing my father's fear of giving "them" ammuni-
tion for attack. I still had to learn that "they" will attack anyway, that I need not be "their" police.

It is from my father's Jewish perspective that I sometimes
think of all the lesbians involved in abortion rights and steriliza-
tion abuse, in battered women's shelters, in rape counselling
centers. Together with their straight feminist sisters, on a grass-
root level, these lesbians managed to start viable shelters, organizations, channels for support. At some point there was always a
direct or indirect charge by someone who wanted to destroy or
render the group's activity ineffective with the charge: "This is
run by lesbians." Sometimes with the collective "I am Spartacus"
consciousness, straight women have refused to betray their
lesbian co-workers. Sometimes, however, they have allowed a
purge in order to "save" the organization. Whenever I hear of
such a purge, I think of my father's admonition: "Don't ever
believe that they fully accept you. In the end, you are still
the enemy."

A couple of years ago, within a relatively short period of time,
I demonstrated in Washington D.C. against Bakke and for affirmative action, participated in an abortion rally and marched
for a Gay Civil Rights Bill in New York City. While many of
the people at the Gay rally participated in both the Bakke and
abortion rallies, I was painfully aware how few of the other
marchers joined us in our gay civil rights struggle. Certain
issues, we seemed to be told, were only *our* issues, supported
only by us. I remember feeling a strong sense of isolation,
wondering if "they" would really defend us, homosexuals
and Jews, from concentration camps. Who were we fighting

with and for what? Who were our real friends and who were our enemies?

In these different contexts my father's Jewish "lessons" replay themselves deep inside of me. Still, I know that they are only partial truths, that they emerged from certain historical periods of specific cultures. He simplified and generalized: "You can *never* trust them. *All* non-Jews are, in their hearts, anti-Semites." By extension, he interprets *any* critical statement of *any* Israeli action as a direct, personal attack on him and on all Jews. His approach has the danger of perceiving attack where it is not, of seeing enemies where they do not exist, of defining the self so broadly that survival is always at stake. Caught in the pain of the past, my father is unable to imagine any other interpretations. He can only see history repeating itself again and again.

I have fought his vision inside of me. But in fighting it, I have frequently made myself vulnerable by not recognizing real attacks on myself and on my people. I have not wanted to see anti-Semitism when it is actually there. I have resisted accepting the fact that history *can*, and does, repeat itself.

The real lesson is how to see and act clearly. To learn from the past so that we do not repeat it, without getting stuck in the past so that we do not repeat it. To see danger when it is there, and not see it when it is not there.

One afternoon, while meditating, I found myself thinking of people I hated, visualizing some of them: the South American military terrorists; Reagan and his cabinet; the oil company presidents; the pompous white male Senators and Representatives making decisions about abortion, Legal Aid, the Family Protection Act, the Clean Air Bill. And I kept thinking, "They are evil, I will not let go of my judgment. I don't want to convince those pigs; I hate them." Since it was New Year's Day, I decided to throw the *I Ching* for an image of the year ahead, particularly for political direction. I threw the hexagram "Inner Truth" (61), which reads in part:

Pigs and fishes are least intelligent of all animals and therefore the most difficult to influence. The force of the inner truth must grow great indeed before its influence can extend to such creatures. In dealing with persons as intractable and as difficult to influence as a pig or a fish, the whole secret of success depends on finding the right way of approach. One must first rid oneself of all prejudice and, so to speak, let the psyche of the other person act on one without restraint. Then one will establish contact with him, understand and gain power over him. When a door has thus been opened, the force of one's personality will influence him.

A friend had recently shared a dream in which Adolf Eichmann appeared. Expecting to hate him, she found herself seeing him as a small, somewhat pathetic human being. Not the devil, not the incarnation of evil. His humanness bothered her. Our dreams and the *I Ching* may give us messages that we may not want to hear.

My history has taught me the danger of scapegoating, of not seeing people as human beings, of objectifying and projecting evil, of not being able—either because of pain, anger, or fear— to see what is out there, what is true. It has also shown me my own ignorance, betrayals, and scapegoating.

I have not come out to my family. I think (and I am perhaps wrong in my perception) that their guilt, shame, fear, and need to assimilate as Jews in an alien land would make my lesbianism extremely painful to them. On some level, I fear perhaps that they might even "betray" me. Yet even without my lesbianism, I have not made them happy, for I did not "Americanize" and assimilate. I went on to graduate school, taught college, did not marry or have children, lived on my rural land. On one level, I certainly seem to have "disappointed" them. But on a deeper level, I feel that they are very proud of me, very loving, very nourishing, very Jewish. This is the level of my mother's strength and wisdom, of my father's hard work and talk of the Russian *shtetl*, of both my parents' non-socialized, non-Americanized essential selves. Under the tangled web my mother's truer voice emerges, a voice which I hear and listen to: "Be strong! Be independent! Be in the world! Don't be a *shmate* for any man!"

Endnotes

[1]Charlotte Baum, Paula Hyman, and Sonya Michel. *The Jewish Woman in America* (Dial Press, 1976).

Lesbians in the International Movement of Gay/Lesbian Jews

Aliza Maggid

The Beginnings of the International Movement

A vigorous discussion followed the regular Friday night service at Congregation Beth Simchat Torah, New York's gay/lesbian synagogue. It was the fall of 1975. People were concerned and angry about the recent U.N. resolution condemning Zionism as racism and about a rising tide of anti-Jewish feeling. A woman rose to speak. "We should respond, and we should do it with other Jews. Let's call other gay and lesbian Jews together and do something about this."

A call went out for people to come to a meeting to strategize as gays and lesbians fighting anti-Semitism. On the weekend of December 5-7, 1975, groups from several East Coast cities gathered at Beth Simchat Torah. Some of the groups that were invited had been in existence for as long as four or five years, but this marked the first call for a national meeting. The gathering was successful, but even more important was the momentum gained, which led to the creation of an international conference in Washington, D.C. in 1976. Once the network was established, international conferences followed in New York City in 1977, Los Angeles in 1978, Tel Aviv in 1979, San Francisco in 1980, and Philadelphia in 1981.

There are now about twenty-three groups affiliated with the International Conference of Gay and Lesbian Jews from all over the United States and Canada, France, England, Australia and Israel. The groups vary in size, style, and purpose. Some are established synagogues, such as those in Los Angeles, San Francisco, and Miami, which are now affiliated with other United States reform congregations in the Union of American Hebrew Congregations. Others lean less toward institutional affiliation and more towards cultural or political expression. Most reflect a mixture of religious, political, social, and cultural emphases.

Jews attending the International Conference prior to 1979 tended to have a liberal political outlook. This was combined with a Middle East stance which supported a Jewish state in Israel, but had little more definition than that. Many of the conference leaders had previous experience in the gay and lesbian, feminist, civil rights, or other progressive political movements, and even more commonly, some involvement with Jewish communal life. When confronted with homophobic or anti-Semitic behavior, the organizational reaction was often activist and political. This was evident in the very formation of the organization.

There are many other examples of this activist response. The most striking are the ones that occurred in Israel after the Israeli Orthodox rabbinate attempted to force the organizers of the International Conference to cancel their meeting in 1978. The group not only held the meeting, but also participated in the first Israeli gay rights demonstration. Later that same week, they opposed the Jewish National Fund when it tried to return a nine-thousand dollar donation the group had made to an Israeli reforestation project. The International Conference continues to fight for the appropriate recognition of that donation and has not only gained organized support in the Jewish community, but has also attracted international media attention.

The Role of Lesbians

Lesbians have been active in the movement from the founding of the first gay and lesbian groups, although initially they were in a minority. At times some of the groups had only one woman; more often women constituted ten to twenty percent of the membership. This was frequently an isolating situation, however lesbians played a central role in building the first groups in Los Angeles and New York, and in each new group that followed.

As the decade progressed, lesbian participation accelerated. By the 1978 conference in Los Angeles the total number of lesbians had reached a critical mass and the first U.S. Jewish lesbian caucus was held. The caucus fomented action towards resolutions on a non-sexist liturgy, women-only workshops at future conferences, and an Equal Rights Amendment (ERA) boycott of unratified states. At the previously mentioned international Israeli conference, heavy-handed attempts by the Israeli rabbinate forced the host committee to scrap its original conference plans. Pressure put on hotels, a kibbutz, and a meeting hall led several facilities to break their contract at the last minute; these facilities had been threatened with the loss of their *kashrut* license which is an absolute economic necessity for such businesses in Israel. On the eve of the conference, a small group of people assisted the Israeli host committee in planning a new schedule. Several lesbians from the United States were central to this group. Their experience in the women's and lesbian-feminist movements were vital in assisting the group to construct a new plan and to hold a successful conference.

Israeli lesbians were among the first to speak with outrage against the actions of the rabbinate. Their organization, separate from the predominantly male conference host organization, had been active for some time in coalition with Israeli feminists and other progressive forces demanding civil rights and equal status for women in Israel. They joined with gay men in pressing for the first gay and lesbian rights demonstration. Despite the many risks they faced in showing up as lesbians at such a public event, they turned out in full force for the rally. These Israeli women also gathered with French and American women in an international lesbian caucus that was unprecedented.

In 1980, lesbian participation came of age when the San Francisco conference was evenly divided in number between gay men and lesbians. In the planning stages of this conference there had been a commitment to increase women's participation. In the process of meeting this goal, two positive trends began within the international organization. The first was a more energetic approach to outreach, encouraging participation by members of the San Francisco lesbian and gay Jewish communities-at-large, and attracting many unaffiliated individuals who worked in cooperation with the hosting congregation. From this broader base a second new trend developed: progressive and lesbian-feminist politics were introduced into the proceedings. An impromptu lesbian caucus met *prior* to the conference to work on implementing new perspectives. They drafted an equal access resolution, calling for child care, sliding fee scales, language (including sign language) interpreters, wheelchair accessibility, a community-based location, and outreach to Sephardic and poor Jews. While many of these provisions are now commonplace demands within the lesbian-feminist community (though they are not always realized), they were new to many of the conference participants. Under the circumstances, it seemed unlikely that such a resolution could pass without heavy lobbying, for which there was no time. Moreover, the inertia to maintain the status quo seemed strong, and only limited funds were available to implement the suggested changes. With little advance warning, ten lesbians approached the microphone at the closing session of the plenary. A spokeswoman argued briefly for the resolution. The chair called for a vote. A large majority of the audience of three hundred favored the resolution and it was adopted. Even the lesbian caucus was surprised at its own victory. A new era of lesbian influence was born.

This had further political repercussions. In previous years, the group had expressed almost unanimous general support for Israel, while little attempt had been made to reach agreement on a detailed Middle East statement. It was impossible to assess the viewpoints of delegates from past conferences surrounding the issue. Clearly, many were knowledgeable and felt strongly about Israel's security. Some had actually made *aliyah*, while others supported the idea of it.

At the same conference, a resolution which supported Israel but otherwise remained vague came before the membership. This disturbed a number of lesbians who were reconsidering their perspectives on Israel's claims to its territories and the rights of Palestinians to self-determination. Some of these women wanted to amend the resolution to address what they saw as serious contradictions within Israeli society: questions of sexism, homophobia, racism, classism, and Israeli-Palestinian relations. When their amendments were rejected, they voted with a few men as a vocal minority against the resolution. While causing controversy, they opened the door for genuine, multi-sided dialogue.

Lesbians with long-term involvement in the international network were taking a more visible stance. Women were the major influence on the creation of a new, non-sexist liturgy used on shabbat. Even now, when egalitarian minyans are becoming common, the sight of several lesbians standing on the bima in one of San Francisco's oldest synagogues gave a profound message about the role of women today. This again became clear when a woman chaired the debate for the election of the steering committee of the newly formed World Congress of Gay and Lesbian Jews. The winning slate was composed of two women and three men; the top position of coordinating secretary went to a woman. In response to these new developments, many Jewish gay men began to question their own roles. A workshop on men and women working together drew a full house, virtually all male. Sometimes there were conflicts and angry feelings, as when several men objected to the use of feminized Hebrew in the blessing said at meals. Throughout the weekend, whenever men and women socialized together, there was discussion of the new involvement of women.

The 1981 Philadelphia conference demonstrated a higher consciousness around the existence of sexism. Strong support was given to the continuation of the ERA boycott against unratified states, to resolutions opposing the Human Life Amendment, and for active women's leadership in all delegations (female chair for the World Congress and the plenary session). For the first time, a female rabbi gave the shabbat service sermon.

Despite the general progress in acknowledging sexism at the 1981 conference, a heated debate concerning six Middle East resolutions demonstrated that sexism had not been eradicated. Several men were very disruptive and prevented women from speaking to these resolutions. The debate eventually concluded with the opposition to the sale of the high-powered armament AWAC's and F-15's to Saudi Arabia, and support of a more general Middle East stance that included a "secure Jewish state in Israel *and* just treatment of Arabs, Jews and non-Semitic peoples in the entire Middle East."

Where Do We Go From Here?

In addition to building our own groups, we must build broad coalitions with people outside our groups. Many of our lesbian/gay groups have been successful in building alliances within the established Jewish community. A large number of gay and lesbian Jews participated in the founding conference of the New Jewish Agenda, a national progressive organization working around a broad range of Jewish issues. Beth Chayim Chadashim in Los Angeles did extensive lobbying in order to be recognized as a member congregation of the Union of Hebrew Congregations. Their groundwork led to a unanimous vote several years later on the recognition of Etz Chayim of Miami, another gay/lesbian synagogue and a similar smooth acceptance for Sha 'ar Zahav of San Francisco.

As Jewish lesbians we face increasing repression and erosion of our rights. We do not have to agree with our allies on every point in order to join in coalition around specific issues. Even when we encounter less than enthusiastic support of a lesbian/gay lifestyle, or when we encounter covert anti-Semitism in other movements, we can continue to work with people, trying to educate them in the process. This requires firmly standing up for ourselves and taking the risk of speaking out. These alliances also require introspection. For instance, as Jewish lesbians working with lesbians of color we must examine our racist assumptions and analyze how racism and anti-Semitism reinforce each other.

As new groups of Jewish lesbians form, a diversity and wealth of human resources will be brought together and put to use in the struggle against the many "-isms" that oppress all lesbians and gays, all Jews, all people of color, and all minorities.

That's Funny,
You Don't Look Like
a Jewish Lesbian

That's Funny, You Don't Look Like a Jewish Lesbian

JEB (Joan E. Biren)

In 1956 I won a prize for my sixth-grade essay on "What It Means To Be An American." It was about the Melting Pot. In this magical cauldron all the "wretched refuse" (my grandparents) would be transformed by the heat of democracy into potential Presidents. Although I later noticed that no Jews or wimmin had ever been President, I still thought I might be the first. That is part of what comes of growing up in Washington, D.C. in a white Christian neighborhood.

My parents encouraged assimilation; insisting that we celebrate Christmas because my younger sister was "too little to understand" why we would not when nearly everyone else did. At first I rebelled: celebrating Chanukah, studying to be Bat Mitzvahed at the storefront synagogue with the radical rabbi who let me carry the Torah, threatening to run off to Israel where wimmin could join the army. But then we moved from the city to the suburbs where there were more Jews. Jewish children there were expected to excel in academics, but not in popularity; to be responsible, but not beautiful; money-grubbing, but certainly not well-to-do. I rejected these stereotypes. I did not want to be restricted, and I translated this into not wanting to "act" or "look" Jewish.

I never actively denied my Jewishness, but it was easy for me to pass. I did not "need" a nose job like some of my friends and relatives. My only "problem" was the curly hair my girlfriends constantly tried to help me straighten. I did not speak with an accent like my cousins from the Bronx and Brooklyn. My father had "americanized" his name—from Birenholtz to Biren (pronounced Byron). I attended a prestigious college. All distinguishing differences were disappearing. I was going to "make it."

The story does not continue as my parents had envisioned. I am a Lesbian. My Lesbianism saved me from melting into conformist oblivion. However, it cost me the closeness I formerly received from many relatives and straight friends. While I could separate myself from them, I did not even want to think about losing my ties to other Lesbians—my new family and friends—because I was Jewish. My denial of my Jewishness was always by silence, by omission: after all, I was not a religious Jew, why bother to mention it?

After living openly as a Lesbian for more than ten years, I now have the strength to affirm my Jewishness. I realize that by facing my internalized self-hatred, I have created new energy to fight all kinds of oppression.

Affirming my Jewish identity has its own problems. After years of assimilating, passing, and dissociating myself from "those other Jews" who were *really* Jewish (*too* Jewish) comes the feeling of embarrassment of not being Jewish *enough*. If you grew up as I did, in a Christian neighborhood, you got your idea of Jewish culture where you could. One of my major sources was Harry Belafonte singing "Havah N'Gilah." Maybe like me you had never heard of the Sephardic language, Ladino, and your entire combined Yiddish and Hebrew vocabulary consists of *shalom, mishuggenah, Chanukah, oy, matzah, l'chaim,* and you cannot spell most of those. Maybe you would really like to check out the Lesbian and Gay synagogue, Bet Mis Hum Hum (Bet Mispachah), but you can't pronounce the name. So, after spending time as an outsider because of being a Jew in a gentile world, it is difficult to contemplate being an outsider as a Jew among other Jews because of not knowing enough about the culture. Can't tell *Succoth* from *Shavuoth* or *kreplach* from *knaidlach*?

I try not to worry and to learn what I can. Lots of us have missed out on big parts of our Jewish heritage. Assimilation is part of the Jewish American experience. But Jewish culture is not just one thing; it encompasses all we are. Many of us have felt different from other Jews and that feeling has helped to keep us isolated. Together we can learn about different ways of being Jewish. Each of us can decide which parts of our Jewish heritage have value for our own present lives. And, as Jewish Lesbians, we can make our own special contribution to the continual redefinition of what it means to be a Jew.

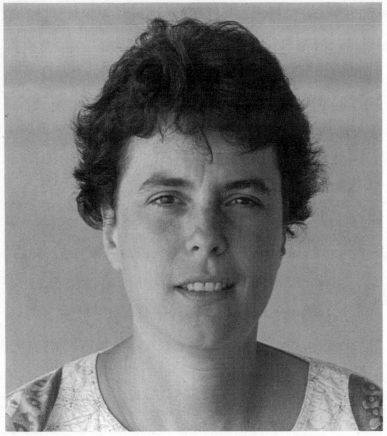

JEB, 1981

"I look more like a Jewish lesbian every day!"

Josylyn and Rachel, 1982

"When Josylyn and I met there was an immediate sense of identification. We were two passionate Third World Jews who didn't fit into the prevailing Jewish stereotypes."

Rachel Wahba

"Most American Jews think that 'looking Jewish' means fitting into the appearance, culture and lifestyles they are most familiar with, that of their immediate forebears who came from Eastern and Northern Europe. Anything else challenges the stereotypes."

Josylyn C. Segal

Leslie, 1982

"The atmosphere at the 1982 Jewish Feminist Conference in San Francisco was electric, reflecting an awareness that we were on the edge of something new: to create what it was to be Jewish/lesbian/feminist. No longer would we be defined by others. Over 1000 of us came together, the overwhelming majority of us lesbians, for three days in which we laughed, cried, fought, played, sang, and danced. We explored the nature of the world's hatred of us as Jewish women (as in the workshop I cofacilitated on internalized anti-Semitism), as well as our love for ourselves and one another as Jewish women. Six years later, I credit this historic event for the depth of pride with which I carry my Jewish identity through my continuing radical-feminist-lesbian-separatism."

Leslie Frann Levy

Evi and Nina, 1989

"I am an Ashkenazi Jew of Russian, Austrian and Polish descent. The struggle is coming to find myself as a Jew, as a lesbian, as a daughter, and as a lover-partner-*esposa*. And being open to the task."

Nina Rachel (Beck), born 1955, Pittsfield, Mass.

"I am a survivor and the daughter of survivors—a 'naturalized' American with roots in Austria, Czechoslovakia, and Poland. I am also the mother of a Jewish lesbian whose courage paved the way for me, and a wonderfully supportive son who recently gave me the gift of lesbian grandmotherhood."

Evelyn Torton Beck, born 1933, Vienna, Austria

Linda, 1987

"I am a lesbian and I am a rabbi. These are words that could not have been spoken in public very many years ago. The fact that I can say the words and not be struck by lightning gives me real hope for the future. It has taken me most of my adult life to feel integrated as a Jewish professional and as a lesbian, but now I'm feeling comfortable and proud of who I am. My partner, Betsy, and I have two sons, Jordan and Zachary. I hope that there is room both in the Jewish community and in the women's community for the life of these wonderful little boys to be celebrated."

Linda J. Holtzman

Wendy with children of the D.C. Jewish Lesbian Group, 1986

"There was a lot of shame in my family as I grew up. Many topics were rarely talked about; being Jews was one of them. I didn't explore any part of being a Jew until I grew up, came out, and on the coattails of my Jewish lover joined a group of women to form a D.C. Jewish lesbian group. As white Jewish lesbian mothers of two adopted Hispanic sons, one of our primary goals is to give our children access to both their birth culture and their adoptive culture without passing on my heritage of shame. So my lover and I have proudly taught our children—among other things—to call us both 'Mommy' (largely through my mother's encouragement) and to know that they are Jewish. Jordan was very self-assured when confronted with greetings of 'Merry Christmas' and questions about gifts from Santa. He said, 'We're Jewish. We celebrate Hanukkah. Not everyone is Christian, you know.' So far so good."

Wendy Melechen with Jordan Rolnick-Melechen

Renee, 1987

"Retired from work but not from life—I'm a political radical, activist, old, Jewish (grand)mother, lesbian lawyer. Being a Jew and female has always been a struggle. When, as a child, I was awarded the Hebrew School medal, everyone (including my parents) told me to refuse it so that a boy (the runner-up) could have it. I resisted the pressure and accepted. Ten years later, when my wonderful Zaide (*evasholm*) died, I was told that I couldn't attend his funeral because I was menstruating. I obeyed 'them' that time, but it estranged me from the Jewish religion and took me more than 30 years to 'return to the fold.' First, in 1976, I joined a gay and lesbian congregation. Then, in 1981, Havurat Achayot, a congregation of lesbian sisters was formed. We still meet, hold services, and celebrate holidays together in Chicago."

Renee Hanover

Michele, Addie, and Libby, 1985

"We're looking at our daughter Addie at her first Gay and Lesbian Pride Day in Washington, D.C. We're wondering what it will be like for her to grow up the child of two white Jewish lesbians in the United States today. Michele grew up Jewish, but Libby's family didn't learn that Libby's mother was Jewish until her mother was 65 years old and Libby was 35 years old, just a few years ago. How do we teach Addie what it means to be Jewish?"

Michele Zavos, Addie Leader-Zavos, Libby Leader

Maxine, 1977

"Anti-Semitism is everywhere; that is why I chose to wear the largest *chai* I could find for my album cover. At the 1977 International Women's Year Conference in Houston, the Ku Klux Klan had infltrated the audience. I was not the only lesbian performing, but I was the only very blatant Jew, and I was the only performer on the Seneca Falls stage who had to be protected by the Secret Service. Outside, the Klan was carrying signs: KILL ALL DYKES KIKES COMMIES AND ABORTIONISTS. Three out of four ain't bad."

Maxine Feldman

Erika, 1982

"In November, 1982 the Ku Klux Klan tried to march in Washington, D.C. Our demonstration stopped their march, but we were teargassed by the police. (My nose and mouth are covered because of the gas.) While I was wearing this sign, another demonstrator spit at me. This showed me that we still have a long way to go before we are unified in all of our struggles. As a Jewish lesbian I have had my own struggles with being accepted because I'm 'only half Jewish.' I hope that some day we will all be accepted and loved for exactly who we are."

Erika Wave

August 23, 1983

When I was first looking for Jewish lesbians to photograph, in 1980 and 1981, it was difficult to find anyone willing to identify herself publicly in this way. After *Nice Jewish Girls* was published in 1982, things began to change. But when I saw this woman with a sign saying "Another Jewish Lesbian . . ." I almost couldn't believe it. "Another"—as though we are so ordinary, as though Jewish lesbians walk around the streets all the time with big signs announcing who we are. I loved the proud feeling of this woman as she walked with the other people who had come to commemorate the 20th anniversary of the great 1963 Civil Rights March on Washington.

JEB

I am a different kind of Jew. Chaya Shoshana, 1989

"The reality of my own experience led me to redouble by efforts to become an effective educator around issues of individual differences and diversity."

Chaya Shoshana (L. Lee Knefelkamp)

Maggie (center), 1980

"It is important to me to be marching (and dancing the hora) with the Jewish lesbian contingent on Lesbian/Gay Pride Day in San Francisco, publicly proclaiming my identity as both Jew and dyke. To the anti-Semite, I am principally a Jew; to the homophobe, a dyke. To me, as I live and experience myself, Jewish and lesbian are not separate. I am not sometimes a lesbian, sometimes a Jew. I am each/both simultaneously in every moment, at all times. I wear my t-shirt declaring 'We are not just good friends' with my Star of David necklace—confronting, in a knowing way, the desexualization and denial of the true nature of women's intimate relationships. We cannot be denied."

Maggie Rochlin

Family Secrets

A Morning for Memories
Ruth Geller

In the middle of the week, Miriam Adler telephoned her sister Shelly to say that she was thinking of driving down that way, and to suggest that they get together for an early lunch. The call was not as casual as appeared, for the two women had not seen one another in six years. Miriam, in fact, had begun to suspect that she'd chosen to vacation at Cape Cod precisely because of its two hour proximity to the small town where Shelly attended college. Shelly, not having expected the call, did not know quite how to respond; she coolly offered to meet Miriam across from the university, in the diner on the hill. Miriam agreed politely, but thought: 'Why doesn't she invite me to her dorm? Why meet in a diner?'

She saw the answer as soon as she arrived. Noisy, crowded with students, the diner was an ideal setting for casual conversation with casual acquaintances and nothing more. She took a seat in a corner booth and prepared herself to wait for Shelly, placed her palms flat on the formica table, then laced her fingers together and sighed in gloomy acceptance.

Miriam was a small, energetic woman of thirty-one, and wore her coarse dark hair short, much the same way she'd worn it for twenty years. She'd found a style that suited her, and kept it. Now, however, a few stark white strands wove through the others. They were curlier than the rest, more interesting, each seeming to spotlight its own circuitous search through the dark.

At times Miriam referred to herself as "prematurely gray." The words were not an accurate description, but rather an ironic tribute of sorts to her mother, who died in her early thirties when Miriam was eight, and who was prematurely gray. Miriam had few clear memories of her mother, but remembered vividly the way she would bend over, point to her hair and say, "See that? Prematurely gray. That's you." For years Miriam had mystified this into an incomprehensible adult statement; eventually she realized that her mother meant simply (or not so simply): 'You did this to me.' It was not so much an accusation as it was a declaration of affection to the independent, rebellious child. "If I weren't so crazy about that ugly kisser of yours," her mother would say in moments of exasperation, "I'd take you right back to the gypsies who sold you to me, and I'd say, 'I don't want this kid, she's more trouble than she's worth.' "

The diner's door opened, and Miriam saw Shelly step into the foyer and pause with her hand on the glassed inner door while her eyes swept the room in careful disinterest. Miriam thought: 'I shouldn't have called her, it was a mistake,' and reached for the menu.

Shelly caught sight of Miriam, her attention apparently absorbed by the menu; and seeing her petite, smartly dressed sister, she felt a sense of physical discomfort, and wished she'd worn something different. Shelly had no sense of color or style, and no matter how she agonized over her wardrobe, she inevitably looked like she'd picked her clothes at random from a heap. Today she wore navy blue corduroy jeans and a purplish blue sweater. Her shirt was a kind of aquamarine. It all clashed slightly, but she'd decided on this outfit precisely because all of the colors were shades of blue. 'Aren't they?' she'd inquired doubtfully into the mirror of her dormitory room. Her response had been a continuation of the resentful commentary that she had played in her mind since Miriam's phone call: 'Well, what does it matter if I match or not, I shouldn't even be going! I want to hear what she has to say, that's all. Phoning me after all this time. . . what does she want from me. . . .'

Miriam looked up, and Shelly approached the table. They greeted each other politely and Shelly sat down, and after an awkward silence, they commenced to fill five minutes or so with small talk: Miriam's trip, Shelly's classes, the rural setting, and even, self-consciously, the weather. They prolonged these topics by studying their menus between comments, but after the waitress took their orders, there seemed little else to say.

Their silence was more obvious in comparison to the other tables where customers, mostly college students, talked, laughed, called across the room to each other. When Shelly's eyes met Miriam's they did so reluctantly; otherwise, they were riveted on various inanimate objects: the stainless steel milk dispenser, the cash register, the transparent glass of water before her.

They had ordered sandwiches, and as the waitress approached with their plates, Shelly said almost to herself, "I think I'll get some buttermilk."

"Oh," Miriam remarked, "that's what *I* was going to get," meaning to imply that they had tastes in common.

Shelly misunderstood and replied tartly: "I'm sure they have enough for two glasses," and gave the order to the waitress.

It was precisely at this point, when Miriam decided to think of an excuse for an early departure, that Shelly asked, "So why did you want to come and see me?"

"Well. . ." Miriam began, but confronted by Shelly's tight-lipped visage, did not know what to say. "It's hard to put it into words with you looking at me like that."

Shelly's expression did not change, and Miriam thought, 'Oh God, it *was* a mistake to come.' She said, "Is it my misperception, or are you angry at me."

Shelly's face was masked by unconcern. "I'm not angry. Why should I be angry. I mean. . . how long has it been since I've even *seen* you."

"Six years."

"Six years," Shelly repeated, as if it proved a point. "Well, that's a long time. I mean, a person up and leaves. . . *How* long ago was it that you left home?" She sounded like a teacher annoyed at her stupid students.

"Thirteen years," Miriam answered, trying to soften her own annoyance with a dry smile.

"Thirteen years," Shelly repeated, as if to say: *Now* do you understand? In case Miriam did not, she summed up her point: "In the past thirteen years, I saw you once, at Daddy's funeral, right?"

The waitress brought the buttermilk. Shelly downed half of hers, put the glass roughly on the table, and waited for Miriam to respond.

"I didn't exactly 'up and leave—' you know," Miriam said evenly.

"Oh no? What would *you* call it?" Shelly asked without emotion, and began eating.

"I didn't have much choice in the matter."

"Mm-hmm."

Miriam reached for the buttermilk and took a sip, and gazed at the thick white liquid. "Tell me something. What do you know about me."

"Not a whole lot. . . . How can I *know* anything about you."

"What I mean is. . . . what did Daddy tell you about me. About why I left."

"Nothing. He said you left, that's all. One morning I got up and he said, 'Miriam's gone, she won't be back.' "

"Well as a matter of fact, it couldn't have happened like that because you weren't at home when I left. You and your mother were staying with her sister Hannah in Chicago. Your mother thought she had leukemia, and she went in to Chicago to see a specialist. Didn't you know that?"

Shelly had taken another bite of sandwich and was in the midst of chewing when Miriam said the word "leukemia"; her jaws stopped for a moment before continuing to chew slowly, as she waited for more information.

"Turned out she was all right," Miriam went on. "The test results came back a couple weeks later." She smiled. "So really, that whole weekend was. . . ." She shook her head and held her hands out in a shrugging gesture, at a loss for words. "As it turned out, I was gone by Sunday morning. You came back that night." She paused, but Shelly did not comment. "So that's all he told you, that I wouldn't be back? Didn't you ask why?"

"Yes. And he told me that you didn't want to live with us anymore."

"Oh, *that's* nice. But it's not exactly the truth. What *happened* was that he said to me," and she recited, "that if I wanted to live in his house, I'd live by his rules. And I didn't want to live by his rules, so I left."

Shelly put a forkful of cole slaw into her mouth, listening.

"God. . . ." Miriam said, and shook her head. "I haven't thought about that weekend in years. . . . He always fell apart in a crisis."

Shelly put down her fork. "What happened that weekend?" she asked, but Miriam seemed not to have heard.

She was looking down at the formica table and smiling. "I remember one time the plumbing broke. I think the pipes froze or something. I was about thirteen. You must've been about three." As though suddenly aware of what a ten year age difference meant, she paused for a moment and stared at the younger woman, then went on: "I remember I woke up in the middle of the night and there was all kinds of commotion, water was spurting out of the handle on the kitchen faucet, and Daddy was acting like the world was coming to an end. And there was your mother, sitting at the kitchen table, looking up plumbers in the yellow pages and saying, 'Irving, go turn off the main water line.' "

Shelly smiled slightly. "And what did Daddy do?"

"Oh, he was going nuts. He was saying, 'The water line! The water line! Where's the water line!' "

Shelly grinned. "Yeah, he used to really get shook up about
things. What did my mother do then?"

"She just sat there with the phone book, saying, 'The water
line is in the cellar. Go get the wrench. . . .' and he said, 'The
wrench! The wrench! Where's the wrench!' "

Shelly laughed. "She should've done it herself."

"Ooh, are you kidding? Not unless she's changed a lot. . . ."

"No, I suppose you're right. Mom *is* a kind of 'lady.' "

"You better believe it. The house could be floating down the
street and she'd be saying, 'Irving, you're making me nervous,
Irving. Go and get the wrench. . . .' "

Shelly laughed again; but she was thinking, 'She's just like
Daddy, never can answer a question right out, always got to
take you on some involved detour. . . .' The laugh was a polite
offering to Miriam, who she knew had expected it, and it was
barely out of her mouth before she cut it off with an impatient:
"So what was the crisis that made him fall apart that weekend."

Miriam nodded slowly. "Right," she said, and nodded once
again. "It's funny. . . . Years later I understood that it had to do
with a lot of other things besides me, like him being upset about
your mother, and being afraid that he'd have to face everything
alone if she was sick, if she was going to die. . . ."

"Face what?" Shelly demanded, and began tapping her foot
impatiently under the table.

"Well. . . you see, this old friend of Daddy's came to see
him. I'll never forget it, I came home Saturday night about five,
and there's Joe sitting in the living room, and I thought, 'You
bastard, you went and did it.' "

"*What* did he do."

"You see, Joe was part owner in a bar, and that Friday night
he'd seen me there." She paused to give Shelly a chance to ask,
'What *kind* of bar,' but Shelly was silent. "I'd just started hanging around in this bar," Miriam went on, "and all the crowd
used to talk about this guy they called 'Joe the Walrus.' They
hated him because he used to charge a buck to get in, and it was
a dinky, run-down place. A dollar was a lot of money in those
days, especially to us, most of us were just kids out of high
school. God, those were the days. . . . Well, one night, it was
that Friday night, somebody said, 'There's Joe the Walrus,' and
I turned around and it was Daddy's friend from the old days."
Miriam shook her head. "I thought I'd die right then and there.
I wanted to melt into the floor. I remember thinking, 'This guy
has the power to change my life.' And the next day when I

walked in and saw him with Daddy, I thought, 'You bastard, you went and did it.' " She paused, waiting for the right moment; and when Shelly's eyes were cast down onto her plate and she was picking up her sandwich, Miriam said deliberately, "There was no need to tell Daddy at all, Joe didn't even know why I was there. But he was a real sicky. It never failed to amaze me that a guy who hated queers so much would own a gay bar."

To allow Shelly a moment to react, Miriam picked up her fork, poked around at her cole slaw, and slid the fork under a few shreds of cabbage. When she looked up, she found Shelly staring curiously at her.

Shelly blushed, and looked down.

Miriam continued speaking. "I think it would've been different had your mom been there. But Daddy blew up. I mean, we weren't on the best of terms anyway. You know?"

Shelly hadn't been listening, and nodded blankly. She liked to think of herself as open-minded, yet felt distinctly uncomfortable. Wanting to deny that Miriam being. . . what she was. . . made any difference, she smiled, looking for the first time directly into Miriam's eyes.

Miriam knew that smile, and did not return it. "Well, we got into a whopper of a fight that Saturday night. And when he told me to get out by morning, I said to him 'I'll get out and you'll never see me again.' And that was exactly what happened." Her eyes filled with angry tears; she clenched her jaws, pressing her lips together. "Stupid. We were both stupid. Stupid and stubborn," she said, and put a forkful of cole slaw into her mouth.

They ate in silence: Miriam frowned, and chewed absentmindedly, Shelly chewed quickly and automatically. Shelly pretended to watch the short order cook behind the counter, but every so often she glanced out of the corner of her eye at her sister.

When Miriam had swallowed the one mouthful, she did not take another, seeming to have forgotten the food. She looked at the sandwich, her eyes unfocused. On the other side of the booth someone sat down heavily; Miriam started lightly, blinking. Then she sighed, and smiled vaguely. "Ah well, it doesn't pay to have regrets. Regrets are the number one cause of ulcers, did you know that, Shel?"

"Shel," Miriam's nickname for her little sister, originated one day when she was tickling Shelly, poking at her ribs, squeezing her knees, all the while saying, "Ooh, look at this Shel, it's nothing but a hard shell. Doesn't anybody live inside? Think I'll knock on the shell and see if anybody's home. . . ." while with her knuckles she tickled the giggling, squirming child.

Miriam did not notice she'd used the name.

But Shelly noticed. "Were you always. . . ." She hesitated, wanting Miriam to finish the sentence, or understand it as it was, and answer it; as Miriam said nothing, Shelly lowered her voice instinctively and asked: ". . . gay?"

Miriam suppressed a smile. "Well, not *always*. . . . "

"No, I know. But. . . when you lived at home?"

Miriam nodded. "When I was older."

Shelly frowned, and searched her memory. . . .

"Why. Does it matter?"

"Oh no," she answered too quickly, with too much conviction.

This time Miriam smiled outright. "Or at least you don't *think* it does. . . ."

Shelly blushed, and continued eating.

Miriam sipped her buttermilk.

"How did you know where to find me?" Shelly asked.

"I got the address from your mother."

"Oh."

"She doesn't seem to have changed at all over the years."

"No, she hasn't. . . ." Shelly smiled in affectionate dismay.

"First thing she asked me after 'How are you,' was: 'Are you married yet?' "

Shelly groaned, laughing.

"Yes. . . . You know, it's funny in a way. . . . She and I, we never got along. I suppose it was because we each had such strong ideas about what the other should be. I mean, *my* mother was kind of. . . rough. You know? She was strong and very determined. And about me, she was very superstitious. You know what the Evil Eye is? Well, she was always afraid that if the Evil Eye knew how much she loved me, it'd get jealous and try to hurt me. So when she was giving me these big hugs. . . you know those big hugs you're always trying to escape from when you're a kid?"

"Mm-hmm. . . ."

"Well, the bigger the hug she'd give me, the worse things she'd say, like: 'You're such a rotten kid, who'd want you. . . .' So to *me* a mother was somebody rough, but somebody who loved you like crazy. And your mother. . . ."

"Is a lady," Shelly supplied.

"Right. And on *her* part, I suppose my father had told her how wonderful it would be, she'd have a ready made little girl. He was such a wonderful con artist. . . . I never was exactly a 'little girl,' if you know what I mean. Not like *she* expected. Or wanted. . . ." Miriam looked at Shelly, the unmatched clothes, the hefty body, the face bare of make-up. "Did she get one in you?"

Shelly sighed in acknowledgment of her own failures. "No. She's always after me to lose weight, to wear make-up. . . . She thinks I'm a disaster area."

Miriam smiled. "You're not a disaster area. Thank you for coming." She would have liked to reach over and pat Shelly's hand, if only in a brisk and unmistakably sisterly way, but restrained herself.

"You're welcome," Shelly said a bit formally, and asked: "But if you don't mind me asking, why did you want to see me?"

Miriam drummed her fingers several times in a deliberate manner on the table. "Did you ever go through the old picture albums? The really old ones, the ones that are falling apart."

'Oh God,' Shelly thought, 'I can't *stand* it, where is she going now. . . .' Accordingly, she presented a silent face to her sister, as though trying to block this new detour.

Miriam, however, did not need prompting. "Well, there's a picture of Daddy and my mother when they first started dating. It must've been after the war, around 1948 or so. They're standing in front of an old Buick—I think it was Daddy's first car. . . . It's really a nice picture. I wanted to ask if you'd get it and send it to me, I'd like to have it." She smiled. "They look like a couple of kids. Blackie and Rose," she murmured.

"Who?" Shelly asked.

"*Who*. . . ." Miriam repeated, bewildered. "What do you mean, *who*."

"Who are Blackie and Rose."

"Daddy," Miriam said. "And my mother." The two women looked at each other without comprehension until Miriam realized, 'She doesn't know *any*thing,' and as if to prove this to be the case, Shelly asked: "Why do you call him Blackie, his name was Irving."

Miriam thought, 'Oh well, I suppose there's no harm now. . . .' and explained, "In those days, he was known as Blackie."

"But why?"

"I'm not really sure. I used to think it was one of those mob names."

"Mob. . . ."

"Yeah, you know, like. . . Scarface, or. . . Fingers. But then later on, I suspected Daddy picked the name himself because Blackie sounds like such a tough guy, and I guess he didn't think anybody in the rackets would take him seriously if his name was Irving."

"*Rackets*. . . . What are you talking about, rackets."

Miriam had been gazing down, reflecting, and didn't seem to hear the questions. "I remember how Zadie hated that name. He used to say it with such. . . contempt. He thought Daddy was a bum. God, they *never* got along. But then Zadie. . . ." She looked at Shelly. "You didn't know Zadie, did you."

"No. He died before I was born."

Miriam nodded. "Well, he was a real old time Jew. A very religious man. He thought America was. . . Babylon. And when he saw how *Daddy* acted, God, he *really* believed it." There was a sad and ironic expression on her face. "He oughta see *me*. . . ." She sighed in resignation. "Oh well. . . ."

Shelly was frowning. "But what do you mean when you say 'mob' and 'rackets'? Daddy was an antique dealer."

Miriam smiled gently. "I hate to break your bubble, dear, but how do you think a slum kid like him *got* all those classy antiques. When he started out, he didn't know a Tiffany lamp from a lava-lamp, but when somebody wanted to get rid of something fast, he had to know what it was so he'd know how much to pay, and where to sell it without any problems. So he learned about antiques."

"Wait a minute, are you saying that Daddy was a fence?"

"Well. . . let's just say he dabbled. I mean, he wasn't Al Capone or anything. He was more like. . . a dabbler. You know, a little bit of this, a little bit of that. . . ."

Shelly's frown deepened. "How do *you* know all this. . . ."

Miriam lifted her hands in a shrugging gesture, as if the answer were obvious. "How do I know," she said. "I pushed the button."

"*What* button."

Miriam folded her arms one over the other, leaning forward slightly on the table. "Daddy used to have a little shop over near Allen Street, you know the area I mean? And in the back of the place there was this phoney wall, and behind the wall there was a back room that was connected on the one side to Joe's Barber Shop, and on the other, to a second-hand bookstore." She spoke in a leisurely manner, emphasizing certain words with her tone, or with her hands. One hand would lift, or the other, or both, as though she were serving up the words, before resting again in the crook of her elbow. "And the three of them, Daddy, Joe, and the other guy, they had all kinds of things back there, a table where they'd shoot craps and play poker on, and a phone, and a two-way radio so the races'd come in and they'd know right away who won. . . ."

"You mean Daddy was a *bookie*!?"

"Well. . . like I said, he was a dabbler."

Shelly looked skeptical. "And what *button* did you push . . . ."

"I used to watch the store after school, and if anybody came in and asked for Daddy, I'd say he just stepped out. And meanwhile I'd press a little button under the desk. A buzzer would ring in the back room, and Daddy would look out through a peep-hole in the wall to see who it was. If he didn't want to see the person, he'd stay in the back room, but if he wanted to see them, he'd walk out through Joe's Barber Shop, and stroll in the door like he'd just come from having a shave. And he was so cool and unconcerned, and meanwhile you knew his mind was going tickticktick. . . ."

She paused, and when she spoke again, her voice was bitter: "That Joe was a bastard, I never *did* like him. One time I was in the store and Daddy had to go someplace. I was only about fourteen, and Joe came in and put the make on me, you know, 'If you're a good girl, I'll treat you right' while he tried to put his hands on my ass. . . I told him, I said, 'You ever try anything like that again, I'll tell my father, he'll kill you.' He would've, too, Daddy would've killed him. I mean, I was fourteen years old. But from that day on, I knew that sooner or later, Joe'd get back at me." She raised her eyebrows. "And he certainly did."

"How?"

"When he told Daddy about me being at the gay bar. I'm sure he made what we were doing sound worse than it was. We were just a bunch of kids sitting around drinking beer, it was no big deal."

"But. . . *weren't* you gay?"

Miriam raised her eyebrows. "That's irrelevant. I didn't deserve to lose my *home* over it." She smiled questioningly at Shelly, as if to ask: Did I?

Shelly flushed again, and picked up her sandwich. "How much of this does my mother know."

"Nothing, as far as I know. He was a whiz at keeping secrets. *And* holding *grudges*," she added sourly.

"Does she know about you?"

"I don't know. I don't think so. Ask her and see."

Shelly nodded slowly, her thoughts already on another question, one that had not been answered. "But why did you want to see me?"

The fingers of Miriam's right hand were curled around the empty glass of buttermilk, and she rotated it, gazing at the thick residue clinging to the inside of the glass. The pattern reminded her of a rippled beach at low tide. "I wanted to ask you some questions, but now that I'm here, I'm not really sure what they were. It's just that. . . ." She smiled at Shelly ironically. "When you're an aged rebel like me, you begin to get curious about the past that you so thoroughly rejected."

She stopped smiling. "That night, that Saturday night when we had that terrible fight, I said a lot of things. . . things that later I was sorry about. And Daddy said a lot of things about family, about. . . . what it meant to be a Jew. . . . At the time, I remember I thought he was a terrible hypocrite: telling *me* about family, and being a Jew, and look at the way he'd lived *his* life, the way he'd treated Zadie, and what he'd done to my mother. I mean, he'd done everything he could to *not* care about family. To not be a Jew. . . . But after I went away, after a long time, I realized that he'd been speaking from experience. He'd learned the hard way, because by then, Zadie was dead, my mother was dead. . . ."

She sighed, but in a moment felt self-conscious, as though she'd found herself expressing her deepest feelings to a stranger. She looked down at her plate. "Look at me, I've been talking your ear off so much, I haven't even finished my sandwich. Oh well, no sense in letting it go to waste." She snapped several napkins out of the container and began wrapping the sandwich.

Shelly laughed. "Daddy used to do that all the time, and my mother would get so mad. She'd tell him that we *had* food at *home*. And he'd say that he didn't care what people thought, he paid for it and he was taking it."

"Oh, baloney, don't let him fool you, he cared all right. Although. . . maybe he changed. I remember. . . . Do you remember his Aunt Molly?"

"Aunt Molly? I don't think so."

"Oh. Well, she lived with us for a while, maybe it was before you were born. She'd just come to America. She was a very educated woman. . . but whenever we'd go out to eat, Molly used to take a couple packets of sugar and stash 'em in her pocketbook. And rolls, too. Daddy used to get so embarrassed! He'd sit there and he'd say, 'Cut it out, Tanta Molly, we have plenty at home.' And she used to say something about sugar being a luxury you couldn't have too much of. When she left, she said to Daddy, 'All your *kvetching*, and look, you got sugar to last a month.' "

Shelly was smiling.

Miriam was looking at, but not seeing, the blank space of table near the sugar bowl. "I remember once Tanta Molly was reaching for the sugar, and I saw some numbers on her wrist. I asked her what they were, and she looked at me—I was just a little girl—and she said, 'That's so I won't forget who I am. . . .' "

Miriam paused, and the diner's careless clatter filled the silence. Shelly was sorry for having chosen this to be their meeting place.

But Miriam seemed to be listening to something else. She smiled and said, "I remember how Tanta Molly used to call me her little *lokshen kugel*. . . . You know, when I think of these things at home, they make me sad. But sharing them, it's different. Maybe that's why I came to see you."

Shelly said, "I hope you come to see me again, Minnie."

Miriam smiled. For a time in high school, she'd fancied herself a beatnik; and with her skinny leotarded legs and big sneakers, she'd reminded Shelly of Minnie Mouse. Sometimes, when they walked down Western Avenue, and Miriam described the thrilling adventures all around them, they were Minnie and Shel, the Great World Explorers.

Shelly asked, "Remember that little deli on Western Avenue, the one we used to pretend was our way station, and we'd stop and get supplies for the rest of our journey. . ." and Miriam smiled.

They sat a while longer and talked a bit more, but it was getting late and each had her own life to return to. Miriam paid the bill (while Shelly, feeling childishly awkward, protested) and they left the diner. They made sure to exchange addresses and phone numbers, and standing on the hill, made sad jokes about hating goodbyes.

Shelly walked down the hill, a touching vision in clashing blues. Watching her, Miriam finally understood what it was she'd wanted from her sister. There was a question she'd had to ask, and she'd found the answers in herself.

The question and the answers were like sweet mournful songs that had been all along inside her: she was Minnie the Explorer, and Molly's *lokshen kugel*; she was her father's rebel girl, and the gypsy child her mother could not bear to give away. She was an observer of her Zadie's righteous wrath. And she was Miriam. She smiled, wondering why she had not seen these simple things before.

The Tree of Begats
Martha Shelley

When they offered me the glass
I turned it down.

The baby sucked a rubber nipple
dipped in wine, and fell asleep again.
Brand-new, red-faced nephew
covered with the fuzz of monkey ancestors,
thrust from a tropical womb
into a blue flannel blanket.
The rabbi tried to bring my godson
closer to the angels,
cutting off that other vestige of an ape,
the little sheath of skin around his cock.

These clean-shaven rabbis merely pretend to reform,
saying in English, "Thank God for a healthy child"
and in the ancient tongue
". . . for giving us a son as our firstborn."

The women, in vernacular,
clustered around a tray of cocktail franks,
glancing sideways at my track shoes
visible beneath a velvet pants suit.
The glass came round.
"All those who want sons, drink,"
the rabbi said. They sipped a bit.
I turned it down.

"Hey, Ma," I said, "I have a radio show."
"Cousin Lynne, I wrote these poems."
"Dad, hey listen, Dad,
I got a yellow belt in my karate class."
"Hey, Ma . . .?"

The women cornered me around the canapes.
"It's your turn now."
"When are you going to make your mother
twice a grandma?"
No way. My womb, like my fist,
is clenched against the world.

Kid sister, I remember being three,
climbing the bars of your crib
teaching you to clap
and sing some garbled Yiddish rhyme.
You asked the wishing well
for a red pinafore.
I, for a microscope.

We rattle around in different cages now.
You almost became your mother's daughter.
I am each day less the wandering lesbian
my father dares not own.

Our eyes meet over a barricade
of sanctified penises
and I ask myself why sisterhood
sometimes feels like a wine glass
crushed in my fist.

The Fourth Daughter's Four Hundred Questions
Elana Dykewomon

*This story was written for lesbians. It is a more or less chron-
ological account of the questions being a jewish dyke has put
me up against in my life.*

*I originally wrote it in response to a letter from Evelyn Beck
announcing this anthology, as I had been thinking about the
issues involved for some time, and had many thoughts to share
with other lesbians about them. After I found out that the anthology was not going to be distributed for womyn-only, I decided not to print this story in it, and instead distributed it in
xerox form.*

*I changed my mind about being included in this anthology
for several reasons, but I still believe very strongly that by stat-
ing for whom we write or work, and why, we help to define our
own work as well as to encourage the growth of lesbian net-
works. I have a lot else to say on that subject, but that's all I
want to say here. I still think this anthology should be distributed
to womyn only.*

*But I choose to be included in it for the following reasons.
Other jewish lesbians who had read the story in its xeroxed
form thought it was important to include. I perceive that this
will be the "source book" on judaism within the lesbian community for some time, and I know that the range of separatist
thought on racial, cultural, and other political issues is too often
discounted by other lesbians because of its absence. Too, having
had a section of* Riverfinger Women *released by non-jewish
women for inclusion in a multi-national corporation's anthology
of "jewish women writers," without my knowledge or consent,
made me want to print what I had to say for myself about being
jewish-born, clearly, and by intent.*

*It is a dangerous business in a dangerous time, working for
lesbians and affirming any racial heritage in white america. I believe two things at once. The first is that we need to take our-*

selves more and more seriously, our work, our communities, our enjoyment, our love, and the danger in which that love places us. The second is that it is crucial to say, yes, I am a lesbian and I am a jew whenever it is necessary to be counted. I felt it was necessary to be counted here.

She was six or seven. She was having trouble with the four questions. Her father beat her. He beat her in the house, and he beat her again on their way to the grandparents. It was hard to learn, she was not good at languages. They made fun of her singing. She was told to go to the guest room until she had memorized it. Later on the guest room would be filled by the coats and smells of twenty women, aunts, great aunts, first second third and fourth cousins. The aunts would dab perfume behind their ears, and unwrap boxes of chocolate matzahs.

She does not know if she dreamt this, but she remembers that Bartons also made a box of chocolate pops in the image of the "four sons." She remembers them clearly, their little chocolate heads with big eyes and yarmulkes staring out of the cardboard filler. In the passover service there is a section on how a man must instruct his sons, and there are four kinds of sons a man may have. She had no choice but to be a son, then, since the aunts were all busy cleaning, carrying, cooking, and there was nothing for a girl to do but open the door for elijah or learn to sing the four questions which the modern age had rendered genderless, to expand the role of the girl child in religion. But a man does not really have daughters, which is true enough.

A man, a jewish man, tells the passover story to his sons. The first is he who does not know how to ask at all (because he will be a laborer, you must treat him gently); the second, he who asks simply (for he will be a dentist, you must tell him only what he can understand); the third, he who asks in detail (because he will be a rabbi, you must encourage him, explaining everything). But the fourth son asks, "What does this mean to you?" Because the fourth son says "you" and not "us," he is called the wicked son, and you must say to him, "it means the Lord God saved me from Egypt." You must say "me" and not "us," for had he been there, he would not have been saved. He would have been an outsider among his people, excluding himself from the life all jews have in common. She remembers, twenty-three years later, how she bit the head off the chocolate fourth son, how then he was inside her, watching the dinner go on.

There were forty people at the table. "Listen to my daughter sing the four questions, go ahead, now, stand up." She sang. She clenched and sang. The only sounds beside her voice were the distant preparations of the black women in the kitchen. "Why is tonight different from all other nights?" Because tonight we eat reclining, to remind us that we are free men. You must say men because that is how it is written. And that is what it means. The aunts bring bowls for the uncles to wash their hands in. Only men may wash. Only grandfather and one great uncle, the rabbi, have pillows. Go on. Eat your soup. Eat your gefilte fish. Your grandmother stood on her feet for three days to make it.

Then suddenly the meal is over and there is the singing. There are songs at the end of the passover book. Judy stands up. The grownups are a little drunk. Everyone loved Judy, or all the men loved Judy, who was her father's cousin. She was a good wife and a good mother, she was one of them and she was a prize, handsome, smart, obedient without being servile. Judy raised her arms. She sang in yiddish, the way Judy's mother had sung while still alive. She threw her head back. Yubabuy, yubabuy, yubbababababababuy! Yubabahba hipbah! Yubabahba hipbah! Yubbababababababuy! Judy snapped her fingers and the muscles in her naked arms jumped.

She remembers this. Judy threw her head back and sang and moved her shoulders, snaked her shoulders in an ancient mediterranean joy. Then Judy patted her on the head before sitting down again beside her husband, before helping later with the dishes.

It is not supposed to be so obvious.

How can it not be obvious?

You must suppress half the facts to avoid sounding blatant. Coming on too strong. Being a spoil sport. After all, you want to leave only the impression. There are woman slaves and behind them another line of woman slaves, and now and then a willing captive princess. Once you may see her in your childhood throw back her head and move as if she were a free womon in her own land. Then she returns to her place. Only brushing the top of your hunger. Startling you awake for a second. O let me leave this feast with you and start a new ritual. But then you are seven, and Judy is old enough to be your mother. So you wish she was your mother. It is the only available choice. Made in secret, by an outsider, the wicked one. While the singing goes on, in yiddish and hebrew.

Her grandmother said in the backyard, "Are you glad you're a girl?" Her brother, the new baby, was screaming in his bassinet, because the men had gathered in yarmulkes to cut off his foreskin. There was a big party for it. The men were happy, drinking, the baby was crying, her mother was walking around trying not to look tired and weak, although she was, tired, weak, and angry about something. "No," she said. Her grandmother pursed her lips. "Why not?" She remembers that she said, "Because when boys grow up they can hitchhike."

It is not only inside itself but outside itself. At first they lived on a block where everyone was jewish, except for one family down the street that was only half jewish and you didn't go play with their children. No one said that you shouldn't but you didn't want to anyway. You didn't want to. Then her family moved to puerto rico when she was eight, and there were no jews in her neighborhood. In her class there was one. The rest were in hebrew school with her, three afternoons a week. In the old synagogue, protected from the road by a row of giant tropical trees. It was very hot upstairs in the classrooms. Her father was delighted when he said her teacher was a sabra, a native israeli. "Now you kids will really learn hebrew." You may say it is a mistake to put in here how he beat her when she could not learn her hebrew grammar. It is not particularly representative of the general fact of her gender. It is only representative of men, after all. He beat her anyway, even if it is not relevant. Among jews there are never manys, only fews, gathering together. Trying to phrase their new questions.

She stood on the stairs of the synagogue. It reminded her of her grandmother's hallway in new york city. Large, old, strange, smelling different, her grandmother's always smelled like chicken soup, even out in the hallway. The temple smelled like oiled wood baking in the heat, smelled like refugees from europe who had become prosperous, but did not look so prosperous on saturday mornings, dark suited, wearing tallises, mumbling along with the rabbi, knowing every word, the murmur rising in the humid air along the banisters. We are different, she thought, caught there on the stairwell, watching the praying men. We are

all different from other people, outsiders, a spy reporting only
to memory, to the sense of difference upon difference. What
does this mean to you? It means if you had been there you
would not have been saved, even though you lived among them,
and did not run screaming down the aisles of the temple in the
middle of sabbath services when you could not stand it anymore, you would not have been saved in egypt even though
you followed in the *siddur* and learned the songs. On the other
hand, you would have gone to the camps, no matter what
you said, you would have been thrust into the boxcars, and
only later did you learn you would have gone first, before
the jews, wearing a pink triangle on your clothes, while your
own family would have watched you go, believing they would
not take the real citizens, the working men, the mothers and
fathers.

And afterwards, every saturday, she would go down to the
house behind the temple, and the rabbi's wife would feed her
lunch, kiss her, as she played with the rabbi's daughter. She did
not go because of the daughter (who taught her to keep score
at scrabble using a thick book and a piece of paper to mark
your total, instead of writing, writing being against the sabbath
rules). She went because of the warm face of the *rebbitzin*,
the way she enjoyed her, encouraged her to show off, the way
she loved her. In her fantasies she developed a secret machine
that turned her from a young girl crippled in an accident where
her whole family was killed (and so had been adopted by the
rebbitzin), into a young man who could walk, who led a secret
life of exciting crime, and with whom the *rebbitzin* could not
help but fall in love. Only she and the *rebbitzin* knew the secret
of the machine where she was changed from child to lover.

Because she was eleven then, and knew nothing besides desire. To be among those womyn throwing their heads back singing. The warmth grown jewish women have in their smiles, some
womon thing that feeds the child. This difference within a difference will make me crazy, she thought. Will make them hate
me.

The crazy years followed. When they had to drug her with
thorazine so that she would wear stockings and a girdle to her
classmates' bar mitzvahs. Many years later, her own mother
had said, in a traffic jam crossing the brooklyn bridge, "The
doctors never did decide what was wrong with you." "What was
wrong with me was that I was born a lesbian," she said. Her

mother flushed a little. "Well I wouldn't exactly say that," she said, as if it were unthinkable that she, who herself had grown up in a kosher household, whose own grandfather had all the toilet paper pretorn on friday so that no one would have to tear toilet paper in his house on the sabbath, could give birth to this throwback, this holdout, this dyke.

To identify as a crazy gives you a home among the crazies. To identify as a jew only gives you a home among the jews. To identify as a lesbian gives you no peace. To choose to be a lesbian separatist places you back among the crazies, who will not have you, and with whom you could not stay, even if they would. To be a lesbian separatist remembering the jews, the jews from which you came and whom you carry in you, makes you remember over and over again being an outsider among outsiders, even when you feel a center, a sense of self that is strong and sure, a clear understanding of all your choices.

Because you were born among them. Because she threw back her head singing. Because your father beat you, outside the temple, on simchas torah. Because you remember the names of all the holidays and you remember that one of your great grandfathers, because he was a rabbi, was dragged by his beard through a small latvian town until he was dead. Then it was up to your great grandmother to take care of the children, to find ways for them to survive, to protect. Because during the last oil crisis there were bumper stickers that read "burn jews, not oil." Because you were the wrong daughter. You had trouble with hebrew. You balked, you ran away, you would not be bat mitzvahed, you did not want to date, you wanted to be strong and alone, if you could not go home with the rabbi's wife, with your cousin Judy. Because once you did go home with your cousin Judy but she did not turn to you in warmth, in recognition, in welcome. She taught you how to make the beds in her house. She told you that there was no question that she loved her husband. That that was what counted.

It is difficult to explain this. She was fifteen, sixteen, seventeen, eighteen, nineteen. She was difficult then. She was the wrong daughter. She was going to school away from her family. Her nonjewish teachers taught her the literature of christian symbolism as the standard by which classics are measured. Her jewish schoolmates took her home on holiday weekends and she was in love with them. One by one she lay in their beds and heard them talk about their brothers and their boyfriends. But a certain light came from them. A certain heat from their thighs which brushed together only accidentally in the most shadowed part of the night. Those girls who did not yet know themselves as slaves.

She was attracted so many times to straight jewish women. That later, when she was still doing it in her twenties she had to say that it was because they were what she was not, but was supposed to have been. A form of primal narcissism. She said that to her italian catholic friend, but she did not believe it, because it was too obvious. After all, one of them had turned out to love her back, even if it didn't last.

There was another thing in it. Or many. First, they were still around straight women, and the straight women loved to lap up that lesbian attention, to flirt with it, and then go home to their boys. Second, she did not yet know many jewish lesbians. And there was something in the jewish women she hungered for besides identification with the straight ideal. One of them later said it was their sense of humor. Another said it was because of the education. Another, that it was a shared value. A value of what? A value of education, she answered. A value of the outsider. But not all of them saw themselves as outsiders, not all of them could say, outside of what.

She had been working at the women's center, every wednesday, with Wendy. Then they went camping in maine. Wendy lived with a man who ran a jewish day camp in the summer. Wendy had been brought up catholic, although she did not discuss it. They were still somewhere in the middle of sisterhood-is-powerful. Around three a.m., on the drive back, Wendy said that she had converted to judaism, because it was against her principles to get married, so she had made that compromise, to make the relationship with her man more easy. What right have you to think you know, Wendy? What a jewish womon is? What right have you to voluntarily join the ranks of slaves when I have spent my whole life rolling in specific jewish anger and pain? What right have you, woman who has worked beside me, to choose to bind yourself to some prick and leave me here alone again? Using a memory that doesn't even belong to you, using my past to do it?

That same year Linda wrote, who had been her college roommate, who had saved her from suicides and held her while she cried, and encouraged her lesbianism since it was not against the california ethic to be queer. But then, a couple of years out of college and Linda started to study talmud, she said it was a pleasure to know the seventy two hundred rules, and you know, it's the seventies, it doesn't matter that the prayers read "thank god i'm not a woman," that's different. Linda came from a family that did not much practice judaism. It was a common thing, that those women began going backwards, having been lost in the melting pot, longing for an at least personalized submission. Linda wrote to say she finally found the boy she wanted to marry, he was a rabbi, they were moving from berkeley to kansas. She wrote to Linda that she never wanted to talk to her again. She had had enough. From the jewish women she had hungered for, from the catholic and christian straight women she had loved. Write when you come out. She said the same thing to Wendy, Miriam, Sarah, Cecily, Amy, Cordelia, and refused every time her cousin Judy invited her to her daughters' weddings. The old warm moment is worn out, girls. A slave who loves her master has nothing to give the outlaw.

And the outlaws? She was then twenty-six, and the womon she loved said, I don't know if a jew and a catholic can live together and survive it. Many tried, it seemed to her, many jews and catholics to live with each other. It seemed that way among lesbians, much more than jews and wasps or even catholics and wasps, from what she could see. A certain fierceness, a certain need for each others' passions, a certain first sympathy that comes from not being the majority, a certain intelligence that comes from being taunted at the great american feasts. But a catholic lesbian can still be a christian whenever it's convenient, whenever she wants to be. And not always know she's doing it, because it's so easy. First the spark, then the differences. In each two, which are different. Differences defended out of pride, out of class, out of confusion, out of denials.

She would like to say that that was why their relationship ended, the intense struggle to live intimately, as dykes, who once were catholic and jew, but there was more to it than that. There are some who do, and not being able to go on has many sources. Still, there is a way a jew is when she's sick and then there is a way a catholic is when she's sick and they are different, they cannot reconcile the difference when they are headstrong lesbians. There is a way a jew is arrogant and a way a catholic is arrogant, and those two arrogances have a hard time meeting. Not that the jewish lesbians always meet. But it is

easier sometimes to say why they fell apart. No you are lying
again, trying to make it neat. There is no easy way to say why
any one love ends badly. It is very hard for them on the edge
of sanity and society to be open, gracious, unafraid, forgiving.
She loved jewish womyn, protestant womyn, catholic womyn,
from many different cultures and classes, many lovings ended
badly, some ended as friends, one love continued. There is no
easy way to say why you still go on loving womyn, why all
womyn whose eyes are strong turn you on, the way they raise
their shiny arms on the dance floor in lesbian bars years later,
dancing as if they were celebrating a victory in the war, when
there is no victory except for the simple fact that they are dancing, throwing their heads back with the song. A song sung in
a foreign country. That her grandmother would not recognize.

It is a hard difference between lesbians. What color, what
country, what class, what region, what religion, what culture.
It should make no difference if you understand that we are
at war, that men made judaism among the patriarchal religions
that crushed the power of womyn, that men trampled the feasts
of the ancient goddesses worldwide, and demanded gods in their
own images, not a fertile profusion of female figures who bled
into the earth. It should not matter when you remember your
aunts at passover passing the platter. It should not matter when
you remember that a boy at the age of thirteen is included in
the religious life of the community whereas a woman may never
take part. It should not matter when you remember the centuries
in which women were actually sold and bought, and then made
to carry on, be the strength of the family. When you know this
and know that every jewish man is your enemy, not just your
father who hit you, who read you "When you ask, 'what does
this mean to you,' to you and not to us, it means if you were
there you would not have been saved," it should make no difference. You were not with them. You were not of them
though you were born among them. The old ecstatic dances
were stolen. Judy was a captive princess who was selling herself, who was selling the ancient dance of the mothers, for a
comfortable prison. The egg, the feast, the light that never goes
out in the temple, all stolen, stolen from you and not just a
thousand years ago but today. While these are being stolen from
you every hour, there is a woman raped sixty times within that
hour, once a minute. So that we will know not to complain.

Not to raise our voices. Not to say, give us back our memories, give us back our centuries, we are taking our lives again, we will never repeat your crummy prayers in your ugly temples where rapists hide in the back corridors.

It should make no difference then. It should make no difference among lesbians. Who have gone this far.

But it does. It is the same american mistake. To believe that having the same understanding, the same conclusion from the same facts, makes us therefore the same. It is anti-separatism to believe that in order to have a motion, it must all be the same motion, that all the words of the new language must come from the same root; it is mindless melting pot politics, to give away what has made you, to come forward pretending you are a blank slate, to expect that all the womyn coming towards you will come empty, blank as the great plains in winter after all the native peoples were killed. To not come towards each other full of ourselves, wanting to taste and smell all the other cultures womyn bring, is a waste. To deny our own cultures is to rob ourselves and each other of the gift we have to give.

But she does not want to be a jew, to be identified as one with her oppressor. However, to say she is not a jew in a country like this means she is a wasp, and she finds that assumption more repugnant. Even to say she is a lesbian means she is a wasp who has fallen from grace, if she does not say she is a jew. To not say she is a lesbian means she is just another woman slave. To not say she hates men means she accepts them. It is the value of the dominant that is assumed.

And because it is the value of the dominant, no womon can ever feel right about sending away her own mother, even though her mother will choose, time and again, the value of her father, the values of her brothers, over the value of the lesbian. Her mother chooses to remain a slave. All the womyn know this and all the womyn are powerless before it. If they must choose to remain connected to their mothers, then they must know their mothers' culture, their grandmothers' culture, the songs of exile and hardship. That each straight woman sings in her own way.

To choose only other lesbians means to deny the centuries of mothers, the centuries of slaves behind her, in their particular prisons, forming their particular prides, leaving inside of the daughters a particular way. But to choose your mother as well as other lesbians renders all lesbians vulnerable to the attacks of men as the mothers transmit them, to the softer ties of false safety, the smell of holiday cooking, the access to the material world the mother woos with, bringing her daughter back home to the dungeon.

She is confused. Her lover walks into the room and she asks, "Why is it better for you to have a jewish lover?" them having discussed it many times.

"I don't know, but it sure is," she says this time. The lover turns from the window. There are so many reasons. From their experiences they try to generalize, about forms of righteousness, ways of sexuality. It is their understanding that christian sexuality condemns you to hell forever, for white protestants it is simply disgusting, for catholics a deep and meaningful sin. It is jewish to acknowledge that sexuality is unclean, makes womyn unfit for religious life, incapable of the higher spiritual, but that is whether they do it or not, a fact of men's fear, not a daily struggle of redemption from flame. The jewish womon is after all expected to be a little zaftig, a little voluptuous, where her protestant sisters are puritanically thin lipped, or caught up in the fierce catholic passions. Then they remember a protestant lover who was funny and imaginative, a catholic lover who taught them to accept their bodies in a new way, a jewish lover who was tight and afraid.

She gives her lover a squint. That is one of the differences. The jewish womyn understand each other in the expressiveness of their faces, a certain facial language comes down to us, a vocabulary of gestures we haven't begun to probe. Not knowing our own phrases, when we squinted at our catholic friends and they raised their eyebrow back, the gesture did not translate, but each of us took a meaning.

Is it better only because it's easier? To begin, to try to come open before the womon so close beside you? Or also because she has the old prayers in her head. Because they can sing camp songs in hebrew to each other riding home at night. Because her lover's mother just missed being killed in a concentration camp, and her own family is always trying to free the relatives still in russia. Because her grandmother kept separate plates. Because nonjewish lesbians like raisin bagels and jewish lesbians barely tolerate them. Because they do not have to explain how these things feel. To be an outsider within an outsider.

Yet she does not want to say she is a jewish lesbian separatist because that means she will only be with other jewish lesbians, which is not what she means. She has spent many years listening, hearing, the stories of what it means, how it feels, to be italian catholic in boston, working class irish in new york, dirt poor protestant in maine, middle class chicana in new orleans, catholic puertoriquena, black atlanta baptist, hopi, navajo, hindu womon trying to make it in a white sorority at oregon state, she is glad to hear these stories, she wants more, she does not want to waste a single flavor, she wants to agree together on what is bitter and imposed, on what is essential, and what is unique. She wants pride in her own story, possibility to see what it means, to have the acknowledgement, the expansion, of other jewish dykes in this chapter. She believes it helps her listen to the other lesbians' stories with cleaner ears.

But she is not sure. She is thirty and does not know the answer. To which question? To the question of how you are a lesbian and a jew but not affirming judaism since it is an explicit battleground in the war aimed at killing you; and still retain that which makes you distinctive, the old song of your mothers as it came through the jews, the need to fight back when that difference which is judaism becomes a point of persecution, to be able to still say when the nazis are marching in oakland, I am a lesbian and I am a jew, and I am fighting back. Without giving any encouragement to jewish men, without making them feel like they still have a claim and a right to you, without denying them in such a way that it causes you to be self-hating.

That question.

She traveled for a year through the southern part of america, and the lesbians there who were not jewish, which was most of the lesbians she met, thought it was strange, exotic, and somehow funny to come from the jews, they thought all jews were good with money and that jews were smart but grasping. They asked, "Did you bring the manishevitz?" and thought it was a joke. They referred to christ being killed by jews in their poems. She did not know if, when they singled her out as a jew, they were confronting the issue or being anti-semitic. She felt they were being anti-semitic. She felt that more and more. She saw the straight media play off jews and blacks, she heard lesbians fall for it.

When jews together joke about being jewish, they are finding out what each other knows, not self-denigration, but exploration. When we joke about where we came from with someone who came from a similar place, we are finding out what to take with us. Finding out what we as lesbians carry into the new country we mean to create with each other, we hope to still be making, keeping all the tastes of ourselves, the sweet profusion of smell, the great variety of color, the great interest of a thousand opinions. Knowing that we find a way to hold on to this not for those who were slaves before us, but for those we are moving towards, the present and future dykes, that we will have together this richness, the many rituals, the many senses of humor, the treasures of memory to share on the road, in the rainy season, in between harvests.

That's the vision.

But right now she lives in a small city, which has a church on every block, a fleet of joy buses for christ, no place to buy chanukah candles, and maybe twenty lesbians, all in the closet. She reads the lesbian papers, the feminist press, and there are beginning to be attacks on jews, and continuing to be attack after attack on lesbians who want to work, live, build their lives with other lesbians.

A young woman came to the door at that moment selling flowers for the christian fellowship. She said, "in conscience, I cannot support the christian fellowship." "Why not?" asked the young woman, "are you jewish? an atheist?" She chooses not to say lesbian, she still had old excuses, the small town, the neighbors, the landlord, why? She said instead, "i'm a jewish atheist." The young woman laughed, as if the idea were very strange. She found she was chuckling a little too, and then her lover called out from the living room, "it's not funny!"

She caught herself in the midst of giving the straight anti-semite the upper hand, so to speak, the last laugh. "She's right, it's not funny," she said, and closed the door.

Affair with a Married Woman

Martha Shelley

A woman from Israel
asks me if there's more to learn
and why they call it *gay*:
My love, you don't need lessons
you could've invented the way—
in three short afternoons
between work and picking up the kids
you learned as much as I did
in as many years
of being queer.

Yes, you know *gay*,
but I need to teach you *queer*
I need to tell you about hostile glares
and false arrests
and you have no defense
a queer can't bear witness
against a lying cop. They call your boss,
you lose your job, there's no redress:
"You can't teach youngsters to be perverts here!"
—or back there—in that Promised Land of ours
the shooting gallery
where patriarchy first took root
and grew its tallest flowers.*

(Thousands of little clay Ishtars
lie broken beneath the phallic minarets.)

*The author notes that she is referring to the entire history of the Middle
East from Sumeria to the present. She does not subscribe to the anti-
Semitic and historically ignorant notion that the Jews invented patriarchy.

Queer means the State takes your kids
or gives your husband custody
and you become a deportee,
an "undesirable alien"
because you desired me.

Queer means a teenage gang
who tried to beat me up and bang me
on the ferry to Manhattan.
Who cared? Passengers stared
at the dyke, who deserved what she got
for dressing like that.

Queer means crazy, it means
the uncle who signed an aunt in
to the looney bin.
(The family still whispers about it.)
Electric shocks prescribed by the Doc
who made burnt offerings of human souls
and sacrificed a woman's brain to Woman's Role.

Queer means burning,
it meant the stake and the rack
when the Doctors wore black
to the Inquisition.
Just yesterday it meant the ovens:
the ashes of a hundred thousand pervert lovers
dirtied the German skies
before the Jews got fried.

You want to be gay and free
you want your husband to leave you be;
be careful—he sits like a jealous Baal
waiting for you to decide
which way to jump.
He has all the trumps on his side.

Gay isn't a game—five thousand years of lies
point at our hearts
like machine guns ready to fire
we have only the fire in our eyes
which they can't see

the fire in our bellies
which they can't feel
a dream of fire—and do we have the guts
to make it real?

Jewish Lesbian Mother

Susan J. Wolfe

Two conversations:

"Doesn't it bother you?" she asks, clearly worried about me.

"Doesn't what bother me?"

"Not believing in an afterlife; not knowing what's going to happen to you after you die?"

A friend adds, "Wouldn't you like to think that you'd go on forever?"

And I explain about the children, about the sanctity of life, about changing things in this world. . . about being a Jew, and what that means.

A close friend remarks, "I just know if I had a baby, I'd never give it away."

In anger, I respond, "I'm sick of women who've never come close to having a child telling me what they would do if they had one."

She declares, "I know you're trying to hurt me, but I don't care."

In tears, I flee the restaurant without explaining about Lesbian mothers and children.

Two conversations, both with friends who are themselves Lesbians. They are the key to the elemental differences I have felt between myself and other women I have called my sisters, differences I have experienced as barriers between us. Always I begin with the assumption that they will understand, or accept me without understanding; always I end by explaining my differences, trying to present the bits and pieces of my self. Until recently, I too accepted the possibility of contradiction in being at once a Jewish mother and a Lesbian, a Lesbian feminist and the mother of a Jewish son.

But I am that being, the Jewish Lesbian feminist mother of a male child. In order to bring the elements of myself together for my sisters, to re-member myself, I can only record the raw emotional data of my existence. For years, I have avoided recreating these moments; I recreate them now, hoping to end the need for explanations.

According to the laws of Judaism and of New York State, I was born Jewish—born of a Jewish mother. Yet the realization of what it means to be a Jew came slowly. In my assimilated Jewish household, little was made of our origins as a people. To my parents, it was more important that we "fit in" with our predominantly Irish Catholic neighbors than that we identify ourselves as Jewish. Jewish holidays were not celebrated, rituals were not performed. The larger "American" culture—the Christian culture—eclipsed ours.

It did not surprise me that my parents chose absorption. I learned early that we were at best invisible, at worst hated by American society. My mother had been forced to lie to the New York Telephone Company; they did not hire Jews, and fired her when they discovered that she was Jewish. I once had heard a Christian non-veteran tell my father (who had fought overseas throughout World War II) that he did not deserve a paid holiday on Veteran's Day, because "it isn't a Jewish holiday." I knew that neighborhood children had taunted and beaten my cousin on his way home from Hebrew school because of the yarmulke on his head. To be Jewish, it seemed, was dangerous.

I have always known that Judaism means more than persecution. Ethical behavior, born of respect for the individual and all forms of life, was expected of me, and was integral to the Jewish sensibility. I remember, as an eight-year old child, running up five flights of stairs after I had been called a *kike*. I asked my mother, "Is it okay if I call her a *mick*, then?" She replied, "No, don't lower yourself. It is never okay to call anyone a name." I was never to retaliate with slurs against someone's racial background, never to lash out without considering the consequences.

Yet my mother managed to imply differences between "us" and "them," Jews and non-Jews. In her view, Christian religious observance emphasized public worship rather than moral responsibility. As Jews, the family was always central—in particular, the children.

On our block no one had much money, but our family handled money differently. My brother and I ate better, wore better shoes, and received better medical and dental care than our white Christian friends. My mother spoke disparagingly of people who didn't understand that children are entitled to the best care and parents are obligated to provide it.

Jewish families who had more money than we provided the poorer Jewish schoolchildren with books, piano lessons and bedroom furniture. If we could not live in a land of milk and honey, these donors would see to it that we would live better lives than our parents. Later, I would wonder if anti-Semitic jokes about Jewish mothers, "Jewish-American Princesses," and Jewish "momma's boys" had all sprung from the same source— a Christian critique and distortion of Jewish values.

Our pets, too, were part of the family. One, a beloved fawn boxer, was slowly dying of an intestinal injury despite every attempt to preserve his life. Finally, when he had lost one-third of his original weight and lost control both of his bladder and bowel movements, my father said, "We'll have to put him to sleep. Even an animal shouldn't be in continual suffering."

When my brother Larry returned from school, his first words were, "Where's Tiger?" Our father did not answer. Larry raised his seven-year old fist and punched him in the jaw; then they hugged each other and wept.

At a Rosh Hashanah service fifteen years later, my rabbi spoke of the rabbi who was late to *shul* because he had stopped to free a dog from a thorn bush. "Life," said the rabbi, "is the most important. . . even the smallest life."

Two statements:

"If I found out my sister was a Lesbian, I'd rape her so she'd know what a real man feels like."

"I *know* you're Jewish, but you're not like the *rest* of them."

The first statement was made by my high school "boyfriend" at a time when I was sexually involved with my best girlfriend (both were Catholic). The second remark was made in various forms by numerous Christian friends throughout my high school years. I do not recall protesting either.

Believing that assimilation meant survival, I spent a great deal of my life denying that my heritage and experiences made me different. While I did not deny my Jewish identity, I declared that identity to be insignificant. By similar reasoning, for over a decade, I experienced strong love for and sexual attraction towards women while denying that I was a Lesbian.

Like most American women of the 1960's, I was unaware of viable alternatives to marriage. When my best friend and lover married my boyfriend during my senior year in high school, I gave up all hope of ever holding on to a woman lover. Marriage would provide a refuge and cover—no one (including myself) would think that I might be a Lesbian; and I desperately wanted children.

When I married, I married Jewish. According to the popular stereotype, Jewish men make better husbands than Christian men. Nothing I observed contradicted that stereotype: in my experience, Jewish husbands seemed less likely to drink or "run around," and more likely to bring their paychecks home. Marrying a Jewish man was both a move towards accepting my Jewishness and a move towards feminism. I married a man who was not likely to interfere with my independence.

At the age of sixteen, I became pregnant because of my boyfriend's refusal to use birth control; since he was Catholic, this would have compounded his "sin." His initial response was "What am I going to do?"; then he insisted on marriage, which I refused. Although my parents offered me an abortion, I chose to carry the baby to term, culminating in the birth of a son. I was awed by the thought that I was "carrying life," and completely naive about the pain my decision would bring. Six days of caring for my child, even in a hospital setting, made it difficult to give him up.

In contrast, my future husband George asked what I wanted to do when I became pregnant a second time. This time, I decided to have an abortion and then marry him.

When wedding plans became overly complicated, we cancelled them and were married in a court house. I had never placed much stock in ritual, but then, I hadn't been raised to practice any. My new in-laws, who had raised their children within the Jewish tradition, were very disappointed; my mother-in-law was to nudge me for two years: "So when are you going to have a real wedding?" (A "real wedding" was, of course, a ceremony performed by a rabbi under a canopy.)

When I became pregnant a third time, my attitude towards ritual shifted. I wanted my child to have a religious background, to be able to choose. The only choices I considered were non-belief and Judaism. I wanted him to know what he *was*, not simply what he was not. I wanted him to take pride in belonging to a people and a religion with a history extending back six millennia.

Finally my mother-in-law was satisfied; we had our Jewish wedding. The bride was six months pregnant; the rabbi, nervous even after checking the original license, married us in my family name, inadvertently changing the groom's. Nevertheless, in the family's eyes, at last we were properly married. Suddenly this had taken on great importance for me.

Yet I was to live, like my parents, as an assimilated Jew—always telling our suburban neighbors that I was not religious, always pointing to my Catholic relatives, excusing myself. I put from my mind my earlier resolution to raise my son Jeffrey within Judaism. We were the only Jewish family in the area, and I convinced myself that Jeffrey would be happier if he did not "feel different." I erected a Christmas tree instead of lighting the Chanukah candles. Each time a new friend made a joke about eating ham as she invited me to dinner, I told myself that I was accepted. I also remembered my mother's admonition: I did not lower myself by replying in kind.

Nor did I speak out when a prospective buyer for our home inquired about the neighbors' religious affiliations, and responded, "Oh, good!" when she was told that we were the last Jewish family. We declined to sell her the house, and forfeited about three thousand dollars in profit. But we did not tell her why.

Welcome the stranger into your house, for remember you were strangers in the land of Egypt.

Let all those who are hungry come and eat.

Plow not the corners of your fields, but leave them for the poor.

After our move to Sioux City, Iowa, a neighbor asked what church we would be attending—in the Midwest, this is considered a polite question. Since I have never been willing to refer to a temple or a synagogue as a "church" I answered, "None." Within the week she was back at our door, toting Lutheran literature, a badge with a picture of Jesus, and a fold-out church with a miniature pulpit for Jeffrey. Thoroughly embarrassed, I explained that while I had had no religious training, my husband had been brought up Jewish, and if we decided to attend services, we would undoubtedly attend Jewish ones. To my surprise, she evinced relief. Her great fear had been that we were atheists, and would thus have "no comfort in affliction."

This incident renewed our resolve to create a Jewish household. Jewish families in the community had already approached us: outnumbered in the city as a whole, they were pleased to discover newcomers. They were following the mitzvot, welcoming strangers. Certainly there was never a Pesach or Rosh Hashanah without an invitation for us to come and share food. We joined the Reform temple and began to attend Friday night services.

What struck me repeatedly as I participated in Jewish rituals and prayer was the emphasis on *life* and the need to preserve it. At each Shabbat service and Seder I heard the commandment to welcome the stranger; entire sermons explained its significance. The stranger was any victim, any outcast. Because we had suffered in bondage in Egypt, we were to offer shelter, food, money, and prayer to all those who were oppressed. This was to be interpreted in the broadest sense; I believe it explains the disproportionate number of Jews in socialist, civil rights, anti-war and various liberation movements.

For a year I taught Sunday school: one class on the significance of the religious holidays and another on ethics. I was learning along with my students; many of them knew more about Jewish holidays than I did. I learned about "the End of the Days," the paradise which was to come to earth at the end of time, brought along by the accumulated total of the mitzvot performed by each individual. Each person could bring this day closer. There was, however, no discussion of an individual soul's fate after death.

In spending time with other Jews, I learned that immortality, such as it existed, lay in one's children or the children of one's people. Like Moses, I might never see the Promised Land; still, "next year in Jerusalem" was a promise for future generations. The Jewish emphasis on children which I had sensed throughout my childhood resonated in the religion and the culture.

My mother had been right: there was indeed a difference between "us" and "them." Unable to affirm directly the strengths that lay in the Jewish culture and Judaism, she affirmed them indirectly through bitter remarks about Christians. She had given me the foundation, though I was not to discover the structure for a decade.

I came to experience pride in the mere fact of Jewish survival. For over five thousand years we have been the object of hatred and fear, the monsters of legend: Christ-killers, drinkers of babies' blood, bestial beings characterized by promiscuity or greed. Surrounded by myths which labeled us murderers while we extolled life, "cheap Jews" while we gave to each stranger of our money and of ourselves, we survived. When the rabbi intoned, "This section of the Bible has been read in every synagogue throughout the world for the last two thousand years," I cried.

Question from a white Gentile Lesbian feminist:

"I do not understand why Black and Jewish women should want to preserve their cultures. What's so great about their cultures? They're all patriarchal. You don't see me fighting to preserve white bread."

Perhaps all states of being contain within them the seeds for change. Certainly an unacknowledged Lesbian lives precariously within her other roles.

At the age of twenty-nine I must have appeared fortunate. One woman told me how lucky I was "to have a husband who understands." George had quit his job in New York so that I could accept a position in South Dakota, then insisted that I take a semester's leave without pay to complete my dissertation. I was a respected member of the community in Sioux City: a wife, mother, temple member, and college professor. (The entire Jewish community, like George and my parents, placed a high premium on education and on the professions. I had gained respect, even prestige, in the move from a non-Jewish neighborhood in New York, where educated women were stereotyped as "pushy" and frigid; one man had once paid me what he considered to be a compliment: "You don't seem like you have that much education.")

Not that my days were without conflict. I feared that my son Jeffrey was slipping away, in part because I felt guilty over my absence—like many mothers who work outside the home. I missed the daily closeness we had shared for the first three years of his life, when we had been a unit unto ourselves, admitting no outsiders. I had been with him for each discovery: sunlight, kittens, yoghurt, stacking blocks. Now I was gone each Monday, Wednesday, and Friday, thirty weeks a year.

I had already drawn away from George, though he had not noticed. Pregnancy and nursing gave me excuses to withdraw sexually; our professional lives led us further apart. And, as if the independence accompanying a career had triggered desire, I was once again drawn to women. My commuting hours, spent lost in Lesbian sexual fantasies, alarmed me. Since I had loved a woman before, I could not pretend to be naive.

For two years I had precariously maintained respectability through silence. A catalytic event challenged my silence. A screening committee considered applicants to replace me during my leave; one applicant was an avowed, outspoken Lesbian feminist.

The chair of the department would not speak to her on the telephone; two members of the committee refused to evaluate her credentials. As the junior faculty committee member, I found her the best qualified applicant, and had no choice but to defend her and her sexuality, the "stranger" in my house. I attributed my behavior to impartial professionalism. She was hired against the protests of half of the committee; I fell in love with the student member who had defended her.

Soon after her arrival, my replacement and I collaborated on feminist and Lesbian research. George, who had persistently urged me to write my dissertation, now waited impatiently for me to "finish" my work, for "things to get back to normal." And, as I led him to believe that there might be an end in sight, I was becoming more deeply involved with my lover.

Within six months George was at the divorce lawyer's, objecting because my "loyalties had shifted." In his view, the two women he saw as my friends, combined with my work, were draining the energy to which he was entitled. I discovered that the feminism of enlightened Jewish husbands did not allow for the woman I was becoming.

I knew I was a hypocrite.

I began to see George as one more sexist male. Judaism with its patriarchal god seemed to offer no solution. Yet I still wanted my son Jeffrey—how I wanted to be with him! I saw the term "Lesbian mother" as contradictory, and viewed the maternal role as one of self-sacrifice and undivided devotion to the child and the nuclear family. As a Lesbian, I foresaw no way to provide the economic security and constant attention I was convinced a parent should. Children deserved the best; how could a Lesbian provide that? I had been socialized well.

Torn by indecision, I wavered for months between determination to fight a custody battle and despair. Iowa had never awarded custody to a known Lesbian mother. I was convinced that George knew about my sexual activities, and was prepared to use it in a courtroom; I could not expose Jeffrey to the pain of a custody battle. At times I broke down completely, falling asleep at the foot of my son's bed after saying goodbye and crying. I told Jeffrey about the divorce; I held him as he wept. I did not fight. The court awarded custody to the father, who immediately moved to Des Moines, leaving Jeffrey to spend five weeks with me.

That fall, I went to a counselor, explaining the guilt I felt over abandoning my child to a father whose values I could not condone, and the anguish I felt for his loss. She advised me that I could give Jeffrey a choice—by offering him a competing set of values. For me these values were learned in childhood, and reinforced by feminism: a respect for life and the individual, the spirit of sisterhood.

A statement, made by Jeffrey's stepmother:

"I think that for Jeffrey and George to identify with being Jewish is a negative identification. They're only identifying with persecution."

Fact: The Michigan Women's Music Festival announced that male children would not be allowed on festival grounds. Male children over the age of six were to be placed in a camp about ten miles away.

Initially my husband's marriage impressed me. Susan had three children: Jeffrey would have playmates as well as a "normal home." Jeffrey lost weight and became more sociable and athletic. Although I was admittedly surprised that George, who had once tried to persuade me to keep kosher, had married a *shiksa*, I assumed that he knew what he was doing.

I kept in touch with Jeffrey by telephone when he could not visit. This necessitated speaking with George or his new wife. I was disturbed at their materiality, the frequent deaths of their pets, and their subsequent indifference to them. I comforted myself that I could provide a counterbalance during the weeks which Jeffrey spent with me.

George and Jeffrey attended church with Susan and her children. I was astounded to hear her equate Jewish identity with masochism and disparage the husband and stepson she claimed to love. George and Susan denied the differences among the children (Jeffrey refers to all her relatives as "grandparents," "uncles," "sisters," and the like). Once again, Jews were expected to be absorbed. This time it was to be my son: third-generation assimilation.

I was furious, but did not want to risk my visitation rights. Instead, I strengthened Jewish identity in my son, pointing out its positive aspects, linking it to the behavior I expected of him. If he repeated a racist "joke" told by his stepbrother, he was rebuked with an explanation linking racism to anti-Semitism and similar cruel, dangerous behavior. At the same time, I began to teach him what I knew about our people, and about feminism.

It has not been easy to be a Jewish Lesbian feminist mother with a son. Forced to choose between my summer time with Jeffrey and attending the Michigan Women's Music Festival, I preserved my sisters' space by staying home. I refused to place my Jewish child in a camp because of his undesirability to lesbian separatists. The festival organizers' ignorance of the Jewish experience with institutionalized camps was disappointingly apparent.

Jeffrey is currently studying for his Bar Mitzvah, despite pressure from his new mother. This Chanukah he requested that I buy him a Star of David: "I want you to buy that for me." I still wonder if I made the right decision in giving him up. Sometimes one must fight for what one has; on the other hand, one must sometimes seem to give it away in order to keep it.

What May Be *Tsores* to You is *Naches* to Me

Dovida Ishatova

Dear Mom and Dad:

So what's a nice Jewish girl like me doing in a book like this? Why, flaunting it, of course, and hoping maybe to meet some other nice Jewish girls. Besides, Jewish girls make such nice lesbians. We're loud, we're boisterous, we know how to cuddle, we know how to squeeze. But to be a Jew, the daughter of a survivor, and a lesbian? How can that be? With a background like mine, how could I have ever wandered so far from the "chosen path"? How could I *not* be in a hurry to replace the family that was killed; give you, my parents, the joy of grandchildren, and myself the security of a nice Jewish boy as a mate for life? But I'm telling you, I *am* a nice Jewish girl. In fact, I'm a very important link in the liberation of women and the liberation of Jews. I should be welcomed into the Jewish community with open arms. I am not a contradiction or an impossibility. What could make more sense than my casting off, in my lifetime, the remaining vestiges of woman and Jew as victim, and asserting my love of self by being woman-identified? I am not here to undermine what is good in Judaism and Jewish culture. I come to shake up that which is no longer useful; the myths about women, the myths about what it means to be Jewish, and the myths about what we must do to survive as a people. Tradition. Yes, I agree that it is important. Tradition carries me back to my ancestors and keeps their wisdom and struggles alive in my heart. But please, spare me the oppressive nonsense about women, children, and men. That has nothing to do with the heart of Jewish tradition—compassion, equality, and freedom.

Across this country, I see Jewish lesbians like myself searching for a Jewish identity that genuinely reflects who we are. This is leading us to explore the more female aspects of the tradition, and to discover the truth about the strong Jewish women of our ancient past—Miriam, Puah, Lilith, Sarah, and the female goddesses and spirits that preceded and became intertwined with Judaism—Shekhina (the female aspect of God), Ashera and Ashtoreth. We are not only reinterpreting the old, but also adding our own visions and rituals, creating a Jewish spirituality that reflects our unique sensibility and awareness as lesbians. We are strengthening the fabric of Jewish identity by stretching what it can include. You taught me the importance of challenging injustice, fighting back, and above all, questioning. I am continually scrutinizing and re-evaluating my life and the world around me. This includes looking at my relationship/ non-relationship with men, and my needs for family and stability. It is you who raised me to be who I am. And that is to your credit.

Dovida

The wisdom and understanding I have gained from both feminism and lesbianism about my relationships with women has dramatically changed my relationship with my mother. As pianists, we are now performing From Mother to Daughter and Back Again *together across the country. The following excerpt from the program reflects my journey to where I am today:*

HENIA
HENIA FLINT
HENIA FLINT GOTTLIEB
HENIA FLINT GOTTLIEB GOODMAN
HELENE

daughter of Esther
daughter of Manes
sister of Caroline
sister of Jacob
sister of Lazar

From a family of fifty
only you have survived
thirty-five years of memories and nightmares
each memory a tear   a tightening in your chest

twenty-five years old and you watched your father beaten
twenty-five years old and you tried to save him who is now
    insane,
out of his mind, yet you remained in yours
How? How did you survive?

twenty-seven years old and you carried the music of Chopin
under your arm to Auschwitz
twenty-seven years old, Dr. Mengele pointed his finger,
and you watched your mother walk the other way and
    disappear forever
Tell me! How did you survive?

On the night of Yom Kippur
you gathered the women and sang *Kol Nidre*
your spirit that belonged to another world,
the world of art and dreams and music,
still alive and helping others find strength.
It was your nature

When someone offered you a chance to escape
you said, "no"—I won't go without my sister-in-law, my aunt,
    and my girlfriend
in so doing, against all odds, you saved them all

Henia
woman of deep melancholy eyes
How afraid I was of your pain
How much you needed me
I was life to you
I was joy to you
I was proof of your victory over Hitler
I was afraid
I was so afraid of you
and how much you looked to me for nourishment
I was just a little baby
and your hunger went far beyond anything I could do
You needed to love and be loved with a desperation that
    suffocated me

and so I grew
I grew walls to keep out the love that frightened me
and I grew horns to match yours as we locked in battle

to match the anger that would have been
suicide had you shown it back then
you saw my anger as the nazi monster
with which you had to plead for life
No   I am your daughter
daughter of your own flesh
I am not the enemy
I do not wish you were dead

You were afraid
afraid of losing me
no place away from you was safe enough for your child
            no place was safe
you were afraid of losing me
through my silence and the ever growing gap between us
yes   I rebelled
I rebelled against anything that had to do with you
I rebelled against being a jew
I rebelled against being a pianist
I rebelled against being manipulated into guilt because of your
     pain
But still, I thought I was to blame
And I felt like a monster for hurting someone
who had already suffered so much

I rebelled   and yet
Here I am today   no longer afraid
of loving you or losing myself
I cry for all the years I couldn't understand
I cry for all the years I couldn't freely love you
you who needed so much love and compassion
to counteract the hunger and self hate
Somehow I've learned to welcome
your tears and your stories
Today I sing praises to your strength
your courage   and your wit
How did you survive?
Was it chance? Was it a miracle?
For one year, in spite of hunger beyond imagination,
you refused to eat the soup that would have made you sterile.
My very existence is a miracle.
How did you survive?
I grope for answers to this elusive question

But without knowing the answer, this I do know—
that you have given me whatever it is that you had
that if it were to happen to me, and if I were favored by chance
I too would survive

By a twist of fate, music saved you
back there in Auschwitz
Is it a coincidence
that through music we have spoken when there was no other
    way?

I am so much your daughter
Henia Flint Gottlieb Goodman
Our lifestyles are different, but our essence is the same
I celebrate how much I am like you
your strength is my strength
your music is my music
I am of your flesh
and I am independent
Today I find myself living out the life you would have led
But it is my life too
I choose it freely

And is it a coincidence
That today I am twenty-seven years old
and I play Chopin?

Coffee and Cake

Harriet Malinowitz

I have not seen my brother Steven since last Thanksgiving, when he forgot to buy the turkey. My mother, my uncle, and I flew out to Tucson for four days. It was one of the very few times all year that it rained, and it rained continuously, the four of us thrown into a more intensive proximity than we'd counted on. I brought a pumpkin bread I'd baked in Massachusetts, carefully wrapped in foil, and winter squash and gourds I'd picked up at farm stands. But when we got there Steven had forgotten to buy a turkey. It was almost midnight on Wednesday.

"It doesn't matter, I'll take us all out to eat," said my uncle—his characteristic gesture, his cure-all for any of life's ills. I had to flush out the raw anger and disappointment in my eyes; I couldn't answer the magnanimity of that offer, the pleasure beaming from my uncle's face at the pleasure he was giving us. There was no way I could tamper with his kindness. Steven, sensing my disturbance, said, "You're only here for a few days, anyway. You wouldn't want to spend a whole day inside cooking, would you?"

The next day we took a dismal ride through the rain to Bisbee, where everything was closed for the holiday. Sitting in the only open restaurant in town, we ate slices of turkey in pasty gravy, canned sweet potatoes, frozen peas. My mother was getting enthusiastic about the salad bar, while I sat beside her, furious, humiliated for her, wishing she could be more collected about the salad bars. I felt the weight of many salad bars behind me. I wanted to tell them not to be too easily satisfied—but didn't know how to press without stabbing. I was afraid of doing some real damage. Instead, I sat there, miserably watching them in their enjoyment as they absorbed the soullessness of all they touched, knowing that I, by proximity to them, absorbed it too. In the end, I made weak jokes caustic barbs punctuated by ameliorating laughs. They sent me puzzled looks but they held me to my laughter. Nobody actually choked on the indignity of the food. The event, after all, was not serious.

Now I am seeing Steven again, after seven months, at my mother's house in Queens. He arrived last night at three a.m. having driven almost continuously from Arizona. I have driven in for the weekend from Massachusetts, and I arrive in time for dinner. We embrace, the ceremony so old that we can use it to camouflage the embarrassment of our real warmth. A dog is barking; it runs in and jumps on me. This is Willie, the puppy Steven has recently bought. It's strange to see a dog in my mother's house; stranger still to see it and Steven playing with each other so intimately. I go into the kitchen, where I find my mother cutting grapefruits. We also kiss each other, and then immediately the dog is there, hurling himself at us in his excitement. Steven appears behind the dog and admonishes him to get down. There are four of us in the kitchen; this morning there was only my mother, but now her daughter has come from Massachusetts, her son has driven all the way in from Arizona, and there is this new personage who runs in and out of the room. He runs in and we pet him, talk to him. He comes over to where my mother is standing and puts his paws up around her leg.

"Sit for Grandma!" commands Steven, and we all begin to laugh.

"Sit for Grandma!" Steven says again, when Willie doesn't pay attention to him, and then he pulls Willie on the floor where they wrestle for a minute. The disciplining parent. My mother is still laughing at hearing the word "Grandma" spoken. I see in her face that this is very funny and very absurd to her, and yet the name itself is like a code word nobody's dared to speak before. Grandma. Someone she wishes to be. She laughs, a little confusedly now, at Willie. Her grandchild? All three of us are redistributing our weight, shifting to make room for a new member of whose inclusion in our circle there can be no question.

I watch Willie and Steven for a little while; then I look again at my mother, who is also watching them, removed from the action now, her lips slightly curving, her eyes soft with absorption. Abruptly, I feel a twinge of fear—the fear that here is a new contingency upon which our survival depends, a new element which must be preserved in our fragile chain of love. I am afraid of the looks upon all our faces, the expressions which confess our helpless awareness of each other.

Steven is teasingly twisting a bone out of Willie's teeth and tossing it so it skims the rug and lands near the piano. We all laugh, and I am afraid. We are too close. I am afraid of their pain. I am afraid too of their joy, because once I see it I know it will be tragic if it goes away. I think of Petra, my lover. With her my fear is of loss, of the unpredictable movements of our personalities. With family, not many changes are expected. The continuance of the relationships is assured; no one else can threaten them. They are utterly pre-determined, pre-guaranteed.

Yet, with all this certainty, all this knowledge, there is still something in the particularity of their pain I can't understand. I see the looks of anguish on their faces, which I perceive even when they are unaware of them. I know too well the delicately honed variations in their expressions. Too well, too, do I know their happy looks. If only I could know for sure that the happy looks would remain, then I could go away, finally, at peace, and not come back.

We don't *want* to be moved by each other. We strive endlessly to be superficially touched, less than profoundly affected. Our joy is always shadowed by death, by geographic mobility, by a dangerous world in which we cannot offer each other real protection, where we play by disparate rules. And I am afraid that later tonight, when my mother goes up to bed and Steven and I go out for coffee, and I finally tell him that I am a lesbian, he won't understand.

One month before, long distance, Massachusetts to Arizona: *This has been a big year for me. A lot has changed. I want very much to talk to you when you come in.*

What is it? Tell me now.

No, it's nothing I can spit out over the phone. I shouldn't have brought it up. I'm sorry. It will have to wait.

But he continues to tease me, playing twenty questions. *Does it have something to do with your career?* Yes. *Is it political?* Yes. *Is it revolutionary?* Yes. *Is it physical?* Yes.

"Now you've got me really confused," he says. "Are you going around planting bombs?"

Yes.

We slide into a booth at The Greasy Spoon Diner. The waitress takes our order: coffee and two slices of hazelnut cheesecake. She puts her pad in her apron pocket, takes our menus, and walks away.

All around us are plump, middle-aged Jewish people of
Queens, drinking coffee, eating cheesecake, babka, apple stru-
del. Tomorrow they will go back on their diets; tomorrow night
they will return and break them. Steven and I both pretend to
feel alienated among them but between us lies the secret of
their familiarity. We've constructed our lives around being different from them, and yet in a minute the pastry smells waft
over and seduce us back. I wonder if the smells make him think
of what I'm thinking: the week we sat *shivah* for my father,
the friends and neighbors and relatives coming to pay condolence calls, bringing cakes and pies from Jewish bakeries all
over the length and breadth of Long Island. About fifty visitors
a day—which means five times throughout the afternoon and
evening sitting down to coffee from the huge borrowed perco-
lator and cakes on fluted trivets carefully lifted from pastel-
colored cardboard boxes tied with flecked string. Did we ever
eat dinner? Lunch? Breakfast? Was it a collective plot of our
guests to ensure our proper mourning behavior by depriving
us of protein and inducing a protracted sugar fit? I don't remember minding or objecting. I only remember loving those
cakes for being so inordinately civilized; for being so attractive; for being so expensive. Within those boxes with their
script saying "Ida's" or "Mitzi's" or "Ratner's," I sensed my
culture.

Yet rarely would my mother have bought such cakes. I had
known them all my life from visitors who brought them, from
houses I had visited as a child in which they were served. That
only my mother, among all mothers I knew, did not identify
herself with those pastries branded our family as an anomaly
within German and Eastern European Jewish society. Sometimes even now I forget that before my struggle to separate and
become an assimilated American, there had been the converse
struggle to integrate, to transcend the limitations of a family
which was ethnically incorrect.

My family: a year ago, Steven's birthday, the three of us in
my mother's house. Steven has been living in the Village for a
year but he has come home to re-live the birthday ritual. My
family, so fond of form, so oblivious of content. My mother
has an Entenmann's Marshmallow Fudge Cake for him. I groan,
remembering to smile humorously as I do so, and she turns to
me with a laugh and says, "Well, it's his favorite." Boys will be
boys. There it sits, sugary, fudgy, tacky in its tin plate. The
candles stuck in this skimpy little mass of junk make me want

to cry—because this is the cake of his dreams; it is the aspiration of his birthday, and she is so acquiescent in fulfilling it. Our mother, who was supposed to teach us about life. And Steven, whose window on Cornelia Street draws in air perfumed with Italian breads, baguettes, challahs, cannolis, rugglach, croissants, tortes, napoleons, brioches. Steven, Steven, Steven! How is it, why is it that the three of us are gathered around this birthday cake in this kitchen, still going through the paces of this ritual? What is it that sabotages our imaginations, preventing us from inventing new celebrations?

Now, hazelnut cheesecake between us on the very un-greasy tabletop in The Greasy Spoon Diner. Steven leans back against the shiny leather seat. "So what's new?" he says.

He is so relaxed that I think he must know. Yet unless I *know* he knows, which I don't know, I have to proceed on the assumption that he doesn't.

I had said to Petra: "The problem is that there are certain words which mean very different things to me than they do to him, and I'm not sure how to use them."

"Like what?" she'd asked.

"Like 'lesbian,' " I'd admitted.

I look at him and decide that that is not a good place to start.

"You remember Petra," I say, and he says yes, he does. The way he acknowledges it, as if clearing an irrelevant detail out of the way so we can get to the point, tells me that he doesn't know at all. So I say, quickly, "Well, last year we became friends and then we became lovers."

Somewhere along the sentence there has been a jolt in his look of blank expectancy; perhaps a fraction of a second before I got to "lovers."

"Really?" he says, in an unnatural voice, and chugs his glass of water like beer.

"Yes," I say, "*really*."

Then I launch into a synopsis of this year of my life, and I hear, as if from a distance, the words and phrases spilling from my mouth: "structuring my life," "defining myself," "made a decision," "political statement." I have become, quite clearly, a paragon of control. I talk and talk, words of power and strength tripping over themselves in their eagerness to make themselves clear. I don't say, "I fell in love with Petra and I was terrified to realize that whether I wished it and willed it or not,

I was a lesbian. That I *had* to learn these things because without
them I couldn't live." No, not me; I was a right-on radical lesbian feminist from the day I was born. On and on I go, skipping
the fright, the confusion, skipping even the love because it is
too bare, too vulnerable, and too true. I tell him only the things
I have learned, the perceptions I have been injecting into my
veins like new, life-giving blood. Maybe if I can reassemble my
molecules so that I look like a Holly Near record, it will all
miraculously click with him.

But that look on his face. A look of shock, and a confusion
he is struggling valiantly to conceal. There is something about
that look—how do I know it? Oh yes, now I remember, it's the
look on the face of the man Marjorie Morningstar marries, after she confesses to him that she's not a virgin. Never again, we
are told, will that look of pure happiness he had when he believed Marjorie to be pure reappear upon his face. I read that
book five times between the ages of thirteen and eighteen and it
always made me feel furiously futile. It was as if I could see that
man standing not very far away from me, and I wanted to go
and shake him, only I knew I'd have to walk all the way around
the world to get to him, instead of simply crossing the street.

Now I get that same feeling, only it is more diffuse and not
really directed at Steven. I suddenly realize it's not going to be
all roses after all. I haven't seen that look on anyone's face yet—
and on his face it cripples me, makes my bones feel weak.

"You haven't told Mom, have you?"

"No, but I'm going to eventually."

"I wouldn't do that. Don't forget you're living in a different
world than she is. She'd be really crushed."

I feel the terrible sense of power I felt in the restaurant in
Bisbee, as he reminds me of the damage I can do. I am sickened
to hear the fear in his voice, to hear his conviction that the possibility of telling my mother is a lethal weapon I possess. I'm
trying to tell him I've been born, while reflected in his eyes I
watch my own death. And this, we both somehow know, is at
the root of the protective instinct we both feel for my mother.
I think of Chava, the daughter in *Fiddler on the Roof* who marries a gentile. Her parents sit *shivah* for her, heartbroken as if
she had died. I used to despise Tevya for that—for being so
fanatic and bullheaded, letting ritual and ceremony prescribe
his feelings for his own daughter. Now I understand how words
like "daughters," "marriage," "family," and "Jewish" came
glued together in their heads, so that when one beam slipped

the whole roof fell in. I wonder if "heterosexual" is glued into my mother's definition of me in the same way. I am sure that it is. Steven's face tells me that it is. Which means that when I cease to be heterosexual, I cease to exist.

"Tell me honestly how you feel," I say. My voice proclaims: Spare me nothing. I can take it. Nothing can mar my confidence, so let's be candid. "Are you really that surprised?"

"Yes," he says, "yes, I am. I'm sorry if I seem negative—this will take some getting used to. If you want me to be honest, I guess I can't help admitting I'm somewhat disappointed."

Disappointed. About what? That I've exploded his illusions about my heterosexuality? That I'm flawed?

"I just don't understand how you can *decide* to *define* yourself as a lesbian," he says, hesitating over the word but coming through in the end. "How can you say that's what you *are*? I've had only heterosexual relationships, but I don't *define* myself as heterosexual. I wouldn't say I *am* heterosexual."

"But you don't have to say it. Everybody assumes it anyway. You're very defined—so defined you never even have to mention it."

He thinks about this. I think what confuses me most in this conversation is the careful consideration he is giving to everything I say. I have had friends tell me about coming out to brothers who were football players and corporate executives, men who simply dismissed them across the board as loony dykes. There is something reassuring about having an antagonist live up to your expectations of him. If my brother were to get belligerent, derisive, or abusive, I could dismiss him with equal conviction. Then I could say he didn't matter. But he matters.

"I guess you're right about that," he says. "I never really thought of it. It's just this idea of a political concept settling who you're going to have relationships with that gets me."

I launch into a lecture about the personal being political, but he's right, because there's one thing wrong with my argument: I have expounded on the political and neglected the personal. It's the one part I can't seem to get out. It's perfectly reasonable that he doesn't understand. I'm touched that he's still trusting in me enough to sit rubbing his cheek thoughtfully as he tries to digest what I have not really prepared for consumption.

So I explain why I feel it's important to fully acknowledge all the components of one's identity. "I'm white, I'm middle-class, I'm Jewish, I'm a woman, I'm a writer, I'm a feminist, I'm

a native New Yorker, I'm a lesbian," I say. "Each of these is absolutely fundamental to my concept of myself as a person in
the world." I add that coming out as a lesbian was what finally
made me throw out the last vestiges of my anti-Semitism. Finding out what lesbian separatism meant made me think of what
Jewish separatism meant to me all my life. The two reflected so
much on each other that I was finally able to look at separatism—
what it was for the separatists, and for the ones being separated
from.

"Sometimes I think of those stories they used to tell us in
Hebrew school, about the Jews in Europe during the war who
were 'safely' assimilated with changed names and false histories,
who finally put mezuzahs up on their doors and got carted
away. They used to make these people sound like heroes, and
I always thought they were just crazy. But now I understand.
Not that I'd be putting any mezuzahs up on *my* door, or coming out if the government were going to execute me for it. I'd
still be scared and cowardly. But I understand the point now. I
understand what it means to deny who you are." There, it was
subtle but he might have caught it.

"I still think it's crazy," says Steven. "You're not denying
who you are to yourself. Why would you willingly bring more
problems into your own life? I think it's more important to
do what you want to do, know who you are in yourself, but
protect yourself at the same time."

I tell him then about Rema, a friend from high school who is
a lesbian now. I saw her once last year, by accident, in a restaurant in Chinatown. She works for a jewelry company, wears
makeup and excruciatingly high heels, and is only out to her
closest friends, who are all lesbians and none of whom consider
themselves feminists.

"I don't see how anyone can live like that," I say.

"I do," says Steven, "I really do. Not everyone's like you.
Not everyone wants to fight. Some people just want to have an
easy life."

"At the cost of feeding the world's stereotypes. Rema gets
chalked up as straight. When people in her office look around
and take stock of the world, they're going to believe it's homo-
geneously straight, as long as everyone in it claims to be. For all
we know, half the earth could be gay and no one will ever
know, because everyone's so busy acting straight."

"But that's her decision," says Steven.

"It's not just *her* decision. Rema's not only perpetuating her own oppression—she's perpetuating mine!" Oh my God—I've actually used the word "oppression." It sounds ridiculous uttered here in The Greasy Spoon, with my brother. It's one of those words you generally pitch only when there's someone around who's trained to catch it.

"But can't you understand why someone might not want to deal with being a social outcast?"

"I'm not an outcast!" I yell, hitting the table. A couple in the next booth turns around and looks at me in surprise. If there's one thing I want Steven to understand, it's that I'm no outcast and have no intention of being an outcast. But how can he truly come to understand this? How can I convey a sense of my own feminism when there is a hurt look in his eyes every time I say the word "men"? I don't mean him—but I don't know how either of us will react to excluding him from the category. How can I possibly make him understand what a women's community means? What it does? Here is a man I don't *want* to be divided from—but how can I help it, within the terms in which I've chosen to view the world now? How can we both remain whole and healthy and still be undivided?

Driving home in the car we talk, unbelievably, of other things. Neither one of us has seized the oars and rowed away, but neither of us has dropped anchor, either. What had to be said has been said; even if it never gets spoken of again, it is there, a little packet of information tied and labeled and irrevocably welded into our relationship. I feel a little ill, physically, although I can't exactly locate the source of my discomfort. I'm not sorry I told him. If I hadn't, I would have gone on month after month, probably year after year, always planning to, perennially on the verge. And that would have been like pushing a rock uphill through all of eternity; or like writing a book that is all preface.

And there he is at the wheel, still driving, still liking me, not going through any red lights. And I still like him too, even if it would be more convenient at this moment not to. I look at him, his face washed in wave after wave of streetlight as we ride down the Queens avenue we have ridden down since we were born. We aren't waiting to grow up any more; we aren't wondering who we'll become, what profession we'll choose, whom we'll marry. These questions haven't been answered; but we've lived long enough to know that life is not a symphony that plays itself out in three movements. The answers, when they come at all, are unearthed in fragments, like archaic fossils or chips of Greek pottery, and at random, often after many days of fruitless digging. And if Steven and I aren't digging in the same place, at least we share some sense of the theory and the process of the dig, and looking back to where we started our eyes come to rest on the same point.

What I didn't know until now, until I came upon this fragment, is that what I hoped for will most likely never happen. Steven and I have already been socialized. Lies, already firmly woven in the fabric of our past together, insist upon the shapes of our present. Yet there are also truths buried in our history which have spun a binding web around us. We are the world's only two bona fide products of the union of Selma and Larry Edelman, the only two ever to have grown up in our house under our circumstances. We are the central intelligence bank of the idiosyncrasies of these two individuals, and we carry these idiosyncrasies around somewhere in our own personalities. At best it is like a legacy, at worst a genetic disease. In either case, certain secrets will always hover between us. Some we'll learn to speak, others will remain silenced, but we will always be pressed into remembrance of their existence by each other's mere presence. There is no one else that either of us can ever be connected to in this way, just as nothing can ever separate us from the common ground of our knowledge—even when the intensity makes us wish to be divided.

My mother used to tell me the story of how I had interrupted my brother's circumcision by crying out at the crucial moment, "The doctor is going to cut the baby!" This was Steven's *bris*, the first major event in a Jewish boy's life and generally the occasion for a party. If he, the boy, had been the firstborn, the *bris* would have been followed by a *pidion aben* a month later. No one in my family has ever been clear on the significance of a *pidion aben*; they only know that it is a tradition, another excuse to celebrate. At the age of thirteen Steven was worth $1500, most of it bonds given to him at his Bar Mitzvah—the ceremony invented so that the Jewish boy can proclaim: "Today I am a man."

I have been told that my turn too will come. My grandmother, who is senile and often doesn't remember who I am, has one message to impart when she recognizes me at her nursing home: "Remember, I want to dance at your wedding." She has said this to me over and over, like a broken record, sometimes a dozen times in one visit. Ninety-one years old and in a wheel-chair, but if I marry she will dance. Sometimes I have the impulse to gather my family and say: "Today I am a lesbian," and see who starts to dance. I would like to see someone rent a catering hall, give me a salad bowl, say, "Mazel tov, mazel tov, health and happiness always!" with tears of joy in their eyes. My birth, my marriage, my death—these are the events which did, would, will chart my existence; they are my demarcation lines on the genealogical map.

"Why is it so important to you to tell the world?" had been Steven's question. "What do you get from it?" And I know the crazy thing I hoped to get from telling him. I hoped to see him dance.

*If I Forget Thee
O Jerusalem*

If I Forget

Evelyn Torton Beck

The entire Israel section of the 1982 *Nice Jewish Girls* was virtually out of date by the time the book appeared. The first edition went to press *before* the Israeli invasion of Lebanon, the second edition *before* the *intifada* (Palestinian uprising) and *before* some Jews in the United States broke their silence and "came out" in vocal support of the Israeli peace movement, a two-state solution, and an end to the occupation in the West Bank and Gaza.

Because this book is also a historical document, I have left this section intact (with the exception of one piece omitted for space considerations). To bring the book up to date, I have added a new poem and a long meditation by Irena Klepfisz documenting the complexity of the changes that have taken place in Israel and analyzing the leadership role taken by Israeli and American feminists.

The *Yerushalayim Midrash*, circulated by the Passover Peace Coalition, encourages us to meditate upon the Hebrew prayer *L'shana haba-ah b'Yerushalayim* (next year in Jerusalem), which is repeated by Jews at the conclusion of the annual Passover seder.

> There is a teaching that Yerushalayim means *ir-ha-shalom* (city of peace). There is also a teaching that Yerushalayim means *yerusha olam* (the world's inheritance). Next year, may Jerusalem be a City of Peace for both peoples. May Israel be a signpost of peace. May all the world rejoice in its heritage of holiness and peace. *

In this spirit and in the spirit of those women in Israel, Jewish and Palestinian, who are struggling together with Palestinian women for a Palestinian state that would coexist *in peace* alongside a Jewish one, I dedicate this section.

May 1989

*The *Yerushalayim Midrash* was created by Arthur Waskow.

221

Next Year in Jerusalem?
Evelyn Torton Beck

For many Jews, the question of Israel is the most complex and confusing aspect of identifying as a Jew today. Israel is undoubtedly a patriarchy and theocracy hostile to women and lesbians; there are also serious problems with its foreign policy and its treatment of Palestinians. Jews of color who live in Israel experience racism, classism, and the elitism of Ashkenazi Jews. This situation becomes even more complex when we realize the strong Sephardic backing of the present Begin administration.

No matter how critical Jews may be of Israel's internal and external politics, most will probably have some positive response to the idea of a Jewish state. It is all too easy for gentiles to forget that the impulse for a Jewish homeland is itself the result of centuries of anti-Semitism and enforced expulsions, that the need for such a state was sharply exacerbated by Hitler's "final solution"—the annihilation of all Jews. I think of this again when I read about the recent bombings of synagogues in Paris, Vienna, and Antwerp, the violent destruction of a Jewish restaurant in West Berlin. The newspapers report that such acts are "political gestures" protesting these countries' relationships to Zionism. These questions haunt me: Why was a *synagogue* bombed? A *Jewish* restaurant? How are these "political" acts of violence and murder different from the old forms of Jew-hating? What makes these acts any less anti-Semitic? Does Israel provide anti-Semites a code word for anti-Semitism as was so clearly the case in Poland in the wake of the recent labor uprisings (which were interpreted as a "Zionist conspiracy" initiated by Jewish agitators)? The rhetoric is all too familiar.

In a recent interview, Jacobo Timerman explores the logic of such accusations: "To say that anti-Zionism is not anti-Semitism is a lie. It is like saying that there is a difference between authoritarianism and totalitarian governments—another adventure in semantics."[1] The degree of public and private hatred unleashed onto Israel seems far out of proportion to what Israel has actually done (in comparison to other countries, such as England, France, Belgium, and the Soviet Union—whose right to *existence* is not questioned).

In the light of this analysis, what am I to make of the anti-Semitic propaganda that is distributed at some meetings where lesbian-feminists work in coalition with other groups? For example, the literature of the John Brown Anti-Klan Committee contains the following:

> Zionism is the enshrinement of white supremacy. . . . Contrary to Zionist claims, they do work with the Klan and other white supremacist groups. The Black liberation struggle and Zionism are diametrically opposed, unlike Zionism and Nazism (or KKKism or fascist jingoism).[2]

Can Jewish lesbians continue to work with groups that call for the eradication of Israel (considered a white supremacist plot) and who equate Zionism with Judaism? The above statement, which pits people of color against Jews, makes it seem impossible for those Jews who in any way support the existence of Israel also to work against racism. Given the large numbers of Jews active in various groups struggling against the American Nazi party, the Klan, and the Moral Majority, this statement is not only false, but also destructive and divisive.

Our vulnerability as Jews is mirrored in the kinds of discomfort we feel while trying to salvage and explain Israel. Timerman believes that liberal Jews of the diaspora, particularly in the United States, feel extreme guilt regarding Israel's reactionary policies. He suggests that such liberal guilt serves only to prevent Jews from criticizing or changing Israel. While he himself chose to settle in Israel after being expelled from Argentina, he is very direct about his criticism of Israel and continues to fight for human rights there as he did in Argentina.

Jewish lesbian-feminists cannot help but feel critical toward the present Israeli government. Yet, Israel mirrors the pluralism behind the initial Zionist impulse. Israel was to be all things to all Jews. Instead, it became simply a nation among nations, nothing more and nothing less. Let us understand its limitations and work to change it to be a place that we can comfortably call a Jewish homeland.

In the past few years, many Israeli lesbian-feminists, who are addressing the homophobia, sexism, racism, and classism of Israeli society, have begun this work. They are also trying to create links with lesbian-feminists in other countries. But these Israeli lesbian-feminists report that they have been ostracized by women from many other countries and are frequently attacked for living in Israel and for being Israeli.[3] In 1981, some European feminists refused to attend an International Women's Studies Conference in Israel because of Israel's annexation of the Golan Heights. Is it not anti-Semitic for women to refuse to work with Israeli feminists solely because of their nationality, especially since many of these Israeli women are courageously taking stances against their government?

Next year in Jerusalem?

Endnotes

[1]Interview by John S. Friedman, *In These Times* (October 14-20, 1981), p. 20.

[2]*The Dividing Line of the 80's: Take a Stand Against the Klan* (1981), p. 16. See also pages 3, 26, and 31.

[3]*Lilith* 8 (1981) has a report of the virulent anti-Semitism encountered by Israeli and other Jewish women at the July 1980 U.N. Mid-Decade Conference on Women (Copenhagen). See pages 30-35.

Letter from Jerusalem
Shelley Horwitz

Dear Evi,

Your recent letter, which posed questions about my decision to make *aliyah* as an American-born lesbian-feminist activist, offered me the opportunity to express the frustration and rage that has been swelling in me during the past four years. I appreciate your willingness to serve as a courier to my Diaspora sisters, who assume that to live in Israel as a lesbian-feminist activist is at best a contradiction, and at worst an impossibility. I often feel as though the Israeli women's struggle is judged by others without consideration of the forces we work against; our lesbian mothers, school teachers, and health workers do not have the economic and political resources backing them, as in the States. When a lesbian either intentionally declares her sexuality or becomes prey to homophobic exposure, the consequences are more severe. For a lesbian to publicly affirm her sexuality, she takes the stance of a courageous fighter. And more and more Israeli lesbians are taking that stance.

In comparison to the United States, we are struggling in a more conservative and traditionally-structured society. Economic survival is harder, creating a greater struggle in developing alternative women's resources. In the past several years, we have created a network of women's centers, battered women's shelters, and rape crisis centers. Our movement has been focussing on issues of violence against women, the maintenance of liberal abortion laws, and the building of a solid national women's movement. Our direction is to lessen the internal isolation of women in Israel, as well as to create greater understanding and connections on an international level. Yet, our struggle seems to be discredited by others because of the fact that we work, live, and identify as Israeli women.

The boundaries between anti-Semitism and anti-Zionism are frequently blurred. Anti-Semitic rhetoric is strong in many parts of the world, particularly America, Europe, and the Middle East. It was present at the 1980 U.N. Conference on Women held in Copenhagen. Since my identification tag cited Israel as my country, I was constantly challenged and confronted with hostility. Without introduction, a British woman demanded to know what territories I was prepared to give back. During a panel discussion on refugees, anti-Israeli diatribes deteriorated into shouts of "down with Zionism," "kill the Jews," and "death to the Jews." In another workshop, a Palestinian woman blamed the Israeli occupation for the sexual inequality of Palestinian women. Although our intention was not to defend Israeli-occupation policy, another Israeli woman and I were denied permission to respond to these statements. I was later grateful to find support among a *chevri* of Israeli and Jewish-American women.

At a lesbian camp in Norway, I was greeted with heavy silence when I stated that I was not in total opposition to the Israeli Defense Force. Even though I am personally opposed to militarism, I believe that Israel's survival is contingent upon the existence of adequate defense. One cannot ignore the fact that Israel is in a constant state of war, perpetuated by countries seeking to annihilate her. We are under moral obligation to defend ourselves.

In order to understand Israel, one must recognize her relation to the Holocaust. Many Jews, both in the Diaspora and Israel, avoid dealing with the Holocaust because it is impossible to shield oneself from the pain of systematic destruction of one's own people, the calculated torture, de-humanization and degradation that has been directed against us, and the silence and complicity of an uncaring world in the face of it. With horrifying clarity, it becomes a bitter lesson about the need for a Jewish homeland.

When Jews mention the Holocaust, or the dangers of repetition, we are accused of functioning under hysteria and obsession. This can be seen as parallel to the accusations of hysteria directed at radical feminists who point out the manifestations of misogyny as a threat to each woman's survival. There is a trend to minimize or deny the actuality of the Holocaust. In both the United States and Germany, revisionist organizations offer monetary reward to anyone who can "scientifically prove" that even one Jew was murdered. These fascists contend that the Holocaust is an invention of an international Jewish conspiracy, to obtain financial retribution. And these accusations and denials are backed with support from liberals such as Noam Chomsky. Again, they would erase us from history and wipe us off the map. The murder of nine million women as witches was similarly denied. As women have been gradually uncovering our herstory (which includes the atrocities committed against us), so must Jews assume a historical responsibility to bear witness and guard against repetition of such events. The lessons of history are important and the past cannot be ignored or politically disowned.

I have often found myself in the position of explaining and justifying my support for Israel. By identifying myself as a Zionist, I am confirming my solidarity with Jewish people and expressing my belief that at this point in history, it is necessary that a Jewish homeland exist. I believe that it is important for Jewish women to support Israel—in addition to working towards important political, economic, and social change. As Jews, our fate is tied to that of other Jews. The fate of the Jewish people is tied to Israel. Zionism is the national liberation movement of the Jewish people. It was created out of necessity and socialist/utopian dreams of equality. Too often, Jews are expected to apologize for and deny our existence, distinctiveness, self-interest, concerns, and identity. Like the class of women, Jews are always expected to be self-sacrificing. Zionists refuse to do so.

So, *nu*, what led me here? Two major aspects of my identity are that of woman and Jew. These are both objective facts. To be Jewish is not something one chooses; one is born into the Jewish people. *What can be chosen is the level of identification and commitment to being a Jew.* One has several options in dealing with the experience of being a Jew in the Diaspora: rejection or denial of one's Jewish identity and heritage, assimilation into the majority culture, or commitment to maintaining one's Jewish identity.

My coming to Israel was such a commitment, an affirmation of my Jewish self. Coming-out as a lesbian was coming home to myself. It brought clarity and a truer sense of being. Coming home to Israel brought a peace and rest to my soul, an end to the deep sense of homelessness and "otherness"—the alienation of the Wandering Jew. An inexorable burden of oppression was lifted, and I could breathe more freely. I am not claiming to be free of oppression in Israel, but on some fundamental levels I feel more whole here. I am more comfortable as a lesbian in Israel (despite the *tsores*) than I was as a Jew in the States, even in gay San Francisco. There I experienced oppression both as a lesbian and Jew; here, I am at least spared the daily confrontation with anti-Semitism.

As a child in Ohio, I was called *kike*, "dirty Jew," "Christkiller," and children asked to "feel my horns." On my way home from school I often defended myself with fists, because my parents encouraged me to have self-respect and integrity, not to allow the *goyim* to harass me. In my neighborhood, Jewish parents organized to protest the fifth- and sixth-grade boys wearing Nazi armbands and proudly displaying other Nazi paraphenalia. Our teachers were oblivious to the impact this symbol of violence had on Jewish students. Other less blatant forms of anti-Semitism were evidenced in the omission of Jewish history from the school curriculum. My history lay in the *shtetls* and pogroms of Russia. My lessons regarding the three thousand years of anti-Semitism were learned at home under the tutelage of my grandmother. The murder of six million Jews was barely referred to in our textbooks. Nor were we taught that the horrors of Nazism were committed specifically and intentionally against the Jewish people.

Later in life, anti-Semitic confrontations continued on a more "sophisticated" level among my "politically-conscious sisters" within the women's movement. While no sister asked to feel my horns, some called me *kike*. They continued to inform me that all Jews are rich and control the media, that we are pushy, aggressive, clannish, superior, smarter than, too intense, talk too fast, and Goddess-killers (a variation on the theme of Christ-killer). Others asked me what difference it makes to be Jewish. This is like asking what difference it makes to be a woman. The very question invalidated my existence and experience.

When I originally left for Israel, I did not intend on making *aliyah*. I went as a tourist for six months, secure with the knowledge that I could return at any time. Even so, I worried about my arrival, knowing that it would confront a lifetime of dreams. What if I didn't like it? What if I liked it but couldn't live openly as a lesbian? And, what if (*oy va voy*) I did like it and wanted to stay? This question worried me as much as the fear of disappointment. It would mean living oceans apart from my family and friends.

Well, four years have passed, and I now consider myself an Israeli. It is possible to fall in love on every street corner—the women are incredibly strong and beautiful. Is this taboo to say?

I love Jewish women, and Jewish women in Israel are even more wonderful. Yes, it is true—we are beautiful, we look, we touch, and we struggle together.

I hope to continue this conversation with you in Jerusalem. Come.

Mazel tov chaverot.

Shelley

A Lesbian
in the Promised Land
Marcia Freedman

An Israeli lesbian is a *lesbit* (lez' bēt). It is a "latinate" word, taken from English and given the standard feminine ending. A feminist is a *feministit*—same story. There are no Hebrew words for us. The Old Testament (and current Israeli law) prohibits male homosexuality, calls it an abomination, an unnatural act. But neither Jewish law nor sacred literature ever mentions love between women.

Lesbit is a general curse word, used interchangeably with *zonah*. Both signify sexual disobedience and therefore disgrace. It is a word to be whispered or hissed. A *lesbit* is a manhater and a pervert. It has a hard sound and is hard to say—that "bēt" at the end does not roll easily off the tongue.

At Rabbinical court. Holit and I have come with one of the women from the shelter. She's come for another of what seems like an endless number of hearings, trying to get a divorce from the wiry, mean-looking guy sitting across the narrow corridor. He, too, has brought a friend. The corridor is filled with waiting women, one driven to hysteria by the endless waiting, the endless delays, the *dayanim* in the long black coats, beards—the black and grey of ancient male plumage. Our *dayanim* know better than most the suffering of Israeli wives. But all they do is reprimand the husbands and send the wives back for another try at *shalom bayt*. The women become desperate, the men crueler. The shelter enrages them; it is beyond their reach and with it, so are their wives.

The mean-looking one is baiting. To Holit he says, "I hear you teach my wife karate. How about a match?" He and his friend stand, move in on us across the corridor. We stand, too, ready to take them on if necessary. The two men back off, shouting, "Do you know what you two are? You're lesbians! Do you know what that means?"

It is hard not to laugh. Of course he doesn't know that we actually do It together.

Maya, who is still my lover despite the ten thousand miles between us, knew that she was a lesbian at the age of twelve, and all through high school she pursued women. Gradually, she learned to believe that she was a freak, an accident of nature, born by mistake. Her hygiene teacher asked her to leave the classroom during the lesson on menstruation; it is for girls only. Maya grew up in a small village near Tel Aviv—a few dozen one- and two-room houses and a *dunam* of land on which to raise chickens or keep a few cows. Maya ate chicken every day of her life. Her mother raised the chickens. Her father was a construction worker—an ideologically preferred job in those days of "building the homeland."

By the age of nine Maya can ride a motorcycle. By sixteen she can fly a plane. By the age of eighteen, she must stop flying planes because the air force doesn't allow women to become pilots. During her teens, she learns the word for herself, *lesbit*, from a magazine article on sex-change operations. It is the first time she has heard or seen the word. It confirms that she was born by mistake. Later, a student at Hebrew University, Maya consults the library. Books on homosexuality are all on the psychology shelves. Maya learns that she has a disease, and that "intelligent lesbians are almost impossible to cure." Maya learns that there are intelligent lesbians. That she has a dis-ease.

There was no Greenwich Village to run off to, no gay bars, nowhere to meet others like herself. Nothing at all in the environment offers validation. So Maya marries and tries to cure herself by bearing three children, each one marking the end of an unsatisfying affair with a straight woman. She expresses her difference with a doctorate in physics, thanks to which she was in America in 1974.

Penina (Pearl) was not so lucky. She was a rabbi's daughter, raised in strict orthodoxy. She was an artist who made her living by creating designs for mass-produced ceramics. Living alone, all alone, without friends and without lovers. She rarely went out. Not by choice but by the coincidence of an orthodox upbringing and lesbian sexuality. Her art is monotone and formal, an art of anonymity. One year ago, in her forties, Penina committed suicide.

During my four years in office, I was not out, not publicly and not to myself. There were rumors, but I was protected by a long-term (the length of my term, in fact) relationship with a man, a journalist well known in the circles that rumored. I told myself, during those years, that I didn't identify as a lesbian because I was not yet sure I was one. But looking back I can see the fear that kept me closeted. The lesbian community then was very small (a few dozen women, at most, scattered over three cities), frightened, often self-hating and mostly non-feminist. The straight feminists, though sophisticated about it, were frightened by lesbianism. Not much encouragement there either. Although I was out of touch with homophobia, and in retrospect entirely naive about what it could mean to my life, I sensed that I walked a thin line and that coming out would have consequences.

I came out, finally, only a few months after leaving politics. 1977, still in the public eye and still wanting to be there, was the year of my first committed relationship with a woman. It was hers as well. Holit, born and raised in America but of the Middle East, like me had been traveling down the road a long time, and we were old and loving friends. And still are, now that we are both in Berkeley. We consider it an irony of life in Israel that she had been my ex-husband's lover before she was mine.

Together we experienced the process of social ostracism that being a lesbian in Israel entails. But not fully, not until we broke up and found, each of us, how alone we had become. A few loyal friends remained, but we were not invited places—public or private—as once we had been. And when occasionally we were, we did not care to go. Too much concealment required. Though everyone supposed we were lesbians, they did not wish to be reminded.

Holit left at the end of that year and went to Berkeley, to heal. After two years she returned, to test her memory of Israel I think, and found that nothing had changed. The isolation, the alienation, the sense of being marginal even among the marginal were waiting for her at the airport. She's back in Berkeley now, and I have joined her. She speaks desperately of "rescuing" the rest of her friends and bringing them over.

Homosexual politics. A bill is introduced to decriminalize the homosexual act. A newly formed gay-rights organization (mostly men) convinced civil-rights advocate Shulamit Aloni to introduce the bill, which she did. The gay-rights group knew of me, as well as another gay Member, but approached neither of us, respecting our closets. Aloni introduced the bill, but did nothing to bring it to the floor for debate. She seemed embarrassed by the huge amount of publicity the bill was getting. I knew that I had to begin lobbying for the bill, and I also knew that I'd be the only one doing so. Taking a deep breath, I stopped the first Member who crossed my path. He is a strikingly handsome man in his seventies, very conservative and very old-fashioned. I spoke to him about the bill and the injustices suffered by homosexuals in Israel. "But there are no homosexuals in Israel," he said—his only words before walking away.

I naively put it down to his naiveté. But soon learned that it wasn't. That just as I'd had to prove there were battered women in Israel, and Jewish rapists and teenage prostitutes, now I'd have to prove there were homosexuals. Not an easy thing to do when all but a handful are carefully closeted, including myself. I contacted the leaders of the gay rights group, proposed to organize the lobbying from my end if they would send in people to lobby the Members. We discussed it for several hours, and I never heard from them again. The bill went out with a whisper.

I laughed at Israeli homophobia and came out proudly when I finally did, one of the handful of uncloseted lesbians in the country. I laughed at my own encounters with homophobia to protect myself, but I couldn't protect my daughter. She had her nose rubbed in it. Soon it drove her away from me, to live with her father, a public act of renunciation, a rejection of the new home I was making with my lover and her children, and a rejection of my rejecting her, so engrossed was I with my new love that for a while nothing else existed. Eventually, homophobia drove her out of Israel, to Berkeley for a year's sabbatical with her father. She meets gay peers, gay adults, learns it's no stigma to have a lesbian mother—it's even a bit of a status symbol in Berkeley, she tells me on the phone. When I arrive that winter for a visit, she tells me she thinks she wants to stay in Berkeley, does not want to go back to Israel. And I promise to come and live with her. My lover will remain in Israel, but I too need to get away.

The homophobia that I'd laughed at had over the years gotten to me in other ways. The society in which I'd been so active now ignored my existence. Where a few years earlier I'd been overwhelmed with requests to speak, I was hardly ever invited anymore. Where I'd had access to the daily press, magazines and the media, I couldn't even get a letter to the editor printed now. The work that I did had to be self-initiated; the environment, self-created. The establishment's doors are closed to dykes who don't know enough to be discreet.

A friend from New York comes to Israel to participate in a peace-movement event. She asks the organizers why I hadn't been invited to speak. "You should never have come out, Marcia," she tells me later.

My daughter. From the beginning, she was on the firing line. When I became a famous feminist, she, not me, personally confronted the hostility I aroused. She was "Marcia Freedman's daughter" and, as such, frightening, different and tainted to many of her classmates and teachers. As was I in the adult world. First for being an angry, noisy and incessant feminist. Then for ending my marriage and exercising my freedoms. And then, finally and the last straw, for being a lesbian. During the heterosexual years it was rumored that I took on eight men at one time. During the lesbian years, it was rumored that I had orgies in which my daughter (aged eleven, twelve, thirteen) participated. For the full year after I came out, she was ostracized by her peers—only a few friends remained loyal (though remain loyal they did). She, as I, had been branded a pervert and a whore (take your pick). No one ever said these things directly to me, but they did to her. One classmate called to ask if it were true that her mother was a lesbian and had I ever tried therapy? It was my child's habit to protect me, so I didn't know much of this while it was happening.

There are stereotypes about Israelis that the Israelis thrive on. That they are direct, speak their minds, do not mince words. That they are practical and efficient. That they are fearless. For some, where these traits are tempered by scruples and sensitivity, the stereotype generates heroes and heroines. For many, however, it is an excuse for self-righteousness and simple rudeness. There are no deviations from their norm; there are no rules they need recognize in punishing deviance.

I knew Leah for three years—we'd worked together and been friends—before I knew that she was a lesbian. Leah, though an active feminist, was a closet dyke. We argue about that incessantly. What good would coming out do, she insists. By keeping her secrets she can have influence, be effective. Which was true. She goes on, visions of holocausts. "If ever we come out, organize as a political force here, we'll be stoned in the streets." In Biblical and Talmudic times, sexually disobedient women were stoned to death. Today, in certain parts of Jerusalem, fanatically orthodox Jews throw stones at the cars driven on the Sabbath and at women immodestly dressed. Perhaps she is right. Goddess knows but she may be right. Certainly on a personal basis, the punishment is severe enough—the traditional Hebrew punishment. You remember—what they did to Spinoza.

Maya's family—mother, brother, sister-in-law and their almost adult children—have been invited to a birthday party. I live there and so am present. Wherever I sit, they gather elsewhere. I join them and they drift away, one at a time. They do not talk to me, speak among themselves as though I am not there. Only the sister-in-law occasionally breaks ranks. It is maddening. It is a microcosm of what surrounds me.

Israel is a post-revolutionary society. Its national liberation movement successful and now into its thirty-third year. Post-revolutionary societies are notoriously oppressive. Israeli children learn in school that "it is good to die for our country." The group takes precedence over the individual, the State takes precedence over all. Israelis have a saying about their country, calling it "a land that devours its inhabitants." The threat of war, the insecurity of being a tiny Jewish minority in the Middle East, is a whip in the hands of political leaders, keeping everyone in line. Education is geared towards science and technology, and minds are trained to accept authority.

This is a harsh picture. It must be tempered by the banalities of daily life, the extraordinary sense of community and the Mideastern sun.

The ḥammam in Jerusalem is a leftover of the Ottoman Empire, one of the few places in Israel to remain authentically Middle Eastern. Most of the time, it is open to men only; twice a week, on Mondays and Wednesdays, it is open to women. There are two kinds of women who come on Mondays and Wednesdays. There are young American-born dykes or Israeli dykes who have found the ḥammam through their American sisters. And there are older Sephardic women, Afro-Asian

Jewish women, most of them beyond their childbearing years, looking seventy or eighty but probably only forty or fifty. From them I learn the beauty of the female body, even at the stage where, I'd been taught, we were supposed to be ugly. I learned how to rub my body down with *leefa* and henna, and I learned to bring a bunch of grapes along with my soaps, lotions and oils.

At first I didn't know and didn't assume that most of the younger women at the *ḥammam* were lesbians. The word was not said between us, hints were not given. The *ḥammam*, where no one touched, was still one of the sexiest places around. On Mondays and Wednesdays a permitted woman's world. A place to relax from politics, to get away from men, to enjoy and indulge my female body—and to look if not to touch. I would go from the hot (hot) tub to an icy cold pool, sit among the older women on heated marble slabs and rub myself down, soap myself, preen, eat grapes, smear henna on someone's back and have mine smeared in return, give and receive a massage, and then go up on the sunroof.

The sunroof is formed from the arched ceilings of the *ḥammam's* rooms. In reverse, those ceilings are the contours of a four-breasted Aphrodite. The older women never go up there to sun themselves, preferring to stretch out on rug-covered mattresses in a cool dark room lit only by a colored-glass skylight. They laugh at our white-skinned passion for the sun. We are sunstarved. We have been sunstarved for generations. We lie exposed to the sun for hours, needing nothing more than to warm ourselves, to darken our skins in the heat. We are most beautiful, most vital, when our skins turn brown.

The lesbians lie upon and around those breasts for hours at a time, bodies oiled and gleaming. They are Jewish women, mostly dark-haired and dark-skinned. With that much Middle Eastern sun twice a week, the bodies are very brown. The sunroof is whitewashed and gleaming in the white light of the sun over Jerusalem. The *ḥammam* is one of the high places.

It would be many years of going to the *ḥammam* before any of us were consciously aware of high places. It would be many years before we arrived at the sunroof and recognized those already there as part of the lesbian community. In the early years, the years that I was in politics, there was no such thing. Each of us thought she was the only one. But those draped brown bodies were not only sexy, they were a ceremony. Rites of absolution and purification are performed at the *ḥammam*.

About ten women meet to discuss the possibility of setting up a lesbian feminist organization. There is to be a national feminist conference in Beersheva the following month. Maya and I propose that the new organization be presented there. But there may be press coverage, and no one is willing to stand up and present it. This is to be a closet organization.

Maya says she will present on condition that the other women will at least stand up in solidarity. Twenty-five women stood up, for almost all of them the first time they'd ever done so. Rather a surprise for the other seventy-five straight feminists present.

Next morning's newspapers carry a report on the conference. Prominently featured is Dr. Amalia Bergman's presentation of the new Lesbian Feminist Organization. The phone begins to ring. Radio, television, newspapers want to speak to Dr. Amalia Bergman. A prime-time talk show wants her to be a guest. We both feel that the hour of reckoning has come, that Judgment Day is upon us. We've agreed that if she goes, we both go. We both have children; Maya has three, and she's afraid of a custody suit. What else do we fear? We never have a chance to find out. My daughter decides for us. She, the oldest of our children, begs us not to come out in the media, and we agree.

Not many Israeli women have identified in print as lesbians—two, maybe three, over the past decade and never more than once.

Two years later, the third annual feminist conference is held. Five hundred women attend, and we, the veteran feminists, are proud of the numbers, of the feminist activity that has been generated. Our movement has become a reality in Israel. Press coverage is slight, a bit of it good, but much of it vicious. Lesbians have grown comfortable with themselves in the context of the women's movement. The arts of concealment are laid aside for the two days of the conference. Women are seen to touch one another, hug, kiss; there are workshops on lesbian feminism and lesbian sexuality. The conference is depicted as a lesbian affair; the women are described as dirty, lascivious; the quotations attributed to them are garbled and foolish. The young women reporting on the conference are horrified by the woman-love they have seen and heard, and they vilify us.

The daughter of one high-placed politician goes elsewhere to live. The niece of another lives with her lover behind constantly closed shutters.

Few lesbians in Israel come out to their parents, a greater worry it seems than coming out to friends or on the job. A straight friend of mine once described Israel as Noah's Ark—everyone comes in pairs, male-female pairs. The country urges its women to marry young, to have three, four children. For the most part, women have not yet begun to question any of this.

If you marry, the State will give you an apartment. The parents will give you a good portion of their life savings to buy a refrigerator, a stove, furniture, maybe even a TV—all very expensive and hard to come by without the help of State and Family. When you have children, the State gives you money. When you have children you pay back the debt to the Family. Lesbians of course either do not marry or, generally, divorce. They do not pay back the debt to the Family or, if they do, they are single mothers struggling to survive. Lesbians do not give their parents *naḥat*. Parents do not often give the lesbians money. A lesbian daughter, acknowledged as daughter but not as lesbian, is a misfortune, a daughter who cannot find or hold a man. Strange and estranged creatures in this society that knows no generation gap, where the value of Family and the value of State is informed by the Holocaust and war.

It's a small and gossipy country. If you don't come out to your family, you don't come out at all.

When we opened the first feminist bookstore in Israel, Maya wanted to call it The Closet and hang the books on hangers in the window. The store soon became a women's center as well and a place where lesbians could say they were lesbians. Lesbian and straight women mixed. Attendance was always highest at specifically lesbian events. The straight women never got tired of hearing about lesbianism. Several crossed over and many like to flirt. The women's center in Haifa soon became known as the lesbian center. When centers opened in Tel Aviv and Jerusalem, the lesbian community began to grow and expand. It became a reality in Israel, both self-perceived and perceived by others. Even-handed articles on lesbianism began to appear in the press from time to time; real-live lesbians were (anonymously) quoted. But everyone is still in the closet and the lesbians in the country who are known to one another still don't number more than a hundred or so.

A community under fire from the straight world, even some of the straight feminist world. The old-time lesbians refer to it as the *hevreh*, the gang, and are glad it has grown. The newly

affiliated see it as salvation, a viable identity. The lesbian feminists are the bridge, and they bear the burden of the crossings
over. The numbers grow. Aided, too, by *aliyah*. Should the
authorities care to check, they would find that the Israeli
women's community is the most successful "absorption" agency in the country. Foreign-born Israeli lesbians, like myself
mostly from America, are a constant trickle of new blood. They
come for a change of scene, or Zionism, or Jewish identity, or
they just drift in. They find smallness of scale, intimacy, a
strong sense of individual importance—all so hard to achieve in
America.

A small community in a hostile environment. And like so
much of Israel, kept going economically by donations from
America. It can feel secure or suffocating. Intimate or oppressive. No matter where you go in Israel, you will never get very
far away from anything you might wish to leave behind. Women
come, but they leave as well. And it is always a wrenching tear-
ing away.

Coming together with Maya is a miracle in the desert. When
we met, there were only a few women over forty in the entire
community (today there are a few more). We felt we'd been
chosen for one another, the chosen of the chosen people. We
compared our lives and saw how our paths had crossed repeatedly, how when we finally found one another we were ready
for the impact. It was pretty heady. Especially in the rarefied
air of Jerusalem where we'd retired for a few days to see how
we felt about continuous time together. It felt wonderful. Especially when we found a house to live in made of stone with
stucco roofs, porticos, balconies, a tower. Our terrace and
garden looked out from the crest of the Carmel over Haifa Bay.
On a clear day we could see into Lebanon. Our garden, wild and
untended, grew oranges, pomegranates and *esquadinias*. Inside
the ceilings were fifteen feet high and the rooms huge. With
partitions and lofts we had a ten-room house for two adults
and four children (thirteen, ten, seven and five).

In that house for the first year our love was larger than life.
We were part of the Middle East—the sights and sounds of modern Israel reduced to the twinkling lights of Haifa Bay at night
or the pollution clouds over the Bay's industry by day. A glar-
ing, unrelenting sun. Lying on my terrace nude, in the full heat
of the sun, was part of my connection with the Middle East. In
it and of it. I may be a fairly well washed-out Semite by now,

after all these generations in Eastern Europe, but a Semite still and at home in that sun.

Our home and our love seemed mythical to others as well as to ourselves. Women came to visit just to see what it all looked like, or to take encouragement from this lesbian marriage. It didn't last, wonderful as it was while it did—reality set in first when my daughter left us, left me, and then when my soul began to cry out for privacy and solitude. Leaving was a painful unraveling and the first step towards leaving Israel, though I didn't realize that at the time. The fabric of life in Israel is tightly woven. When I began to consider leaving, I was centrally involved in at least a half dozen projects, two relationships, and I'd spent the past fifteen eventful years of my life in Haifa. I had never been more deeply and intricately connected to a place, not since childhood. Any who have done so know how hard it is to leave, and how hard to stay away. There are few objective reasons why this should be so, especially for women and even more especially for lesbian feminist women. Israel is a hostile and barren climate for dykes.

Eve. *Em Col Hai*. The Hebrew Mother of all living things. Our Mother, Her daughters, in captivity in the Promised Land. Eve's punishment, our punishment is explicit in Genesis: sexual slavery. "Thy desire shall be to thy husband, and he shall govern thee."

We Semite women are drawn to the Land again and again. What is the gut force that attracts us, holds us, even as we know we should go elsewhere for a while? We are Semitic Canaanite women and the Middle East is our habitat, even though, in its contemporary manifestations, we are not welcome. Our bodies are at home in the sun.

Not our Promise, but yes our Land.

Letters from My Aunt

Maida Tilchen with Helen D. Weinstock

In June 1974, I began a wonderful correspondence with my Aunt Helen. She has recently celebrated her sixty-second birthday, and lives in Israel. As you will discover from these letters, my aunt is a lesbian.

Every lesbian and gay man has probably wondered whether she or he has a gay relative. Aunt Helen had always been my most mysterious relative, and I often wondered about her. Unlike my other aunts, who were married and lived in New York, she never married and lived in San Francisco. My only significant childhood contacts with Aunt Helen were through letters, where I learned about her pets and motorcycles and camping trips. In my grandparents' apartment were several beautiful Japanese artifacts which she had sent them in the late forties during the Occupation. Occasionally my family received Hanukah cards signed "Helen and Marion"; once I asked my mother who Marion was, and my mother blushed and mumbled something about it not being important for me to know.

By the time I came out and began to wonder about the possibility of Aunt Helen being lesbian, I had completely lost contact with her. Then, in June of 1974, I unexpectedly received a letter from her. I was thrilled. While I hoped to discover whether she was a lesbian, I decided to proceed very slowly. As you will see from the letters, we were both groping towards coming out to each other. Once that landmark was passed, we opened up. We have since become confidantes for each other's love affairs, dreams and troubles.

My letters to Aunt Helen have become my journal of the last six years. Her letters to me began the recording of a fascinating and fully-lived life of a Jewish lesbian. The following are selections from our earliest letters, and then some of her later letters about her life as a lesbian in Israel.

Helen to Maida: June 1974

Frankly, I don't know where to begin. . . . I have lost all contact with your branch of the family. In her last letter, your sister gave me your address but not a word as to your activities—and how does someone you scarcely know go about asking personal questions? She did not mention if you are married; if you are, I hope this will reach you under the name of Tilchen.

In my reply, I told Helen what I had been doing with my life, including the following:

Maida to Helen: July 1974

Another thing that has been happening in my life is that I have lost interest in communes and got interested in the women's liberation movement. I got involved in women's liberation in Bloomington, Indiana, about seventy miles from the rural town I was living in as a VISTA. I now live in the Bloomington Women's Center with Fran Koski, who was my best friend in high school. I work on our monthly women's newsletter, and help arrange and publicize meetings.

I am really excited to write to you because I think my life is going to be a lot more like yours than my mother's. I wish you'd tell me more about your life. What kind of social life did you have in California? I think of it as a place where nonconformists disappear to and lead great lives. Please don't hesitate to ask me personal questions as I trust you and want you to know me better.

Helen to Maida: July 1974

How happy I was to receive your letter and to know that I am not the only oddball in the family. So much of what you write reminds me of things I also did—and so much that you have done sounds wonderful—thoughts of "If I could have. . . ." My parents did not allow me to take an academic high school course or go to college. When I was young there was no VISTA (I was thinking of joining it before I came to Israel). I graduated from high school with a commercial diploma, in the midst of the Depression, hating office work. After a few miserable experiences, I managed to get away from it. Jobs were very hard to get: 1) the Depression, 2) lack of experience, 3) very active anti-Semitism. Advertisements could actually state "White Christians only." I have washed spittoons in a pool parlor, packed rolls of hard candies, worked as an engine lathe operator (*that* I liked), a wirer and a solderer. I also sold door-to-door all sorts of crap and crud including Fuller brushes. For a few summers I worked as a Coney Island barker or talker. Was offered a job as a freak—"the girl with a hole in her tongue. Watch as a hook is inserted and she swings a bucket right through the air!" I chickened out only because it might've embarrassed the family if someone saw me. At that time the whole family was living in Brooklyn. Oh, in case you are wondering—I do not have a hole in my tongue. It was a gimmick (disappointed?). I often say, "I've been everything but a prostitute or a thief." That's not true. When I was in New Orleans my friend lost all our money in a poker game, and all our friends were broke. She and I were the only ones who had a room so everyone slept there crosswise on the big bed and made the rounds of the market area returning with such diverse and exotic articles as *pâté de foie gras*, cheese, loaves of bread, fruit and vegetables. Finally, I got a job as a waitress and she in a hot dog joint and we were able to enter a market without looking first for the fuzz.

Women's lib is not a new movement. It's just the name that's different. Way back when (even before my time) the women were called Bloomer Girls. It was their activities that earned women's suffrage. . . certainly no man has gone to much trouble to free us from bondage unless he was forced to by women. I don't know much about your father's family and their hangups, but I do know my father has never forgiven me because I never married and never did anything to increase the tribe of Israel which is the "duty" of every Jewish female. Would like very much to see your women's lib newsletter. Incidentally, do you find many gay women in your group and do you run into problems because of this?

My feelings about women's lib are these: the goal should be for complete legal and social equality of opportunity. I agree with you that women in power should not be just like men in power. There is a difference between the sexes besides the merely biological.

Was just about to close when I realized I hadn't told you anything about coming to Israel so I'd just as well babble on some more.

Had been sharing quarters (on Hartford Street in San Francisco) for a number of years with a friend whom I'd originally met at a New Year's party of a sort for Women's Lib club before the name Women's Lib became popular. Marion was born a Catholic, but wasn't a practicing one and her family was very close to me.

If there was a birthday party or a christening or a wedding or a wake, it was taken for granted that I would be there with the rest of the family, and on my birthday all of them came to celebrate with us. I don't remember exactly how the idea of coming to Israel originated, but we felt it was one of the few countries in the world with ideals. . . .

Maida to Helen: December 1974

To be perfectly frank, I am very curious about you. I spend a lot of time thinking about the different ways women might live their lives and yours is unique from most women your age that I have met. If you don't mind telling me, I'd like to know how you feel about the choices you've made in your life: to live far from your family, to live in a "bohemian" city like San Francisco. It seems from your letters that you committed a lot of yourself to your former roommate, Marion. As I am very close to Fran, I can understand that. I think we might be very much alike.

Helen to Maida: January 1975

I will start by answering the end of your letter first, which will either clarify things and make communication between us more free, or if I completely misunderstand you, will (possibly) end all further correspondence.

Marion and I met at a New Year's party of the Daughters of Bilitis in 1958. Although it's been some time since I was in the States, they were quite an active group of feminists at that time, and I imagine they are still in existence. I had been living alone (voluntarily) for some years and was not planning on any "commitments," but eventually we decided to live together and did for about eight years. . . . Maybe when I read this letter over in the a.m. after a good night's sleep, I will get cold feet and write something more innocuous. After all, the last time I spilled the beans (to my father) the well-known shit hit the fan.

Marion left Israel (after a year??) saying she would study Hebrew in the U.S. and study for conversion to the Jewish faith (not for religious reasons, but because she wanted to become an Israeli and she felt she would be able to adjust better if she "belonged"). And so the months went by: at first, many letters with plans for our future, which slowly died down. . . . I did make sacrifices for her, and her for me, but in the end, I guess I was more committed to my country than to her. Marion was not the first woman in my life, but I think she will be the last. I put my all into this relationship and it was not enough. Perhaps I am too old to allow myself to be torn asunder again. I fill my time with work, lectures, concerts, camping trips, and platonic, casual acquaintances. It is a fairly satisfactory life, although a bit juiceless. How do I feel about the choices I have made? Perhaps, had we not come to Israel, we might still be together. Who knows? But one cannot live one's life dreaming of the perhapses which are strewn throughout our careers on this globe. Perhaps, if my parents had permitted me to study to be a teacher as I had wanted, perhaps, perhaps. I could name you a dozen crossroads with the signpost of "PERHAPS," and have long learned not to dwell on the perhapses but to go on from where I am at present—and to enjoy what is available. That is not to say that I will not strive for better, and perhaps, for something slightly beyond my reach, but never to look backward and dwell morbidly on what is lost and cannot be regained or changed.

Maida to Helen: January 1975

I wanted to write immediately to assure you that the "well-known shit" will not hit the fan in this case. We are lesbians, yay! I had no specific reason to believe you were one but I suspected it from your lifestyle. I really want you to know how thrilling this is for me and Fran—especially for me. We want to ask you some questions. Don't feel you have to answer them. We don't know any gay women older than us, and that's why we're asking you. You are a heroine to us because you made your own life at a time when it was much harder to do than it is now. Please tell us about your childhood, and how you "came out." We are really curious about the bar scene. Was it the style in San Francisco to associate with gay men? We do, but many women here don't. Tell us more about the earlier days of D.O.B. The image of D.O.B. now is that it was conservative and aimed at "adjustment." Right now many lesbian and gay groups have the "I'm gay and proud" philosophy. Was there ever a split like that in D.O.B.?

Helen to Maida: January 1975

If you had seen one picture taken of me when I was four or five years old you would not have had any doubts. I believe that homosexuality is, in the majority of instances, a result of environmental influences and from the earliest days it was said of me, "Helen is just like her father." I remember once when I was around seven and getting my hair cut that the barber asked how the back was to be cut and my mother said, "pointed, like a boy, because she likes it like a boy."

I read Krafft-Ebing when I was fourteen and attended psychology lectures with my mother. She was devoted to a Freudian psychologist, Dr. Arthur Frank Payne, who spoke on the radio and also did public lectures. After one lecture on dream analysis I wrote him. He had mentioned a book, *The Sacred Fire* (I can't remember the author) and I wanted the author's name. I also described a dream of mine (I was fifteen). He said my dream showed me to be a woman of marriageable age—in plain words (which he did not use) he said I needed to get laid. However, he forgot to give the information on the book, so I never read it. As for his dream interpretation, I thought it was as funny as could be.

About the same age, I was in Girl Scout camp. I was aware of the fact that the bugler and the director's daughter were lovers, but it seemed a perfectly normal thing to me and I didn't pay it any special attention. Also, one of the other girls was having sex relations with another girl whom she seduced. (You notice the difference in how I refer to each of these groups? The first two were lovers, the second sexual experimentation.) Years later, when I was working in Coney Island, I saw the aggressor of the second group. She was married and had a daughter, whereas the first two were gay. In the Girl Scout camp I was not with the "in" group. Part of it was because of being Jewish, part because I had no spending money to buy handicraft materials and other luxuries. I opened a shoe-shine business and earned pocket money. Many of the other kids thought I was being "Jew-stingy"; aside from that I got along well with the girls and played an active part in the midnight taffy pulls, night raids, athletic competitions. . . but I was always conscious that SOMETHING was going on that I was missing out on.

I think the next thing of importance was my experience with Myrtle. We were both around seventeen years old and lived in Brooklyn, I on Union Street, she on Eastern Parkway. We were very close friends. Both of us devoured books although I had read much more extensively; she had no background in psychology whereas I had been through much of Freud, Jung, Adler, Krafft-Ebing and had frequently attended lectures. Myrtle was rather introverted. I forget whether her mother was a widow or a divorcee but I know that there had been no father figure around for many years and her mother had a strong personality. I was "analyzing" Myrtle and helping her to come out of her book world and mix with people and I was keeping a typewritten record of her progress (the self-confidence of the young never ceases to astonish me). One evening while her mother and future step-father were playing cards in the kitchen, Myrtle and I were lying on the couch together. How it started I don't remember, but before I knew what was happening we were making love... neither of us had any previous experience... it was an overwhelming tide of emotion. It was the first time I was truly aroused except for fantasies. Eventually, I had to get up and go home.

The next day as I was working in my father's store, I kept thinking of it. I could not believe it. I thought, "I must have dreamed it all." Finally I phoned Myrtle and asked, "Was I over at your house last evening?" She said, "Yes." I asked, "Did anything unusual happen?" She said, "Yes, are you sorry?" I said, "No, I'll be over again tonight." So began my first satisfactory sexual relationship. For some months Myrtle and I were inseparable; however, I finally became conscious that our relationship had deteriorated intellectually. We no longer discussed books, music, psychology. Any time we were together alone it was sex, sex, sex. Also, I became worried that this might have a detrimental effect on her life. Funny, although I knew she wasn't gay, I never thought of myself as gay or not. I have often been insightful of others but unaware of my own mental processes. Anyway, I saw that we were really becoming enslaved by sex to the detriment of all other aspects of our relationship and that we were excluding other people from our lives; so still in the framework of my "analyzing" treatment I explained to her that this, which had been between us, was only a normal phase which many teenagers go through and that it was time to return to a normal life. Gradually, I saw to it that we did not meet as often and there was less opportunity and less temptation for us to indulge in our favorite activity. It was not as easy for me as it may sound, but I sincerely thought it was a normal phase.

A number of years later (I think it was around 1943) I brought a WAC sergeant I was going with to visit my parents and we stopped to visit Myrtle and her mother who lived a few doors up. It was shortly after this that Myrtle joined the women's army and I've often wondered if there was any connection—I mean, if meeting the sergeant influenced her to join.

Her mother and I had become very good friends and I had told her about being gay (that was after I had been to Japan). She told me that she had one sexual experience with a woman (they were both hard up and no man was available) and it had been terrific, but I never told her about my relationship with her daughter. Myrtle did eventually marry. When her mother died, many years later, I lost track of Myrtle. I never saw her again after she married but she lived a very adventurous life in the wilds of Alaska and later in some midwestern town.

After this episode with Myrtle, I went about building a "normal heterosexual" life, dating boys. I did meet, date, and go to bed with two fellows, during this period, but despite my deep liking for them I felt absolutely no physical response to their lovemaking—not disgust—just nothing. In time I dropped the sexual bit entirely, putting it out of my mind. There was so much more to do in life: books, music, bicycling, hiking, and thoughts to share with friends. I did enjoy parties and dancing. I became quite adept at the smooth "goodnight" at the doorstep, perhaps with a light kiss. Not that boys disgusted me or seemed repulsive; they just brought forth no pleasurable physical response at all, so why bother?

When I was twenty-one I moved out of my parents' home and into a French pension on 33rd Street between Eighth and Ninth Avenues. There I met Vijeko, a man about twenty years my senior. He was Chief Engineer on a ship, an educated and sensitive man. We went to concerts, to the opera and ballet. We went rowing in Central Park, hiking in the country, wandering around the city. He became my lover and I loved him deeply: he never knew that I felt absolutely no sexual response to his lovemaking.

One day when Vijeko was away on a cruise, I saw a new tenant coming into the lobby of our building. He was a young man, pretty rather than handsome. I immediately felt that I must meet him and managed to get introduced. His name was Adrian, and in the course of our conversation he mentioned that he was going to attend a masquerade the next night. I thought, "If he is going as a woman, I know he is one of THOSE." I had until then never knowingly met a homosexual (I did not know the word "gay") but felt fascinated by this young fellow.

Sure enough, he was planning to go as a woman, so I invited him to my room offering him the loan of my hat and other accessories, which he accepted gratefully. I did not understand why I was so attracted to him—it was certainly not on a male/female level—all I knew was that I had to get to know this fellow better, that it was important for me.

Two days later he returned from the masquerade. When I asked him about it, he asked me if I was gay. I told him I did not know the word so he explained it. "You know," I said, "I never even thought about the possibility." I told him about Myrtle and about my reaction (or lack of it) to male lovemaking. Finally, I said, "Can you introduce me to a lesbian? I would like to find out."

The next day he introduced me to the only lesbian he knew. She was a hustler who preyed on women and although I did not know that at the time, I did recognize that she was not anyone with whom I'd be able to establish any meaningful relationship. However, I was determined to find out about myself and took her home with me. Despite the fact that this was just plain SEX with no pretense of romance, I was surprised to find that I had more a physical response to her than I had had to Vijeko whom I truly loved. I had no interest in ever seeing the woman again; my question about myself had been answered, and the next weekend I went down to Greenwich Village and began the search for my future life. That is when I really "came out."

Your article which included descriptions in old paperbacks of gay bars makes them appear real spooky.[1] I never was in places such as they describe or at least the places I was in were not furtive—or maybe I was so uninhibited that I wasn't aware of these aspects (the fear, the denigration). I guess you could say my final "coming out" was through the bars and once I knew my way around, they were comfortable places to be in and to relax in. Until I found my way, I sort of wandered on the fringes like a kid peeking in the window at a wonderful party she did not know how to join.

Then I saw Katie. She was about my height (five feet) with shoulder-length black wavy hair and huge, very dark eyes, and she was deaf. She always seemed to be in the midst of a group and everyone, even the not-deaf, seemed to know the hand-sign language. For weeks I haunted the bars where she went, hoping for some way to meet her. Very late one night, I saw her walking alone in the street. I ran quietly, until I almost caught up with her, then I walked quickly past her. She whistled after me and SHE picked me up (not bodily). We became "THE COUPLE" of Greenwich Village. Actually, she knew very little about

what gays do in bed and much of what she did know was only
by hearsay (like "cunnilingus causes insanity"). Since I knew
even less, we had a fairly satisfactory sex life; however, she was
very much a role player and I was forbidden to make love to
her. She appeared one day with her hair slightly trimmed. She
claimed she had gotten paint on it. Gradually it got shorter.
Eventually she looked like a cute little boy and all my feeling
for her faded away; however, the last time we were together
I did get her "turned over" and did all the things I had been
fantasizing for months—including the proof that it does not
cause insanity.

Although I would have preferred a more female-to-female
relationship, role-playing was the way of life amongst all the
lesbians I knew. One was expected to be either "butch" or
"femme." Those who did not conform were contemptuously
referred to as people who didn't know their own minds, so
since I was not attracted by imitation men, I became "butch."

Gay boys and girls mixed quite freely. Only a small minority
confined themselves solely to their own sex (socially; I am not
talking about sexually), and quite often I was the only female
in a group of boys and "passed" as one of them. I lived with
Kay for some years, and since she worked evenings, often went
out with a group of boys to strictly boy bars. Only my personal
friends knew I was a girl and the men brought drinks for me and
my friends in an attempt to try to "make" me.

I wasn't hassled much by "dirt" (as we called men who were
looking to beat up gays, male or female) because it was known
that I had a pal who was from a family pretty high up in organized crime. He and I would go drinking together—just sitting
and having a few beers and looking over the gals—but no cruising
when we were together. If any guy had ever roughed me up, my
friend would have taken care of him. Also, I had one or two
acquaintances on the vice squad and the regular police would
tip me off before any raids, so my friends and I never got caught
in anything like that.

I was lucky also that the families of all the women I have ever
lived with have always accepted me as one of the family, and
that until Marion came to Israel with me, my family had always
been very pleasant to all of the women they met. I never got the
heavy pressure to get married that many gays suffer from. One
lover I had used to come to Pesach Seders with my family (she
wasn't Jewish). When I finally left her because of her alcohol-
ism, her mother said, "Even if you and Kay get a divorce, I still

want us to be friends"—almost causing me to drop my tonsils into my soup, as I didn't know she knew.

As far as my parents are concerned, I believe my mother knew from the time of my early childhood, even before I did. But hers was an instinctual knowledge. I think she just accepted me as I was and never asked questions, or subconsciously did not allow herself to think about it. She and my first "permanent" lover were very good friends and often went to the beach together when I was away from New York but we have never discussed homosexuality and I don't know whether she has named it to herself in relationship to me. My father is, supposedly, more worldly than my mother, but he was shocked, and disinherited me when I told him about Marion and myself.

I put in many hours as a volunteer for the Air Force at the start of World War Two. I was the third female examined for the women's army—and the first rejected due to almost non-existent vision in my right eye. The war years I spent doing volunteer and defense work, and giving a pint of blood every two months (I have a fairly rare type) until I became ill and was given a choice between going to the hospital or going to a warmer climate. No Blue Cross in those days, so I thought, "if I have to spend all that money, I'd just as soon enjoy it." So that was the first time I left the New York-New Jersey environs, to go to Miami. When the war ended I went to Japan to work for the United States government. Planned to go to Germany on the same type of job but fell in love with San Francisco and never got to Europe. I did return to New York and started my nurse's training there, but the climate was again too much for me. I decided to return to San Francisco where I belonged. Graduated as a registered nurse in 1954.

I worked for the U.S. Army in occupied Japan. I was exposed by a very unbalanced bisexual woman with whom I refused to have relations. My girlfriend (a Japanese medical student) was raped by the CID (intelligence) officer assigned to the case in order "to teach her how much better a man was than a woman." She was a virgin. Why didn't I do anything? During the occupation our wonderful GIs ran amuck in Japan and did what they damn well pleased. They would get on a Japanese bus and demand cameras, wrist watches. They raped, stole, just plain took. At best, they offered girls food and other scarce necessities in exchange for their "favors." All this had the unspoken approval of the United States Army. Homosexuality at that time was strictly illegal and had any big outcry been made, Mariko and her family (her father was a dentist) would have been disgraced for life, and she would have had to drop her medical schooling. By agreeing to leave quietly, I managed to get a high officer in psychiatric services to promise protection for Mariko against future harassment (the rapist had threatened to return weekly and Mariko was about to commit suicide). I tried to get her to the United States after that, but the immigration laws were very strict. I knew that Mariko was basically a hetero (we had discussed this a long time back) and that we were a unique experience in her life. I felt that she could marry a man and that it was not correct to allow her to spend the best years waiting. It was one of the most difficult letters I have ever written. I heard from a mutual friend about a month later that she had suddenly married, and I never heard from her again.

In its earliest years, D.O.B. was a progressive group and accepted anyone who wanted to join—from way-out role-players to straight women interested in homosexual problems or women's problems in general. As time went by, a small nucleus of the more active ones sort of took it over; women who came to all meetings and worked on all projects. As is true in most group activities and clubs, it gradually became more conservative; the more colorful people and "social misfits" being discouraged. Once, I think it was the first national D.O.B. convention, we were the hosts in San Francisco and local members were asked to accept, as houseguests, members from out of state who had no place to stay. I noticed that most of the others chose conservative-looking people. One guest whose description sounded as though she might stick out like a bearded queen at a women's lib party (that doesn't sound odd enough) was sympathetically discussed by all, but no one chose her. So your dopey aunt volunteered—and she was somewhat of a social problem. The poor thing did try so hard. She actually bought a dress—the first in her life (and she was in her thirties). I had to show her how to put on a brassiere. This incident cooled me to D.O.B. It showed them to be a bunch of snobs. Soon after this I sort of dropped out of their "active" list and just occasionally came around on their big social nights, and then eventually just the New Year's parties.

Glad to hear that you have seen *The Ladder*.[2] We used to assemble, fold and staple the sheets together. Is it still mimeographed? No, I think we had some other type of duplication even then. My name on the *Ladder* mailing list was "Dorothy Winton." Of course, I knew Phyllis Lyon and Del Martin. Are they still together? It was at one of their New Year's parties that I met Marion.

Helen to Maida: February 1975

About my Zionism: you may be disappointed to know that except for a spell when I was seventeen years old and planned to come to Palestine (one of my friends went and came back with malaria so my parents wouldn't hear any more about it), I really didn't think much about the subject at all. While I was in Japan in 1948 I wasn't even aware of the War of Independence, and while I was in San Francisco I had practically no connection with Jewish life whatsoever. Although Herzl's picture always hung somewhere in the apartment of my parents and my father was a member of the Farband, he never discussed these matters with me—in fact, I don't remember him discussing any matters of economics, politics, or religion with me. It was the fact that my parents went to Israel so often (after the 1960s) and that my sister and her family were immigrating that put the idea in my head. Marion had never travelled and was very enthusiastic about it once I broached the subject. Also, she felt as I did, that this was one of the—if not the only—countries in the world with ideals. When I came here on tour in 1969, I really began to get enthused—I felt as though, at last, I had come home. Even now, despite the struggle and some bitter and lonely times, I cannot conceive of returning to the U.S. to live.

This thing of finding a place you fit is of primary importance. Filled with much idealism, I left the U.S. and a good-paying job. There are in this country kibbutzim such as I dreamed of. They are the new kibbutzim in the north along the Syrian border or in the southern part of the Negev. They are the kibbutzim of the young couples who still have ideals and are willing to sacrifice for them. They do not accept new members over the age of thirty. Galil Yam, where I was, was started by a group who had fled from the Polish pogroms. Later, it received a large group of German refugees. Marion and I were the only ones whose mother tongue was English and neither of us could speak Hebrew well enough to be able to hold more than the most elementary conversations. When she returned to the U.S., I decided to leave the kibbutz in order to take an intensive course in Hebrew after which I got a job in a hospital—which paid fairly well, but I still didn't feel that I "fit." In fact, I was beginning to say to myself, more and more often, "What in the hell am I doing in this country? For what did I sacrifice my good stateside job, comfortable apartment, my station wagon, my Vespa scooter and all my friends?" I had started to investigate the longest and cheapest routes to the U.S. when I found my present position. I am not saying it is perfect. The pay is not great and the hours are all split up, but the work fits me and I fit it. I feel I am needed where I am and that I am doing a good job as the school nurse. We have approximately 150 Israeli boarding students, another 150 who live nearby and come in daily, sixty new immigrant children from Russia, France, Argentina, and the U.S. It is an agricultural high school.

Maida to Helen: April 1975

Lately, we've been so busy with school work that we hardly socialize at all. However, starting next week there's going to be a weekly gay coffeehouse in a church. There's also a gay conference being planned for October. Fran and I are probably going to put together a workshop for it on lesbian literature. The Free University lesbian class has one more activity this semester, a weekend camping trip. I am sending a copy of the "Bloomington Women's Handbook" which I worked on.

Helen to Maida: May 1975

I was very impressed with your "Women's Handbook," and by the many organizations and activities in your area which are devoted to various aspects of woman's life. When I think of the changes in college atmosphere and society's attitudes from the days of my "coming out," I feel as though I have lived in days mid-Victorian. What growth, what freedom, and what opportunities for progress are open to you. . . and truly, how lonesome it makes me feel. You know, when Marion left I closed the door on any emotional involvement and have made no efforts to find gay people. I have tried to fill my time with work, books, trips and casual acquaintances (no sex) and to stifle my need for a closer relationship. Now, reading your letters and the women's handbook, I become aware of the lack of—I think "camaraderie" might fit best in English—of my own kind. It's sort of like, when I was in the U.S., I knew I was a Jewess, but made no special effort to BE a Jewess; however, when I came here I knew I was with my own, that something had been missing. Now, having buried my woman-feeling for so long I feel

the need to have people around with whom I could feel free—
and I don't know where to find them. I doubt you could
help me, but perhaps amongst all the organizations with which
you have contact, there may be either someone who has been
to Israel or who knows of people in Israel. If you can find out
anything, I would very much appreciate it.

Helen to Maida: December 1975

I FOUND THEM. Enclosed please find advertisement from
the Jerusalem *Post*.

> IF YOU ARE interested in changing the legal status
> of Homosexuals, in Israel, contact S.I.R. (Society for
> Individual Rights) P.O. Box 46039, Tel Aviv.

I nearly popped my buttons, sat down and answered it. Letter
ran sorta "Would like to know what the legal status of the
homosexual is in Israel" and asked whether S.I.R. here was re-
lated to the S.I.R.[3] in the States. The last, to let them know
that I had been involved in the States, that I was aware of S.I.R.
there. No reply for some time. In the meantime, there was an
ad for a Women's Rights outdoor meeting and march. Got to
that and managed to find the right people who invited me to a
gathering after the march at a private home. Although I suspected most of the females were gay, after over five years of no
contact, I was hesitant about coming out and asking. They are
to write me with more information on the women's liberation
movement. Anyway, I finally got a letter from the S.I.R. group
and have since met the girl who seems to be the chief secretary,
recruiter and bottle washer. In October the organization was
legally registered under the name of Society for the Protection
of Personal Privileges.

Maida, you cannot imagine how excited I am about all of
this. I never had any identity problems in the States and lived,
almost completely, out of the closet. Then, suddenly, to be
boxed in and apparently nailed shut down into that closet.
Every woman I met in this country seemed to be busy making
babies, or if she had no husband, was busy searching for one, or
sometimes was busy making babies without any legal husband.
Once or twice I saw a couple who looked as though they might
be one of ours, but they always seemed to be checking the locks
on their closets and I didn't dare to try the door.

Helen to Maida: February 1976

As we rejoin Aunt Helen in her adventure in SPPP land, she has so far met Ziva, twenty-five years old who appears to be doing all the work of the SPPPs, and Elly, a thirty-six year old journalist, and Haim, in his twenties, a typical gay cruiser and habitue of the parks, etc. Both Ziva and Haim live with their families. Ziva's know, Haim's don't. So came the big night and I went to the opening gathering of the guys and gals of the SPPP. There were more than fifty fellows—and only four females (including myself). Two of the women were visiting from Norway so this would be their only time with us. Some straights from the suicide prevention clinic came later, but if they were thinking of referring some of their problem people to us, I doubt if they were too impressed by what they saw. I expected the police to break in at any moment and a riot to break out. It may have been great cruising and fun for the boys, but to me it was a bore. I arranged a meeting with Ziva and Avi (a fellow active in the more serious aspects of the group) and tried to explain the necessity of an all-female group. Under the present set-up we will only end up as the women's auxiliary of a male dominated organization. However, Ziva is so heterosexual-society oriented that she let Avi do all the talking. They do not feel that there are enough females in the area to make it go and could not see that any one who might consider it would be immediately discouraged by the overwhelming majority of faggots.

Two meetings later we did meet with a group of women who live in the area—not at the club, but in the home of one of them. They also are strong for a strictly female organization. Because of my work, the fact that I live very far from Tel Aviv, and that my car has developed a stubborn streak and refused to function, I have not been able to get back to them.

Helen to Maida: November 1976

I got the day off especially to go to the feminist meeting. Not many of the feminists I had met were there—lots of new women and many of them English speaking which is not usual. One group of four looked interesting and one of them was wearing a woman power pin (fist within the woman sign) and one a gay pin (signs joined). So I got into that group. The gay-sign gal is a non-Jew from Ireland and she lives with the woman-power (Israeli born) woman. We had a terrific discussion and it went on after everyone had left and they practically had to sweep us out of the coffee house.

This weekend we had the first meeting of our consciousness-raising group. About ten women were to come but we were only five—I don't know exactly what a CR meeting is because I've never been to one but we didn't CR—just talked about what we might be able to do with the group. Two of the women are strict separatists—they don't even want to talk to men unless there is no alternative (like at work). I consider all sexes as just humans and enjoy social contacts, irrespective of sex, with intelligent, congenial people. Ruth is an enthusiastic feminist (she recently spent time in jail and still has to face a hearing on charges of spraying feminist slogans on Jerusalem walls). Hanna is bisexual, and wants one day to marry and have children—with an understanding, probably gay fellow, so she can hop the fence. From this nucleus we hope to make the lesbian feminist group.

Helen to Maida: January 1977

Saturday night there was a meeting of the male and female gays of Jerusalem. There is going to be another meeting in two weeks and a party next week—all of this I will miss because I have to work. Maybe I could get a few hours free but the round trip takes two to three hours. You know, I'm getting cheated all around. I was in the U.S. before the word "gay" was even known to straights and left just when it started to become an almost acceptable thing and now it seems to be the "in" thing to be in the States. Came here when everyone was still locked in their double-doored safety vaulted closets and worked hard to get the movement started in Tel Aviv. I had more free time then. Now that things are opening up in this country gaywise, I am really tied down to my job. I'd really like to say "fuck 'em all, I quit," but I don't have that sense of irresponsibility.

Helen to Maida: April 1977

I went to an interesting wedding. One of the lesbians married a gay fellow. Golda Meir came to the wedding. The bride's father has some connection to her, I never asked what. Golda was not, insofar as I know, aware of the fact that these people are gay. One of the gay fellows who also came is a motor scooter teacher. When he found out I used to ride he invited me for a spin so we left the hot and smoky hall. I tucked up my long maxi gown, put on my helmet, and off we went, all around Tel Aviv. Seven years since I'd been on a motor scooter. It was great!

Between 1977 and 1980, Aunt Helen and I continued to exchange letters. In these letters, she describes her growing involvement with ALEF (the Israeli lesbian-feminist organization) and the International Conference of Gay and Lesbian Jews. Aunt Helen writes also of her difficulty in making friends her own age, since most of the politically aware lesbians she encountered were considerably younger and less experienced than she.

Helen to Maida: December 1980

In response to your question about the role of Jewish lesbians in my life:

Besides Myrtle, the other Jewish girl was Katie.

I nearly forgot about Ida in San Francisco. She had a son about my age. This was right after I returned from Japan. I guess I was about thirty. She had known many men, and had never gone with a woman before me. For years we had a very warm relationship, of which I am sure her family was aware. I nursed her through her radical cancer surgery. She was a big, heavy, wonderful woman.

Those were my three Jewish women. Actually, when I came out in the forties, my friends were very un-race, un-color conscious. We felt that as gay people we should support each other. Gay fellows and gay women were friends and went in mixed groups. I know there were a lot of Jewish lesbians around the Village. I remember a discussion about the preponderance of Jewish gay women. No, I can't say there was anti-Semitism in Village gay life, at least I wasn't conscious of any. However, I was aware of it when I worked for the Army, specifically regarding the observance of Jewish holidays.

Did my need to have lesbian allies override any anti-Semitism? It never came up. I had lovers, short and long term: Caucasian, Japanese, Black, Brown, Red, Native American and except for the three Jewesses, I was seldom aware of their religions. I never knew whether Mariko was Buddhist or Shinto. In Israel, we come in all shades, from the fairly dark Yemenites and Moroccans to the blonds. I'm sorry to say there is a certain amount of estrangement between the darker Sephardim and the lighter

Ashkenazi. This is true amongst the gay women to a certain extent, but you will find it more often within the straight feminist movement.

As for my current life, I've not had any time for complications, which, although it has its good points, does tend to take the spice out of life. I hope to find the spice-pot in the near future.

In June of 1981, Aunt Helen returned to the United States for the first time since 1970. By coincidence, her first week back was New York City's Lesbian and Gay Pride Week. She attended her first women's music concert (an Alix Dobkin performance) and her second Lesbian and Gay Pride march. As Aunt Helen and I marched up Fifth Avenue, she was impressed with the diversity of the marchers; she proudly joined with the Gay Nurses, Gay Community News, *and the Lesbian and Gay Jews.*

Since the 1981 International Conference of Lesbian and Gay Jews was to take place the following weekend in Philadelphia, the New York march had a large contingent of Jews from around the world. I was quite amused when Helen tried to explain in Hebrew to her two native-born Israeli friends why the contingent was singing "Go Down Moses."

Aunt Helen and I celebrated our reunion (we had not seen each other since 1968) by walking around Greenwich Village, where she had come out, forty-one years ago.

Endnotes

[1]The article referred to was published in *Lavender Culture*, eds. Karla Jay and Allen Young (New York: Harcourt, Brace Jovanovich, 1978); "Some Pulp Sappho," by Fran Koski and Maida Tilchen, pp. 262-274.

[2]*The Ladder* was a magazine published by the Daughters of Bilitis (D.O.B.); it began publication in 1956 and ceased in 1972.

[3]S.I.R. was a gay rights group.

Yom Hashoah, Yom Yerushalayim: A Meditation

Irena Klepfisz

Wednesday, January 18, 1989:

A breathless week. Monday met Rita Falbel and Donna Nevel to review text of new flyer for the Jewish Women's Committee to End the Occupation. We sat in a Jewish deli and after a while I noticed that the waiters were eavesdropping. Turned out they were Palestinians. One of them had been imprisoned. Can imagine the history and finally his exile. Listening to him made our work seem less abstract.

Talked with Rita and Donna about trying to reach the mainstream community. We're thinking of organizing women rabbis, reaching Hadassah women, planning monthly events. We're reassessing the vigils, trying to figure out how to make them more effective. It's hard to believe we've been doing this for over nine months.

Tuesday went to a reception for Dr. Mariam Mar'i and Edna Zaretsky, the Palestinian and Jewish Israeli women of New Jewish Agenda's Women-in-Dialogue Tour. I became upset because someone made analogies to the Holocaust and Nazis, said that Israeli leaders had to be put on trial and sit in glass cages, an allusion to Eichmann's glass cage. I am always aggravated by such remarks. I tolerate certain Israelis being called fascist and I feel clear that there are fascist elements in Israel, but I can't bring myself to call them Nazis. It's wrong. Since this was a reception, I decided not to question it.

I discussed it later, with little clarity, with some women when we were heading downtown to the Village Gate to hear Mariam and Edna speak publicly. They talked about indoctrination, the failure of the educational system, the stereotyping prevalent in Israel. They were excellent, but I felt exhausted and left early. Had a lot of work waiting at home, including a speech for today's rally to protest the arrest and harassment of members of *Yesh Gvul* [There's a Limit], Israeli reservists refusing to serve in the Occupied Territories.

Got up at 6:30 this morning. Wasn't that happy with the speech—but it was okay. Hard to keep writing statements. Kept reminding myself about the waiters in the deli.

Rally was at noon in front of the Israeli Consulate. There were newspeople from Channel 4 and they spent most of the time with a woman who said we were disgusting. I really lost it when she called us anti-Semites. I can take self-hating Jew, but I can't take anti-Semite. So I screamed back and everybody started trying to cool me out. I was in a rage. Turned out she was a survivor. I expect the newspeople felt she had a special view on the subject or was more informed or had more of a right to have an opinion. I don't know quite what. But clearly whenever any issue about Israel is raised, survivors and the Holocaust come to the foreground almost immediately. Why not? They're permanently linked. But the rally was good. Excellent press coverage, solid attendance. It was a beautiful day. Everyone energetic, up despite the fact that we're all on overload.

This afternoon planned to finish some poems and to work on my Yiddish translations. But Deborah (editor at Beacon) called about *The Tribe of Dina*. She added that the deadline for the Israeli piece for *Nice Jewish Girls* is February 1. I panicked. Israel has taken over my life. One more speech, one more essay, one more press release. Another meeting, another rally to prepare for. My Yiddish work and poetry get postponed again.

I have not resolved this tension within myself. Beginning with Israel's invasion of Lebanon I have become increasingly involved in peace work. Since the *intifada* (Palestinian Uprising) began, I haven't been able to pull myself away from it. I can't bear what Israel is doing. I can't bear that teenagers are being killed, homes demolished, all education brought to a halt. I feel an urgent need to deal with this. At the same time, I'm never quite comfortable doing direct political work. I am most at ease in my role as poet and writer. I want so badly to return to my poetry and translations. I believe American Jews are engaged in a spiritual life/death struggle. The dissolution of secular Jewish identity, the rupture created by the Holocaust and one still not healed, the disappearance of Yiddish, the death of the generation of survivors linked to Yiddish culture—all have contributed to this crisis. But I have not found a way to balance my concern for the Israeli/ Palestinian struggle and the one here. Most of my energy, my passion is now directed toward peace work. And there seems no end to it. I felt relieved that the rally went well and was worthwhile. But then felt despondent after seeing the *Times* article about Israel becoming tougher in the Territories. Plastic bullets are killing more Palestinians than regular bullets ever did. December and January have had the heaviest tolls since the *intifada* began. Thirty-one in December. Over 20 already this month— and it's only the 18th. There's no way to turn away from this.

*   *   *   *

As I reread this journal entry, I am conscious how different my life is now compared to what it was when *Nice Jewish Girls: A Lesbian Anthology* first appeared in 1982. I think back to a certain day. Wednesday—late afternoon. Spring. About eight contributors to *NJG* were gathered in a coffee shop on New York City's West Side to prepare for that evening's reading at Womanbooks. We had just heard that Israel had invaded Lebanon. We felt bewildered. Should we go on with the program? If yes, should we acknowledge what was happening? How? But beneath these lay the quintessential Jewish questions: Why did the actions of one group of Jews in one part of the world affect another? Were we, American Jews, responsible or accountable for the invasion by Israeli Jews? We knew, of course, that many would claim we were. We ourselves were unclear and fluctuated between complete dissociation and intense guilt.

The evening was fraught with irony. *NJG* represented a major step toward claiming pride in Jewish and lesbian identity. It was spurred by the women's and lesbian/feminist movements' tolerance of anti-Semitism and indifference (sometimes hostility) to Jewish attempts to strengthen Jewish identity. Sometimes anti-Semitism was expressed through rigid anti-Zionist statements that demanded dissolution of the Jewish state. Much of this was beneath the surface, but many Jewish feminists and lesbians were conscious of it, sick of it; increasingly, Jewish lesbian/ feminist groups were being organized both as a defense against anti-Semitism and as a source of nurturance for discovering Jewish attachments and the past. A number of these groups were also assessing the spiritual wounds left by the Holocaust. Jewish lesbians were frustrated by the fact that many viewed the

Holocaust as an event limited to European Jews, with no connection to American Jewish life. All in all when *NJG* was first published, Jewish lesbians were angry both at the women's movement and at the Jewish community for its homophobia. Though anti-Israeli sentiments were a concern to us, they were not our sole preoccupation.

Israel's invasion of Lebanon changed everything. Those of us present for that Womanbooks reading faced a new and ponderous question: How were Jewish lesbians to express pride in their Jewishness when Israel was invading another country, killing another people? That night at Womanbooks I made a statement for the group, acknowledged what was happening in the Middle East, expressed our concern, and then—because there was nothing else we could do—we went on with the program. None of us was ready to launch a full discussion of the Middle East, and the facts about Israel's invasion were few and very scattered. I still remember how terrified I was when I made the statement. I was afraid someone would scream at me, throw something. Nothing like that happened, but from then on throughout the invasion and occupation I experienced constant fear whenever I called attention to my Jewishness in public.

All of us became better informed that summer and fall, though no one was prepared for the news of the Sabra and Shatilla refugee camps massacres. During that period *Di Vilde Chayes*, a Jewish lesbian group that I belonged to (six out of seven of us were contributors to *NJG*),[1] put out three statements, each one as mistimed as the next. The first, written before but not published until after the invasion, made us seem indifferent to the brutal events. The second, written before but not published until after the massacres, again made us seem indifferent to the plight of the Palestinians. Both statements were criticized by Jews and non-Jews for failing to take a position on a Palestinian State and the question of the Occupied Territories. It was not until we wrote our third and final statement around November that we were able to pull together our concerns about anti-Zionism, anti-Semitism, and a Palestinian state alongside Israel.

Like *NJG*, our statements were directed at the lesbian and women's community. They were published all over the country in feminist papers, and they provoked heated debate among Jewish and non-Jewish lesbians and feminists. *Di Vilde Chayes* felt beleaguered, constantly under fire. Often we were misunderstood because we insisted we were still proud of our Jewishness even though we abhorred what was happening in Lebanon. We refused to back down on our belief that Jews, despite everything, deserved a Jewish state; yet we were becoming more explicit in our expression of solidarity with Palestinians and those who were fighting for the Palestinian right to a homeland.

I remember this period as being particularly painful. Jewish women, Jewish lesbians seemed bitterly divided. No one had a formula for uniting us. I had no formula for uniting what seemed to be contradictory parts of myself. I felt confused, often ashamed and could not bear to read the news. I also felt disoriented. I did not know how to switch my focus away from anti-Semitism, from the wounds of the Holocaust, from my work on strengthening Jewish identity. The events in Israel had pushed me in directions that I never would have predicted. Wanting to show solidarity with Zionist sisters whose Zionism did not, I felt, make them automatically racist, I called myself a Zionist—even though I had been raised as a Bundist and taught that Jews did not need a separate Jewish state. Wanting to feel solidarity with other Jews despite what was happening in the Middle East, I attended my first synagogue service—even though I was raised and have always remained antireligious, intransigently secular. This occurred in the fall of '82 right after the camp massacres, and there was great anxiety that Jewish institutions would be attacked. In New York City policemen had to guard many synagogues during High Holy Days. I was living in upstate New York and felt an intense need to be with Jews, so I went with three other lesbians to a small synagogue in Glens Falls for Yom Kippur. It was in this context that I heard my first Jewish service and was surprised to find that I recognized music I had not realized I knew. Being Jewish seemed different at that moment from anything it had ever been before. It felt unfamiliar—even alien. When a few days later I heard that the Glens Falls synagogue's walls had been painted over with swastikas, my Jewishness felt familiar again.

*   *   *   *

In the winter of 1984–85 I traveled with Melanie Kaye/ Kantrowitz to Israel and a lot of my confusion abated. Our trip had a specific purpose: to find material from progressive Israeli women for a book we were coediting, *The Tribe of Dina: A Jewish Women's Anthology*. Melanie and I made contact with Israeli activists, met Israeli lesbians, visited the West Bank. The situation at that time was very bleak, worse than we had imagined. We had expected to find a strong, energetic left movement. But the recent Israeli elections had placed Meier Kahane in the Knesset, and Labor and Likud had been forced into a paralyzing coalition. We found most people were depressed, frustrated, unclear what direction to take. We paid tribute to the Holocaust by visiting *Yad Vashem* and later learned of the bitter anger of the Sephardim about the way the Holocaust of European Jews was memorialized and the oppression of Arab Jews ignored. I was particularly impressed with this as I listened to Sephardic women describe their experiences and their treatment by Ashkenazis. On the West Bank we found—not surprisingly—Palestinians living in Palestinian cities. Hebron, Ramallah, Birzeit—how could anyone claim these were Jewish territories? The Jewish settlements, surrounded by barbed wire, seemed bizarre, out of place. Though I had understood the politics of this long before, the trip made the politics more concrete.

Despite this, I came back more knowledgeable, more solidly grounded in my belief that it was possible to be strongly Jewish identified, to believe in the necessity of the State of Israel, and to fight for Palestinian rights. The activists that I met gave me confidence that a peace movement existed, that many Israelis wanted the establishment of a Palestinian state, and that they needed American Jewish support. I also felt a new, strong connection to Israeli activists—particularly the feminists and lesbians. The trip was a turning point in my commitment to the issue of peace in Israel and in Palestine. I had moved very far from that night at Womanbooks.

* * * *

The 1984 trip was not my first. I had been to Israel in 1963. I stayed with my friend Pearl, whom I had met when she was studying in the States. Like me, Pearl was born in Poland and was a child survivor of the Holocaust. Pearl had once told me that when her family first settled in Israel, they were given a house and that for weeks— perhaps months—after they moved in, a Palestinian woman would come and sit on the steps and weep. It had been her home.

Pearl's story brings the Holocaust again to the forefront in dealing with Israeli politics. Jewish survivors and Palestinians who are stateless press against each other although I would wish them to become disentangled; the powerful lessons each evokes and teaches me remain intertwined.

I was particularly conscious of this in 1987 when I attended the International Women's Writers Conference in Jerusalem.

Toward the end of my stay, a group of American and Israeli Jewish writers and I met with two Palestinian women in East Jerusalem. One of them had been in Nairobi in 1985. She, like the Palestinian woman in Pearl's story, was born in a neighborhood that one of the Israelis was living in, a neighborhood now completely Jewish. During our meeting, the Palestinian women asked us to promote the cause of their people. I was deeply moved by this encounter and by the knowledge that women who had attended the Nairobi conference had been affected by it and were now trying to make contact with Jewish women. The next day I took a tour of the Jewish settlements around Jerusalem. I was shocked at their size; they were cities, fortresses. I realized for the first time that the term "settlement" was a euphemism.

This last trip took place in April, the month when Jews commemorate the Holocaust. While there, I became aware that the Israelis were already preparing to "celebrate" the 20th anniversary of the reunification of Jerusalem. I saw the two holidays as symbolic and wanted to put them in perspective. I remembered what the Palestinian woman had said: "Write about what you see. Write what is happening to us." And I did.

Yom hashoah, Yom yerushalayim (1987)

In late April, Israeli Jews and Jews all over the world observed Yom hashoah, *the day commemorating the Holocaust, the murder of their six million.*

As a Jewish child-survivor born in Warsaw during the war, mourning the Holocaust is an important part of my yearly cycle. Coming in the beginning of spring, it reaffirms my belief that Jews need a safe homeland in a world that for centuries has proved hostile; it makes me consider once more the enormity of our loss, its irretrievability, and the moral lessons to be drawn for the present and future.

One of these is that the cry "Never Again!" applies not only to ourselves but to others. Never again are we Jews to be deprived of the life, culture, and religion we choose to be ours; never again are any other people to be deprived of their life, culture, and religion.

Yet as we move toward summer, as Peres and Shamir struggle for power, as peace and security for all in the Middle East remain elusive, the Israeli government prepares for another holiday on June 5, Yom yerushalayim—*the reunification of Jerusalem. That this day is designated for celebration ought to cause deep sorrow, for* Yom yerushalayim *veils a reality that should be mourned—*

the 20th anniversary of the Israeli military occupation of the West Bank.

I know that there are American Jews and allies who deny out of fear and shame the validity of the term "military occupation." Yet as hard as it is for those of us who are rooted in our Jewish communities, who share a commitment to Jewish survival and a Jewish state, we need to use this term openly.

The Israeli military occupation is just that: The Palestinians on the West Bank are under military law, without a civil judicial system, frequently denied rights to lands on which they and their ancestors were born. Like any military occupation, the Israeli is brutal and arbitrary. It arrests and detains without charges hundreds of "suspicious" civilians. In 20 years, it has generated over 1000 regulations, which only recently were coded, published, and made available by Raja Shehadeh, the Palestinian attorney. Like any military occupation, the aim is to divest the occupied of will, collective identity, and cultural autonomy. This is done through the disruption of daily life, the control of educational institutions, and the systematic degradation of the Palestinian people. Predictably, the response and counter response have been escalating violence and oppression.

One insidious example: The act of tree planting, so cherished by American Jews as a way of supporting Israeli and Jewish aspirations for nurturance and stability, has been perverted. Today on the West Bank, the presence of olive trees is often considered illegal. Palestinian orchards, as well as newly planted trees, are being uprooted and transplanted on Israeli soil. Why? If the land remains uncultivated for three years, the Israeli government can claim it. If the land sports no house, it too can be claimed; and if there is a house, the house may be bulldozed. Land on the West Bank is slowly being dragged from Palestinian control. Slowly, slowly push "them" back and back until the land is empty—as some have pretended it was from the start.

Need I say that this contradicts what I have always been taught were Jewish values: the sense of justice, of legal order, of respect for other human beings, the necessity for culture, roots, and self-determination? And we need to keep hold of this contradiction as we move from Yom hashoah toward Yom yerushalayim to remind ourselves that the six million who died were ordinary men, women, and children who simply wanted to go on with their lives and were not permitted to do so.

Yet it is in their name that both the U.S. and Israeli governments (for different reasons) justify current Israeli policies on the

West Bank and thereby deny the decent and ordinary life that each Palestinian, like any other human being, yearns for. American Jews and non-Jews must recognize that the invocation of the Holocaust by our government does not necessarily express a concern for Jewish survival. Certainly the Iran/Contra affair has proven the cynicism with which U.S. policymakers regard Israel— a puppet that carries out actions declared illegal by Congress.

During a recent trip to Israel with a friend who was visiting for the first time, I saw a dramatic enactment of the way the Holocaust is pitted against the occupation. On her last afternoon, my friend was given two choices: to tour Yad vashem, Israel's museum and research center for the Holocaust, or to tour the "settlements"—a euphemism for the stone fortresses that ring Jerusalem outside the Green Line. There was not time for both. In this instance the forced choice between honoring and mourning our dead and acknowledging and addressing present wrongs was simply a matter of bad planning.

Both the American and the Israeli government present us with a similar false choice. They plan upon real fear of genocide and desire for security, and they press us to choose "us or them." They pretend that the military occupation on the West Bank is somehow an answer to Yad vashem. It is not, for the last 20 years have brought neither safety nor security. Sabras, Holocaust survivors, and later refugees fleeing anti-Semitism have lost sons and daughters in the struggle to contain the Palestinians. Hardly a single Israeli Jewish family has been spared. And the violence continues.

Some will consider my words disloyal to Jews and to Israelis. But many Israeli Jews acknowledge these things openly. In April, more than 20,000 Israelis and Palestinians came to a peace festival in Neve Shalom, the Israeli Arab/Jewish town, to express their support of the possibility of Jews and Palestinians living in peace. In May, Arab and Jewish university students together protested discriminatory tuition charges. Most American Jews and allies ignore such realities. They ignore the very present, if splintered, peace movement in Israel made up of more than 50 Arab/Israeli and Palestinian/Jewish peace organizations that are groping toward a nonviolent political solution (a fact rarely discussed in the American media). They forget that thousands of Israelis do not want to see another generation killed or maimed but want peace now and an end to the present occupation; they forget that many of these Israelis support self-determination for Palestinians side by side with Jews. Our loyalty should be to these

Israelis and Jews, for they are the repositories of the values we call Jewish.

Some maintain that you can't talk to the Palestinians; they're all terrorists. Yet talks between Israelis and the PLO have been going on for years; it is only governmental hypocrisy that obscures this reality, most recently with the government choosing to press charges against Israelis who met openly with PLO representatives in Rumania.

I have also heard many urge the Palestinians simply to emigrate to other Arab countries. This shows ignorance of (or disrespect for) the political and cultural diversity of the Middle East. Would anyone ever suggest to Swedes that they resettle in Norway because it too is a Scandinavian country?

Other debates about Israel focus on innocence. But there has been so much violence on both sides that such debates have no meaning. The issue is no longer who is to blame, is most innocent, or has fanned the hostilities. The issue is to recognize the undeniable fact that the Israeli military has wielded power over the West Bank for the past 20 years and that it must stop.

The Jewish Women's Committee to End the Occupation

In April 1988, exactly a year after my trip to Israel, I helped found a new political group—the Jewish Women's Committee to End the Occupation of the West Bank and Gaza. It happened like this: Since the *intifada* began in December 1988, there were intensified efforts to pressure Israel to withdraw from the territories and to recognize a Palestinian state. In February, New Jewish Agenda had staged a protest opposite the Israeli Consulate in mid-Manhattan. A short time later we heard news of Beita, where Israeli teenagers had been protected by Palestinian villagers from extremists. This did not stop the Israeli Defense Forces from blowing up houses in the village in retaliation for the death of an Israeli teenager who'd been shot by her Israeli guard after he (the guard) had been hit by a stone thrown by a Palestinian. Grace Paley called me and wanted to stage a vigil in protest. I was unenthusiastic. We'd hold the vigil and the next day we would read of more outrageous actions.

In analyzing my response I realized that an ongoing vigil might be more effective because the situation was continuous. Clare Kinberg from New Jewish Agenda and Grace agreed. We were, however, unclear about the makeup of our vigil. Should it be just women or men and women together? That week, Lil Moed, peace activist in Israel, gave a talk at Agenda's office and brought news of the work of two Israeli women's groups: Women in Black, who were holding weekly vigils in front of Shamir's house protesting Israel's actions in response to the *intifada*, and SHANI, Israeli Women's Alliance Against the Occupation. It made sense to organize an American Jewish women's vigil in solidarity with Israeli women working for peace.

That is the genesis of the Committee. We needed endorsements for the first flyer, so I began calling Jewish women in New York City. Everyone on the list was already sympathetic, so I did not hesitate to state our position: end the violence now, support an international peace conference and a two-state solution. But whenever I had to say what we were actually going to do, I would take a deep breath, for our weekly Monday-night vigils were to be held at 515 Park Avenue, the offices of the Conference of Presidents of Major American Jewish Organizations, an organization that claims to speak for American Jewry and always endorses Israeli government action in regard to the Occupied Territories. I know the deep feelings most Jews—including myself— have about public criticism of other Jews even when they disagree with them.

By selecting the Conference offices as the site of the protest, we had decided that, instead of pressuring Israel directly, we would pressure the established American Jewish community that promotes/justifies/supports the policies of the Israeli government. American Jews need to start dealing with their involvement with Israeli policies. Given the support American Jews extend to Israel, we cannot claim neutrality on this question.

So within a space of six days the Jewish Women's Committee was formed, and on Monday, April 25th at 5 o'clock, the day after the first major Jewish rally protesting Israeli policies in the Occupied Territories, 11 Jewish women—a number of them lesbians—gathered in front of the offices of the Conference of Presidents. At first it all seemed just like other demonstrations. You confer with the police, establish the rules about where you stand and where you leaflet. You approach people. Some take the lavender flyer, some don't. Some Jews don't like it and crumple it in disgust. All of this was expected.

What I did not expect was the intensity with which my doubts kept surfacing. I did not doubt for one moment that the occupation in Gaza and the West Bank and the second-class status of Palestinians within the Green Line were evils to be struggled against. No extenuating circumstances could justify morally what we had witnessed during the past five months of the *intifada*—Palestinians (many of them children) killed, maimed, illegally imprisoned and tortured; their homes demolished, their schools and shops closed. Yet despite my conviction that these evils had to be stopped, I found that standing in front of a Jewish organization, *publicly* questioning its integrity was not easy. A number of Jews came by and asked "Aren't you ashamed?" and I wondered if what we were doing was right. In the past I had always felt secure in my devotion to my Jewishness, to the Jewish people; I had never felt shame. Yet standing on line those first few weeks, I felt shame over what Israel was doing and also some shame about myself. This was a sense of my Jewishness that was completely new to me.

The confusion I felt during the initial vigils was intense. But equally intense was my reaction to those Jews who insisted on referring to the Holocaust, insisted that the Holocaust precluded our taking this kind of political action. Their fears and anger were unqualified. The first day a Jewish man came up to me and said: "I wish you were buried in Poland like my parents." Other Jews also wished another Holocaust upon us. Still others said our action would only lead all Jews, including us, "back to the ovens." Over and over again, in one form or another, we were told that the vigil was not only disloyal, but a form of collaboration with contemporary and historical Nazis. We were told that to give the Palestinians a state was to give Hitler his final victory, that our behavior was desecrating the Holocaust of the '40s and ensuring the Holocaust of the '90s, perhaps even the '80s. I was stunned and offended by these extreme remarks, but I did not find them ridiculous. Shame was a new feeling for me as a Jew, but, like the Jews who cursed us, fear has been my Jewish companion for as long as I can remember, and I understand its power. I soon came to recognize that the strange mixture of both shame and fear was the basis of a new aspect of my Jewishness, a mixture that brought into stark relief my feelings about Israel and about my background as a survivor.

* * * *

I want to come to grips with this mixture, the shame, the fear, and also the anger—for I have a lot of anger toward the Jewish community. It's a community I fight for and deeply love, but which, I remind myself, loves me only conditionally. I need to remind myself how I feared this community's rejection when I first came out as a lesbian. My being a child survivor, my family's activism in the Jewish underground during the war, my own strong attachment to Yiddish and activism in promoting *yidishkayt* and strong Jewish identity—none of these were sufficient armor against homophobia. Today I feel I have gained acceptance, but it was a tough process; I have scars and remember with bitterness many moments of pain.

The vigil brought new fears and anger to the surface. At the big April 24th rally I had feared the counterdemonstrators and their propensity toward violence. They screamed with such venom, such hatred for others—Arabs, Palestinians, Jews who disagree with them. They were ready to send us all to gas chambers and relished the idea. These Jews deliberately evoked fear: "Think, be like us—or die!" My fear of these Jews, the militant right, is rational. They are dangerous.

But I fear not only these Jews; I fear also those kinder Jews who taught me my moral and political lessons, and this fear is more difficult to describe and explain. Do not speak ill of a Jew in public, they taught; and I have always obeyed. The command had nothing to do with social graces or pride. It was a command meant to help me get through life more safely. Publicly criticizing Jews gives fuel to the anti-Semites and endangers the Jewish community. It's a centuries-old rule for survival. Backed by the knowledge that anti-Semitism can turn into the Holocaust, the rule has even greater force for us in the post-Holocaust era than it did for our parents and grandparents. Anyone who breaks the rule places the Jewish people in danger and shows lack of respect and love for them. The response must be murderous rage. By participating in a vigil in front of the Conference of Presidents, I break the rule. I am afraid of the rage this may unleash as well as the unintended danger it might bring to Israel. After all, I might be wrong.

But the tangle of emotions does not end here, for I also fear history. I fear that I will misinterpret the present and not recognize my rightful role. This is a fear I have had all my life. Knowing that the world was passive and indifferent while 6,000,000 Jews died, I have always considered passivity and indifference the worst of evils. Those who do nothing, I believe, are good Germans, collaborators. I do not want to be a collaborator.

So in trying to determine the right actions for myself in regard to Israel, I too leap to the Holocaust for analogies and models, and I am trapped. On the one hand, I face the wrath of my own people; on the other, the wrath of history. I don't know how to find a balance. I want to be able to act with conscience, I want to remain part of the community. I don't know how to decide, how to feel certain and centered in my decision. These were the knots of feelings that emerged in the early days of our vigils as I listened to the remarks and arguments of passersby and staff workers from the building.

In reviewing my feelings, am I being finicky? Palestinians are dying. Israel seems ready to break apart. Jews and Israelis worry about possible civil war. Should I be spending time examining my Jewish fears? I think I should because they remind me I have not left the tribe, that I am not as far from some of those Jews who confront us on line as I would like to think. I have to understand their emotions if I ever hope to reach them. They form the bond that connects us across the great political chasm that separates us. To deal with the Israeli/Palestinian situation effectively, I need to calm their fears as much as I need to calm my own. I need to convince them of what I have to convince myself again and again. That Jews must choose and risk for peace. That we must choose justice despite our fears. That our fears are real, rooted in history, but that they cannot control us or stop us from making just choices.

Choices

During the Holocaust, choice was the nightmare. Whether through direct order by a Nazi or through the tangled strategies for survival, making decisions—who to take on a journey, who to leave behind, to set out early or late—was always the nightmare.

When I was little, I asked my mother over and over: "If the Nazis made you choose between me and my father, who would you choose to be killed?" At age 10 I had absorbed the full horror of the choices Jews faced—the life/death choices. I knew the idea of the third way was myth, romance. Someone stood and pointed and said: "*Choose! Choose now or they both die!*" I was, of course, testing my mother, trying to find out how much she loved me. In my fantasy I mistakenly thought she had power. "And if you had to choose between me and Elza," I would persist, "who would you pick?" Elza, orphaned daughter of family friends, my almost-sibling and therefore a rival for my mother's love. "*Pick me! Pick me!*" my 10-year-old heart would beat and yearn, never fully understanding what it was I was asking, but clearly tapping the core of the Holocaust nightmare.

For most of my life making decisions has been fraught with tensions way beyond what others regard as appropriate. I fre-

quently experience as crisis what seems much simpler for other
people. It is a psychology rooted in the past, not the present. It is
something I need to watch.

Have Jews in the Diaspora and Israel permanently adopted
this life/death psychology? Are we unable to see the present for
what it is? Are we always looking at it through the immediate
past, through the Holocaust? Is this why we do not perceive that
the third way is not myth, that there is a third way in Israel,
that there must be?[2]

Israel and the Holocaust: Analogies

I was always taught: never use Holocaust terminology to describe other situations; *never* in relation to Israel's own actions.
never, that is, unless you want to support Israel, justify its
policies; then always bring up the Holocaust, point to what we
have endured, claim that we will never again endure it. For this
reason fund raising for Israel is frequently done in the name of
the Holocaust. That is considered legitimate.

But what is not legitimate is expressing concern for Palestinians, for criticizing Israeli policy in the context of the Holocaust
experience. Over and over we are told not to make comparisons,
and most Jews balk when they hear them. Yet isn't it impossible
not to make comparisons? Two events—the Holocaust and the
creation of Israel—occur during the life span of one generation
and are historically linked. Israel, after all, became the asylum
for survivors of the Holocaust, many of whom were not Zionists
but had decided they were better off taking their chances in a
Jewish state.

So whether we like it or not, the Holocaust and Israel are
intimately connected in our minds and history. I think of the
Holocaust and wonder what would have happened if Israel had
existed in 1939. I think of Israel and wonder if it would have
existed without the Holocaust or what kind of a country it would
be now without the European survivors and their children. In
what way would its national character, its psychology, its consciousness of tragedy and its self-image, rooted in fending off a
second Holocaust, be different? Israel and the Holocaust form a
natural association. What is problematic is the hardening of that
association into an analogy between Israelis and Nazis, an analogy that enrages because it nullifies the Holocaust. If Israelis or
Jews are really Nazis, then the murder of 6,000,000 of their parents and grandparents is not so tragic after all.

When anti-Semites use the analogy, their intent is to negate German and world guilt. But when concerned, passionate Jews use the analogy, they are not only saying what they believe, they are also trying to express their outrage over Israeli action and to shake other Jews out of their apathy over the fate of the Palestinians. As a strategy the analogy is misguided; it detracts from the issue. Instead of focusing on the Palestinian struggle, Jews spend all their energy disproving the analogy and finding satisfaction and comfort in the fact that Israelis are not Nazis. This is disturbing and makes me wonder how close Israelis need to get to being true Nazis before other Jews begin to voice their objections. When we reject the analogy (as we should), and say that Israel is a democratic state and then turn away from the Palestinian struggle, are we not saying we are willing to object to Israeli policies *only when* Israel does finally resemble a completely fascist state? Do we want to wait that long? Exactly how many Palestinians must die before we speak up? One million? Shall we wait till the whole Palestinian population on the West Bank and Gaza and all those in camps are murdered? Is there not evil that we must object to *before* it reaches the level of Nazism?

"What does it remind you of?" I ask my mother, and read her the *Newsday* article of the Palestinian men in Rufus; rounded up by the Israeli police, they're told to lie face down in a nearby field. "I know what it reminds me of," she answers and says nothing more. Given the images etched on our collective consciousness, how can this *not* remind us of the Holocaust? What is it that we have been asking everyone to remember? Is it not the fields of Ponary and those nameless fields on the outskirts of dozens of *shtetlekh* that we've all pledged to remember? Am I to feel better that the Palestinians from Rufus were not shot by the Israelis but merely beaten? As long as hundreds of Palestinians are not being lined up and shot, but are killed by Israelis only one a day, are we Jews free from worrying about morality, justice? Has Nazism become the sole norm by which Jews judge evil, so that anything that is not its exact duplicate is considered by us morally acceptable? Is that what the Holocaust has done to Jewish moral sensibility?

* * * *

I was especially conscious of Jewish sensitivities around using the Holocaust in analyzing Israeli policies toward the Palestinians when in April 1988 I was asked to speak at a ceremony marking the 45th anniversary of the Warsaw Ghetto Uprising. I accepted because I considered it an honor. But I was also conscious that the *intifada* was already in its fifth month, and I couldn't imagine speaking without making reference to it. I had to find a way to bring up the *intifada* without offending the survivors and without disrupting the memorial itself. I had to find a way to express my morality, which is rooted in the Holocaust, without evoking the hated analogy.

Though I had fears that I would not be skillful enough and might offend despite myself, more than anything I felt angry at myself for being fearful and also angry at this community of survivors with its rules and taboos that restricted open discussion, that always threatened excommunication, that was willing—if I did not please—to label me the enemy. Even more, I was angry that there should be any question at all as to the rightness in condemning Israeli actions in regard to the Palestinians.

The evening of the memorial, the Norman Thomas High School auditorium is crowded with 500 to 600 people, mostly survivors and children of survivors. I am sitting on stage. I am nervous, but as often happens, anger fuels my courage.

But from the start I'm caught off guard. The evening begins with the ceremony of lighting candles for the six million. Six elderly survivors are called to the stage, among them survivors of Auschwitz, Bergen-Belsen, the Lodz Ghetto. They walk slowly, light the candles, then stand behind the candelabra. I suddenly feel again what this all means and am in awe. This woman was in Auschwitz. Imagine what she saw. That man was in Bergen-Belsen. Imagine what he lived through. Imagine what they all lost. Someone sings the *kaddish*. I feel I'm about to cry.

I remind myself that survivors who suffered the experiences of the Holocaust should not be expected to be morally superior. Surviving Auschwitz does not make anyone an expert on anything, not even on surviving Auschwitz. But also I must never forget the obvious: that survivors who are stubbornly wrong about Israel and its oppression of Palestinians are still survivors, Jewish men and women who suffered the experiences and losses of the Holocaust. The fact that they are not morally superior does not erase their suffering. Sometimes, in my passion, I am guilty of that erasure. I realize this as the survivors leave the stage. It is uppermost in my mind when I deliver my speech.

45th Anniversary of the Warsaw Ghetto Uprising: April 19, 1988

I was honored to be asked to speak on the anniversary of the Warsaw Ghetto Uprising, but I was also afraid. The anniversary has always been a painful day, reminding me of what my mother and I barely escaped and what my father, my aunts, cousins, and grandparents did not survive. When I was a child, our early post-war memorials made vivid the horrors and atrocities, the deprivations that Eastern European Jews endured, and they terrified me. I feared that memory would suddenly, perhaps the next day even, become a reality. I am no longer a child, but I still think a great deal about the relationship between the past and present and would like to talk about that now: its meaning to those who are survivors, or children of survivors, or American Jews deeply connected to our Jewish history.

Today, April 19th, is the 45th anniversary of the Warsaw Ghetto Uprising, the act of resistance that has come to symbolize the period known in English as the Holocaust. During the initial postwar years, many of you were reluctant to speak about that period, while others were reluctant to listen. Since then there has been a major change, and the Holocaust has become the property of history—the object of historians, scholars, archivists, and filmmakers. And this is just, because the Holocaust must be known fully. It must remind us—Jews and non-Jews—of how far human beings can go in their dehumanization of themselves and in their attempts to dehumanize others who are different or alien. Jews especially must remember what was lost and must continue searching for ways of healing ourselves as a people.

But for those who are survivors, the Holocaust can never be transformed into history and will always remain simply der khurbn (the destruction). Whatever the long-term effects on the descendants of European Jews, whatever the effect on Jewish history and the history of humankind, for survivors der khurbn will remain an individual, personal experience. It permanently changed and shaped our lives.

Perhaps this is obvious. And yet, I sometimes think that this most obvious fact is often forgotten in the whirl of rhetoric and research by political scientists and historians. Too frequently the Holocaust is spoken of in statistics, in analysis of power and powerlessness, too often evoked by photographs of lines of anonymous naked men and women or mass graves. Yet der khurbn that survivors experienced is not general but very specific. It is reflected

*in precious sepia photographs pasted into incomplete family al-
bums. It consists of identifiable names, of familiar faces of family
members, of named streets, stores and schools, teammates, friends,
libraries, doctors, hospitals, lectures, marches, strikes, political allies and enemies—the people, places, and institutions that make
up the fabric of any human being's ordinary, everyday life. It is
these specifics and the loss of that ordinary life that survivors
remember and mourn. And not just today, but during all those
frequent moments when memory of childhood or ghettos or camps
is triggered by something in the present—an angle of someone's
jaw, a special shade of color, a faint smell of certain food, a dream.
During those daily moments when the fabric of our present life
tears apart, survivors mourn and mourn again.*

*What we grieve for is not the loss of a grand vision, but rather
the loss of common things, events and gestures. We do not grieve,
for example, that Anne Frank had no opportunity to become a
great writer, but rather that Anne Frank did not continue her
schooling and learn more of the world about which she was so
insatiably curious, that she did not spend more time with her
friends and enjoy the normal process of growing up free to exper-
iment, to experience the pleasures of success, the difficulties of failure. We mourn that Anne Frank was denied an ordinary, anonymous life. And looking at that lost experience, I have come to believe that ordinariness is the most precious thing we struggle for,
what the Jews of the Warsaw Ghetto fought for. Not noble causes
or abstract theories, but the right to go on living with a sense of
purpose and a sense of self-worth—an ordinary life. It is this loss
we mourn today.*

*But memorials are for both the living and the dead. Forty-five
years after the Uprising of the Warsaw Ghetto, those of you who
thought the ordinariness of life was lost forever—perhaps even felt
it would be immoral for it to be reestablished—are reminded today
that it was not. Our present life bears little resemblance to your
life in 1939 or 1945, for it is grounded in different soil and society,
expressed in a different language. Yet certain things, the building
blocks of our life, are the same: ties to community and friends and
commitment to a Jewish future are firmly rooted among us. We
survived and somehow went on with the business of living. And
the dead, if they could, would approve. I cannot imagine for one
moment that my father or any one of my family would have wanted
anything else for my mother and me, just as I am sure that all
those who died during that period would have wished only the
fullest of life to all survivors and their descendants. This new life*

was truly an unexpected, astonishing gift, particularly when you passed it on to us, the next generation. It was a major step toward securing Jewish survival.

Yet what seems even more astonishing is that the business of living after our tragedy and loss has turned out to be not all that different than what I imagine it must have been before the war. Miraculously, we were given opportunities for pleasure and joy, something that many of you perhaps thought might have vanished from your lives forever. On the other hand, if we imagined the war's agony would make us immune to future misfortune, we found out we were wrong. We were just as susceptible to failure and illness, to pain and suffering as we had been before the war. We found we were not shielded from having to make difficult political and moral decisions or from making mistakes. Der khurbn seemed to have balanced nothing out. It could be said that we were forced to face life once more as if this tragedy had not happened. Yet we know it did, and it happened to us. We bear its physical and psychological scars; and though we have gone on living, we are not the people we were or might have been.

One difference is that we, a generation further removed from the actual experience of der khurbn, live with the knowledge of the war and the murder of six million. Like others, I ask myself what this knowledge and this anniversary mean to us and what they will mean to future generations. Our parents and friends, I know, had to use all their energies to come to value present life as much as the life before the war, to keep memories from overwhelming them and locking them into the past. We of a younger generation have a different task. Our energies must be directed toward holding on to the past in such a way that it is not an event apart from our everyday life, but rather is intertwined in the present and future.

Like many child survivors and children of survivors, I have not found it easy to do this. But I have concluded that one way to pay tribute to those we loved who struggled, resisted, and died is to hold on to their vision and their fierce outrage at the destruction of the ordinary life of their people. It is this outrage we need to keep alive in our daily life and apply to all situations whether they involve Jews or non-Jews. It is this outrage we must use to fuel our actions and vision whenever we see any signs of the disruption of common life: the hysteria of a mother grieving for the teenager who has been shot; a family stunned in front of a vandalized or demolished home; a family separated, displaced; arbitrary and unjust laws that demand the closing or opening of shops and schools; humiliation of a people whose culture is alien and deemed inferior; a people left homeless, without citizenship; a people living under military rule. Because of our experience, we recognize these as evils, as obstacles to peace. At those moments of recognition we remember the past, feel the outrage that inspired the Jews of the Warsaw Ghetto, and allow it to guide us in present struggles.

Like most of you, I consider April 19th a sacred day specially designated for mourning, a day for Jews to reflect on their history quietly and without distractions. But the present presses in on us, insists on our attention, and we do not mourn in a vacuum. Forty-five years after the Warsaw Ghetto Uprising, Jews all over the world are faced with serious moral and political issues. These are becoming more and more urgent and are very much on our minds. I know that the Israeli/Palestinian crisis is an explosive topic and I will not dwell on it. But I have referred to it not out of disrespect for this evening's memorial—this event is too important to me—but because of what the history of der khurbn and what many survivors taught me, taught all of us: silence about any form of injustice is wrong. Many of us are confused about what to do, what to say. We need inspiration and models, and I know of no better source on which to draw than the Warsaw Ghetto Uprising.

Today when we light candles in memory of the six million, we renew our commitment never to forget the grave moral lessons learned at a price no one should have to pay. These lessons we need to cherish and keep close to our hearts together with the family, friends, communities—all those we loved—who were not saved. On this 45th anniversary when we have gained new strength, have recovered as much as could be expected from such trauma, we commemorate and honor our six million, express gratitude for the astonishing gift of the new life given to our people, and renew our dedication to preserving, for ourselves as well as for all others, that precious ordinary life that is everyone's right and of which we were once so brutally deprived.

* * * *

Afterwards, backstage, many members of the chorus thank me. "Thank you for saying *that*," they say to me. "I'm so grateful." I go down into the auditorium. People ask me for copies of the speech. Survivors whom I know from Poland hug and kiss me. "It was good," they say. "It was just right." "I'm proud of you." There are people who think bringing up the *intifada* was inappropriate, but they were not offended and I learn that later there is a lot of discussion. I am pleased. Discussion is what I had hoped for.

A friend who watches everyone's response says afterwards: "It's so clear they adore you." I don't think it's adoration, but deep love. I am, have always been, the child that survived. I suddenly realize that the depth of their love reflects the depth of their sorrow. I cannot make up for any of it, but I am proof to them that they have lived on. As a child, of course, I hated this—found it a burden. But this year on April 19th I am moved beyond my anger at this community and feel again the meaning, the grief behind *der khurbn*. In my ardor on behalf of the Palestinians I want to make sure I don't lose touch with these feelings again.

Looking back I am also struck by how many of those present did actually feel relieved that I referred to the Palestinian struggle. Many of them want to take a moral stand but are afraid or confused or frightened by history—much as I have been. There is more dissent than any of us working on this issue realize. It is not just among the fringes, as leaders of mainstream organizations would like us to believe. It is deep within the community. We need to learn how to bring it to the surface and how to break the taboos, the rules, without losing our credibility.

* * * *

Progress is hard to measure at this level. A 20-minute discussion that provokes thought rather than anger, that brings someone closer to thinking compassionately or realistically or morally about Palestinians and their need for a state of their own, is a victory. It is one of hundreds, perhaps thousands, of unrecorded events that form a chain reaction that ultimately will change history, will bring about a Palestinian state. I am particularly aware of these kinds of events and of their cumulative potential when I think about the vigils of the Jewish Women's Committee in relation to various women's groups that have been organized here in the United States and in Israel. For me, the Israeli women's groups are a critical link in this chain.

Women in Black began in Jerusalem shortly after the start of the *intifada* in December 1987. Ten women gathered opposite Shamir's house. They were dressed in mourning and stood silently, their only message on small posters: *Dai lakibush!* (End the Occupation). Today, in May 1989, they still stand every Friday, but now number 150 and have sister chapters protesting in Haifa, Tel Aviv, and Beersheba.[3] They do not argue politics with anyone, they do not answer insults. Though we sometimes have difficult moments at our protests at the Conference, they do not compare to what Women in Black must endure. They are spat upon and cursed as whores, as traitors. Right-wing Israelis constantly threaten them with violence and force the police to move in. The police themselves are not always sympathetic or cooperative. It takes great courage to stand there week after week taking the abuse and risking the violence. The photographs that I've seen of these vigils are inspiring.

Last summer and fall, a number of these Israeli women happened to be in the States visiting relatives. They would join us at the Monday night vigils and tell us of conditions in Israel and of the progress of their protest. I was moved by their appreciation of our work here, by their delight that *their* work was known and supported. They talked proudly of support groups in France and in Italy. We in turn told them of similar groups in Santa Cruz, Ann Arbor, Boston, Washington, D.C., Berkeley, and Los Angeles and of plans in other American cities to organize Jewish women around this issue.

A number of these Israeli women were also members of other women's organizations. SHANI, the Israeli Women's Alliance, was also organized in response to the *intifada*; it has paid solidarity visits to Palestinians in hospitals and schools on the West Bank and is dialoguing with Palestinian women. Members of SHANI are simply ignoring official political obstacles separating Israelis and Palestinians. SHANI also organizes lectures and group discussions for Israeli women and tries to break down many of the same attitudes and fears discussed in this essay.

The Women's Organization for Women Political Prisoners, made up of Israeli Palestinian and Jewish women, is another group founded since the start of the *intifada*. Committed to improving the conditions in women's prisons, it brings to the forefront the suffering of Palestinian women illegally imprisoned under the military administrative detention regulations, many of whom are held in filthy conditions without charges and without counsel. WOWPP is trying through vigils, protest letters, and telegrams to alleviate the brutalities of imprisonment.

Among all these women are many Israeli Jewish lesbians who in the last few years have established an active lesbian organization, CLaF. Based in Tel Aviv, it now has over 150 members. As politically conscious Israelis concerned with the conditions of Israelis and Palestinians, CLaF members claim that one cause of the "sexist nature of Israel" is the "constant atmosphere of war and subsequent dominance of the military in the whole culture [and] a prevailing nationalism fueled in large part by the military occupation of the West Bank, Gaza Strip and Golan

Heights." Their statement goes on to say that Israeli lesbians are not optimistic about changing the sexism and the religious tyranny of the Rabbinate in the near future; "much of our energy goes into resisting the Israeli oppression of Palestinians." Because there is no way to be openly gay in Israel, these lesbians are politically active in other women's and mixed groups.[4]

It is evident that throughout Israel women are protesting, organizing, resisting. Many of them, we are told, have never been politically active before, but all are sick of the violence, the human cost of this seemingly endless confict. They are committed to organizing a powerful Israeli women's peace movement and bringing about a two-state solution. And their actions are, I believe, being paralleled here in the States. In both countries, Jewish and Palestinian feminists and lesbian/feminists are doing grass-roots work. This is very moving, for it is hard to be involved in this peace work without being conscious of the networking and bonding that are taking place among American Jewish and Palestinian women and Israeli Jewish and Palestinian women inside and outside the Green Line. This bonding is strengthening to Jewish women in our struggle against the Jewish mainstream in both the United States and Israel, in breaking down our sense of isolation and fears of disloyalty. Increasingly we feel more confident in our challenges to the establishment, and the work helps us create a supportive Jewish women's community of our own. Despite daily frustrations, there is more optimism among many Jewish women activists; it parallels the optimism resulting from the more positive recent developments among the Palestinians and the PLO.

The bonding among women activists has special significance, I believe, for American Jewish feminists and lesbians because we are furthest removed from the crisis. Our perception of Israelis and Palestinians and our evaluation of possible solutions are partly shaped by our distance, by our living in a gentile society that is not always sympathetic to our differences as Jews. As my Israeli friend Pearl once wrote me: "*We* in Israel must *live* with the consequences." And I thought, yes, the risk is the Israelis' both in war and in peace. It is Israeli Jews, not American Jews, who will suffer the consequences of a negotiated peace if it should fail. American Jewish women's increased contact with both Israeli Jewish and Palestinian women makes concrete the hardships and risks on both sides.

But it is also clear to me that Jewish fears of annihilation, of another Holocaust, cannot change the inevitable. A Palestinian

state *will* be established. The Palestinians need and want independence, and they will get it. The only question is how much
more they will have to suffer for it. In our struggle to understand
ourselves and other Jews, we must not forget that it is the Palestinians who are suffering grave injustices, whose lifelong damage
will not be undone even when a Palestinian state is finally established. I read in the paper that 16-year-old Madwan Abu Sabah
was shot dead near Hebron. I know his friends and family will
always mourn. I read that 17-year-old Ahment Abu Mustafa from
Khan Yunis died in an Israel hospital and know his friends and
family will always mourn. I learn that 22-year-old Munira Daoud
of Beita has been imprisoned because she threw a stone when her
brother was shot by the Israeli settler guarding the teenagers.
She was later arrested and her home bulldozed. I think of her
parents, her husband, her children. They will never forget her
brother, the pain of her imprisonment, the destruction of her
home. It is easy to lose touch with the daily events that make up
the Palestinian tragedy as we try to change Jewish attitudes, try
to find the right road through the labyrinth of Jewish fears, de-
fenses, and taboos. We must remember that every morning flesh-
and-blood Palestinians wake up and face another bitter day's
hardships—food and medicine shortages, the gaping emptiness
created by the death of a daughter, son, cousin, friend, neighbor.
Every morning Palestinians wake up and begin to try to adjust
to the wounds that will remain with them for the rest of their
lives.

Yes, Jews must learn to say without excuse, without equivoca-
tion: Despite our history and our powerlessness in the past, despite all the injustices that we have endured—today, now, the
Palestinians are the victims of oppression and their oppressors
are the Israelis. The Palestinians must have Palestine, and there
must be peace between Palestine and Israel.

May 1988

Endnotes

[1]Other members of *Di Vilde Chayes* were Evelyn Torton Beck, Nancy
Bereano, Melanie Kaye/Kantrowitz, Bernice Mennis, and Adrienne
Rich. Gloria Z. Greenfield was a seventh member who dropped out after
a few months.

[2]I am indebted for the idea of "the third way" to Raja Shehadeh,
Palestinian attorney and activist, in his book *The Third Way*, reprinted
under the title *Samed: A Journal of Life in the West Bank* (Quartet
Books, 1982).

[3]As far as I know, the founding members of Women in Black were

Israeli Jews. They were soon joined by Israeli Palestinian women who became members of the groups and active participants in the demonstrations.

[4]Quotations attributed to CLaF are from its statement of purpose. Addresses for these organizations are as follows: *CLaF*, POB 22997, Tel Aviv 61228; SHANI, Israel Women's Alliance Against the Occupation, POB 9091, Jerusalem; *Women's Organization for Women Political Prisoners*, POB 31811, Tel Aviv 61318; *The Jewish Women's Committee to End the Occupation*, Suite 1178, 163 Joralemon, Brooklyn, NY 11201.

East Jerusalem, 1987: *Bet Shalom* (House of Peace)

Irena Klepfisz

In 1987 in East Jerusalem a group of Jewish women writers (American and Israeli) met with Palestinian women to express feelings and responses to the Israeli occupation of the West Bank and Gaza. I was very moved by this meeting, but could not write about it until after the intifada had begun. I was particularly affected by one of the Palestinian women, to whom this poem is dedicated.

To a Palestinian woman who I am afraid to name

Whether we like it or not
we must sit here.   What we feel
does not matter. We are the heirs
our legacy is in the air we breathe
the ground we stand on.

One of us lives   in the neighborhood
you were raised in
where you took   your first steps
and met the world
Then everyone left.
Your uncles and aunts
carried their belongings
and left.   It was '48.

You ask us:
> *Do you understand   can you imagine*
> *what it must feel like to me?*
> *to all of us?*

I do not go back to those neighborhoods.
I just don't feel right.
Do you understand
what it means to all of us?

We understand   we remember history
and understand it all:
the need for safety   a safety
no one else can take away.
The need for control
not waiting on line   to get attention
or for the consciences of others   to awaken.
We understand what it means to have children
who die   children who live and learn to be proud
of who they are.

Doubts   break through.
This is in the air   the reluctance
to have understanding be enough.
We ask: didn't you omit
part of the picture
didn't you leave out a piece   along the border
a piece of sky   the very peak of a mountain
the bus bombed   the children in the schoolhouse
peaceful farmers   ploughing fields—
you left out part of the picture.

Understanding wraps us again   tightly
toward each other.
We remember the camps: during   and after.
During: there was murder   and resistance
more murder   *and after:*   there was determination
sneaking in at night   no lights burning
the small boats   the landings on the beach
when everyone else had said: don't go there
or there   or there   or who wants them anyway
they've always been trouble   *and again after:*
bombings   massacres
we understand   the actions of a desperate people.

Doubts break us apart
we can barely breathe.   We ask:
why are you our problem too?   we can hardly hold
our own.   Why can't you just blend in
with your own kind?

Whether we like it   or not
we must sit here   and this is in the air.
You say to us:
    You must understand
    how it is for me.
    You are writers
    Write about it.
You mean: Our voices carry.
Yours alone does not.

All of us part.   You move off   in a separate
direction.   The rest of us return
to the other Jerusalem.   It is night.
I still hear your voice.   It is in the air
now   with everything else   except sharper
clearer.   I think of your relatives
your uncles and aunts   I see the familiar
battered suitcases   cartons with strings
stuffed pillowcases
children sitting on people's shoulders
children running to keep up

Always   there is migration
on this restless planet   everywhere
there is displacement   somewhere
someone is always telling   someone else
to move on   to go elsewhere.

Night.   Jerusalem.   *Yerushalayim.*
Jerusalem.   If I forget thee
Oh Jerusalem   Jerusalem   Hebron
Ramallah   Nablus   Qattana   if I
forget thee oh Jerusalem
Oh Hebron   may I forget
my own past   my pain
the depth of my sorrows.

Appendix:
Cast a Critical Eye

Though these essays may not have been written from a specifically Jewish lesbian perspective, they will be of interest to readers of this anthology.

I. B. Singer's Misogyny
Evelyn Torton Beck

Isaac Bashevis Singer, who recently won the Nobel Prize for Literature, is the one author by whom thousands of people the world over will measure both Yiddish literature and Jewish culture. Unfortunately, readers who are unfamiliar with Jewish history and culture may assume that Singer's portrayal of prewar Polish Jewry is an authentic representation of reality. It is, instead, a rather distorted picture of *shtetl* and city life, reflecting fringe elements of that society rather than the norm.

Singer is not interested in the ordinary life of the average Jew. His preoccupation with sex, for example, was hardly characteristic of the hard-working Jews of Eastern Europe, who had to wage a daily struggle for mere survival. His focus is not on the values or realities of Jewish life but on the aberrations of human psychology. Unlike nineteenth-century Jewish writers who, while critical of Jewish life, believed in Jewish values and in the possibility of preserving them, Singer is a pessimistic modernist who believes all humans are essentially depraved.

While Singer presents men in terms of their individual psychological aberrations, he treats women as a class, making far more frequent use of clichés and stereotypes in depicting them than in depicting men. Singer's vision—combining the traditional Jewish image of woman as subservient and inferior with the misogynistic view of woman's nature in the philosophies of Schopenhauer, Nietzsche, Freud and Weininger—represents a powerful assault on the Jewish woman.

Singer's thinking, epitomized in "Zeitl and Rickel" is that "old maids, you know, also end up half crazy. But when a woman who has had a man is left alone, it goes to her head." The result, in this Singer story, is a lesbian relationship, which Singer views as the ultimate aberration.

The strong, assertive, independent, or what Singer calls "mannish" women in the body of his work all come to a bad end and inevitably bring suffering not only on themselves but also on those around them. Elka, the wife of Gimpel the Fool, is a rolling-pin wielder who lies, cheats, and cuckolds her husband: "Her mouth would open as if it were on a hinge and she had a fierce tongue." The tragicomedy of her evil shrewishness lies in what Singer sees as the wrongful reversal of roles: "When you're married the husband's the master," Gimpel reasons plaintively.

The best known of these strong women, "Yentl the Yeshiva Boy," comes off relatively well in comparison to some of the others, but even here Singer hardly shows enthusiasm for the young woman's remarkable intelligence. In recognition of her capacity for and interest in learning, her father quips:

Yentl—you have the soul of a man.

So why was I born a woman?

Even heaven makes mistakes.

Singer, who controls the narrative, seems fully to agree with this explanation. For all the apparent sympathy for Yentl's situation, her inclination to study in preference to mending socks is presented as if it were a kind of failing in *her*.

The only genuinely positive images of women—Teibele in "Short Friday" or Esther in *The Magician of Lublin*—are those who faithfully carry out their traditional subsidiary roles and devote their lives entirely to the care of men, no matter what the cost to themselves. Singer's formula seems to read: men serve God; women serve men.

Who can understand the feminine soul? Even an angelic woman shelters within herself devils, imps, and goblins. . . It is all part of the perversity so characteristic of the female's nature.

Shadow of a Crib

For Singer, the natural perversity of women lies chiefly in female sexuality, which he seems to regard as a natural "flaw" in women that poses a constant threat to men. They must ever protect themselves against it.

The most persistent of Singer's stereotypes, one that almost subsumes all the others, is woman as temptress. (Of course, in a society that encouraged its men to become scholars rather than providers, women frequently became the economic mainstays of their families, and not the sirens-in-search-of-sex that Singer would have us believe.) In "The Captive," an elderly Circe-like woman tries to enslave the narrator/writer into faking her dead husband's memoirs:

> She took my arm and pressed it to her body...A few times her leg brushed against mine....A sudden lust for that ugly creature seized me.

Since Singer does not seem able to see past women's bodies, he presumes that they cannot ever forget their own sexuality either, no matter how inappropriate the situation would appear to be, nor what their age or occupation. Even when the woman is a poet engaged on a purely intellectual mission, as in "The Colony," she behaves lasciviously, as if such behavior were a female reflex to the presence of any male:

> Sonya kept talking....At the same time she patted, pinched, and pulled my hand; she even dug the nail of her index finger into it. The calf of her leg she pressed against mine.

Her behavior is described in terms that make the overture repellent; there is even the suggestion of sadism in the detail of nails digging into flesh: the woman's sexuality is an assault.

> Reb Bunim also had a daughter, and women, as is well known, bring misfortune.
>
> *The Destruction of Kreshov*

Like so many other male writers, Singer sees the world as essentially male-centered and clearly views women as "other"—separate, subsidiary, apart, alien. He betrays a deep mistrust, revulsion and hostility toward women, especially those who stray in any way from their prescribed roles or cease to organize their lives around men.

Singer portrays women almost entirely as the sum total of their biological functions and in terms of their relationships (or lack of them) with men. He uses physical details of women's bodies as signposts of their personalities. In describing unattractive women—particularly older ones whose physical aging often seems to discredit them or make them seem absurd—there are always sagging, wrinkled breasts, grotesquely swollen bellies, female odors, and menopausal instability.

Whenever a woman fails to carry out her physiological destiny (remains a virgin too long, cannot conceive) it is presented as the woman's failing for which she can compensate only by showing extreme loyalty and support to her male partner.

In some stories, Singer equates sexuality with the world of demons who lie in wait for their human prey; the witch is a symbol of human depravity. It is useful to compare here the different treatment Singer accords witches of the two sexes: when men are witches, they are more often explicit incarnations of the devil; their evil comes from sources outside themselves. When women are evil, they seem to be depraved in their human essence. In spite of their greater capacity for evil, female witches have less power than male witches, and are all ultimately under the power of Satan himself. So man rules, even in the witch world.

As a witch, woman is given magical powers to heal but also to harm (midwife *and* abortionist); she is also, of course, accused of sexual aberrations. Cunegonde, in "The Destruction of Kreshov," is a good example of the witch type—isolated, old and ugly, the object of public scorn and suspicion, she is brutally killed by the angry fiancé of a woman she has ostensibly tried to help.

While Cunegonde, Hodle and other Singer witch figures are based in the *shtetl* and have their origin in traditional folk material, Singer also attributes witch-like characteristics to women in stories with a modern venue. For example, in "Alone," the Cuban caretaker of a deserted hotel in Miami is described as:

> a deformed creature. . . with a hunched back, disheveled hair. . . long hairy arms and crooked legs. . . (who) stared at me intently, *as silent as a witch casting a spell.*

In the flash of a sudden storm, this woman becomes "the witch crouched low like an animal ready to seize its prey."

Singer's males almost always seem helpless in these situations and are forever entangled with women's sexuality—obsessively, one might even say. The pattern that emerges most often in his stories has the central male figure or narrator caught in a web of his own making, trapped in relationships with several women, all of whom want him. Asa Heshel in *Family Moskat*, Herman Broder in *Enemies*, Yasha in *The Magician of Lublin* and, most recently, Aaron Greidinger in *Shosha* are prime examples.

> Leib returned to his cherished vision: Rooshke lay there, dress up, legs stretched out, the knife in her stomach with only the metal handle sticking out. . . . He had been having a long dream, all about Rooshke, a strange one, for he had been slitting her throat and at the same time making love to her.
>
> *Under the Knife*

Singer's men's arousal at women's sexuality and their inability (or unwillingness) to deal with their own feelings leads to hostility to women. Male anger at female sexuality is the theme of "Under the Knife," one of Singer's most savage stories. Here the protagonist plots revenge against his woman "for being too tough," that is to say, for jilting him. Even in *Shosha*, where the narrator ostensibly loves his childlike wife genuinely, the marriage initiation is a rape:

> I awoke excited. I grabbed Shosha, and before she could even wake up, I mounted her. She choked and resisted. A stream of hot blood burned my thigh. I tried to pacify her but she broke out in a wail. . . . It was all out of love, I cried.

In so frequently associating male lust with violence toward women, Singer diverges most strongly from traditional Jewish life and comes closest to the Western pornographic imagination. While he does not go as far as to suggest that deep down all women actually want to be raped, he does seem to believe that women enjoy being victimized, degraded, and overpowered by men. The narrator of "A Quotation from Klopstock" boasts that "A few fiery slaps worked like a charm. After slaps she started to kiss. . . . I knew well how to manage my women." The protagonist of "The Briefcase" provides a good summary of this attitude: "I wronged everybody, but all these women continued to shower me with love." In "Blood," another of Singer's most brutal stories, Risha, applauding her lover's sexual prowess, uses the language of his trade (slaughtering): "You

sure murdered me that time." And in "The Dance," an abused
wife becomes an abused mother after her husband dies:

> I made myself a doormat for him. I suffered all his caprices.
> Even before he asked for something I gave it to him. Once
> when I handed him his slippers, he took one and smacked
> me in the face with it. *It was my fault. Not his.*

In causing the victim to blame herself, Singer is not only creating a distorted image of the Jewish woman as emotional cripple.
He is also granting license to her oppressor.

> We often drew [our] situations from your stories in the
> Yiddish papers. I wonder if you realize how much litera-
> ture influences life.

As this quote from one of Singer's characters shows, the
author is well aware that literature and life are mutually inter-
dependent. For this reason, the images in a fictional world can
never be dismissed simply as harmless creatures of the imagination. Unchallenged stereotypes help to keep groups in inferior
positions, be they Jews in a gentile society or women in a
patriarchy. But while American Jews have long recognized the
power of art, and have unhesitatingly spoken out against novels
and films that perpetuate derogatory images of Jews, they
have remained disturbingly complacent when faced with similarly damaging stereotypes about women.

Singer seems to be responding favorably to the feminist challenge, at least on the level of official pronouncement. At a public lecture in New York City last fall, he went so far as to say
that Judaism had made an "historical mistake" in not teaching
women Torah, that the denial of women's rights had contributed
to assimilation, that he welcomed giving Jewish women full religious rights in the synagogue (including *aliyoth* and ordina-
tion), and that a reversal of these inequities would be "wonderful for religion and justice." (*JTA*, 11/8/78)

As encouraging as such remarks may be, they nonetheless
stand in stark contrast to Singer's most recent fictional writings,
which continue to present the male/female dichotomy in un-
changed sexist terms. While it is possible to explain this gap between the written and the spoken word as the result of the time
lag between the two media, it seems more likely that this dis-

crepancy is exactly what it appears to be—an unresolved contradiction.

Acknowledging that women have been deprived of their rights within Judaism is an essential step toward the creation of a changed consciousness. But it is only a beginning. For Singer to be able to portray women as full human beings, as subjects seen in relation to themselves and each other rather than as appendages or complements to men, would require a deeper revision and a determination to shed years of acculturation. We can only hope that in time, Singer will influence Singer, and that his theory and his practice will become more fully integrated.

Blaming the Jews
for the Birth of Patriarchy

Judith Plaskow

There is a new myth developing in Christian feminist circles.
It is a myth which tells us that the ancient Hebrews invented
patriarchy: that before them the goddess reigned in matriarchal
glory, and that after them Jesus tried to restore egalitarianism
but was foiled by the persistence of Jewish attitudes within the
Christian tradition. It is a myth, in other words, which perpetuates traditional Christianity's negative picture of Judaism by
attributing sexist attitudes to Christianity's Jewish origins, at
the same time maintaining that Christianity's distinctive contributions to the "woman question" are largely positive.

The consequence of this myth is that feminism is turned into
another weapon in the Christian anti-Judaic arsenal. Christian
feminism gives a new slant to the old theme of Christian superi-
ority, a theme rooted in the New Testament and since reiterated
by countless Christian theologians.

Invidious comparisons between Judaism and Christianity
most often appear in one particular context in feminist work.
Writers exploring the Jewish background of Jesus' attitudes toward women frequently exaggerate the plight of women in Judaism in order to make Jesus' position stand out more positively
in contrast. If Jewish women are unclean chattels, then Jesus'
treatment of them must be revolutionary. "Jesus was a feminist,"
as Leonard Swidler put it.

Understanding Jesus' relations with women in the historical
context of contemporary Judaism is surely a legitimate and important task. But many feminist accounts of Jesus' Jewish
milieu suffer from three serious scholarly errors or oversights
which are rooted in biased views of Jesus' Jewish origins.

First of all, a number of discussions of Jewish attitudes towards women use the Talmud or passages from it to establish
the role of Jewish women in Jesus' time. The Talmud however,
is a compilation of Jewish law and argument which was not giv-

en final form until the *sixth century*. Passages in it may be much older or at least reflect reworkings of earlier material. But this can be determined only on the basis of painstaking scholarly sifting of individual texts. Such sifting clearly has not been done by authors who can blithely refer to the whole Talmudic tractate *Sabbath* as contemporary with Christ or who can say that certain taboos against women were incorporated into the Talmud "and from there passed on into Christianity."

Similarly, references to rabbinic customs or sayings as contemporary with Jesus also reflect a misunderstanding of the development of Judaism. The Rabbinate emerged as an institution only after the fall of the Temple in 70 C.E., and it took considerable time before rabbinic authority was consolidated and came to represent more than a minority opinion within the Jewish community.

Secondly, it is deceptive to speak of rabbinic opinion, customs, or sayings as monolithic. Even if one assumes that the Talmud gives an accurate picture of Jesus' Jewish background, the Talmud is at least as ambivalent as the New Testament on the subject of women. Yet writers dealing with Jewish attitudes towards women often select only the most negative rabbinic passages on the topic. Their treatment of Judaism is analogous to conservative Christian arguments for the subordination of women which quote only certain verses from Paul. Perhaps the most egregious instance of this type of distortion of Jewish tradition is Virginia Mollenkott's statement that "the Rabbis" would have been shocked and alienated by Christian belief in the mutual love and service of husband and wife. Is she speaking of "the Rabbis" who said "Love your wife as yourself, honor her more than yourself," or "If your wife is small, stoop and whisper in her ear"? Certainly, there are many dreadful rabbinic sayings about the relationship between husband and wife, but there are also a large number of precepts celebrating the joys of a loving match. And if the negative statements influenced Jesus and the New Testament authors (a questionable assumption!), then the positive ones must have as well.

The third error frequently made by feminist scholars is more subtle. It lies in comparing the words and attitudes of an itinerant preacher with laws and sayings formulated in the rarefied atmosphere of rabbinic academies. Many discrepancies between Jesus and "the Rabbis" on the subject of women can be explained by the fact that Jesus was constantly in contact with real women, speaking to and about them in the context of concrete situations. Rabbinic discussions about women, on the other hand, were often largely theoretical, taking place in institutions where no women were present. Where we do have rabbinic stories of actual male/female interaction, we find that rabbis too—whatever their ideological statements—were capable of reacting to women as persons. The often-quoted story of Jesus' compassion for the woman taken in adultery (John 7:53ff), for example, finds a parallel in a rabbinic anecdote told of Rabbi Meir. A man became so angry at his wife for staying out late attending Meir's sermons that he vowed to bar her from the house unless she spat in Meir's face. Meir, hearing of this, sent for the woman and told her that his eyes were sore and could be cured only if a woman spat on them. The woman was then able to go home and tell her husband that she had spit on Meir seven times. The theological point of this story is not the same as the New Testament one. But it is not very different in showing a rabbi react with concern and sympathy for the trials of an ordinary woman.

These deficiencies in feminist scholarship are serious, and they suggest the need for major revisions in the treatment of Jesus' Jewish background. Required, first of all, is honest, balanced, non-polemical discussion of those texts which are in fact contemporary with Jesus. Such discussion should take into account variations in Jewish practice in different areas of the ancient world as well as differences in the setting and audience of Jewish and Christian material. Only when Christian feminists have deepened their understanding of Judaism can they honestly evaluate the uniqueness or non-uniqueness of Jesus' attitudes towards women.

At the same time that Jesus' milieu is being reevaluated, the Talmudic rabbis ought to be compared with their true contemporaries—the Church Fathers.

Admittedly, this task is less rewarding than comparison of the Talmud with Jesus: examination of rabbinic and patristic attitudes towards women leaves neither Christians nor Jews much room for self-congratulation. Rather, what is immediately striking is the similarity between the two traditions—in both, the developing association of women with sexuality and the fear of woman as temptress. Christianity compensates for the image of the temptress with that of virgin; Judaism, with the good wife with whom sex is permitted and even encouraged. But while these images saddle women with different disabilities and provide them with different opportunities, it would be difficult, and certainly pointless, to label one superior to the other.

The persistence of biased presentations of Judaism in feminist work is disturbing. But were sloppy scholarship the only issue at stake in feminist anti-Judaism, it could easily be corrected. Much more important, the popularity of such research indicates a profound failure of the feminist ethic. The morality of patriarchy, Mary Daly argues, is characterized by "a failure to lay claim to that part of the psyche that is then projected onto 'the Other.' " Throughout the history of Western thought, women, Blacks, and other oppressed groups have had attributed to them as their nature human traits which men could or would not acknowledge in themselves. Sexuality, bodiliness, dependence, moral and intellectual failure were all peculiarities which belonged to everyone except ruling class males. The feminist ethic, in contrast to this, is supposedly an ethic of wholeness, an ethic based on the withdrawal of projection and the recognition that the full humanity of each of us embraces those despised characteristics patriarchy ascribed to a host of "Others."

Christian feminist anti-Judaism, however, represents precisely the continuation of a patriarchal ethic of projection. Feminist research projects onto Judaism the failure of the Christian tradition unambiguously to renounce sexism. It projects onto Judaism the "backsliding" of a tradition which was to develop sexism in new and virulent directions. It thus allows the Christian feminist to avoid confronting the failures of her/his own tradition. This is the real motive behind biased presentations of Jesus' Jewish background: to allow the feminist to present the "true" Christian tradition as uniquely free from sexism. Otherwise, why not present positive Jewish sayings about women along with the negative ones? The former are just as conspicuous as the latter in English anthologies of rabbinic thought. And why not compare the Talmud with the Fathers instead of Jesus? Clearly, because that would not permit as dramatic a contrast between the two traditions.

The "Other" who is the recipient of these projections is, of course, the same Other who has received the shadow side of the Christian self since the beginnings of the Christian tradition. Feminists should know better! During the period when witch persecutions were at their peak, witches and Jews were the Church's interchangeable enemies. When the Inquisition ran out of Jews, it persecuted witches—and vice versa. This fact alone should alert feminists to the need to examine and exorcise a form of projection which bears close resemblances to misogyny. But besides this, what Other is more truly a part of the Christian than the Jew? Where else should the withdrawal of projection *begin* than with Judaism. Yet women who are concerned with the relation between feminism and every other form of oppression are content mindlessly to echo traditional Christian attitudes towards Judaism.

The purpose of these criticisms of feminist scholarship is not to suggest that traditional Jewish attitudes towards women are praiseworthy. Of course, they are not. But Christian attitudes are in no way essentially different. They are different in detail, and these differences are extremely interesting and worthy of study. But weighed in the feminist balance, both traditions must be found wanting—and more or less to the same degree. The real tragedy is that the feminist revolution has furnished one more occasion for the projection of Christian failure onto Judaism. It ought to provide the opportunity for transcending ancient differences in the common battle against sexism.

Blaming the Jews for the Death of the Goddess

Annette Daum

Christ, Carol P. and Judith Plaskow, Eds.: *Womanspirit Rising: A Feminist Reader in Religion* (Harper & Row, 1979).

Engelsman, Joan Chamberlain: *The Feminine Dimension of the Divine* (Westminster Press, 1979).

Goldenberg, Naomi R.: *Changing of the Gods* (Beacon Press, 1979).

Ochs, Carol: *Behind the Sex of God* (Beacon Press, 1977).

Patai, Raphael: *The Hebrew Goddess* (Ktav, 1967; pap.: Avon, 1978).

Ruether, Rosemary and Eleanor McLaughlin, Eds.: *Women of Spirit: Female Leadership in the Jewish and Christian Traditions* (Simon and Schuster, 1979).

Starhawk: *The Spiral Dance: A Rebirth of the Ancient Religion and the Great Goddess* (Harper & Row, 1979).

Stone, Merlin: *When God Was a Woman* (Harcourt Brace Jovanovich, 1978).

Strober, Gerald S.: *Portrait of the Elder Brother* (American Jewish Committee, 1972).

Swidler, Leonard: *Biblical Affirmations of Women* (Westminster Press, 1979).

There has been an explosion of exploration by feminists seeking alternatives to theologies rooted in and reflecting the male experience. These ten works, and most especially the two anthologies—*Women of Spirit* and *Womanspirit Rising*—provide a diversity of religious options while making obvious the differing agendas of the reformists and the revolutionaries.

The reformists, mostly Christian feminists, are examining their heritage, researching and reconstructing the past in an effort to remove layers of sexism in religion and to uncover what they regard as the essential core of their traditions. While rejecting any misogyny within their faith, they remain loyal to their religion, seeking change from within the system.

The revolutionary feminists reject such loyalty, considering all religious tradition irredeemably sexist, and turn to other sources in their search for spirituality. Some, seeing divinity within women, seek new symbols, new rituals based on women's experiences, dreams, fantasies and literature. Others, seeking freedom from the past, are returning to ancient symbols of womanspirit such as witchcraft (*The Spiral Dance*) and Goddess worship. Some even suggest that a modern form of polytheism is necessary to reflect the diversity of imagery. Still others offer Jungian psychology as a replacement for religion, although Naomi Goldenberg warns in *Changing of the Gods* that this system supports stereotyped notions of masculine and feminine.

A common thread weaves through this diversity of material: Judaism is singled out by many feminists—reformists and revolutionaries, religious and anti-religious—as the source of society's sexism.

In their desire to prove that Christianity is not innately sexist, some Christian feminists have all too often unintentionally but unquestioningly incorporated the anti-Semitic prejudices of Christian male theologians of the past. References abound in their works purporting to trace the sexism of Christianity to its Judaic heritage. Paul's negative statements about women are attributed to his Jewish heritage, while Jesus is depicted as standing in opposition to Jewish society in his support of women.

Even Leonard Swidler, who acknowledges in *Biblical Affirmations of Women* that Jesus was "an observant, Torah-true Jew... standing very much in the Jewish, Pharisaic tradition of his day," claims that Jesus was unique among his peers in his positive attitudes towards women. Not even Jesus' expressions of concern for the widowed, long a part of Prophetic tradition, are attributed to his Jewish heritage.

The term "Judeo-Christian heritage" crops up again and again in these books, as if Judaism and Christianity were one. This simplistic usage ignores the fact that Jews and Christians do not share a unified common historical experience, nor do we interpret in the same way the Scripture that we do share. Judaism and Christianity are not monolithic in their treatment of women and also discriminate against women in different ways. The sexism in Christianity, therefore, cannot be attributed solely to its Jewish roots, as many of these authors do.

The old Christian charge of Deicide, that the Jews murdered God incarnate in the ultimate masculine body form of Jesus Christ—rejected in recent times by many denominations—is now being resurrected by some revolutionary feminists in different form: the accusation that the Hebrew people were responsible for the destruction of the ultimate feminine deity, the Goddess.

Merlin Stone, in *When God Was A Woman*, describes the Hebrews as ruthlessly supplanting Goddess worship with the monotheistic *male* Hebrew deity:

> Into the laws of the Levites was written the destruction of the worship of the Divine Ancestress, and with it the final destruction of the matrilineal system.

While acknowledging that the elimination of Goddess worship started long before the appearance of the Hebrew people and continued until the last Goddess temple was destroyed by the Christians in the fifth century, C.E. Stone fails to note (as Raphael Patai does) that monotheism involved the destruction of all idolatry of *both* male and female deities.

This charge of Goddess-murder has been added to the feminist arsenal of accusations against the Hebrew people.

The most blatant distortion of Judaism occurs when feminists apply modern standards of morality to the beliefs and practices of ancient Israel. Abraham, the Patriarch of Judaism, Christianity and Islam, the revered model figure who demands justice even from God, is depicted by some Christian feminists as despicable for behavior that recent archeological evidence indicates was probably customary for those times in that milieu.

No re-evaluation by feminists has had a more negative impact than that regarding the *Akedah*, the Binding of Isaac. Referring to this event as the "Sacrifice of Isaac" reveals the bias of the focus. Stone acknowledges that testing by divine powers in connection with the revelation of moral truth was common to many cultures, but interprets the *Akedah* solely as a harsh test of blind obedience, missing the point. Carol Ochs, in *Behind the Sex of God*, mistakenly assumes that the *Akedah* has the same meaning in Judaism as in Christianity and also represents the ultimate patriarchal expression of religion:

> The meaning of the test is that Abraham must prove his allegiance under the new patriarchal system. . . . In order to

prove that Abraham is not rooted in the older [matriarchal] tradition, God demands that he renounce the most fundamental tenet of the matriarchal religion and kill his own child.

She understands the rite of circumcision, a custom also common to surrounding cultures, as a substitute for child-sacrifice, but fails to note that this ritual, which seals the covenant relationship in Judaism, is consistent with the requirement that Abraham and his descendants obey God and *refrain* from child-sacrifice.

Neither Stone nor Ochs considers the significance of God's dramatic intervention to prevent the sacrifice of Isaac. According to Jewish tradition, the crucial moral truth revealed is God's *opposition* to human sacrifice. This contrasts with Christian theological focus which depicts Christ as the "Lamb of God" whose sacrifice is *required*.

The information Stone provides about Judaism is selectively judgmental. She describes as "shocking" Biblical laws regarding virginity before marriage but applies no such pejorative adjective to describe ancient sacred sexual rites associated with Goddess worship in pre-Biblical days—which included the ritual sacrifice of the annual male consort of the High Priestess. Stone further suggests that eventually other rituals, such as castration, were substituted for human sacrifice, indicating also that men may have made themselves eunuchs to serve as attendants to the High Priestess. She exhibits no revulsion or concern about these practices, which could surely be considered more abhorrent by modern standards than the requirement of pre-marital virginity by females.

Some feminists have fallen into ancient masculine anti-Semitic traps unworthy of their scholarship. Stone perceives the myth of Adam and Eve as an assault upon Goddess religion and thus, by inference, the basis of women's debasement. And Ochs, in what is perhaps the ultimate expression of Christian feminist chauvinism, portrays Mary as a goddess figure—and as the antithesis of Eve:

> Through Eve all women are cursed and through Mary all women are blessed. . . . Mary through her gift of Jesus . . . . restores humankind to its sinless state.

While the popular notion among many Christians attributes the subjugation of women to the Eve/apple story from Hebrew

Scriptures, new research by Biblical scholars indicates that such an interpretation is unjustified and that the original meaning of the text is egalitarian.

Stone regards both Judaism and Christianity as anti-sexual, but attributes this solely to Hebrew culture and disregards entirely the impact of Hellenistic emphasis on body/mind dualism. However, Rosemary Ruether, the Christian feminist co-editor of *Women of Spirit*, correctly calls attention to the profound effect of this philosophy on the development of sexism in Christianity. Hellenistic philosophy equated the human body with carnal impulses, regarded it as evil, and associated with women; it placed these attributes on a lower level than the intellectual and spiritual realm, which was reserved for men by men. Ruether more carefully identifies Christianity as the heir of this philosophy, of neo-Platonism and "apocalyptic Judaism."

She sees the ascetic movement in Catholicism as a liberating force for women, offering them options of freedom from unwelcome marriages and providing them with the opportunity to lead a holy life of greater independence, self-development and study. This was achieved at the price of their sexuality.

Another pitfall many of these authors fall into is their tendency to interpret Hebrew Scriptures in the worst possible light and to contrast this interpretation with the most positive evaluation of the New Testament.

Even Elizabeth Fiorenza, Associate Professor of Theology at Notre Dame, who calls on the Church in her piece in *Womanspirit Rising* to "abandon all forms of sexism" as it has "publicly repented of its anti-Semitic theology," falls victim. She claims that the baptismal formula in *Galatians 3:28*, which states that for all who have accepted Christ, "there is neither Jew nor Greek; there is neither slave nor freeman; there is neither male nor female" demonstrates Christianity's egalitarian commitment, and she offers conclusive evidence of women's participation in the early Church. Many scholars, however, see the verse in *Galatians* as a reference to the hope that social discrimination will cease in the *next* world.

Fiorenza compares that verse to what she describes as "accepted social discrimination in the Judaism and Hellenism of the times." She bases this conclusion on the similarity of prayers thanking God for being human, not beasts; Jews, not heathens; free, not slaves; men, not women.

Her comparison, however, is between different categories of writing. The New Testament, sacred to *all* Christians, is contrasted with one minor prayer designed not for synagogue use, but as an optional private prayer for the home. And, indeed, only one group of Jews—orthodox males—include this prayer in their liturgy today (Reform Judaism rejected it and Conservative Judaism eliminated it), a fact apparently unknown to Stone who states, without qualification, that this prayer is still recited by Hebrew males every day.

While no amount of apologia can eliminate the underlying chauvinism of this traditional prayer, a better comparison could be made between *Galatians* and Jewish writings of an equally sacred nature. *Genesis 1:27*—a revolutionary statement of principle that men and women were created equal at the same time by God, in the image of God—would be a more valid comparison.

Stone and other feminist writers assert that the position of ancient Israelite women was worse than that of women in surrounding cultures. Swidler also indicates that this position was worse during the end of the Second Temple Period, with further restrictions imposed upon women partially as a result of the increasing persecution of Jews by pagans and Christians after the destruction of the Second Commonwealth. These evaluations pose a challenge to the assertion by Jewish authorities that the position of Jewish women was superior to that of other cultures.

The question of what is truth and what apologia will haunt us until more Jewish feminist scholars devote time and energy to the painstaking job of research. Historically denied access to education in Torah and Talmud, Jewish women have very few scholars equipped to challenge and remove centuries of sexist translation, interpretation, commentary and customs.

Jewish feminists are caught in a dilemma. Most of the research reviewed here has been conducted by Christian women who have a long history of involvement in scholarship within their faith groups. We owe our Christian counterparts a tremendous debt of gratitude for their pioneering work in developing feminist insights into Scripture which enhance our personhood as women. But there also is deep resentment that these same insights threaten our personhood as Jews.

This new feminist theology, which unfortunately incorporates old anti-Semitism, will be taught to generations of Christians to come unless there is open conversation between Jewish and Christian feminists, free of diatribe or polemic, to bridge the gap in understanding and foster a joint unbiased approach to Biblical interpretation in the future. Only when we can openly acknowledge that neither Judaism nor Christianity has lived up to its expressed ideals in the treatment of women will we be able to unite in our demand for justice in the name of God who demands justice for all.

Contributors' Biographies

Pauline Bart is a Brooklyn-born sociologist, mother of two, and casualty of the fifties. She spent that decade in a tract house in Culver City, California, being a permissive mother and a messy housekeeper. In 1961 she returned to graduate school and wrote her dissertation on depression in middle-aged women ("Portnoy's Mother's Complaint"). After receiving her doctorate she held three jobs in four years because of general discrimination—in addition to her gender, her age, her writing about women, and to quote the elitist institution where she lectured, "after all, it was a question of image. We couldn't have our first woman be a Jewish mother." Pauline has written on women's health issues ("A Funny Thing Happened on the Way to the Orifice"), on menopause ("Taking the Men out of Menopause"), mental health, and sexism in social science. She is also coauthor of *Stopping Rape: Successful Survival Strategies*. At present she is a professor of sociology in the departments of psychiatry and sociology at the University of Illinois at Chicago. She is a mother and a grandmother.

Evelyn Torton Beck, scholar/teacher/activist, is professor and director of the Women's Studies Program at the University of Maryland–College Park and a member of the Jewish Studies Program. She is the author of *Kafka and the Yiddish Theater* (1971), coeditor of *The Prism of Sex* (1979), and translator from Yiddish of stories by Isaac Bashevis Singer. She has lectured and written widely on Jewish women's studies, lesbian studies, anti-Semitism in the women's movement, feminist transformations of knowledge, feminist perspectives on Kafka, and women in the arts. She is currently at work on a book, *From "Kike" to "JAP,"* analyzing the forces that came together to construct the stereotype of "Jewish American Princess," hoping by this work to disrupt them.

Nina Rachel (Beck) is currently living in Oakland, California, with two cat-children, Mathilda and Elilah. Grateful for the support of a loving, clean, and sober lesbian community and for the rich, warm love of Carolina Delgado. "We are both brave womyn who reach beyond the boundaries and limits set for us by our cultures, daring to live the dream of our hearts, willing to walk the road into the unknown."

Annette Daum (1930–1988) was coordinator of the Department of Interreligious Affairs at the Union of American Hebrew Congregations. She also served on the Task Force on Equality of Women in Judaism.

Elana Dykewomon is the author of *Riverfinger Women* (1974), *They Will Know Me by My Teeth* (1976), and *fragments from lesbos* (1981). She is the current editor of *Sinister Wisdom: A Journal for the Lesbian Imagination in the Arts and Politics.*

Marcia Freedman lived in Israel from 1967 to 1981. She is one of the founders of the Israeli women's movement and was elected to the Israeli Knesset (parliament) in 1973. In 1977 she left mainstream politics in order to devote her time to feminist organizing. Her first project was to establish a national Women's Party to run in the elections of 1977. This was followed by the establishment of Israel's first shelter for battered women, its first women's center and bookstore, and the establishment of the Women's Aid Fund, which was instrumental in pioneering a network of feminist activities including a rape crisis center, other women's centers, legal aid, a national feminist quarterly, a press collective, and annual feminist conferences.

Ruth Geller was born in 1945 and began writing in 1970. Her first novel, *Seed of a Woman*, was all set to be published when the publisher went out of business. She published the novel herself (along with a collection of short stories, *Pictures from the Past*) and hated self-publishing so much that she was delighted when her third novel, *Triangles*, was published by Crossing Press. Unfortunately, *Triangles* is now out of print. Her fourth book, *The History of the Syracuse Peace Council*, was supposed to be published, but then the organization that hired her ran out of money. After 20 years, Ruth thinks she's worked long enough and that it's high time she found her audience. She hopes to find it with *A Letter to My Son*, written to the child she gave up for adoption in 1966.

Shelley Horwitz was born in 1954 in Toledo, Ohio. Jewish-identified and proud, she became a *garinim* addict in 1978. Living in Jerusalem, she has been involved in a four-year monogamous love affair with Israel and teaches Israeli children. As an active feminist, she looks forward to the continuing development of Israel's lesbian community. Her future plans include a trip to the United States for *shlichut lelesbiot* (lesbian immigration outreach) and *hasbara* (dispelling of myths) to strengthen Jewish-lesbian ties internationally.

Dovida Ishatova is a pianist, composer, piano tuner, and ardent cat lover living in the Boston area. This essay is her first major work since an eighth-grade paper on "The Causes of World War I" (currently out of print).

JEB (Joan E. Biren): In my first books of photographs, *Eye to Eye: Portraits of Lesbians*, published in 1979, the only Jewish lesbian was me and I didn't identify myself as a Jew because it never occurred to me to do so then. When my second book, *Making a Way: Lesbians Out Front*, was published in 1987 it included photographs of more than 20 Jewish lesbians of whom 13 chose to identify themselves as Jews in their short statements in the text. It feels good to be able to see change so clearly. My new work, which reflects a Jewish consciousness, is a one-hour documentary, *For Love and for Life: The 1987 March on Washington for Lesbian and Gay Rights*, now available on videotape from Moonforce Media, P.O. Box 2934, Washington, D.C. 20013.

Melanie Kaye/Kantrowitz worked in the civil rights movement in Harlem in the early sixties and has continued as an activist in antiwar, feminist, and progressive Jewish politics, including Middle East peace work. She is the author of a book of poetry, *We Speak in Code*, a collection of short stories, tentatively titled *Some Pieces of Jewish Left: Secular Tales for Modern Times*, and she coedited *The Tribe of Dina: A Jewish Women's Anthology*. From 1983 to 1987 she edited and published *Sinister Wisdom*, one of the oldest lesbian/feminist journals. She holds a Ph.D. in comparative literature from the University of California, Berkeley, and teaches women's writing and women's studies in the graduate program of Vermont College.

Irena Klepfisz was born in Warsaw, Poland, in 1941 and came to the United States at the age of eight. She is a poet and author of *Keeper of Accounts* (1983), *Different Enclosures* (1985), and co-editor of *The Tribe of Dina: A Jewish Women's Anthology* (Beacon Press, 1989). An activist in both the Jewish and lesbian/ feminist communities, she has lectured, written, and led workshops on feminism, office work and class, homophobia, Jewish identity, Yiddish culture, anti-Semitism, and the Middle East. She received her Ph.D. from the University of Chicago and has taught English, Yiddish, women's studies, and creative writing. In 1988 she received an NEA Fellowship in poetry and in 1989 served as translator-in-residence at YIVO Institute for Jewish Research focusing on Yiddish women writers. Two companion volumes—one of her collected poems, the other of her collected essays—will be published by Eighth Mountain Press in the spring of 1990.

L. Lee Knefelkamp (Chaya Shoshana) has lived Jewishly for half of her forty-four years. She is a convert to Judaism and a scholar, educator, and academic administrator who sees her work as fundamentally rooted in *Tikkun Olam*. She works to make colleges and universities places where goodness happens and where diversity is taken seriously.

Aliza Maggid is a founding member of Am Tikva Boston, a lesbian and gay Jewish group. She is a longtime feminist activist and builder of alliances between many groups of people on a community, national, and international level.

Harriet Malinowitz lives in New York City. Her fiction, articles, and reviews have appeared in *Chomo Uri, The Massachusetts Review, Conditions, Sinister Wisdom,* and in *Love, Struggle and Change: Stories by Women,* ed. Irene Zahara. She is currently writing lesbian stand-up comedy and teaching English in a New York labor college.

Bernice Mennis lives in the southern Adirondacks where she shares land with a group of close friends. She teaches writing and literature in a community college, a prison, and a neighborhood community center.

Judith Plaskow is associate professor of religious studies at Manhattan College. She is coeditor of *Womanspirit Rising: A Feminist Reader in Religion* and *Weaving the Visions: New Pat-*

terns in Feminist Spirituality and author of *Jewish Feminist Theology: Standing Again at Sinai.*

Adrienne Rich is a poet, essayist, and activist, now living in California. She is actively involved with New Jewish Agenda, and teaches part-time at Stanford University.

Josylyn C. Segal was raised both in New York City and the Poconos, Pennsylvania. Her undergraduate study utilized both Brandeis University and Beacon College, where she focused on social psychology and women's studies. Josylyn currently resides in southern California, where she plays soprano saxophone and congas, is creatively unemployed, and is an aspiring writer trying to move back to northern California. "Interracial Plus" is her first publication.

Martha Shelley was born in Brooklyn in 1943 into a working-class Jewish family. For many years she enjoyed gay spinsterhood and a glorious career in politics and communications, Radicalesbians, Gay Liberation Front, RAT Newspaper, WBAI-FM (producer of lesbian-feminist shows), and the Women's Press Collective. Now she is living with a lover and three kids, and looking for a good-paying job. She has published two books of poetry, *Crossing the DMZ* (1974) and *Lovers and Mothers* (1981). Both books are available from Sefir Publications, 729 55th Street, Oakland, CA 94609.

Savina Teubal is a Sephardic Jew, born in Manchester, England, of Syrian parents. She was brought up in Buenos Aires, Argentina, where she published fiction and a book of short stories (in Spanish). She left Argentina for political reasons during the Peronista era. Savina has lived in the United States since 1959 and has dedicated the last 10 years to researching and writing about the matriarchs of Genesis. In 1984 Swallow Press published *Sarah the Priestess*. Savina is now working on *The Book of Hagar.*

Maida Tilchen, a longtime lesbian activist in Bloomington, Indiana, moved to Boston in 1980 to become a writer and promotions manager for *Gay Community News* (the national weekly newspaper for lesbians and gays). Her writing has appeared in several lesbian and gay publications, including *Lavender Culture* and *The Lesbian in Literature* (third edition).

Helen D. Weinstock was born the middle daughter of three. With neither the power of the eldest nor the privileges of the "baby," she was tossed into the faceless clerical pool in the midst of the Great Depression. To escape the army of nine-to-fivers, Helen washed spittoons in a pool parlor, was a "barker" in Coney Island, worked in a candy factory, waitressed, operated a lathe, became a radio electrician—all in various parts of the United States and Japan. She graduated as an R.N. in San Francisco in 1954. Since 1970 Helen has made her permanent home in Israel, where she primarily works in the clinics of outlying agricultural settlements.

Rachel Wahba is a psychotherapist in private practice in San Francisco, where she also serves as a clinical supervisor at Operation Concern: A Gay/Lesbian Mental Health Agency.

Susan J. Wolfe, a Jewish lesbian feminist from a working-class background, has given birth to two sons, one born "out of wedlock." Neither lives with her now. She is professor of English at the University of South Dakota, where she teaches linguistics and women's studies. Coeditor of *The Coming Out Stories*, she has also written on the relationship between language, gender, and society. She is coediting an anthology of lesbian-feminist literary criticism.

Suggestions for Further Reading

Intersection of Judaism/Lesbianism/Feminism

Aliza, Arich and Hannah. "A Feeling of Family: Boston Gay and Lesbian Jews Attend World Conference." *Gay Community News,* 29 August 1981, p. 10.

Anonymous. "Dilemma of a Jewish Lesbian." *Chutzpah: A Jewish Liberation Anthology,* ed. Chutzpah Collective. San Francisco: New Glide Publications, 1977, pp. 30-31.

Baetz, Ruth. *Lesbian Crossroads: Personal Stories of Lesbian Struggles and Triumphs.* New York: Wm. Morrow & Co., 1980. See interview with Jane Salter, a blind Jewish lesbian.

Baracks, Barbara and Kent Jarratt, eds. *Sage Writings: From the Lesbian and Gay Men's Writing Workshop at Senior Workshop in a Gay Environment.* New York: Teachers & Writers Collaborative, 1980. See Gerry Faier, Ruth Herstein, and Florence Holland.

Bart, Pauline. "Depression in Middle-Aged Women." Originally entitled "Portnoy's Mother's Complaint." *Woman in Sexist Society,* ed. Vivian Gornick and Barbara K. Moran. New York: Basic Books, 1971, pp. 99-117.

Bauman, Batya. "Ten Women Tell... The Ways We Are." *Lilith: The Jewish Women's Magazine* 2, Winter 76/77, pp. 9-10.

_____. "Women-Identified Women in Male-Identified Judaism." *On Being a Jewish Feminist: A Reader,* ed. Susannah Heschel. New York: Schocken Books, 1983, pp. 88-95.

Beck, Evelyn Torton. "Daughters and Mothers: An Autobiographical Sketch." *Sinister Wisdom* 14, 1980, pp. 76-80.

_____. "Teaching About Jewish Lesbians in Literature: From 'Zeitel and Rickl' to 'The Tree of Begats'." *Lesbian Studies,* ed. Margaret Cruikshank. Old Westbury, NY: The Feminist Press, 1982, pp. 81-87.

Becker, Robin. *Backtalk.* Cambridge, MA: Alicejamesbooks, 1982.

Bloch, Alice. *Lifetime Guarantee: A Journey Through Loss and Survival.* Watertown, MA: Persephone Press, 1981.

_____. "Scenes From the Life of a Jewish Lesbian." Reprinted in Heschel, *On Being a Jewish Feminist,* pp. 171-176.

Bulkin, Elly. *Lesbian Fiction: An Anthology.* Watertown, MA: Persephone Press, 1981. See especially Irena Klepfisz, Francine Krasno, and Lynn Michaels.

Bulkin, Elly and Joan Larkin. *Lesbian Poetry: An Anthology.* Watertown, MA: Persephone Press, 1981.

Cowan, Liza and Penny House. "Anti-Semitism in the Lesbian Movement." *Dyke: A Quarterly* 5, pp. 20-22. (The journal is now defunct.)

Dykewomon, Elana. *fragments from lesbos.* Langlois, OR: Diaspora Distribution, 1981.

——————. *They Will Know Me By My Teeth.* Northampton, MA: Megaera Press, 1976. (Available from Diaspora Distribution.)

Feinstein, Sarah. "It Has to Do With Apples." *Lesbian Insider/Insighter/Inciter,* No. 4 (July 1981), p. 1.

Freespirit, Judy. *Daddy's Girl: An Incest Survivor's Story.* Langlois, OR: Diaspora Distribution, 1982.

Geller, Ruth. *Pictures From the Past.* Buffalo, NY: Imp Press, 1981.

——————. *Seed Of A Woman.* Buffalo, NY: Imp Press, 1981.

Katz, Judith. "Nadine Pagan's Last Letter Home." *Sinister Wisdom* 19, 1982.

Kaye/Kantrowitz, Melanie. *We Speak in Code: Poems & Other Writings.* Pittsburgh: Motheroot Publications, 1980. (Available from *Sinister Wisdom.*)

Klepfisz, Irena. *periods of stress.* Brooklyn, NY: Out & Out Books, 1977.

Litman, Jane. "How to Get What We Want By the Year 2000." *Lilith: The Jewish Women's Magazine* 7, 1980, pp. 21-22.

Miriam, Selma. "Anti-Semitism in the Lesbian Community: A Collage of Mostly Bad News By One Jewish Dyke." *Sinister Wisdom* 19, 1982.

Nachman, Elana. *Riverfinger Women.* Plainfield, VT: Daughters, 1974. (Forthcoming edition will be available from Diaspora Distribution.)

Parnok, Sophia. "8 Poems." Translated by Rima Shore. *Conditions: Six,* 1980, pp. 177-193.

Rich, Adrienne. *A Wild Patience Has Taken Me This Far.* New York: Norton, 1981.

Rukeyser, Muriel. *Collected Poems.* New York: McGraw Hill, 1979.

Seagull, Thyme S. "My Mother Was A Light Housekeeper." *The Woman Who Lost Her Names: Selected Writings By American Jewish Women,* ed. Julia Wolf Mazow. New York: Harper & Row, 1981, pp. 177-191.

Shelley, Martha. *Crossing the DMZ.* Oakland, CA: Women's Press Collective, 1974. (Available from Sefir Publications.)

——————. *Lovers & Mothers.* Oakland, CA: Sefir Publications, 1981.

Shore, Rima. "Life in America." A one-act play. *Conditions: Three,* 1978, pp. 62-85.

——————. "Remembering Sophia Parnok." *Conditions: Six,* 1980, pp. 177-193.

Teubal, Savina J. *Sarah the Priestess: The First Matriarch of Genesis.* Ohio: Swallow Press, 1984.

——————. "Women, the Law and the Ancient Near East." *Fields of Offerings: Studies in Honor of Raphael Patai on the Occasion of His Seventieth Birthday.* Fairleigh Dickinson University Press, 1982.

Tilchen, Maida. "JEB Talks—Picturing Lesbians." *Gay Community News,* 8 August 1981, p. 11.

——————. "Speaking Out: Jewish Feminists Discuss Anti-Semitism." *Gay Community News,* 14 March 1981, p. 5.

Toder, Nancy. *Choices.* Boston, MA: Alyson Press, 1980.

Young, Elise. *Medusa's Hair: Poetry of Lesbian Re-Envisioning.* Middlefield, MA: Mountainwind Products, 1980. (Available from Diaspora Distribution.)

Intersection of Jewish Women/Women of Color

Green, Tova. "Rediscovering My Jewishness." *A Working Conference on Women and Racism: Newsletter of the New England Women's Studies Association,* 4 March 1981, p. 8.

Morales, Rosario. "Double Allegiance: Jewish Women and Women of Color." *A Working Conference on Women and Racism: Newsletter of the New England Women's Studies Association,* May 1981, p. 8.

Sinclair, Jo (pseud. for Ruth Seid). *The Changelings.* New York: McGraw Hill, 1955. (Though this book shows a close friendship between two young girls, one Jewish and the other Black, the picture of the adult Jewish community is extremely negative and limited.)

――――――. *The Wasteland.* Philadelphia: Jewish Pub. Soc., 1988.

Smith, Beverly with Judith Stein and Priscilla Golding. "The Possibility of Life Between Us: A Dialogue Between Black and Jewish Women." *Conditions: Seven,* 1981, pp. 25-46.

Yanina. "Reflections: A Black Lesbian Relates With Her Jewish Grandmother-in-Law." *A Working Conference on Women and Racism: Newsletter of the New England Women's Studies Association,* May 1981, p. 8.

Jewish History

Angel, D. Marc. *The Sephardim of the United States: An Exploratory Study.* New York: Union of Sephardic Congregations, 1974.

Azaryahu, Sarah. *The Union of Hebrew Women for Equal Rights in Eretz Ysrael: A Selected History of the Women's Movement in Israel (1900-1947).* Translated and with an afterword by Marcia Freedman. Haifa: The Woman's Aid Fund, 1980.

Barnett, Richard, ed. *The Sephardi Heritage.* New York: Ktav Publishing House, 1971.

Baum, Charlotte, Paula Hyman and Sonya Michel. *The Jewish Woman in America.* New York: New American Library, 1975.

Belth, Nathan C. *A Promise to Keep: A Narrative of the American Encounter With Anti-Semitism.* New York: Quadrangle, 1979.

Canetti, Elias. *The Tongue Set Free: Remembrance of a European Childhood.* New York: Continuum Publishing Corporation, 1980.

Dawidowicz, Lucy S. *The War Against the Jews 1933-1945.* New York: Bantam, 1975.

Dobroszycki, Lucjan and Barbara Kirshenblatt-Gimblett. *Image Before My Eyes: A Photographic History of Jewish Life in Poland, 1864-1939.* New York: Schocken Books, 1977.

Fein, Helen. *Accounting for Genocide: Victims—and Survivors—of the Holocaust.* New York: The Free Press, 1979.

Fenelon, Fania. *Playing for Time.* New York: Berkley Publishing Co., 1979.

Gilbert, Martin. *The Jews of Arab Lands: Their History in Maps.* London: Board of Deputies of British Jews, 1976.

Glückel. *The Memoirs of Glückel of Hameln (1646-1724)*. New York: Schocken Books, 1977.

Greenberg, Blu. *On Women and Judaism: A View from Tradition*. Philadelphia: Jewish Publication Society of America, 1981.

Grosser, Paul E. and Edwin G. Halperin. *Anti-Semitism: The Causes and Effects of A Prejudice*. Secaucus, NJ: Citadel Press, 1979.

Hazleton, Lesley. *Israeli Women: The Reality Behind the Myths*. New York: Simon and Schuster, 1977.

Howe, Irving and Kenneth Libo. *How We Lived: A Documentary History of Immigrant Jews in America 1880-1930*. New York: Richard Marek Publishers, 1979.

Henry, Sondra and Emily Taitz. *Written Out of History*. New York: Bloch Publishing Company, 1979.

Kolmar, Gertrude. *Dark Soliloquy: Selected Poems of Gertrude Kolmar*. New York: The Seabury Press, 1975.

Laqueur, Walter. *A History of Zionism*. New York: Schocken Books, 1978.

Lavender, Abraham D., ed. *A Coat of Many Colors: Jewish Subcommittees in the United States*. Westport, CT: Greenwood Press, 1977.

Lee, Albert. *Henry Ford and the Jews*. New York: Stein and Day, 1980.

Levin, Nora. *The Holocaust: The Destruction of European Jewry 1933-1945*. New York: Schocken Books, 1975.

—————. *While Messiah Tarried: Jewish Socialist Movements 1871-1917*. New York: Schocken Books, 1977.

Marrus, Michael R. and Robert O. Paxton. *Vichy France and the Jews*. New York: Basic Books, 1981.

Memmi, Albert. *Jews and Arabs*. Chicago: J. Philip O'Hara, 1975.

Potok, Chaim. *Wanderings*. New York: Alfred A. Knopf, 1978.

Quinley, Harold E. and Charles Y. Glock. *Anti-Semitism in America*. New York: Collier, 1979.

Roth, Cecil. *Doña Gracia of the House of Nasi*. Philadelphia: Jewish Publication Society of America, 1977.

—————. *A History of the Marranos*. Philadelphia: Jewish Publication Society of America, 1932.

Senesh, Hannah. *Her Life & Diary*. Translated by Marta Cohn. New York: Schocken Books, 1973.

Steinberg, Lucien. *Jews Against Hitler: The Seminal Work of the Jewish Resistance*. New York: Gordon & Cremonesi, 1978.

Tillion, Germaine. *Ravensbrück*. Garden City, NY: Anchor Books, 1975.

Zborowski, Mark and Elizabeth Herzog. *Life is With People: The Culture of the Shtetl*. New York: Schocken Books, 1962.

ADDENDUM TO BIBLIOGRAPHY—1

Articles

Beck, Evelyn Torton. "Unity in Diversity." *Selected Papers from the 1983 New York State Women's Studies Conference: Women in the Eighties, Strategy for Solidarity*, April 1983. Available from Elaine Ognibene, English Dept., Siena College, Loudonville, NY 12211.

_____. "Between Invisibility and Overvisibility: The Politics of Anti-Semitism in the Women's Movement and Beyond." *Working Papers in Women's Studies*, Spring 1984. Available from the Women's Studies Research Center, University of Wisconsin, 209 North Brooks Street, Madison WI 53715.

_____. "No More Masks: Anti-Semitism as Jew-Hating." *Women's Studies Quarterly*, Vol. XI, No. 3 (Fall 1983).

_____. "From Kike to 'JAP.'" *Sojourner*, Vol. 14, No. 1 (September 1988), pp. 18-20.

_____. "The Politics of Jewish Invisibility." *NWSA Journal*, Vol. 1, No. 1 (1988), pp. 93-102.

Brown, Fern. "As a Jewish Lesbian: Questions of Race and Anti-Racism." *Common Lives/Lesbian Lives*, No. 3 (Spring 1982), pp. 42-46.

Douglas, Carol Anne and Alice Henry. "Jewish and Arab Women's Dialogue." *off our backs*, January 1983, pp. 6-7, 27.

Freespirit, Judy. "Letters on Anti-Semitism and Editing." *Common Lives/Lesbian Lives*, No. 6 (Winter 1982), pp. 44-47.

_____. "Flashbacks from the Jewish Feminist Conference, June 1982." *Common Lives/Lesbian Lives*, No. 7 (Spring 1983), pp. 86-90.

Henry, Alice. "Racism and Anti-Semitism in the Women's Movement." *off our backs*, August/September 1983, pp. 3-4.

Lerner, Elinor. "American Feminism and the Jewish Question." *Encounter of Jew and Gentile in America*, ed. David Gerber. Champaign, Ill. University of Illinois Press, 1984.

Mushroom, Merril. "Merril Mushroom Is a Jew." *Common Lives/Lesbian Lives*, No. 7 (Spring 1983), 78-85.

Pratt, Minnie Bruce. "Who Am I If I Am Not My Father's Daughter? A Southerner Confronts Racism and Anti-Semitism." *Ms.* (January 1984), pp. 72-73.

Proudfoot, Philippa and Maria Scipione. "Racism and Anti-Semitism in the Women's Movement." *New Women's Times*, September 1983, pp. 4-7.

Siegel, Rachel Josefowitz. "Preliminary Reflections on the Jewish Mother and the Jewish American Princess: Images of Combined Sexism and Anti-Semitism." *Selected Papers from the 1983 New York State Women's Studies Conference: Women in the Eighties, Strategy for Solidarity*, April 1983.

Smith, Barbara. "A Rock and a Hard Place: Relationships Between Black and Jewish Women." *Women's Studies Quarterly*, Vol. XI, No. 3 (Fall 1983).

Stein, Judith A. "Telling *Bobbeh Meisehs:* Notes on Identity and the Creation of Jewish Lesbian Culture." *Common Lives/Lesbian Lives*, No. 8 (Summer 1983), pp. 7-13.

Willis, Ellen. "The Myth of the Powerful Jew." *Beginning to See the Light: Pieces of a Decade.* New York: Alfred A. Knopf, 1981, pp. 228-244.

Books

Balka, Christie, and Andy Rose, eds. *Twice Blessed: On Being Lesbian, Gay, and Jewish.* Boston, MA: Beacon Press, 1989.

Bulkin, Elly, Barbara Smith, and Minnie Bruce Pratt. *Yours in Struggle: Three Feminist Perspectives on Anti-Semitism and Racism.* Brooklyn, NY: Long Haul Press, 1984.

Bloch, Alice. *The Law of Return.* Boston, MA: Alyson Publications, 1983.

Coming Out, Coming Home. Distributed by New Jewish Agenda, New York. Copies $.50 each; bulk rates available.

Geller, Ruth. *Triangles.* Trumansburg, NY: Crossing Press, 1984.

Heschel, Susannah, ed. *On Being a Jewish Feminist: A Reader.* New York: Schocken Books, 1983.

Katz, Esther and Joan Ringelheim. *Women Surviving the Holocaust: Proceedings of the First Conference.* Institute for Research in History, 432 Park Avenue, New York, NY 10016.

Kaye/Kantrowitz, Melanie, and Irena Klepfisz, eds. *The Tribe of Dina: A Jewish Women's Anthology.* Boston, MA: Beacon Press, 1989.

Klein, Judith Weinstein. *Jewish Identity and Self-Esteem: Healing Wounds Through Ethnotherapy.* 1980. (Available from the American Jewish Committee.)

Klepfisz, Irena. *Keeper of Accounts.* Watertown, MA: Persephone Press, 1982. (Available from *Sinister Wisdom.*)

Kreitman, Esther. *Deborah.* London: Virago, 1983.

Laska, Vera, ed. *Women in the Resistance and in the Holocaust: The Voices of Eyewitnesses.* Westport, CT: Greenwood Press, 1983.

Loewenstein, Andrea. *This Place.* Boston, MA: Routledge & Kegan Paul, Pandora Books, 1984.

Rich, Adrienne. *Sources.* Woodside, CA: The Heyeck Press, 1983.

ADDENDUM TO BIBLIOGRAPHY—2

Alarcon, Norma, et al. *The Third Wave: Feminist Perspectives on Racism.* Latham, NY: Kitchen Table, 1990. Includes material on anti-Semitism as well as the Middle East.

Beck, Evelyn Torton. "Naming Is Not a Simple Act: Lesbian Feminist Community in the 1980s." In Christie Balka and Andy Rose, *Twice Blessed.* (See Addendum 1.)

Cantor, Aviva. *The Jewish Woman (1900–1986): A Bibliography.* 2d ed. New York: Biblio Press, 1987.

Elwell, Sue L., ed. *Jewish Women's Studies.* 2d ed. Lanham, MD: University Press of America and Biblio Press, 1987.

Falk, Marcia. *The Book of Blessings: A Feminist Jewish Reconstruction of Prayer.* San Francisco: Harper & Row, 1990.

Friedman, Marcia. *Land of Exile.* Ithaca, NY: Firebrand Books, 1990.

Hamelsdorf, Ora, and Sandra Adelsberg. *Jewish Women and Jewish Law: Bibliography.* New York: Biblio Press, 1981.

Kaye/Kantrowitz, Melanie. "Class, Women and 'The Black-Jewish Question.'" *Tikkun*, Vol. IV, No. 3, pp. 97–101. See also Cheri Brown in the same issue.

———. *Some Pieces of Jewish Left: Secular Tales for Modern Times.* San Francisco: Spinsters/Aunt Lute, 1990

Klepfisz, Irena. *Collected Poems* and *Collected Essays.* Portland, OR: Eighth Mountain Press, 1990.

Lipman, Beate. *Israel—the Embattled Land: Jewish and Palestinian Women Talk about Their Lives.* London: Pandora, 1988.
Newman, Leslea. *A Letter to Harvey Milk* and *Good Enough to Eat.* Ithaca, NY: Firebrand Books, 1988.
Plaskow, Judith. *Standing Again at Sinai: Rethinking Judaism from a Feminist Perspective.* San Francisco: Harper & Row, 1990.
Potter, Claire, ed. *The Lesbian Periodicals Index.* Tallahassee, FL: Naiad Press, 1986.
Schneider, Susan Weidman, ed. *Jewish and Female: Choices and Changes in Our Lives Today.* New York: Simon & Schuster, 1984.
Schulman, Sarah. *The Sophie Horowitz Story.* Tallahassee, FL: Naiad Press, 1984.
———. *Girls, Visions and Everything.* Seattle: Seal Press, 1986.
———. *After Delores.* New York: New American Library, 1988.
Shipler, David. Arab and Jew: Wounded Spirits in a Promised Land. New York: Penguin, 1987.
Zahara, Irene. *Jewish Lesbian Stories.* Freedom, CA: Crossing Press, 1990.

Small Press/Periodical Addresses

Alicejamesbooks, 138 Mt. Auburn Street, Cambridge, MA 02138.
Alyson Publications, 40 Plympton Street, Boston, MA 02118.
American Jewish Committee, 165 East 56th Street, New York, NY 10022.
Biblio Press, 27 West 20th Street, rm. 1001, New York, NY 10011.
Big Mama Rag, 1724 Gaylord Street, Denver, CO 80206.
Board of Deputies of British Jews, Woburn House, Upper Woburn Place, London WC1H OEP.
Bridges: A Journal for Jewish Feminists and Our Friends, P.O. Box 10, Nehalem, OR 97131.
Common Lives/Lesbian Lives, P.O. Box 1553, Iowa City, IA 52244.
Conditions, P.O. Box 56, Van Brunt Station, Brooklyn, NY 11215.
Crossing Press, P.O. Box 1048, Freedom, CA 95019.
Diaspora Distribution, P.O. Box 19224, Oakland, CA 94619.
Eighth Mountain Press, 624 Southeast 29th Avenue, Portland, OR 97214.
The Feminist Press, CUNY, 311 East 94th Street, New York, NY 10128.
Firebrand Books, The Commons, Ithaca, NY 14850.
Gay Community News, 62 Berkeley Street, Boston, MA 02116.
genesis 2, an independent voice for Jewish renewal, 30 Old Whitfield Roac, Accord, NY 12404.
Lilith: The Jewish Women's Magazine, 250 West 57th Street, New York, NY 10019.
The Heyeck Press, 25 Patrol Court, Woodside, CA 94062.
Jewish Lesbian Daughters of Holocaust Survivors, P.O. Box 6194, Boston, MA 02114.
Kitchen Table: A Women of Color Press, P.O. Box 908, Lathem, NY 12110.
Long Haul Press, P.O. Box 592, Van Brunt Station, Brooklyn, NY 11215.
Moonforce Media, P.O. Box 2934, Washington, D.C. 20013

Motheroot Publications, 214 Dewey Street, Pittsburgh, PA 15218.
Naiad Press, P.O. Box 10543, Tallahassee, FL 32302.
National Yiddish Book Center, Old East Street School, P.O. Box 969, Amherst, MA 01004.
New Glide Publications, 390 Ellis Street, San Francisco, CA 94102.
New Outlook: Middle East Monthly, 9 Gordon Street, Tel Aviv, 6358, Israel.
off our backs, 2423 18th Street, N.W., Washington, D.C. 20009.
Piecework Press, Box 2422, Brooklyn, NY 11202.
Plexus, 545 Athol Avenue, Oakland, CA 94606.
Response, 15 East 26th Street, Suite 1350, New York, NY 10010.
Sefir Publications, 542 25th Street, no. 335, Oakland, CA 9612.
Sinister Wisdom, P.O. Box 3252, Berkeley, CA 94703.
Sojourner, 380 Green Street, Cambridge, MA 02139.
Teachers & Writers Collaborative, 84 Fifth Avenue, New York, NY 10011.
Tikkun, 5100 Leona Street, Oakland, CA 94619.
Union of Sephardic Congregations, 8 West 70th Street, New York, NY 10023.
Womanews, P.O. Box 220, Village Station, New York, NY 10014

Special Issues of Journals and Newspapers focused on Jewish Women and Anti-Semitism

Big Mama Rag, July 1982
genesis 2, March 1981
New Outlook, June/July 1989
off our backs, February/March 1972
off our backs, April 1982
Plexus, September 1982
Response: A Contemporary Jewish Review, No. 44 (Spring 1983)
Sojourner, July 1983
Womanews, December 1981

Tapes

"Feminist Jewish Women's Voices." A presentation by the Jewish Caucus of the National Women's Studies Association. Includes the stories of Jewish women who are secular and religious, Ashkenazi and Sephardi, rural and urban, American-born and Holocaust survivors, lesbian and heterosexual, as well as those who represent different class backgrounds. Available for $6.95 from NWSA, University of Maryland, College Park, MD 20742.

"Jewish Lesbian Culture and Anti-Semitism in the Lesbian Community." A presentation by Minneapolis Jewish Lesbians. Available from Radical Rose Recordings, SDO 1, P.O. Box 8122, Minneapolis, MN 55408.

"Celebrating our Diversity." A 2-hour videotape and workbook (1988) by L. Lee Knefelkamp that explores what bias is and how to eliminate it. Discusses Anti-Semitism. Distributed by the Association of College Unions International, 400 E. Seventh, Bloomington, IN 47405.

Glossary

Akedah, biblical account describing God's command to Abraham to offer his son Isaac as a sacrifice. Divine intervention prevented consummation at the last minute. Abraham's willingness to make this sacrifice was regarded in Jewish tradition as the supreme example of readiness to submit to the will of God.

Aliyah, Jewish immigration to Israel. The term also designates the calling up to the altar to read from the Torah.

Aliyot, plural of *aliyah.*

Asherah, Canaanite fertility and mother goddess, popular throughout the Ancient Near East. Jezebel introduced Asherah to Israel's court worship. Manasseh placed an idol of Asherah in the Temple, which was later removed by Josiah.

Ashkenazi, the term specifically denotes German Jewry and their descendants in other countries. From the fifteenth to sixteenth centuries, the center of Ashkenazi Jewry shifted to Bohemia, Poland, and Lithuania. In Slavonic territories, the Ashkenazis' use of Yiddish became prominent. After the Chmielnicki massacres in 1648, Ashkenazi Jewry spread throughout Western Europe. Toward the end of the nineteenth century, Ashkenazi Jewry massively emigrated from Eastern Europe. Before World War II, ninety percent of the world's Jewish population was Ashkenazi.

Ashtoreth, Canaanite goddess of love and war.

Baal, designation of great weathergod of Western Semites. During the early centuries of Jewish settlement in Canaan, Baal's worship became very alluring.

Bar Mitzvah, term denoting liability to observe precepts of Judaism, occurring when a boy passes his thirteenth birthday. He then ranks as an adult, becomes included in the *minyan* for public services, and wears the phylacteries at morning services. The bar mitzvah boy reads from the Torah and speaks on a biblical or rabbinic topic at the public or family celebration.

Bashert, inevitable, (pre)destined.

Bat Mitzvah, the age (twelve years and a day) at which the girl attains religious maturity. The ceremony varies from her reading from the Torah (prohibited in Orthodox congregations) to holding collective ceremonies or calling male relatives to read from the Torah.

Bet Mispachah, the house of the family.

Bima, the raised platform in the synagogue from which the Torah is read. In Sephardi and some Ashkenazi synagogues, it is also from where the cantor conducts service.

B'nai Brith, founded in New York in 1843, it has developed into the world's oldest and largest Jewish service organization. Its objectives are moral, social, plilanthropic, and educational.

Bris, the ceremony of circumcision where all or part of the foreskin covering the glans of the penis is removed on the eighth day after the birth of a son. This ceremony, required by Jewish law, symbolizes the entrance into a covenant with God.

Bubbe, grandmother.

Bund, Jewish socialist party founded in Russia in 1897. It was particularly influential in Russia between 1905 and 1920, and in Poland until World War II. Committed to Yiddish, autonomism, and secular Jewish nationalism.

Chai, life. As a letter in the Hebrew alphabet, it is often worn by Jews to symbolize life.

Challah, braided white bread glazed with egg. Eaten on Shabbat and other holidays.

Chanukah, Festival of Dedication or Feast of Lights, commemorating the victory of the Maccabees in recapturing Jerusalem from the Syrians and purifying the Temple. In celebration of their one-day's supply of oil miraculously lasting eight days, this festival is celebrated by lighting the menorah candles on eight consecutive nights.

Chevri, group.

Chochem, wise one; sage.

Chutzpah, nerve; impudence; unmitigated gall.

Daven, to pray.

Dayanim, Dayenn, rabbinical court judge.

Diaspora, the lands of the Jewish dispersion; settlement outside of Israel.

Di bubbe est a zeml, the grandmother eats a roll.

Dunam, one thousand square meters.

Elijah, a fiery ascetic prophet, he is seen as the herald of the Messiah. A glass of wine is traditionally poured for him at the Passover Seder, and a chair is prepared for him at the circumcision ceremony.

Em Col Hai, the mother of all life.

Erev Rosh Hashanah, eve of Rosh Hashanah, the Jewish New Year. Jewish holidays are celebrated from sundown to sundown.

Erev Yom Kippur, eve of Yom Kippur, the Jewish Day of Atonement. This is the most important occasion of the religious year. All work is forbidden, as are eating, drinking, washing, the wearing of leather shoes, and sexual activity. The day is spent in prayer.

Esquadinias, loquat tree, an ornamental tree originally from the Far East. It produces a small yellow fruit.

Galut, exile; the condition of Jewish people in dispersion.

Garinim, sunflower seeds.

Gefilte fish, a Jewish specialty consisting of ground cod or white fish mixed with eggs and matzoh meal, boiled in broth, and served cold with horseradish (particularly on Shabbat).

Goy, a Gentile.

Goyim, plural of *goy.*

Goyish, characteristic of Gentiles.

Hammam, Turkish baths consisting of several pools of varying temperatures, a steam bath and a room of heated marble slabs.

Hanukkah, see Chanukah.

Haroset, a mixture of wine, chopped apples or dates, and nuts eaten at the Passover Seder as a symbol of the mortar Jews manufactured during their slavery in Egypt.

HaShem, synonym for God, often substituted for the name of God when speaking out of context of formalized prayer (it is forbidden to speak God's name).

Hatikvah, Israel's national anthem, meaning hope.

Hevreh, social group; peers; those congregated for a meeting.

High Holy Days, Rosh Hashanah and Yom Kippur.

Kaddish, prayer which glorifies God and which has come to be used as the Mourners' Prayer in the belief that by praising God the souls of the dead will find peace.

Kashrut, kashruth, the set of dietary laws governing eating habits, including injunctions against mixing meat and milk, against eating shellfish and animals without split hooves and who do not chew their own cud.

Kibbutz, collective agricultural community in Israel where childcare and eating arrangements are collectivized and where socialist principles govern.

Kike, a derogatory term for Jew which originated from the practice of illiterate Jews marking their signature with a circle (*kikel* in Yiddish) rather than an X.

Knaidlach, matzoh balls, or dumplings made of matzoh meal and eggs, served in soup.

Knesset, Israel's parliament.

Knishes, pieces of dough filled with meat, potatoes, or barley (kasha); baked or fried.

Kol Nidre, prayer lamentingly intoned at the commencement of Yom Kippur. Declaration of annulment of all vows made before God.

Kosher, term used to describe food permitted and prepared according to Jewish dietary laws.

Kreplach, noodle dough stuffed with any combination of kasha, liver, or cheese; boiled and served in soup (usually chicken broth).

Kvetching, nagging; complaining; whining.

Ladino, Hispanic language written in Hebrew characters, developed at the end of the Middle Ages. After Jews were expelled from Spain in 1492, various dialects of Ladino crystallized in the new lands of settlement: North Africa, Balkan states, Turkey, the Middle East, and later in the United States and Latin America. The first printed book in Ladino appeared in Constantinople in 1510; widespread literature developed in subsequent centuries. Ladino is also referred to as Judeo-Spanish, *Romance, Judezmo,* and *Spaniolish.*

Latkes, pancakes usually made with potatoes and served with apple sauce or sour cream. Eaten especially during Chanukah.

Leefa, loofah.

Lilith, the first woman, said to Adam, the first man: "We are equal because we both come from the earth."

Lokshen kugel, noodle pudding.

Lubavitcher Hassidim, a sect of Judaism: *Hassidim* are pious Jews who emphasize the mystical and spontaneous aspects of communication with God; the *Lubavitchers* are a group of *Hassidim* who work to make Jews more observant of Jewish law and custom.

Magen David, six-pointed star used as a symbol of Judaism. In ancient times, it was used for decorative and magical purpose by Jews and Gentiles; Christians used it during the Middle Ages. Its use as a specifically Jewish symbol began in the seventeenth century. During the nineteenth century it was adopted by the Zionist movement, and is now the emblem of the Israeli flag.

Mahalath, mother of a group of demons and ruler of one of the seasons.

Mame, mother; mommy.

Mame loshn, mother tongue, especially the Yiddish language.

Matzah, matzo, unleavened bread made chiefly for Passover, representing the hurried exile of Jews from Egypt when there was no time to allow the bread to rise.

Matzo brei, matzo soaked in egg and milk, fried, and often served with jelly for breakfast (especially during Passover when only unleavened bread may be eaten).

Mazel tov, congratulations, good luck.

Mazel tov chaverot, good luck, sisters.

Menorah, seven-branched oil lamp. On Chanukah, an eight-branched candelabrum with a ninth candle (for lighting the other eight) is used.

Mezuzah, small rectangular piece of parchment inscribed with the passages Deuteronomy VI.4-9 and XI.13-21, and written in 22 lines. The parchment is rolled up and inserted in a wooden or metal case and nailed in a slanting position to the right-hand doorpost of every orthodox Jewish residence as a talisman against evil.

Minyan, a quorum of ten men required by Jewish law for a proper religious service.

Mischling, mixture.

Mishugge, Mishuggenah, crazy, crazy one.

Mitzvot, commandments, usually referring to good deeds, such as helping one in distress; of the 613 *mitzvot* listed in the Bible, 248 are positive commands.

Mohn-cake, poppyseed cake.

Naches, Nahat, joy; contentment; gratification.

Nu, go on! well? designating mild impatience.

Oleha hashalom, may she rest in peace.

Oy gevald, an exclamation of horror, astonishment, dismay.

Oy va voy, woe is me!

Passover, English for *Pesach,* the festival commemorating the liberation of the Jews from their bondage in Egypt. It lasts seven days, and during the first two nights, a ritual meal *(Seder)* is held, where the story of the bondage and liberation is recalled. A particular set of dietary laws governs food consumption during this week.

Pesach, see Passover.

Peyes, long, uncut locks of hair which Orthodox Jewish males grow in front of their ears in accordance with the Biblical proscription "they shall not cut the corners of their beards."

Pidion aben, ceremony which takes place one month after the *bris.* A parent buys the son from the rabbi as a symbol of God's ownership of all children and in observation of the commandment to remember God's sparing of the Jewish first-born sons in Egypt.

Pilpul, techniques of talmudic disputation utilizing subtle differentiations, in arguments; sophistry.

Ponim, face.

Rabbonim, rabbis.

Rebbitzin, rabbi's wife.

Rosh Hashanah, the Jewish New Year; the time when God opens the Book of Life and judges each individual's deeds of the past year over a ten-day period of repentance which culminates in *Yom Kippur.* Thus Jews wish each other a good inscription for the coming year as a new year's greeting.

Ruggalach, pinwheel pastry made of dough, cinnamon, nuts, and brown sugar.

Sabra, nickname for native Israeli, referring metaphorically to the cactus ("prickly pear"): prickly exterior and tender heart.

Schmaltz, fat or grease; extra, gaudy ornamentation; sweet talk or flattery.

Seder, the religious home service/evening ritual meal recounting the liberation from Egyptian bondage, and celebrated amidst festivity on the first and second nights of Passover.

Sephardim, descendants of Jews who lived in Spain or Portugal before their expulsion in 1492. Sephardim established communities of numerical, economic, and scholastic importance in North Africa, Italy, the Near East, Western Europe, America, and the Balkan states (especially Constantinople, Salonika, Izmir). The distinctive language of the Sephardim is *Ladino.* Together with other non-Ashkenazi Jews, Sephardim constitute seventeen percent of world Jewry and approximately half of the population of Israel (but there the term refers to all Arab and Oriental Jews). Three percent of the Jewish population in the United States are tallied as Sephardic.

Shabbes, Shabbos, Jewish sabbath which begins on Friday evenings at sundown and continues through sundown on Saturday. All work—including writing, cooking, sewing, etc.—is forbidden at this time.

Shalom, a common greeting.

Shalom bayt, domestic harmony; peace of the house.

Shavuoth, festival of weeks, feast of the harvest celebrating bringing in the first fruits of the field.

Shekhina, divine presence; Holy Spirit who is visible on earth and who in late Midrash literature appears as a feminine figure, compassionately intervening with God in defense of mortals.

Shep nachas, reap joy.

Sheitel, wig worn by Orthodox Ashkenazi wife in obedience of the Mishnaic law which forbids a married woman from showing her hair outside of her house.

Shiksa, Gentile woman.

Shivah, "to sit shivah" refers to the traditional Jewish mourning ritual which requires the deceased's immediate family to stay together for seven days, receive condolence visits, say *Kaddish* (the Mourners' Prayer) every morning, and refrain from work.

Shmate, rag; often used disdainfully to describe a piece of clothing.

Shtetl, small-town Jewish community in Eastern Europe, where Yiddish culture flourished. Shtetls were obliterated by the end of World War II.

Shul, synagogue.

Shvester, sister.

Siddur, daily prayer book.

Simchas Torah, a joyous holiday on the last day of *Succoth* on which the reading of the Torah is both completed and begun anew.

Succoth, a holiday in which wooden huts with thatched roofs covered with green twigs are built to commemorate the Jewish wanderings in the desert after emancipation from Egyptian bondage.

Tallis, prayer shawl.

Talmud, the body of teaching which comprises the commentary and discussions of the meaning of the Torah.

Tanta, tante, aunt.

Torah, a parchment scroll containing the first five books of the Old Testament.

Tsores, woe; troubles; misery.

Tzimmes, a sweet dish made from stewed dried fruits and vegetables. Used metaphorically to describe a fuss.

Vaser, water.

Vos vil di bubbe?, what does the grandmother want?

Warsaw Ghetto, established by German Nazis in October 1941, for Warsaw Jews and deportees from other parts of Poland. The population reached 450,000. Starvation and inhuman living conditions resulted in over 100,000 deaths by the summer of 1942. Approximately 300,000 were deported to Treblinka extermination camp between July and September 1942. Armed Jewish resistance began in January 1943. A courageous revolt began on April 19th, lasting until June. Over 56,000 Jews were either killed or deported during the revolt.

Yarmulke, traditional skull cap worn by Jewish males during prayers; observant Orthodox men always wear it. The *yarmulke* is worn as an acknowledgment of God's presence above and as a demonstration of respect for God.

Yente, an overly talkative woman who likes to gossip.

Yiddish, language of medieval German origin used by Ashkenazi Jews over the past thousand years. Began in the tenth century in Middle Rhine region, and spread with Jews in their wanderings throughout Europe. Written in Hebrew characters. By 1939, there were 11 million Yiddish speakers. However, the forces of the Holocaust, Soviet anti-Semitism, anti-Yiddish forces in Israel, and assimilation throughout the world have drastically reduced the number of Yiddish speakers in the world.

Yom Kippur, Day of Atonement; a twenty-four hour solemn day of fasting, praying, and repentance which ends the ten Days of Awe (beginning with *Rosh Hashanah*) and during which time every Jew makes peace with all friends and foes so that the Book of Life can be closed by God with a positive inscription for the coming year.

Zaftig, plump; voluptuous.

Zogt, says.

Zonah, whore; prostitute.

Zuntig, bulbes; muntig, bulbes; dinstik un mitvokh, bulbes, Sunday, potatoes; Monday, potatoes; Tuesday and Wednesday, potatoes.

Credits

If I am not for myself who will be?
If I am only for myself what am I?
And if not now when?

—Rabbi Hillel